H. Stonehewer Cooper

The Islands of the Pacific

Their Peoples and Their Products

H. Stonehewer Cooper

The Islands of the Pacific
Their Peoples and Their Products

ISBN/EAN: 9783744722032

Printed in Europe, USA, Canada, Australia, Japan

Cover: Foto ©Suzi / pixelio.de

More available books at **www.hansebooks.com**

ORAL LANDS OF THE PACIFIC.

LAGOON OF MANGO.

THE

ISLANDS OF THE PACIFIC

THEIR PEOPLES AND THEIR PRODUCTS.

BY

H. STONEHEWER COOPER.

'To burst all links of habit—there to wander far away,
On from island unto island, at the gateways of the day.'

WITH TWO ILLUSTRATIONS.

A New and Revised Edition of 'Coral Lands.'

FOR CIRCULATION IN AUSTRALIA.

LONDON:
RICHARD BENTLEY AND SON,
Publishers in Ordinary to Her Majesty the Queen.
1888.

NOTE.

This Edition is especially issued by the Proprietors of the Copyright for circulation in the Australian Colonies only.

PREFACE.

(TO THE SECOND EDITION.)

NOTWITHSTANDING the almost prohibitory price at which the first edition of 'Coral Lands' was issued, the very flattering reception which my work has received from both the public and press has resulted in its now being altogether out of print. Every day public attention is being more and more directed to the infant Colony of Fiji and the surrounding groups in the Pacific.

The importance of Polynesia will not perhaps be thoroughly understood by the majority of my countrymen until the completion of the Panama Canal has placed these rich archipelagoes on the direct route from London to our Australian Colonies.

In the meantime a popular edition of such a work as 'Coral Lands' may tend to prepare the public mind for estimating the full value in every sense of the islands of the great South Sea. The information afforded in this edition has been brought down to the latest news from the Pacific, and the whole work has been thoroughly revised.

PREFACE TO THE SECOND EDITION.

In this revision I have been assisted by many good friends. For the most recent returns of the exports and imports of the colony of Fiji, I am indebted to the indefatigable Colonial Secretary, the Hon. John B. Thurston, C.M.G.; while in regard to some interesting Samoan data, I have to acknowledge the kind assistance of Mr. H. Phipps Allender.

The beautiful lagoon of Mango, which forms the frontispiece, was sketched from a photograph by my friend M. Frédéric Sang, of the Salon, Paris. For the index appended to this edition I am indebted to Mr. F. W. Jordan.

H. STONEHEWER COOPER.

CHURCH END, FINCHLEY,
June, 1882.

PREFACE.

(TO THE FIRST EDITION.)

THE original pioneers of the Pacific were exceptionally unfortunate.

In the church of St. Francis, in the town of Nombre de Dios, on the Darien isthmus, is a painting of Vasco Nunez de Balboa. With infinite labour he has dragged the timbers of his vessel across the mountains of America, and now, clad in complete armour and standing up to the waist in salt water, with a sword in one hand and the Papal flag in the other, he is depicted as taking formal possession of the islands of the Pacific on behalf of the Apostolic See of Rome. He died under the headsman's axe in 1517, for an unjust charge of treason, four years after his great discovery.

Magalhaens, who passed, in November, 1520, through the straits which bear his name, died the next year in a miserable skirmish with some Indians. Alvaro de Saavedra died upon his return voyage from Mexico to Manilla. It was Saavedra who proposed to the King of Spain to cut through the isthmus of Darien, and very circumstantially described the route between the San Miguel and Atrato, a favourite one at this hour.

Alvaro de Mendana, who discovered the Solomon Islands in 1567, afterwards planned and attempted a scheme for their colonisation. On his second voyage, however, in 1595, he was unable to find them, and a settlement was tried at Santa Cruz. At that place he died, leaving his wife in command of the colony; but disease and other disasters soon caused it to be abandoned, and the survivors, sick and dying, sailed away for the Philippines, taking Mendana's body with them. The vessel, carrying the corpse of the pioneer, was last seen in full sail drifting towards a reef, but the body of Mendana had the ghastly companionship of a crew of dead men—for no living man was on board the ill-fated discoverer's ship; with their late commander they had all gone on the more extended voyage of eternity.

Dampier, our countryman, died in obscurity, we know not how or where.

Fernando Quiros, who gave his name to an island which yields an annual income of some thousands sterling, has left us this record at the hands of Cardinal Valenza: 'I have seen, in a wine-shop of Seville, one Fernando Quiros, who had been an adventurer in the Indies and beyond, and who told me he had seen there people who did eat their wives and other relatives, in place of consigning them to tombs, which did not so much surprise me, seeing that the same thing has been related of the ancients.' Quiros commenced life as a common sailor, and became an admiral. Torres, who gave his name to the Australian Straits, was Quiros's lieutenant, and Torquemada his historian. This 'man in the wine-shop' died in obscurity in Panama.

Roggewein, who discovered Samoa, was imprisoned in Batavia, and died in wretchedness.

Of Cook's sad end I need not speak.

The French circumnavigator, M. de la Perouse, perished off the island of Vanikoro, one of the Santa Cruz group; while Dumont D'Urville, the Polynesian naturalist and traveller, was burnt to death on the Paris and Versailles railway.

To these men, and many others who seem to have given their lives for the Pacific, we owe a deep debt of gratitude, for they serve, though dead, as finger-posts to a world of wealth.

Spain is no longer a colonising power, and though the discovery of the Pacific is due to the Latin race, the utilisation of that discovery will almost certainly be the work of the Anglo-Saxon.

With the hope of assisting in that work, morally and commercially, I have written 'Coral Lands.'

PREFACE TO THE FIRST EDITION.

To the Agent-General for New Zealand, Sir Julius Vogel, K.C.M.G., I must also tender my grateful thanks for much valuable information on the trade of the South Sea Islands, notably in Mr. Sterndale's report to the Government of New Zealand, which I have followed in my treatment of some details. To my old friend Mr. Archibald J. Dunn, I am indebted for valuable assistance. To Messrs. Thos. P. Elphinston of Fiji, and T. S. Kelsall of Samoa, I am also much obliged; and I should add that some of the commercial matter on Fiji has appeared in the columns of the *Field* newspaper above my signature.

If the following pages have any tendency to advance civilisation—by which I mean religion, law, order, and freedom for all—and which includes legitimate commerce in the great Pacific, the end for which this book was written will have been accomplished.

H. STONEHEWER COOPER.

CHURCH END, FINCHLEY,
September, 1880.

CONTENTS.

CHAPTER		PAGE
	INTRODUCTION	v
I.	FROM THE GOLDEN GATE TO FIJI	1
II.	THE FIJI GROUP	8
III.	CORAL AND CORAL REEFS	12
IV.	THE CESSION OF FIJI	18
V.	THE CANNIBAL OUTBREAK OF 1876	34
VI.	LEVUKA	43
VII.	LIFE IN LEVUKA	50
VIII.	RELIGION, PAST AND PRESENT	59
IX.	FIJI IN CANNIBAL DAYS	67
X.	FUNERALS IN TAVIUNI	74
XI.	FIJI LIFE, PAST AND PRESENT	85
XII.	THE FIJIAN OF TO-DAY	91
XIII.	MORE ABOUT THE FIJIAN OF TO-DAY	96
XIV.	MEKE-MEKES	108
XV.	BRITISH NATIVE POLICY—FIAT JUSTITIA	119
XVI.	ZOOLOGY AND BOTANY OF FIJI	131
XVII.	A VERY SUGGESTIVE CHAPTER	140
XVIII.	MORE HINTS FOR CAPITALISTS	161
XIX.	LAND TITLES	171
XX.	A SAMPLE OF POLYNESIAN WANDERINGS	175
XXI.	A LITTLE 'BLOW'—AND SOME LIGHT FROM THE CANDLE-NUT AND OTHER THINGS	184
XXII.	SAVU SAVU TO TAVIUNI	192
XXIII.	MANGO AND MANGO COTTON	203

CONTENTS.

CHAPTER		PAGE
XXIV.	THE REWA.—LET FIJI FLOURISH . . .	206
XXV.	THE SAMOAN OR NAVIGATORS' ISLANDS . .	211
XXVI.	LIFE IN SAMOA	219
XXVII.	GODEFFROY AND CO., THE SOUTH SEA KINGS .	232
XXVIII.	THE CAREER OF 'BULLY HAYES' . . .	240
XXIX.	PEARL FISHING AND 'BEACHCOMBERS' . .	245
XXX.	WHAT B CHE-DE-MER IS, HOW IT IS CAUGHT, AND WHAT IS DONE WITH IT	263
XXXI.	TURTLE AND SPONGE FISHING . . .	279
XXXII.	A GLIMPSE OF TONGAN HISTORY . . .	286
XXXIII.	TONGAN TRADITIONS	301
XXXIV.	NEUTRAL TONGA	308
XXXV.	THE LINE ISLANDS	312
XXXVI.	'FROM ISLAND UNTO ISLAND AT THE GATEWAYS OF THE DAY'	323
XXXVII.	POLYNESIAN TRADITIONS	344
XXXVIII.	WHO BUILT THOSE FORTS?	350
XXXIX.	THE SOLOMON ISLANDS	360
XL.	THE SOCIETY ISLANDS	363
XLI.	IS NOTHING TO BE DONE? . . .	370
	APPENDIX	375

INTRODUCTION.

THE peoples of Polynesia may be divided into three distinct classes. In the western islands from the east end of New Guinea and Australia eastward, including Fiji, we find a nearly black frizzly-haired people. In all the eastern islands there are large brown straight-haired people (found also in New Zealand); and in the western islands north of the equator, there is a smaller brown straight-haired people. The black frizzly-haired people, who are nearly the lowest type of humanity in existence, are called Papuans.*

On some of the islands the men collect their hair into small bunches and carefully bind each bunch round with fine vegetable fibre from the roots up to within about two inches from the head. Dr. Turner, in his 'Nineteen Years in Polynesia,' mentions having counted nearly seven hundred bunches on the head of one young man. This strange custom gave rise to the long popular belief that the hair of the Polynesians grew in tufts. Dr. Turner also calls attention to the strange resemblance existing between the hair of these people thus dressed and the conventional representation in the Assyrian sculptures.

In the physiognomy of the Papuan people there is great difference. The lips of a typical specimen are somewhat thick.

* From '*Papuah*, frizzled, woolly headed.'—*Marsden's Malay Dictionary.* According to Spencer, the Fuegians, Andamans, Veddahs, etc., are of a lower type than the Papuans.

b

The nose is broad, often arched and high, but coarse. The jaws project, and they may as a rule be said to be prognathous. They are generally small in stature; and in islands where the natives are comparatively large-sized, there is always evidence of their mixture with another race. The typical Papuan is small, thin-limbed, and physically weak. They are savage, bloodthirsty, and inveterate cannibals. They are also broken up into hostile tribes, speaking languages with a structural resemblance, but wide verbal differences, owing to long isolation; in fact, the people in one valley frequently had no communication with the people in another, except when at war with them.

Women hold a very low position among the Papuans, and are merely the slaves and tools of the men. Their domestic instincts are not greatly elevated above those of the lower animals. In the Papuan mode of government might is right. Both intellectually and religiously the natives are of a low type, and they possess few of the traditions, poems, and songs common to many barbarous races. In arts and commerce they are also backward, although with occasional exceptions.

Throughout the whole of the Papuan region, there are traces of more or less mixture of the people with the large brown straight-haired people referred to, whom Mr. Whitmee calls the 'Sawaiori,' and other writers the Mahori races; and this is especially noticeable in Fiji, and in the Solomon Group. The word 'Sawaiori' is taken from the three representative peoples of the race, those belonging to *Sa*moa, Ha*waii*, and Ma*ori*.

The Papuans of the Pacific are believed to belong to the same race as those in New Guinea and other parts of the Indian Archipelago; in fact, they may be divided into Eastern and Western Papuans. That they were the earliest occupants of the various places where remnants of the race are now found, and that they have in many places been partly or wholly overrun and displaced by more recent races, is, in my opinion, unquestionable.

The average height of the Sawaiori races is five feet ten inches, and they are proportionately well developed. Their colour is brown, lighter or darker according to the amount of exposure to the sun. The hair is black and generally straight, but sometimes wavy, with a tendency to curl. The features are fairly regular, and the eyes dark; the jaws do not project, except in a few instances; the lips are of medium thickness, thicker than those of Englishmen; the nose is short, but somewhat wide at the base, and the forehead is moderately high, but rather narrow. Politeness is one of their marked characteristics, and women occupy a position hardly inferior to men. Rank and hereditary titles exist, and a different language is used in addressing chiefs from that employed to common people.

If a chief possesses a dog, the animal must be spoken of by a different name from that given to a common man's dog. In Samoa, for instance, there are four different words for 'to come,' appropriated to four grades of people—*sau*, for a common man; *maliu mai*, for a person of respectability; *susu mai*, for a titled chief; and *afio mai*, for a member of the royal family. When addressing a person in respectful language, the Samoans never use the personal pronoun in the singular number, but always in the dual—the dual of dignity.

The way in which landed property is held and transmitted, resembles its tenure by the Israelites under the Mosaic laws. The land in the islands is divided among families, each of the members having an equal right to its use. The patriarch, or recognised head of the family, however, alone properly exercises the right to dispose of, or to assign it temporarily to persons outside the family or clan. I expressly use the word 'clan,' as the family among the Sawaiori people consists of all the connections by blood or marriage. Elaborate traditions, both in prose and poetry, exist among them, and have been retained with the greatest accuracy for centuries.

The Sawaiori people have always been great navigators, and are skilled in boat-building. They think highly of themselves, and some are decidedly conceited. As a heathen race, they are strict in their religious observances, and they are easily influenced by Christianity.

In the western portion of Polynesia, north of the equator, there is a wide belt of atolls or lagoon islands, inhabited by a brown race of men, in colour resembling the Sawaioris, but of smaller stature and less robust. These Mr. Whitmee, in a paper read before the Philological Society, classes as the Tarapon race, from *Tara*-wa and *Pon*-ape, names of two representative islands in the Gilbert and Caroline Groups respectively. They differ more from one another than the Sawaioris do. The natives of the Carolines are larger and finer men than those of the Gilbert Group, and are yellower in colour. The Tarapon people are decidedly a mixed race, and in many respects resemble the brown people of the Malay peninsula more nearly than they do the Sawaiori race. The Tarapons are all navigators, and many of them build large boats or proahs, not unlike those found in Indian seas.

It is more than probable that, at an early period, the ancestors of the Sawaioris, the Tarapons, the Malays, and also the Malagasy of Madagascar, dwelt together in the islands of the Indian Archipelago.

From some cause or other, probably from war, a portion of that people migrated eastward to Polynesia. Finding the islands in the west occupied by the black Papuan race, they went on until they reached some of the islands in the centre of Polynesia, perhaps Samoa, and there they settled. From this point they spread abroad to the distant eastward islands: some went north-east to the Hawaiian Archipelago; some south-west to New Zealand; and a few others, at various times, migrated westward into the Papuan area, and either formed colonies there or mixed with and intermarried among the Papuan people; some have also, in comparatively recent times, gone north-west, and mixed with the Tarapon people, who entered Polynesia much later than the Sawaioris. These Sawaioris being isolated from contact with other people, have retained their primitive manners nearly unaltered.

The changes which have taken place among the Papuans since their settlement have probably all been for the worse, for want of circumstances to call for the use of knowledge or of habits originally possessed. The absence of Sanscrit elements in their language proves that their migration must have occurred before Sanscrit influenced the languages of the Indian Archipelago.

At a later period a second migration took place from the Archipelago, westward across the Indian Ocean to Madagascar. This, we may conclude, was in post-Sanscrit times—for there are a few Sanscrit elements in the language of Madagascar. Later still, another migration from the Indian Archipelago went eastward, settling on the north-west islands of Polynesia, commonly known as Micronesia.

The bulk of these people probably came from the Philippines or some other island in the north-eastern portion of the Archipelago. The few Papuan elements which now appear in the Tarapon people may have existed in the original people before they migrated. Since their settlement in the Pacific there has been a considerable infusion of other blood among them—probably Chinese and Japanese.

To make this division of races in the Pacific clear to my readers, I give a list of the principal Archipelagos under the different heads of Papuan, Sawaiori or Mahori, and Tarapon or Micronesian.

PAPUAN.

New Ireland.
New Britain.
Papua or New Guinea, mixed with Sawaiori.
Solomon Islands ,, ,,
Santa Cruz, mixed with Sawaiori.
New Hebrides ,, ,,
Loyalty Islands ,, ,,
New Caledonia ,, ,,
Fiji Group ,, ,,

SAWAIORI OR MAHORI.

New Zealand.
Kermadec.

Tonga Group.
Samoa Islands.
Phœnix Islands.
Cook Islands.
Society Islands.
Austral Islands.
Marquesas and Tuamotu Groups.
Hawaiian Islands, North Pacific.

TARAPON OR MICRONESIAN.

Gilbert or Kingsmill Islands, North Pacific.
Marshall Islands.
Caroline Islands.
Mariana or Ladrone Islands.

The Rev. S. J. Whitmee thus describes the three great varieties of speech which are used by the races in Coral Lands—Papuan, Sawaiori, and Tarapon:

'The following are the broad characteristics of the Papuan languages . . . Consonants are freely used, some of the consonantal sounds being difficult to represent by Roman characters. Many of the syllables are closed. There is no difference between the definite and indefinite article, except, perhaps, in Fiji. Nouns are curiously divided into two classes, one of which takes a pronominal affix, the other which never takes an affix. The principle of this division appears to be a near or more remote connection between the possessor and the thing possessed. Those things which are intimately connected with a person, as the parts of his body, etc., take the pronominal affix. A thing possessed merely for use would not take this. For example, in Fijian the word *luve* means either a son or a daughter, one's child, and it takes the possessive pronoun after it, as *luvena;* but the word *ngone*, a child, but not necessarily one's own child, takes the possessive pronoun before it, as *nona ngone*, his child, *i.e.*, his to look after or bring up. Gender is only sexual. Many words are used indiscriminately as nouns, adjectives, or verbs, without change, but sometimes a noun is indicated by its termination. In most of the languages there are no changes in nouns to form the plural, but a numeral indicates number. Case is shown by particles which precede the nouns. Adjectives follow their substantives. Pronouns are numerous, and the personal pronoun includes four numbers, singular, dual, trinal, and general plural, also inclusive and exclusive. Almost any word may be made into a verb by using with it the verbal particles. The differences in these particles in the various languages are very great. In the verbs there are causative, intensive, frequentative, and reciprocal forms.'

With one exception the soundsfound in the Sawaiori languages may be expressed by the Roman letters, with their ordinary values. This exception is a sound which we call a break; a kind of a pause in the breath, which is between an aspirate and a *k*. A *k* sound takes its place in some of the languages. In those languages in which this sound occurs we usually write it by a comma inverted, as in the name Hawai'i. The vowel sounds are all simple, as in Spanish. Every syllable is open. To this there is no exception. Some words consist entirely of vowels. Phonetic changes have taken place according to law, so that a given word in one language may have its form in any other language, if it be found in it predicated. As a rule the accent is on the penultimate syllable, but in a few cases (chiefly when the last syllable ends in a diphthong or a long vowel, which is really a double vowel) on the ultimate. Very rarely, in some languages the accent may be on the antepenult. There is an indefinite as well as a definite, and in some cases a plural, article. But some nouns are formed from the verb by taking a suffix, and some adjectives are formed from the noun in the same way. There is some variety in the way of indicating number in the noun. In Samoa many nouns have special plural forms. The cases are indicated by prepositions. Proper names in the nominative cases take a prefix, as *O Tahiti, O Samoa*, etc. Adjectives follow the substantives. The pronouns are numerous. Personal pronouns are singular, dual, and plural. The form of the plural in some languages shows that it was originally a trinal. In the verbs the distinctions of tense, mood, and voice are indicated by particles prefixed and affixed. Number and person are generally regarded as accidents of the subject and not of the verb. To this, however, the Samoan forms an exception; in this language many of the words have a special plural form. In all the languages there is a causative, which is formed by a prefix to the verb. There are also intensive or frequentative and reciprocal forms of the verbs. The intensive consists usually in a repetition of the active verb; the reciprocal is usually formed by both a prefix and postfix. Verbal directive particles are freely used to direct towards, away from, or aside. In some languages—especially in that of Samoa—many ceremonious words are used to persons of rank. Words which form part of the name of a chief are often disused during his life, and in some places they are disused after his death.

'In the Tarapon language,' says Mr. Whitmee, 'consonants are used more freely than in the Sawaiori languages. They have some consonantal sounds which are not found in the latter, such as *ch*, *dj*, and *sh*, which may perhaps be regarded as intermediate between the Sawaiori and Papuan, although not nearly so strong as in the latter. Closed syllables are by no means rare. Occasionally double consonants are used, but there is a tendency to introduce a slight vowel sound between them. In all of these particulars there is an approximation to the Papuan. Most words take the accent on the penult. In some of the Tarapon languages there appears to be no true article. Gender is sexual only. Number in the noun is either gathered from the requirements of the sense or is marked by pronominal words or numerals. Case is known by the position of the noun in the sentence, or by prepositions.'

In the language of Ebon, one of the islands in the Marshall Archipelago, nouns have the peculiarity which I mentioned as being characteristic of the Papuan languages, viz.: those which indicate close relationship, as of a son to his father, or of the members of a person's body, take a pronominal affix, which gives them the appearance of inflections. I do not know of the existence of this peculiarity in any other Tarapon language, but would not make too much of negative evidence.

Many words may be indiscriminately used as nouns, adjectives, or verbs, without any change of form. In some languages the personal pronouns are singular, dual, and plural. In others there are no special dual forms, but the numeral for *two* is used to express the dual. In the Ebon language there are inclusive and exclusive forms of the personal pronouns, which, as far as I have at present been able to ascertain, do not occur in the other Tarapon languages. The verbs usually have no inflection to express relations of voice, mood, or tense, number or person, such distinctions being expressed by particles. In the Ebon language, however, the tenses are sometimes marked; but even in that the simple form of the verb is frequently given. All verbs have directive particles. In Ponape—one of the Carolines—many words of ceremony are used only to chiefs, exactly as they are used so largely in Samoa. The custom of tabooing words which occur in the names of chiefs is also found there.

It may be useful for any philological readers of Coral Lands if I enumerate the principal works bearing on the languages of the South Sea.

The first in time and importance is the comparative sketch of the grammar and dictionary published in the 'United States Exploring Expedition during the years 1838-42, Ethnology and Philology,' vol. vii., by Horatio Hale, Philologist to the Expedition (Philadelphia, 1846). In this grammar and dictionary, Mr. Whitmee remarks, in a paper read before the Philological Society of London, 'Mr. Hale collected together the information which had up to that time been gathered by the missionaries respecting the languages of several groups. He also carried on independent investigations during his cruise, both in the languages which had been studied by missionaries and in others up to that time unknown. The vast amount of information thus brought together he generalised in a moderately full grammar which has up to the present time been the chief standard work on the whole Malayo-Polynesian (or Sawaiori) family of languages. His dictionary also has been of very great value, although I think it of less value than the grammar. To say that Mr. Hale's work is now behind our present knowledge of these languages is to say only what every student would hope and expect to be the case. But even now, the student of the Polynesian philology who has separate grammars and dictionaries of all the languages in his hand may still learn something from this work which he cannot afford to overlook. The volume containing it is, however, very rare and difficult to obtain.'

As regards Tahiti and the Marquesas, P. L. J. B. Gaussin's *Du Dialecte de Tahiti, de celui des Iles Marquises, et en général de la Langue Polynesienne* (Paris, 1853), is a work which is of interest and especial value in regard to the Marquesas.

Dr. Friedrich Müller's sketch of the Sawaiori languages, in his 'Voyage of the Frigate *Novara*' (*Reise der Fregatte Novara*, Vienna, 1867), has some value.

As this subject must possess great interest for many, and, with a view to popularising, as far as I can, a study which must tend towards the opening up of the beautiful region about which I write, I make no scruple in reproducing here the admirable list of books of reference on the languages of Polynesia, for which I acknowledge myself indebted to the author of the paper just quoted. In addition to the works already named, the chief works on the particular languages of the Malayo-Polynesian or Sawaiori tongue are as follows:

On the *Maori* of New Zealand the grammar by R. Maunsell, LL.D. (Auckland, N. Z.; 1st ed., 1842; 2nd ed., 1862). Kendal's Grammar, 1820, may be consulted, and Archdeacon Williams's 'First Lessons in Maori' (1872); Bishop Williams's Dictionary (1st ed., 1844; 3rd ed., edited by Archdeacon Williams, 1871) is very good, and moderately full, giving many examples of the use of words from Sir G. Grey's 'Mythology and Traditions of the New Zealanders' (London, 1855), which greatly enhances its value. Sir George Grey's 'Maori Poetry' (New Zealand, 1853), and his 'Proverbial and Popular Sayings of the Ancestors of the New Zealand Race' (Cape Town, 1857), will be found useful and instructive.

In the *Hawaiian* language there is an excellent grammar by the late Judge Andrews, and Professor W. P. Alexander has published an admirable little 'Synopsis of the most essential points in Hawaiian Grammar,' for the use of his students in Oahu College, while Andrews's 'Dictionary of the Hawaiian Language' (Honolulu, 1865) may certainly be regarded as by far the best dictionary of any Polynesian tongue which has been published. It may be mentioned here, though I omitted to mention the fact when sketching my short stay in the Hawaiian Islands, that newspapers are regularly published in its language, and the Bible has, of course, been translated.

A short grammar and small dictionary of the language of *Samoa*, by the Rev. G. Pratt, was published in Samoa in 1862. This being out of print, Mr. Pratt has prepared a new and enlarged edition, which I believe has been published by Messrs. Trübner and Co., of London. This new edition contains all the words which have been collected by the united efforts of the missionaries; but, although he is the editor and proprietor of the copyright of this work, Mr. Whitmee thinks that the definitions of words are briefer and the examples of their use fewer than are desirable. In some respects the Samoan is one of the most important of the Sawaiori or Malayo-Polynesian languages, and there can be little doubt that it is the parent of some of the members of this family, such, *e.g.*, as the Tokelau and Ellice Islands dialects. I have heard it stated, moreover, that the Samoan version of the Bible published by the indefatigable British and Foreign Bible Society is one of the best versions of the Protestant Bible extant. Still more recently, in 1880, Father Violette has published in Paris an English, French, and Samoan Dictionary, with a Samoan grammar, the merits of which I have had no opportunity of judging.

Of the *Tongan* language a vocabulary by the Rev. S. Rabone was published in Vavau in 1845. This is far behind the knowledge of the language now possessed by some of the missionaries. Mr. Whitmee tells me that he has been engaged on a 'Comparative Polynesian Dictionary,' in conjunction with the Rev. J. E. Moulton, and says, modestly enough, 'From Mr. Moulton's ability and thorough knowledge of the language, I am sure this will be a very valuable contribution to our knowledge.' We may safely add the name of the Rev. S. J. Whitmee after that of the Rev. J. E. Moulton in this quotation.

A grammar and a dictionary of the *Tahitian* language were published in Tahiti in 1851; and the Rev. J. L. Green, of Tahiti, has been at work, in conjunction with Mr. Whitmee, upon the last-named gentleman's 'Comparative Dictionary.' Gaussin's 'Grammar of the Tahitian' can be safely relied on, and Buschmann and Baron William von Humboldt, in their works on the Marquesas, also deal with the language of Tahiti.

Of the *Hervey Islands* dialects, of which the principal is that of Rarotonga, no dictionary has been published, but a brief grammar by the Rev. A. Buzacott was published in the island in 1854. The assistance of the Rev. W. W. Gill, B.A., has been secured for the 'Comparative Dictionary,' which will take some time yet to complete.

In regard to the *Marquesas* I have already mentioned Gaussin's work, and I learn there is also an *Essai de la Langue des Iles Marquises* in existence, but do not know when it was published or where. The *Aperçu de la Langue des Iles Marquises et de la Langue Taïtienne, par J. Ch. Ed. Buschmann* (Berlin, 1843), contains, besides the last-named gentleman's essay, a short French Marquesan vocabulary and some Marquesan and Tahitian texts, with interlinear French translations. To these are appended a grammar of Marquesan and Tahitian, and a vocabulary of the Tahitian by Baron William von Humboldt, which will be found useful. Abbé Boniface Mosblech's book, published in Paris in 1843, under the title of *Vocabulaire Océanien-Français et Français-Océanien des Dialectes parlés aux*

Iles Marquises, Sandwich, Gambier, etc., is by no means a perfect work, but at present it is the only published dictionary of the Marquesan language. The services of M. Pinard, who has resided some time in the islands, have, however, been secured for the 'Comparative Dictionary,' and he will contribute material from the two dialects known to exist in the group.

The same gentleman will also furnish that portion of the same important work which deals with the *Rapanui* and *Gambier Islands.* Most of the people of the *Tuamotu*, or Low Archipelago, are now speaking the Tahitian language, and I conclude that M. Pinard's contribution on the Gambier Islands dialect is likely to be all that will be obtained from that widely scattered cluster of small islands.

As regards *Niuè* (or Savage Island, sometimes spelt Nieue), a grammar of its language has been prepared by the Rev. W. G. Lawes, who was many years a missionary there, for incorporation in a proposed 'Comparative Grammar.'

The languages of the *Tokelau*, or Union, and the Ellice Islands are approximate to the Samoan. Yet they use more sounds than are found in most of the other Sawaiori languages. Samoan books have been used in both of these groups, and most of the people now use that language. I learn that a moderately full vocabulary has been secured for the 'Comparative Dictionary.'

As I have already stated, the Fijians, as a Papuan (or Melanesian) people, are much crossed with Sawaiori or Malayo-Polynesian blood, so that in the language of Fiji we find many Sawaiori words. This occurs, too, again in *Rotuma* (a volcanic island to the north-west of the Fiji Group and recently annexed to the British Empire in answer to the prayers of the inhabitants, in consequence of the unseemly squabbles between the followers of the Catholic and Protestant missionaries), in the language of which island there are a few Sawaiori or Malayo-Polynesian words to be found.

Again, in *Uvea*, one of the Loyalty Group, and at *Futuna*

Aniwa, *Mel*, and *Fil* (the two latter places belonging to the island of Efate, in the New Hebrides), there are colonies of brown Polynesians who speak dialects of the Sawaiori language.

In regard to the Tarapon or Micronesian languages we know but very little. Mr. Hale published a brief vocabulary of the dialect spoken in Tobi, or Lord North's Island, as also another of the language of *Mille*, an island in the Radack chain of the Marshall Archipelago.

Of the language of *Ponape*, one of the Caroline Islands, we know more than of any other dialect of the Tarapon tongue. In 1858 the Rev. L. H. Gulick, M.D., published a small grammar of the Ponape language. In 1872 a revised edition of this, together with a Ponape-English and English-Ponape vocabulary, was published in the 'Journal of the American Oriental Society' (vol. x.), and gives us a fair knowledge of this language.

In 1860 the Rev. E. T. Doane, a missionary residing on *Ebon*, or Strong's Island, one of the Marshall Group, published in *The Friend*, at Honolulu, a brief sketch of the Ebon language.

It should be added that papers on some of the languages of Micronesia (or Tarapon region) have been published in the *Journal du Muséum Godeffroy*, at Hamburg. Number I. of that serial for 1873 contains a brief German and Ebon vocabulary by J. Kubary, and Number II. of the same year contains a comparative vocabulary of German, Ebon, and *Yap* (of the Caroline Islands).

The languages of the Papuan, or Melanesian, or Negrito-Polynesian peoples we know more about. The work first in importance on these languages is *Die Melaneischen Sprachen nach ihren Grammatischen Bau und Polyneischen Sprachen von H. C. von der Gabelentz* (Part I., Leipzig, 1860; Part II., Leipzig, 1873). In the two parts of this work most of the material available for studying the Melanesian or Papuan languages has been worked up. Part I. contains the *Bau* of Fiji, the *Annatom* (or more correctly *Aneityum*), *Erromanga*, *Tana* and *Mallikolo* (sometimes spelt *Malicolo*) of the New Hebrides, the *Mari* and *Lifu* of the Loyalty Islands, the *Duauru* dialect of New Caledonia, the *Bauro* and *Guadelcanor*, or *Gera*, of the Solomon Group. Part II. is chiefly derived from the late Bishop Patteson's vocabularies, and contains more or less information on the languages of *Fate*, *Api*, *Pama*, *Ambrym*, and *Vunmarama* (north end of Whitsunday Island), in the New Hebrides, the *Lifu* and *Uea* (now written *Uvea*) of the Loyalty Islands, the *Yehen*, or *Yengen*, of New Caledonia, the *Bauro*, *Mara*, *Ma-siki*, *Anudha*, *Mahaga*, and *Eddystone Islands* of the Solomon Archipelago.

As regards *Fiji*, Mr. Hale published a grammar and dictionary in his great work already mentioned. There is also a very good grammar and dictionary by the late Rev. D. Hazelwood (second edition edited by the Rev. J. Calvert, without date). Both these works deal almost exclusively with the *Bau* dialect. As I have already stated, the Bau has been adopted by the missionaries, and into this portions of the Scriptures have been translated.

I have in my possession an admirably got-up Fijian Catholic Prayer-book, *Ai Vola ni Lotu Katolika*, printed in Sydney in 1864, which is a very complete book of devotion.

There is a useful little grammar of the language of *Mota*, one of the *Banks Islands* (London, 1877); and it should be noticed in Dr. R. G. Latham's 'Elements of Comparative Philology' (London, 1862), that the author devotes three or four pages each to the Sawaiori and Tarapon languages, while he gives twenty pages (329-349) to those of the Papuan or Melanesian peoples.

All that is known of the Admiralty islanders is, I believe, confined to the paper of Mr. H. N. Moseley, F.R.S., published in the 'Journal of the Anthropological Institute' for May, 1877. In the eighth volume of the German 'Journal of Ethnology' (1876), Captain H. Strauch gives us a comparative summary of seven languages belonging to *New Guinea*, *New Hanover*, *New Ireland*, *New Britain*, and the *Solomon Islands*.

The above is a list of the most important contributions to the philology of the Pacific. A large field is still open, however, to students of the present day, while good service will ere long be rendered to Polynesian history by the publication of a detailed catalogue of every known work upon Australia and the Pacific, which I understand that Mr. E. A. Petherick has had in hand for many years, and for which he has collected materials in different parts of the globe.

THE

CORAL LANDS OF THE PACIFIC.

CHAPTER I.

FROM THE GOLDEN GATE TO FIJI.

THE completion of the Trans-Continental Railroad of America opened a new era for the islands of the Southern Sea. The great through route to Japan, China, New Zealand, and Australia, *viâ* San Francisco, is now an accomplished and very successful fact.

The steamers of the Pacific Mail Company have brought the Sandwich Islands within thirty days of London, and, although the service to Fiji is for the present suspended, there can be no question that the growing importance of our recently acquired territory—to say nothing of the surrounding groups—will necessitate its resumption at no distant date. A glance at the map will show anyone the advantages of the San Francisco route for reaching quickly those marvellous clusters of islands which lie just in the track of ocean travel between the Pacific slope of the United States and the ever-growing colonies of Australia and New Zealand.

A pleasant run of a little over seven days brings you from the City of the Golden Gate to Honolulu, the capital of the Hawaiian kingdom, delightfully situated on the island of Oahu, one of the thirteen which compose the Sandwich Group. Eight of these islands are inhabited. The chain runs from south-east to north-west, in lat. 19° 22′ N. and 155° to 160° W. long. All the islands are very mountainous, and of volcanic origin.

The pleasant little town of Honolulu, which boasts a population of about 15,000 souls, is built on a level piece of land, backed by a low range of green-clad hills, topped here and there by peaks of volcanic rocks. The harbour affords a good anchorage, and there is an excellent wharf for the large trans-Pacific steamers. All the Pacific Mail Company's Australian steamers coal at Honolulu; so the through passenger has at least a few hours wherein to enjoy the scenery and gain some little knowledge of this most interesting Archipelago.

In ancient days the different islands of Hawaii had their separate kings and constitutions; but Kamehameha the Great, 'the Napoleon of the Pacific,' united all the islands under his rule. He levied great armies, sometimes 7000 strong, and his victories are celebrated in the national songs with majesty and power. He founded that dynasty which has stood for seventy years, and which, compared with the Governments that went before it, has been clement and civilised. From Vancouver's Island Kamehameha heard tidings of the grandeur of the Christian races, and he asked for Christian teachers to instruct his own people. Some American missionaries first tried the experiment; but, as a test of their Divine mission, they were ordered to throw themselves from the top of a precipice into the sea, and on their declining to do this, their pretensions were rejected, and the king remained unconverted.

Kamehameha III. became some sort of a Christian, and made Christianity the national religion. At the present time there is a Catholic mission in the islands, but the Anglican religion is dominant.

The old Paganism was of a virulent kind, rejoicing especially in human sacrifices. Rows of altars, on which eighty victims are known to have been offered at once, are still existing in one part of the islands; and there is a legend that King Umi, having vanquished six kings, was sacrificing captives on these altars when the voice of his god, Kuahilo, called to him to furnish more victims. Fresh human blood was made to stream from the altars, but the insatiable demon called for more, till Umi had sacrificed not only all the captives, but all his own men; and Kuahilo continued to thunder from the clouds until no living being was left but the king and the sacrificing priest.

It was my good fortune to arrive at Honolulu on the king's birthday, and we had hardly got to the wharf before a battery above the town thundered out a right royal salute.

The form of government is an elective monarchy, the present King David Kaluakua having been raised to the throne in 1874. His majesty is tall and well-built, a little over six feet in height, of an olive complexion, with crisp, curly hair. All our saloon passengers were entertained with a sumptuous luncheon, after having assisted at the *levée* which the king held at the palace, a one-story building, surrounded by gardens rejoicing in all the luxuriance of tropical floriculture. His majesty was attended at the *levée* by his ministers and high officials, mostly English or American, gorgeously got up in blue and gold; while the court flunkies were unexceptionable, both as to calves and hair-powder. A good military band played on the lawn during lunch, and a detachment of the Hawaiian army, which numbers about 200 efficient troops, clad in a uniform something like that of the French infantry, and armed with the Remington breechloader, formed a guard of honour.

Honolulu is well laid out, and the roads are perfect. The Parliamentary buildings are of substantial character, in the Italian style, and from one of the flank towers a fine view is to be obtained of the town and its surroundings. There is a very fair Museum attached to this block; and, though unpretending as compared with the regal pomp of the palace, the Government buildings are all that can be desired.

The stores and commercial edifices of Honolulu are far beyond the average, and when going into some of them you can hardly realise that you are visiting the self-same group in which, less than a hundred years ago, Captain Cook, the celebrated navigator, was murdered. He was killed on the island of Hawaii—formerly spelt Owyhee, which is the largest in the group, and has an acreage of 2,500,000. The other islands are Maui, 400,000; Oahu, 350,000; Kauai, 350,000; Molokai, 200,000; Lanai, 100,000; Nichau, 70,000; and Kahulai, 30,000 acres. The census, taken at the end of 1878, shows a total population of 57,985. The natives and half-castes decreased from 51,531 in 1872, to 47,508 in 1878.

Naturally, the trade is nearly all in the hands of our cousins the Californians, but until quite recently a very fair trade was done with the Australian colonies by the steamers of the Pacific Mail route.

My stay in Honolulu being regulated by the coaling of our southern-bound boat, my personal knowledge of the Sandwich

Group is, of course, confined to the island of Oahu; but, from other experiences in similar places, I know that what applies to one island in a group applies to the rest.

The Kanakas, who at present populate Hawaii, are, as a rule, well made and intelligent. That there is a cross of the Malay and Indian blood in them few can doubt. They are advanced in civilisation. They speak generally very little English, and that of the basest pigeon sort; but are most remarkably clear in the pronunciation of the word 'dollar.' The men wear a shirt and pantaloons, and are not averse to a wreath of flowers in their hair; the women—not strikingly handsome—affect a sort of bathing-gown costume of some gaudy-coloured print. Their eyes and expression are bright and cheerful; but, to the Anglo-American, to see the Hawaiian ladies riding astride is somewhat of a surprise.

After lunch at the palace we 'did' the regular Honolulu 'Rotten Row;' that is, having bargained, at considerable expenditure of time, money, and temper, with a Kanakan representative of the International Cabby Association, we secured a buggy and drove to Pāli, about six miles distant from the north of the town. The villas of the white residents and native chiefs line the side-walks for some distance ere you get quit of Honolulu, and are generally admirable specimens of tropical house-building, surrounded with lovely gardens. About half-way to Pāli you pass the residence of Queen Emma, who was very popular when in England some years ago. The view from the ridge of volcanic rocks at Pāli, to which there is a gradual ascent, is a grand one. The road abruptly terminates with huge masses of rock on either side, and below is a sheer fall of some 1400 feet to a plain, which stretches for some miles of cultivated soil to the North Pacific shore, the islets clustering round the coast perfecting the picture.

The cultivation of sugar, coffee, and rice is carried on with much success, and large fortunes have been made by Americans and others ; but until quite recently the great difficulty has been labour. To meet this, the Government have encouraged Chinese immigration by giving $25 to every celestial who lands. The passage from China to Honolulu costs a coolie about $45, which amount is advanced by one of the six large coolie companies in the Canton province who rule this business. The $20 due by the man is repaid to the company's agent out of wages.

The number of Chinese in the Hawaiian Group is about 6500. The whites and Kanakas speak highly of their general conduct, and—owing, I suppose, to the laziness of the native islanders—there is none of that bitter feeling of unsuccessful rivalry displayed by the working-classes on the Pacific slope of the States.

The average rate of wages paid by the sugar and rice planters is from $10 to $15 per month, with rations, and about 6000 coolies are employed in this fashion.

In California, the Chinaman's wage averages from $25 to $30 per month. It is nominally much more, but all holidays are deducted, and with the ordinary coolie these are numerous enough. The Californian coolie, however, has to find himself, and the necessaries of his celestial existence are much dearer in 'Frisco than in the Sandwich Islands.

Taking everything into consideration, I think the Chinese emigrant is better off in Hawaii than anywhere else.

A reciprocity treaty exists between the Hawaiian kingdom and the United States, the effect of which is of course to confine nearly all the trade to San Francisco and other American ports ; the consequence being that you have to pay Californian prices for many things which, if shipped from a British port like Sydney, would be only a fraction over London figures. I was told the treaty was made in haste ; it will probably be repented at leisure.

The climate is one of the loveliest on earth. It is almost absolutely equable, and a man may take his choice between broiling all the year round on the sea-level on the leeward side of the islands at a temperature of eighty degrees, and enjoying the charms of a fireside at an altitude where there is frost every night of the year. There is no sickly season, and there are no local diseases. The trade-winds blow for nine months of the year, and on the windward coasts there is abundance of rain, and a perennial luxuriance of vegetation.

The native population is rapidly on the decline, nor as far as I could learn is any adequate explanation offered of the fact. Captain Cook gave his estimate at 400,000 ; so there has been a terrible falling off. There is a capital hotel in Honolulu, called the Hawaiian, where we had a first-class dinner at the termination of a tiring sight-seeing day. After some twenty-six hours in the pleasant harbour of Honolulu, we returned to our old amusements of lounging, smoking, and gossip. The Pacific deserved its name. We had smooth seas, warm suns and fresh breezes all the way, and the evenings were distinguished by some most gorgeous sunsets, one of which was combined with the mirage of a city, perfect in nearly all its details of trees, houses, and waterfalls. The same night, when it was quite dark (there is no twilight in the Pacific), a most brilliant meteor passed directly over our quarter.

About thirteen degrees south we met the homeward-bound mail steamer, the *City of New York*, and, in a sea like glass, exchanged letters—thus a letter of mine, posted, so to speak, nearly 1000 miles south of the equator, and 170° W. long., reached friends at Hampstead, London, in thirty-seven days going of course *viâ* San Francisco and New York.

We had just a glimpse of the Union Islands, and passed quite close to Savaai, the largest island of the Samoan Archipelago; and after rounding, a few days later, the whole of the Fiji Group, to the east and south, we arrived off the harbour of Galoa, in the island of Kandavu—the port where the Fiji-bound passengers used to leave the 'Frisco steamer for the local communication with Levuka—about eight o'clock one fine evening in November. Rocket after rocket was sent up to arouse the inhabitants of that busy centre—Kandavu boasts (or perhaps boasted, as no mail-steamers call there now) one very small hotel and three white men's houses—but to no purpose. They were either fast asleep or had forgotten us.

'What do these people care,' said Captain Dearborn, 'for the result of our Presidential election, or whether Russia and England are at peace or war? Not a cent, sir—not a cent!'

CHAPTER II.

THE FIJI GROUP.

THE island of Kandavu is twenty-five miles long, and throughout its whole length is high and mountainous, except a small part at its centre, near Malatta Bay, which is divided from Galoa Bay by an isthmus of a few miles in width. Galoa Bay itself is a noble harbour towards the south-east, and it is said that the whole of the British navy could safely ride in it; but of this I have my doubts, knowing from statistics what the British navy comprises. Galoa looked quite busy, as the stately American mail-steamer headed for its exquisitely wooded shores. There was the *Australia*, a splendid steamer under the British flag, waiting for her New Zealand mails, while H.M.S. *Nymphe* was not far off. Some native craft (canoes with outriggers) dotted the surface of the bay, the occupants of which, girls and men, with their hair profusely adorned with gaily-coloured flowers, came aboard with baskets of cocoa-nuts, oranges, and pine-apples for sale; others had Fijian clubs and curios of all sorts, while model canoes were eagerly purchased by the Australian-bound passengers of the *City of Sydney.*

These humble traders were my first Fijian acquaintances, and handsome specimens they were. The men stood nearly six feet in height, of a dark-brown skin, and by no means forbidding in countenance; their hair, frizzed like a barrister's wig, was also dark brown, and their simple attire was a *sulu*, or fathom of *tappa*, a native cloth of spotless white made from the bark of the mulberry-tree, which they wore round the loins; the women, at any rate in Kandavu, adding a short sort of calico pinafore. Both sexes wore earrings, and some had necklaces of sharks' teeth. They moved about the deck quietly and respectfully, but seemed perfectly at home. On board the *City of Sydney* was the menagerie attached to the American circus of Messrs. Cooper and Bailey, who were *en route* for Sydney, and the Fijians were profoundly astonished at the camels, lions, tigers, and elephants they thus beheld for the first time.

'There's the *Star of the South!*' said Dr. Brower, a Fiji-bound fellow-traveller; and straining my eyesight I discovered, under the shelter of the land, a little steamboat, evidently taking things very easily.

'Well!' I rejoined, thinking perhaps she was the harbour-master's steam-tender.

'Oh, she's our mail-packet!' was the startling reply. 'She's not what you may call a very quick steamer, but it's infinitely better than having two or three nights in a sailing-cutter.'

How often in my Pacific wanderings, with particularly uncertain communications, have I not longed for the luxury of that feeble little steamship, the *Star of the South!* She boasted a tonnage of 175, with a nominal and delightfully uncertain horse-power of 45.

My Fiji-bound fellow-passengers insisted on my tasting 'Fiji cider,' which a native had brought off with him. They stood by me while I drank, and then asked how I relished it. I replied diffidently that I had no doubt Fiji cider was an acquired taste, but to me it seemed a curious compound of soapsuds and salt.

Dr. Brower gave a hearty laugh, and said I was not far out in my opinion of *angona.* I shall have something more to say about this beverage by-and-by.

The passengers for Fiji having safely reached the Levuka 'mail-boat,' the *City of Sydney* steamed majestically away for the port of her name. The *Australia* soon followed suit for Auckland; while the engineer of the *Star of the South* boarded H.M.S. *Nymphe,* apparently to request the loan of a little coal to take us and Her Majesty's mails to Levuka—distant some ninety miles. He was gone a considerable time, and it was long past noon before we headed our ship for the capital of Fiji.

We had a favourable passage, though accompanied by a good deal of drenching tropical rain. We were a representative crowd, the travellers who had come *viâ* 'Frisco being largely augmented by Fiji residents, and others who had been stopping in the 'colonies,' as the various provinces of Australia and New Zealand are called in Fiji and the adjacent groups. There was the Governor's secretary, Mr. Arthur Gordon, who so well earned his C.M.G. for the services he rendered the Government in the suppression of the cannibal outbreak of 1876. There were also Mr. Liardet, R.N., He

Majesty's consul for Samoa; Mr. Hedemann, the senior of one of the leading mercantile firms in Levuka; and many others. We talked of Fiji, and of Fiji only, till it was quite late, and then turned in.

By half-past six on the following morning the *Star of the South* had accomplished her ninety miles. We had passed through one of the entrances of the coral reef, and were at anchor in the harbour of Levuka, situated on the island of Ovalau (eight miles long by seven wide), one of the most central of the Fiji Group. It was pouring with rain. Hastily collecting my baggage I was soon ashore, and proceeded to read, mark, learn, and inwardly digest all that was to be read, learned, marked, and digested about fair Coral Lands.

The Fiji Group comprises more than eighty inhabited islands in the South Pacific, between longitude 176° east and 178° west, and latitude 16° and 21° south, and is situated 1760 miles N.E. of Sydney, and 1175 N. of Auckland. Viti Levu (or Big Fiji), the largest island of the group, is half as large as Jamaica, and larger than Cyprus; the second island of importance, Vanua Levu, is three times the size of Mauritius, and ten times that of Barbadoes; and the aggregate area of the whole is greater than all the British West Indies.

There are about 7,000,000 acres in Fiji, of which less than one-seventh is claimed by Europeans. The soil is mostly volcanic, of the richest possible description.

The country is well watered by numerous rivers, several of them being of respectable size. The Rewa in Viti Levu is navigable by vessels of light draught for 50 miles, and on the banks of this river there are thousands of acres of the richest alluvial flats, with soil 14 or 15 feet deep.

The climate is healthy. Ague, malarious fever, and other diseases common to tropical countries are almost unknown in

Fiji. For nine months in the year the cool south-east trade-winds make one doubt the reading of the thermometer, which ranges from 55° to 95°, with a pretty regular daily average of 75° to 80°. The rainfall varies in different localities, the lee-ward side of the large islands being much drier than the wind-ward. It is estimated to average 100 to 110 inches per annum. The average velocity of the wind at Bua in Vanua Levu in 1878 was 15 to 20 miles an hour. In addition to the islands named, the principal centres for white men are Taviuni, Koro, Vanua Balavu (of which the capital is Loma Loma), Mango, Lakemba, and Chichia.

The population may be set down at 118,000 natives, 2000 Europeans or whites, and 2000 Polynesians, coolies, etc.

CHAPTER III.

CORAL AND CORAL REEFS.

THE formations of coral in the Polynesian Groups are produced by the ceaseless work of the zoophytic animals called polyparia. Dr. Dana describes the polyp as 'an aquatic animal of the *radiata* type, having in general a cylindrical body, at one extremity of which is a mouth surrounded by one or more series of arms or tentacles.'

The water of the sea holds in solution a great quantity of calcareous or lime matter, which is absorbed for their sustenance by these little tenants of the deep; and as the coral and shells remain after their occupants are dead and decomposed, the bed of the ocean is constantly receiving additions from this source; shells also, and the teeth and skeletons of fishes, contribute some portion to the ever-growing stock. These relics accumulate in large masses, which rise to the surface in moderate depths of water, and which also form islands, on which the usual plants and animals exist. The shapes of these coral formations are various—flat, tubular, oval, and irregularly rounded at their circumference—and are almost invariably supported by an under-water elevation, such as extinct volcanoes or underlying rock. It is thought that these aggregations are stratified rocks of limestone, and that all calcareous formations have proceeded from the putrid bodies of fish.

Polyparia are composed of two separate parts : an external living fleshy envelope bearing and containing polypi, and an internal firm, solid, and inorganic axis. The base of the attachment is large, the stem fixed, the branches subdivided, calcareous, and mostly jointed. The animals inhabit the concretions in minute cells, and draw their nourishment through an aperture.

The formation of the coral-reefs consists of the shells of myriads of these little beings, resembling plants without leaves. Coral itself is, in fact, an animal growing in plant-like form, and seems to be a connecting link between the animal and vegetable kingdoms.

The sea is found to be deficient in lime-salts near the islands of the South Pacific. Chemically the common reef corals consist almost wholly of carbonate of lime, the same substance, in fact, which constitutes ordinary limestone. The currents of the Pacific are constantly bringing new supplies of sea-water (on which the tiny insects live) over the growing coral beds, and the whole ocean is thus engaged in contributing to their nutriment.

The coral-reefs around the islands are guardians of the low lands against the incursions of the sea. In Fiji they are often miles from the shore, the water inside the reef being usually calm, while that without, if there be anything like a breeze, is immediately agitated. One of the most beautiful sights in the Pacific is to watch the big white-crested breakers dash themselves against these reefs.

Sometimes a reef in Polynesia is thirty feet wide, and the rolling billows of the Pacific—extending occasionally in an unbroken line for a mile along the reef—are arrested by it, and, curving towards the shore, form a graceful liquid arch, which glitters in the sunlight. The beautiful water-structure then disappears with a loud and hollow roar into the reef, only to be succeeded by another and another.

In every reef there is a provision for the ingress and egress of craft by openings in the lines of coral, and the traveller will hardly fail to notice that these openings are almost invariably opposite some valley where streams of fresh water flow from the mountain.

The tallest cocoa-nut trees grow on small islands. In some of the breaches in the reef they serve as lighthouses or beacons, and show the native fisherman where he can get shelter and replenish his stock of fresh water. These islands have a coral formation, and their origin is doubtlessly due to the decaying vegetation or wood dashed in by the sea, and seeds washed to the reef from the beach.

Dr. Darwin divides coral-reefs into three classes: an atoll (or a sort of ring of coral surrounding a lagoon), which only differs from a barrier-reef in encircling no land; while a barrier-reef differs from a fringing-reef in being placed at a much greater distance from the land, in consequence of the probable inclination of its submarine foundation, and in the presence of a deep-water lagoon-like space within the reef. I have before remarked that the polyparia cannot exist at much more than a hundred feet below the surface. There can be no difficulty respecting the foundations on which fringing-reefs are based;

whereas with barrier-reefs and atolls there is a great difficulty on this head. In barrier-reefs, from the improbability of the rock of the coast, or of banks of sediment, extending in every instance so far seaward within the required depth in which the polyparia can work; and in atolls, from the immensity of the spaces over which they are interspersed (they spread, in a rough line, 4500 miles in length), and the apparent necessity for believing that they are all supported on mountain summits, which although rising very near to the surface level of the sea, in no one instance go above it.

Dr. Darwin considers this a most improbable supposition, and holds that there is but one alternative—the prolonged subsidence of the foundations on which the atolls were primarily based, together with the upward growth of the reef-constructing corals. On this supposition, every difficulty vanishes. Fringing-reefs are thus converted into barrier-reefs; and barrier-reefs, when encircling islands, are thus converted into atolls, the moment the last pinnacle of land sinks beneath the surface of the sea.

By this hypothesis alone can be explained the existence of breaches opposite valleys, to which I have already alluded. Little direct proof of subsidence can, however, be found in the case of atolls and barrier-reefs, whereas the presence of upraised marine bodies on the fringed coasts show that these have been elevated. The recent finding of fossil coral at a considerable height in the island of Viti Levu would, in my opinion, indicate that the lands encircled by the barrier-reefs were elevated in like manner. This coral was found by a friend of mine in 1876, during the campaign against the cannibals.

The same authority goes on to say: 'We thus see vast areas rising with volcanic matter every now and then, and bursting forth through the vents or fissures with which they are traversed. We see other wide spaces slowly sinking without any volcanic outburst, and we may well feel sure that this sinking must have been immense in amount as well as area, thus to have buried over the broad face of the ocean every one of those mountains above which atolls now stand like monuments marking the place of their former existence.'

Thus on the island-mountain of Taviuni we find the remains of an extinct volcano. Taviuni has perhaps reached its elevation; while, on the other hand, the fringed-reef Samoan Islands are in the immediate vicinity of several submarine volcanoes. About fourteen years ago the water to the eastern end of the Samoan (or Navigators') Islands was seen to be much agitated; a dense mass of steam rose from the surface, and the water was found to be boiling hot.

With the subsidence of the atoll islands in the Pacific comes a proportionate rising of other parts of the world, notably on the western coast of South America, which forms the greatest volcanic chain in the world; and Dr. Darwin states that not only is this rising of the South American coast a well-known geological fact, but that certain islands to the north-west of the Pacific, especially some of the Philippines and Loo-choo Islands, have extensive strata of a modern date.

It has been noticed that the action of the submarine volcanoes and consequent elevation of the earth has been followed by that tremendous agitation of the water called a 'tidal wave.' This great heaving of the bed of the ocean is felt all over the Pacific, north to south, east to west, and especially on the coast of South America. It sweeps away some of the atolls and affects the fringed-reef groups, while it is hardly noticeable in those possessed of barrier-reefs.

Thus in May, 1877, when I was sailing in a cutter in the Fiji Group, there was a terrible wave which swept away thousands of the inhabitants of the atoll islands, some of which disappeared altogether, did a great deal of damage among all the islands possessing only fringed reefs, and struck the west coast of South America with fearful execution.

In Fiji, with the exception of an unusually high tide nothing was noticed in that part of the group in which I was sailing; but a friend of mine, who had been cruising in the neighbourhood of the Navigators', told me he had passed through a perfect sea of pumice-stone on about the 8th or 9th of May.

The Fiji Group illustrates all the varieties of coral-reefs. For instance, Koro has a fringing-reef excepting on its western side. The island of Angau is encircled with a coral breakwater, which on the southern and western sides runs far from the shores, and is a proper barrier-reef; while on the east side it is a fringing-reef. The Argo reef, east of Lakemba, is a large barrier. It is actually a lagoon island twenty miles long, with some coral islets in the lagoon.

On the southern shores of the big island of Viti Levu the coral-reef lies close to the coast, and the same is seen on the east and north extremity of Vanua Levu. On the west side of these islands this reef stretches far off from the land, and in some parts is even twenty-five miles distant, with a broad sea between. This sea, however, is obstructed by reefs, and along the shores there are the ordinary fringing-reefs.

To recapitulate this matter of reefs. Reefs around islands may be (1) entirely encircling, or they may be (2) confined to a larger or a smaller portion of the coast, either continuous or interrupted; they may (3) constitute throughout a distant barrier, or (4) the reef may be fringing in one part and a barrier in another, or (5) it may be fringing alone; the barrier may be (6) at a great distance from the shores, with a wide sea within, or (7) it may so unite to the fringing-reef that the channel between will hardly float a canoe.

CHAPTER IV.

THE CESSION OF FIJI.

THE first known European who mentions Fiji is the Dutch navigator Tasman, who in 1643 passed between the islands of Taviuni and Kaimea, and the straits to this day bear his name. He christened the group Prince William's Islands. Captains Cook, Bligh, and Wilson are among the early discoverers who mention the group.

Colonel Smythe, of the Royal Artillery, was despatched in 1860 to report on a proffered cession to this country, and his account was very unfavourable to its acceptance by Great Britain. But since that date fuller information reached those interested in the distant Archipelago. In 1860 there were forty tribes all more or less independent, but only twelve chieftains possessed any real power. The head of these, Cacobau, chief of Bau, called himself Tui Viti, or King of Viti (the leeward portion of the group), but his claim was never admitted by the chieftains of the Windward Islands.

Dr. Seeman, who visited Fiji in company with Colonel Smythe, was of opinion that Cacobau had a perfect right to the title, as tributes more or less direct were paid to the chief of Bau. He further concluded that at one time Fiji was a powerful homogeneous kingdom, and adds: 'The hypothesis advanced derives additional strength from the fact of all Fijians, though scattered over a group of more than two hundred different islands, speaking one language, having a powerfully developed sense of nationality, and feeling as one people. No ancient Roman could have pronounced the *civis Romanus sum* with greater pride or dignity than a modern Fijian calls himself "Kai Viti," a Fijian.'

In 1808 a brig called the *Elisa* was wrecked off the reef of Nairai, and the escaped crew and passengers, mostly runaway convicts from New South Wales, found there were seven powerful chiefs in the group, that of Verata being leader. The sailors and convicts, however, under the command of a certain Charley Savage, took the side of the Bau people. Powder and shot soon settled the question of ascendency, and since the loss of the *Elisa* Bau has retained it. The chief of Bau at this time was a certain Na Ulivou, and was a brave leader of men. So great was his success that he was accorded the title of *Vuni Valu*, 'Root of War,' or, as some translators have it, 'Source of Power'—a distinction which has since been hereditary in the chiefs of Bau.

Internecine fighting chiefly constituted the Fijian life of those days, but the Vuni Valu of the time maintained the position he had won. He died in 1829, and was succeeded by his brother Tanoa, who, after a troubled reign, five years of which were passed in exile, died on the 8th of December, 1852.

In the meantime a Wesleyan mission had been founded at Levuka in 1835, and the last of the convicts had died in 1840. That year Commodore Wilkes, of the U.S. Navy, visited the group, where the white population was slowly but steadily on the increase.

King Tanoa, the father of ex-King Cacobau, was a fine old Fijian cannibal, one of the olden time; in other words, he was a desperate heathen man-eater.

Cacobau succeeded him, and was acknowledged by many of

the chiefs as Tui Viti, or Chief of Viti. In the concluding years of his sovereignty Cacobau found his throne anything but a bed of roses; in fact, until he ceded his kingdom to Great Britain, he was always in hot water.

Any sketch of Coral Lands would be incomplete without the story of Cacobau's experiences with the Tongan chief Maafu. This latter personage began life in 1842 by hiring himself and companies of his people to the unprincipled scoundrels who at that time were carrying on the trade of the South Sea Islands. These gentry, when persuasion failed, tried bullets; and Maafu, to put it pleasantly, became a first-class sandal-wood appropriator. A New Zealand Government blue-book calls the business by an uglier name.

Maafu first appeared in Fiji in 1847, having been exiled from his native country by his royal relative King George, who sagaciously thought his room safer than his company. He took up his abode at Loma Loma, and, espousing the cause of the weaker of two fighting Fijian chiefs, he defeated his enemies and at once became master of the whole of the islands of Vanua Balavu. He soon wanted a 'rectification of territory,' and naturally determined to seize the entire group of Fiji. To this end he began building a schooner of about thirty-five tons' register, and taking other steps which demonstrated that fire and sword were to be carried all over the islands.

The first appointed British consul, however, put a stop to his proceedings, and 'the Bismarck of the Pacific' was quiet for a short time. Everything comes to him who waits, and Maafu had not to wait very long. Fiji about 1859 was like some of the South American republics, where you may count on an annual revolution, accompanied by civil war, as safely as on the return of Eastertide.

Two chiefs on the northern side of Vanua Levu differed,

and their subjects prepared to club each other to death. Maafu was equal to the occasion, and, sending friendly messages to one of the chiefs named Bete and his ally Bua, a triple alliance was formed, and the whole of the northern district of Vanua Levu (called Macauta), as well as a small province in the south, quickly succumbed to the well-led legions of the all-conquering Tongan. Vanua Levu acknowledged a sort of vassalage to King Cacobau at Bau, who began to think Maafu was going a little too fast. At the division of the spoil the parties did not quarrel, but any reference to the claims of Cacobau was scornfully omitted.

Cacobau's sovereignty even of Bau now trembled in the balance; for Maafu at once despatched an expedition against the island of Benga, not very far from the southern coast of Viti Levu, the inhabitants of which instantly surrendered. The British consul, Mr. Pritchard (who was the means of attracting the cotton industry to the group) had just returned from England, where he had taken Cacobau's offer of cession to the Queen, and, believing that the offer had been accepted, brought Maafu to his senses with the aid of one of Her Majesty's war-ships. Maafu endeavoured to renew his intrigues, but another of the Queen's steamers interfered, and he had the common sense to perceive that fighting Fiji chiefs and the British forces are two very different things.

Maafu resided in Fiji until his death (which happened a few months ago), and was chief of the Windward Group. He was not only a man of great ability, but of very advanced intelligence, and his advice was often sought on native matters by the Fijian Government.

In the deed of cession to Great Britain, Cacobau's name of course appears first, and then follows that of Maafu. When the unconditional cession was under consideration, Cacobau said to Maafu: 'If you and I are of one mind, we need not ask another chief in Fiji.'

King Cacobau had other troubles besides those springing from Maafu's rivalry. His squabble with the United States was indirectly the means of bringing his so-called kingdom under the British flag. In 1849 there were about fifty whites resident at Levuka, among them the American consul, whose house was burned to the ground through an accident in firing a cannon on the 4th of July; whereupon the natives improved the occasion by carrying off whatever they could lay their hands on. In 1851 an American war-ship, the *St. Marys*, visited the group, and Mr. Williams, the U.S. consul, applied to the commanding-officer for compensation, which he estimated at the very precise sum of $5001 38c.

The history of how this claim of $5000 became swollen to $45,000 is anything but creditable to the American citizens concerned. Advantage was taken of another robbery by the natives, and, through the influence of an American naval officer, poor Cacobau was forced to sign a document acknowledging the justice of an unfair claim. Her Majesty's commissioner in 1861 reported: 'From all I can learn, one-third of the sum demanded by the United States Government would be amply sufficient, both as compensation for the loss of property and as a fine.' And in 1874 the Queen's commissioners say in their report: 'We have nothing to add to the statements previously made to Her Majesty's Government and published in England on the subject of the claim of the United States against King Cacobau—a claim which was unfairly made and unfairly pressed, and which has led to speculations of a questionable character.'

These comments are literally true. Certain Melbourne speculators conceived the idea of obtaining a cession of land from King Cacobau, in consideration of which they were to settle the claims of the American Government. Cacobau jumped at the proposal, and though (as the despatch of the British consul, Mr. Thurston, dated June 1, 1866, amply demonstrates) he had no power to do so, he ceded to the Melbourne gentlemen, as agents for a certain company 'about to be formed,' a large tract of territory, said to amount to 200,000 acres.

In the despatch just mentioned Mr. Thurston conclusively shows how the so-called cession was obtained, and what a vigorous protest he made against the conduct of the Vuni Valu and the British adventurers. But the Polynesian Company became an accomplished fact, and the American claim was settled in great part. Ninety thousand acres were stated to be conveyed to the Polynesian Land Company, and the Australians, who would not listen to the reiterated warnings of a British consul, were a short time since endeavouring to push their 'claim' against the Imperial Government.

This series of transactions caused Fiji to figure prominently if not very brilliantly before the civilised world.

On the establishment of the San Francisco and Sydney mail service, Lieutenant George A. Woods, of the Victorian navy, was sent down by the Steamer Company to superintend the survey and arrange for the lighting of the group. In those days the steamers from San Francisco made Levuka a port of call. Having in the performance of his duties attracted the attention of King Cacobau, his assistance was asked in the formation of a government, which, after some very natural hesitation, Mr. Woods proceeded to give. It would be an endless task to unravel the tangled skein of causes which broke up the Woods Administration, but the fact remains that, notwithstanding Mr. Woods' own untiring efforts, and those of his able coadjutor, Mr. Thurston (the present Colonial Secretary), the Government was unpopular with the whites, who did their best to destroy it. The lives and property of British, German, and American subjects were at stake, armed mobs of whites paraded Levuka beach, there was no security existing, and Fiji was getting to be a by-word and a scandal. After a great deal of time had been spent in negotiation, the unconditional surrender of the sovereignty of the islands was accepted by Her Majesty, and, on the 30th of September, 1874, they were formally ceded to England. In my opinion, a very few years will show that one of the most valuable cessions ever made to this country was effected on that day.

Sir Hercules G. R. Robinson, G.C.M.G., the Governor of New South Wales, proclaimed Her Majesty as sovereign, and, returning to his duty at Sydney, left Mr. E. L. Layard, C.M.G., to be Administrator of the group, pending the arrival of the late Governor, Sir Arthur H. Gordon, G.C.M.G.

On the 12th of January, 1875, H.M.S. *Dido* arrived at Levuka from Sydney, having on board ex-King Cacobau, and his two sons Rokos (or Princes) Timothy and Joseph, who were suffering from measles. It seems from the official despatches that the medical officer of the *Dido* thought they had been for some days quite well, and no caution was given to Mr. Layard or the Colonial Secretary that there was any fear of infection. The consequence was that before the young men landed numerous shore-boats and canoes had come out with both Europeans and natives, who were allowed free access to the ship. The two young Fijians of blood-royal went shortly afterwards ashore in their own boat, and the luckless *Dido* embarked 100 Polynesians to return to their own homes. Mr. Layard was only too true a prophet when he said: 'If the seeds of the disease are carried by them to the Polynesian

Islands the effects will be most disastrous among the natives.' He added: 'I have thus done all I can to prevent it spreading to other groups of islands, but to stay its progress here is impossible—it is everywhere. The natives will not do as they are told, but will expose themselves to cold and wet, to allay the feverishness. Some actually creep away at night from the guard we have stationed over them, and go and lie down in the sea or creeks; this brings on dysentery and congestion of the lungs, of which Ratu Savanatha died. We have published and distributed plain directions for its treatment; but, I regret to say, some evilly disposed white persons have told the natives not to take our medicines, as they were only meant to augment the disease, which has been purposely introduced to enable us to kill them, and get their lands.'

This last statement seems incredible. Political hatred may go a long way, but that in its malevolence it should deliberately assist in the destruction of a race of human beings, passes European comprehension. Yet there is the damning record contained in a Government blue-book. I believe the total number of deaths from this epidemic was at least 30,000! The white inhabitants did their utmost for the poor sufferers, and directions for remedies were posted on the trees all over the islands. Eye-witnesses have described the scenes of horror that were of daily occurrence, and the following extracts are taken from letters written by a Wesleyan missionary, the Rev. A. J. Webb:

'A calamity of the most serious kind has swept down upon this beautiful group of islands, and its ravages will have to be computed not by hundreds, but by thousands. We are having the same disease here that has been prevalent in the Colonies; but the mortality is heightened by the habits, the ignorance, and the lack of aid which is ever to be found in a large native population.

'By most remarkable fatuity persons sick of measles were allowed to disembark from the *Dido* and land the dire disease upon the shore of their country, and perfectly free intercourse took place between the King's family and their compatriots from different parts of Fiji. Ere long the people lay down in masses, and a most extraordinary scene was presented of whole towns with the houses closed, the lanes and squares silent as death, and the inhabitants all down. Old men and infants, young men, and mothers of families, one heap of illness. On Bau it seemed as though the curse that alighted on Sennacherib's army was repeated, and there was a weird quiet about the place that struck very peculiarly upon one's feelings. Daily the canoes were to be seen carrying the dead to their breezy resting-places on the opposite shore, and day and night was the death-drum beating, and the wails of the mourners rose on the air. Strong winds and heavy rains added to the horrors of the situation; and the Bauans almost starved for food, the people being unable to get to the mainland where their gardens were. All our servants were laid up, and we had to nurse them for weeks with food and medicine. My wife was weak, and nursing and other work fell on me, there not being another soul to do it. Hard worked in the day, and with broken rest at night, I passed through some weeks the like of which I hope never to see again. In our own land there is always a large proportion of healthy persons who act as a relief to the many stricken by disease; but here you have a whole country down, men, women, and children all round you, dying every day. Your best friends among the people dying, and those you have taken the greatest pains with. Two, both fine young preachers, have died on my own premises; and so fetid did they make the houses they died in, that I have had to destroy the walls to let the trade-wind purify the air. . . . Two of our children have had the measles, and are not quite recovered yet. Reports still come in from different parts of Fiji; and at Rewa the workings of the disease and its accompaniments are simply horrible. It is to be feared that the frightfully impure state of some of the villages may engender typhus fever, which would sweep off numbers that measles and dysentery have spared. The imported labourers are dying on the plantations, the occupations of the planters are seriously interfered with by disease, and, in fact, Fiji has received a most serious wound through the introduction of this disease, and a partial paralysis must occur in all commercial operations and in inter-island navigation.'

Next we have the terrible testimony of Captain Barrack, a planter, who writes from his estate in Savu-Savu Bay, Vanua Levu:

'I am sorry to say that the country is in a deplorable state; I hardly know how to describe it to you. The greatest trouble is to get the dead buried. The whites have done all they can in their several neighbourhoods, and in most cases get them over the measles; but a malignant type of dysentery follows, they get unmanageable, and the result is death.

'They likewise seem quite indifferent about one another, and, unless some white person is near, neglect the sick, and sit and look at them dying for want of a drink or a bit of food. It is a sad tale, and I don't know who is responsible.

'The whites, too, have had their trouble with sickness, and many have been carried off. We have to be very thankful, for, although Mrs. Barrack has been daily amongst the sick, none of our family have been ill as yet. Neither have any of our Tanna men; but we can hardly expect to escape altogether.'

With reference to this awful scourge, I cannot resist quoting Mr. Layard's testimony to the gallantry of Mr. James Harding, an officer of the Armed Constabulary of the late Government. The mountains of Viti Levu, or Big Fiji, were the last refuge of the cannibals. Although constantly warned by the Woods Administration, they persisted in making murderous raids; and just before annexation an expedition under Mr. Harding, and numbering only 210 armed natives, had signally defeated some 3000 of the cannibals, who suffered immense loss. Mr. Layard himself met the chiefs, and Mr. Thurston selected ten of them to accompany the Europeans to Levuka, to show them something of civilisation. During their visit they caught the measles. Mr. Harding was among the mountains when they returned, and here is the official record:

'I fear we shall have sad accounts from the interior. Mr. Harding reports from the centre of the mountains of Viti Levu that all the chiefs who came down to Levuka at my invitation have the disease, and that it is spreading rapidly. They attribute it to poison and treachery. Mr. Harding, at the imminent risk of his life, is remaining among them to endeavour to restore confidence.'

Whether the spread of the measles had anything to do with the final cannibal outbreak of 1876 I do not know.

Sir Arthur Gordon reached Levuka on the 24th of June, 1875, in Her Majesty's ship *Pearl*, and landed on the following day at the Government offices at Nasova, a sort of suburb of Levuka, where he afterwards resided. He was, of course, received with viceregal honours, and the native troops were passed in review. On the 26th of June he received the Vuni Valu, who presented, through his herald, a root of *angona*, as a symbol of friendship, peace, and submission. A piece of the *angona* was offered to the Governor, who replied: 'I accept this; may Fiji be happy.'

The Governor then invited the Vuni Valu and his chiefs into the Government buildings, where a short interview was held, at the termination of which the Vuni Valu, having taken leave of his Excellency, addressed the assembled natives, who in all were about 500 and said:

'Listen, men of Gali Vuka Levuka, and Gali Vuka Bau; the Governor has arrived in Fiji. I am happy to-day because I have seen him. The chiefs of the provinces are not here; you only, the men of Ovalau and Bau, have seen the Governor. His arrival is for the good and prosperity of Fiji. You will have to obey the law. Law is a good thing; it is the refuge of every man. In law little men and big men are all alike. Every man is responsible for what he does and no more; chiefs or other persons who are impudent will be punished. The Governor has come to do good; see that he is obeyed, for he represents the Queen. The aspiring man, what can he do now? The land is ruled by the Queen—here is her Representative. We ruled the land formerly; well, we still remain in the land, but our rule is gone—it is given to the Queen. By-and-by a day will be appointed for all the chiefs to assemble here and meet the Governor; to-day we only do so. I am happy because the Governor is here. These are my words to you, men of Bau and Levuka.'

On the 2nd of September Sir Arthur Gordon received some 200 of the planters, dealing, of course, mainly with those topics of most interest to the white settlers. On the

11th of September the sovereignty of Queen Victoria was in the most formal manner acknowledged by Cacobau; and his Excellency's account of the ceremony by which he was, according to the native ideas, invested as *Vuni Valu*, is so graphic that I give it *in extenso.*

Cacobau became a Christian in 1854, and is considered a very devout member of the Wesleyan Church. He is above the middle height, with white whiskers and moustache, not unlike those of the German Emperor. His sons were educated at Sydney, and speak English fluently, Roko Timothy being an exceptionally tall handsome man of noble carriage. Cacobau receives a pension of £1500 a year from the British Government, and was presented with a very smart sailing yacht. The Rokos to whom the Governor alludes are the chiefs of the provinces into which Fiji is divided.

Sir Arthur's despatch is dated Nasova, Sept. 20, 1875, and addressed to the Earl of Carnarvon, at that time Secretary for the Colonies:

'Shortly after my arrival here, Cacobau (who has, on every occasion since the cession, consistently shown the utmost anxiety to confirm and strengthen the authority over the natives of the Government by which his own has been superseded) suggested that, after the public reading of my commission, I should go through a ceremony which, he said, rarely took place, but which had been performed at his own inauguration as Vuni Valu, and which he assured me would pledge all the chiefs and people to me as their feudal superior. This ceremony, I found, consisted in drinking a bowl of *angona* in the presence of the chiefs, whilst they saluted me with their hands in the manner in which an inferior among the Fijians salutes his chief when drinking.

'After consulting those best acquainted with the natives, and having been assured by them that the performance of the ceremony would undoubtedly afford me a great hold over both chiefs and people, I assented to Cacobau's proposal; and on the 11th instant the ceremony took place at Bau, a locality selected by me for its performance, on account of its being the ancient capital, the traditional head-quarters in former times of cannibalism and heathen superstitions, and a place still of so much importance that its common people are regarded as chiefs in other parts of the group.

'Bau is a small island some twenty miles from Levuka, very near the mainland of Viti Levu, and entirely covered with houses, which cluster round a low hill in its midst. Its aspect, always picturesque, was rendered doubly so on the occasion of my arrival, by the crowds assembled to witness my landing.

'As I stepped from the boat in which I had sailed down from Levuka, Cacobau, after saluting me with the "tama," or cry of respect, took me by the hand and led me, still holding it, through the streets of the town. We walked thus along a broad road, shaded in some places by trees, past the sites of heathen temples, now destroyed, past the upright stones which mark the ancient places of sacrifice, and at length reached the entrance of his own residence.

'The way was lined by men and women in clean bright dresses, and seated on the ground in perfect silence, in the crouching attitude of Fijian respect.

'On entering the house I was conducted to the daïs, Cacobau taking his own seat below me on the floor.

'An interesting conversation ensued, in which the Vuni Valu very emphatically repeated many times, and I have no doubt with perfect sincerity, the expression of his satisfaction at the assumption of sovereignty by Her Majesty, a satisfaction which he thought that the majority of the chiefs shared with himself, although they did not see so clearly the advantages of the change. He denounced by name, and more than once, two or three of the great chiefs who led drunken and irregular lives, and insisted on the necessity of religion, morality, and sobriety in anyone placed in command, in a style which, his past history considered, was sufficiently surprising, but was, I believe, thoroughly true and real.

'Before I left he asked permission to send the criers through the town, announcing the ceremony of the next day, and they were so engaged until far into the night.

'The following morning the Vuni Valu assembled all the high chiefs, and lectured them on their duties under the new state of things, their ignorance, shortcomings, and foolish anticipations, after a fashion which those who heard it describe as in the highest degree striking and effective.

'In the afternoon the great chiefs, to the number of about 200, took their seats in a double row in a circle on the ground, under the shelter of a great awning of mat-sails, erected in the *rara* or public square of Bau. Outside the awning were the townspeople and my native guard, and at a little distance, on a small rise of ground, Cacobau's wife, Adi Litia, with her family, ladies, and servants.

'The *angona*, having been made to the accompaniment of the usual chanting, was brought in a small bowl to Cacobau by a young chief of high rank, and by Cacobau handed to me, amid the profoundest silence. As I began to drink, at Cacobau's signal and himself leading, the assembly raised the hand-clapping and shouts which imply acknowledgment of superior rank and position; and on their cessation, as I ceased to drink, I was much struck by the sudden momentary buzz of suppressed but excited conversation, which contrasted strongly with the silence observed both before and subsequently.

'The address, of which I enclose a copy and translation, was then read in Fijian by Mr. Carew.

'After this I proceeded to administer the oath of allegiance to the Queen to each of the ten *rokos*, reappointing each, with one exception, to his former Government by the delivery of a staff, accompanied by a few words of admonition, with their hands placed within my own.

'It was curious and interesting to watch them, as each successively sat before me, with the *bulis*, or district chiefs of their respective provinces seated behind him. There, somewhat ill at ease, in a place where, though treated with much outward politeness, he is naturally regarded with much bitterness and ill-will, was Maafu the Tongan, the bold and ambitious foreigner who has secured a master's hold upon the half of Fiji; and there were others with whose names I will not weary your lordship, but among whom "the King of the Reefs" (Tui Thakau), with great awe of the oath on his handsome Assyrian face; the wise and good Tui Bua, the most reflective man and best Governor I have met in Fiji, in countenance resembling a Spanish ecclesiastic of the sixteenth century; and Na Cagi Levu, the energetic and large-limbed chief of Kandavu, were perhaps the most remarkable.

'The ceremony concluded with the formal donation on my part of a large present of cloth to the principal chiefs, and the presentation to me of an address from the native clergy of the district, which, according to a promise made by me to them, I enclose to your lordship in original, that your lordship may see how clear and good a handwriting that of a native Fijian may sometimes be.

'Cacobau seemed much relieved and in much better spirits

when the whole affair was over. He had urged it with much persistence on some of those present, from whom he had wrung but an unwilling acquiescence in its performance, and who would fain have avoided any overt admission that they had accepted a stranger for their master. The fact of this reluctance justified Cacobau in having insisted on the importance of the acknowledgment. None were at last absent whose presence was of the slightest consequence, and the significance in the eyes of the native population of the public act of homage rendered not only, as on my arrival, by Cacobau himself on behalf of others, but by all the assembled chiefs, can hardly be overrated.

'Cacobau declined to wear at this ceremony the vast train of *tappa* in which it was formerly his custom to appear on state occasions, saying that "the time for such things was past," and appeared, as did nearly all the other chiefs, in a long *sulu*, of many folds of chief's *tappa*, a light-brown with black spots, reaching nearly to the feet, almost the only exceptions to this costume being that of some of the native magistrates, and some of the chiefs from the Lau Islands, who wore black *tappa*, and the native ministers, who were for the most part dressed entirely in white.'

CHAPTER V.

THE CANNIBAL OUTBREAK OF 1876.

Thus with every mark of respect and submission by both whites and natives was the British Government established in Fiji. There was still, however, in the highlands of Viti Levu a force of cannibals, ready and anxious to rush down on the unarmed Christians of the coast, and so provide the material for their horrible man-eating feasts. Mr. Walter Carew was despatched by the Governor into the interior of Viti Levu, and made a most interesting report to his chief. The highlanders thought that the epidemic of measles was the result of the anger of the heathen gods at so many of the Fijians having embraced Christianity, and it was evident that an outbreak was contemplated.

Very wisely, Mr. Carew requested a native missionary to leave the people to themselves for a while, and not to push Christianity against their wish, and stated that the Government expressly forbade any attempts of this kind—that religion must be left to the individual will of every person, but that the law must be obeyed. After clearly explaining the submission of the Vuni Valu and the supremacy of the Queen, Mr. Carew added that it would be 'easier for them to attempt to stay the heavy breakers on the beach than to attempt by their insignificant scheming to thwart the benevolent intentions of the Government on behalf of the people.' Mr. Carew suggested to his Excellency that a meeting of the chiefs of the cannibals should be held, and that under the presidency of the Governor a complete understanding should be arrived at. This advice was taken, and on the 5th January, 1876, Sir Arthur Gordon met the Kai Colos, and made them a very effective address, warning them in the plainest language of the consequences of insurrection. But all was of no avail. The heathens of Viti Levu could not and would not tamely allow their island to be ceded to a Christian Queen. They had been accustomed to regard with the most perfect contempt those who had *lotu'd* or become Christians; they had been used to sweep down on the Christian villages, and after murdering all who resisted, imprison the rest, and reserve them for a series of cannibal orgies. Under the reign of a Christian monarch (these people had never recognised Cacobau, who was only a king *in* Fiji, and not king *of* Fiji) Christians would certainly get the upper hand, and to do simple justice to the cannibal Kai Colos, the Christian natives did unquestionably indulge in very unwise boasting and rejoicing, which, of course, was gall and wormwood to the mountaineers.

The Christian settlements in Viti Levu extend from the coast upwards, and there are thus points over a great sweep of country where the *lotu* people and the 'devil'-worshippers infringe upon each other. The line is not a hard and fast one, extending round any definite point of the mountain range, but follows the ridges of the mountains in a broken line, now dipping deeply towards the coast, now retreating into the misty peaks which may be dimly seen as one sails along the island-shores, or explores the inland territory. All the mountaineers are not cannibals, nor are all the towns and villages in the plain Christian, nor, indeed, were all the cannibal towns disaffected. The intense enmity which has always existed between these two widely differing portions of the native population broke out afresh just after our rule began. The 'devils,' as they themselves expressed it, felt they must go in for a *moka*—a word which has exactly the same signification as the Malay 'running a muck.' Doubling round a strong camp of armed police, which the Governor had established at the first rumours of their disaffection, they descended the Sigatoka river (a large navigable stream, some hundred miles long), and attacked and burnt several of the native Christian towns which were especially obnoxious to them; but their sudden and unexpected attack was bravely met and repelled, though not before many innocent women and children had been slaughtered. The great chiefs, anxious to repay the confidence the Governor had reposed in them, rallied the men of their respective districts, and drove back the mountaineers upon the central police camp in the vicinity of the mountains; thence the force issued forth, and on one or two different occasions grappled with and punished the mountaineers. This was in April, but a more serious affair occurred in May. The Governor determined on again personally conferring with some of the mountain chiefs, and accordingly, after a two days' journey on foot, he reached the mountain town of Nasaucoko. The country through which his Excellency passed on his arduous duties, consisted, he says, 'for the first 12 or 14 miles, of open rolling plains, covered with grass, thinly dotted over with *pandanus.* Here and there, in the neighbourhood of villages or watercourses, trees are to be found. The hills then rise somewhat suddenly, and at the height of about 2000 feet from the sea is an extensive plateau, from which higher mountains spring. Clumps of wood become more frequent at a distance of 20 miles from the sea.

'The highest pass crossed was about 2500 feet by the barometer, and the highest of the surrounding mountains were probably about 1500 or 2000 feet higher. Nasaucoko itself is situated in a fine broad and fertile valley, into which the waters of the plateau leap in two magnificent cascades. The fort is strong for a native place. It is surrounded by an earthen wall about 7 feet high, plentifully loopholed, and surrounded by a palisade; outside the wall is a deep ditch, beyond which is another palisade. A third palisade surrounds the place at a distance of about 60 or 70 yards.'

At this fort of Nasaucoko, his Excellency had a conference with the leading mountaineer chiefs. Some of them, notably Kolikoli, the chief of the mountain tribes on the river Sigatoka, announced that they believed the Government to be good, and intended to remain quiet. All was going well, and Sir

Arthur had every reason to congratulate himself on the result of his labours, when Mudu, chief of the Quali Mari, declared that he was of a very different mind. He hated Christianity, and he hated the Government, and he had only attended the meeting in the hope that Kolikoli had called them together to concert measures for an immediate attack on the Christian camp at Nasaucoko. Another mountaineer took the same side, and the meeting broke up in confusion.

His Excellency then returned to Nadi, a settlement on the west coast of Viti Levu, and at the mouth of the river of that name; and afterwards had a three days' journey to Cuvu, a town close by Nadroga, a harbour to the south-east of the same island. On his line of march, a village, about a mile from where the viceregal party were supping, was burnt by the cannibals, and the insurrection commenced in earnest.

The various *rokos* or chiefs were now called upon to contribute their men for the war. They came from Vanua Levu in the north, and from Kandavu in the south, over a distance of 150 miles by sea, at the order of the new Kovanna, as they termed the Governor, who had shown sympathy with their race, and confidence in themselves. The armed police, under Captain Olive, had been encamped at Nasaucoko. Two columns were formed: one, composed of the 'regulars' or armed constabulary, under the command of Captain Knollys of the 32nd Regiment, was to advance against the mountaineers in their fortresses; the other, consisting of Nadrog and Sigotoka men, was to operate against the Quali Mari tribe, who had committed the ravages on the Sigatoka river. This was under the direction of Mr. Gordon, the Governor's private secretary, who was appointed deputy-commissioner of Viti Levu for the emergency. A force of auxiliaries, under Mr. Le Hunt, occupied the former police camp at Nasaucoko, while Mr. Walter Carew visited the tribes on the Rewa river to the south-west of the island, to claim their neutrality, and to endeavour to prevent the mountaineers escaping in that direction under cover of their friendly protection.

The difficulties of the Fiji Government at this time could hardly be exaggerated. It had neither troops nor war-ships. The arms which the colony possessed were a very few rifles, and some hundreds of old flint guns, and percussion Enfields, which had been handed over by the late Government. The New Zealand Government most promptly sent a few dozen Sniders, and of course these were turned to the best possible account. The wisdom of the native policy of Sir Arthur Gordon and his advisers was never more apparent than in this little war. The fighting men on the side of the Government were called out by their own chiefs, who led them, fed them, and controlled them, in native fashion. The chiefs were counselled and directed by the officers I have named, who in their turn were prompted by the experienced wisdom of Mr. Carew.

The campaign was opened by Mr. Gordon, who found the 'devils' occupying in force some village about 14 miles from the native town of Sigatoka. Two smart skirmishes ensued before the strongholds were attacked, and in both cases the cannibals were promptly driven back. The first village fort being taken, they retired to their great stronghold, Mantanivatu, which was on a high rock and covered with dense wood. It was regarded as impregnable, for art had very cleverly (for Fijians) supplemented nature. The firing of the Sniders was however too much for the mountaineers, who, of course, had only the old muzzle-loading muskets; and although they defended themselves with great bravery, the rock was scaled and captured by the Government forces, after a brief hand-to-hand struggle, in which the formidable Fiji club played a very conspicuous part. About fifty of the cannibals were slain, and many prisoners were taken. The main body escaped to other towns of the same district, but they were quickly followed up, and the bulk were either captured or surrendered to the chief of Beimaua, who acted with the Government. Those captured included the principal chiefs of the revolted cannibals, and also the leaders of the atrocities on the Sigatoka river. The Government loss was one man killed, and a very few wounded.

Mr. Gordon having so successfully concluded the task confided to him, of capturing the strongholds of the Quali Mari and dispersing the rebels, returned to the coast with the principal prisoners in charge of his militia. The rest of the prisoners were brought down by the returning forces to Sigatoka, and there lodged in the 'Bure,' or devil temple, which is still preserved in that now Christian town.

The captured mountaineers, filing in with bound hands and dejected countenances, were no longer the proud Quali Mari of the hills. Their hair, which in war they mass up in stiff locks so as to give their heads an enormous and leonine appearance, was cut off, and their proud boasts were silenced. Women and children carrying their household goods on their backs, followed with the women who had accompanied the Government force, and all went to the same villages. There were no taunts or cruelty to the prisoners or their women. They were taken care of in the villages of the conquerors, until the Government decided to let them return to their homes.

A very different fate, however, was in store for the murderers of peaceful women and children. Thirty of them were tried before Mr. Gordon as a deputy-commissioner of Viti Levu, and were found guilty of murder. The sentence of death being submitted to the Governor, he selected fourteen of the most guilty for capital punishment, of whom four were hanged and ten shot.

The operations of Captain Knollys against the Kai Colos were also very successful. Close to the stronghold of these cannibals was the town of Nadrau, and owing to the careful manipulation of Mr. Carew and Captain Knollys himself, the chief of that place had been retained on the Government side. The mountaineers being asked if they intended to *soro*, that is, send in their submission with presents as tokens of their sincerity, replied that they meant fighting, and when they were killed their women would fight. The boast was not verified, however, for when Captain Knollys was ready to give the assault, the Kai Colos fled from their famous town, taken by surprise at last—for their kava (the *angona* liquor) was ready to drink, and their yams were baking. They were finally hemmed in by the Government troops, and reduced to surrender from some caves in which they had taken refuge.

Peace was soon restored to Viti Levu, and quiet has reigned there ever since.

The town of Bukutia, in the Sigatoka district taken by Mr. Gordon, had never been captured in any of the tribal fights, and was regarded as a sort of sacred place by the cannibals. When it was surrounded by the Government forces, the 'devils' consulted their chief priest as to the meaning of these strange portents. From the top of the lofty rock he announced in the quiet evening air the response of the oracle to his dispirited followers.

'My house,' he cried, 'is not accustomed to be burned.'

His words were heard by friends and foes alike; and scarcely had the echoes died away, when a great shout rose from the Christians surrounding the rock:

'Wait until to-morrow!'

The unexpected response seems to have struck terror into priest and people, for during the night the town was evacuated, and the 'devil' temple, unaccustomed to be burned, was duly committed to the flames.

The chiefs invariably harangue their followers before an assault; these harangues are usually eloquent, and delivered with great vigour. They walk along the front of the lines beseeching, taunting, breaking out into great leaps and bounds, expressive of the activity they intend to display, and inciting their followers to imitate them. This may be regarded as an appeal to the old savage elements, for when it is finished, a more dignified ceremony is observed.

The Christian teacher comes forward, and all the soldiers kneeling down with their faces to the earth, he pours forth a prayer for success in battle. The teachers are not slow to shoulder a rifle themselves, and some of them had to be reminded after the fight that it was their special duty to show care for the wounded, and prevent cruelty to the vanquished.

Mr. Gordon set them an example which at first they could scarcely comprehend. A poor baby was shot on its mother's back during the flight, the ball passing across its stomach. The mother threw it down as dead, but it was found alive, and the utmost care was taken of it; and when at length it died, it was wrapped in Mr. Gordon's mat.

The cannibals did not show similar humanity. They captured a teacher belonging to the British forces. The unfortunate man was rather shortsighted, and had walked inadvertently into the enemy's camp. He was clubbed, carried off, and eaten. His bones, with the marks of the fire on them, were found when the town was captured shortly afterwards.

It is a strange reflection that the men who captured the town were themselves cannibals only a few years before, but had become as well disposed and obedient subjects of Her Majesty as if they had been born of Christian parents, and surrounded with all the traditions of a Christian country. Cannibalism is a thing of the past, and there is no fear of any further rising of the people. Before annexation, insular prejudices, like the clannishness of the tribes, prevented united action; but now that they are face to face with an imperial power, those few among them who still refuse to accept the Christian *lotu* have not only been reduced to submission, but in the vast majority of cases that submission has been cheerfully given, and they know and feel it to be a great change for the better.

CHAPTER VI.

LEVUKA.

LEVUKA presents a very pretty aspect from the anchorage inside the coral reef surrounding the island of Ovalau. There are two good entrances through this reef, called respectively the Levuka and Wakaya Channels, the latter being named after a small but most beautiful island, lately the property of my friend Dr. Brower, at one time consul for the United States in the group. A noble background of steep hills is covered with luxuriant tropical foliage, whose rocky peaks attain an altitude of something like 1500 feet; two well-defined spurs mark two distinct bays, and then white-painted wooden houses with balconies extend for upwards of a mile. Nestled snugly on the hillsides are the houses of the principal merchants, and the piers running out from the beach tell of the pushing Anglo-Saxon and his trade.

At the south end of the beach is Nasova, the residence of

the Governor and the chief officers of state, together with their official places of business. This viceregal quarter is guarded by a few sentries of the native armed constabulary—clad in blue tunics and carrying rifle and bayonet. The Custom House, Post Office, and bureau of the Department of Law are at the northern end of the town, beyond which is the original Levuka of the natives.

Two creeks—formerly mountain torrents—run into Levuka Bay, known respectively as Totoga and Levuka, the former nearly subdividing the entire length of the capital of Polynesia. Of good stores, hotels, and boarding-houses there is no lack; notably, the hostelries called the 'Levuka,' the 'Royal,' 'Polynesian,' and 'Steam-packet,' all of which have first-class billiard-tables. The shops and stores are so numerous, that it would be difficult to mention even the leading ones by name.

There is a plentiful supply, at very moderate prices, of all articles in ordinary use. Groceries and drapery are exceptionally cheap. Levuka boasts of one or two milliners and dressmakers, a first-class photographer (who also attends to the repairs of watches and clocks), a 'practical' tailor, and a really admirable barber's shop kept by a gentleman of African blood, whose boast it is that he was the first 'white man' that ever crossed some Fijian mountains—in what island I forget.

Saddle-horses for ladies and gentlemen can be had at the moderate charge of 10s. a day, while an omnibus runs from one end of Beach Street to the other.

There are two well-known auctioneers, while Mr. F. Spence devotes his entire attention to the collection of the splendid ferns in which the group abounds. Beach Street is, of course, the principal promenade, and gossip during and after business hours is a great source of amusement.

When I say that, in a population of some 700 souls, there is a capital club, two boat and yachting clubs, besides cricket, archery, and shooting clubs; that Levuka possesses an admirably conducted mechanics' institute, with a good reading-room and library; that concerts, professional and amateur, are neither few nor far between; and that the *valse à trois temps* is thoroughly appreciated—I fancy my readers will agree with me that emigration to 'cannibal' Fiji is not altogether such a miserable prospect as they perhaps imagined.

In addition to a Town Board with a warden, Levuka rejoices in that peculiarly British luxury, a School Board. There is a well-conducted gaol and lock-up, but very few whites, I am glad to say, have patronised 'Seed's Hotel,' as the *Fiji Argus* called the institution under control of the Chief of Police.

The Good Templars have a hall, in which temperance lectures and entertainments are frequently given.

The principal wharf is at the south end of the town, and is carried out to a depth of more than six fathoms of water, so that the Sydney steamers of 1500 tons come alongside to discharge and receive cargo. Two ship-building slips have been erected in consequence of the great increase of this branch of Polynesian industry.

Levuka may be called the Babel of the Pacific. The white population is a wonderfully diversified one, for in a small township of about 700, there are representatives of nearly every civilised community: English, Scotch, Irish, Germans and French abound, while Russians, Swedes, Norwegians, Danes, Dutch, Italians, Spaniards, United States citizens, West Indians, Canadians, South Americans, Australians, Chinese, Hindoos, etc., are numerous. Among the Polynesian races, representatives may be found of nearly every group or island in the broad Pacific. Fijians, Samoans, Tongese, Tahitians, Caledonians,

Tokalaus, Marquesans, Solomon Islanders, Santos, Maralebs, Aobans, Sandwich Islanders, Savage Islanders, natives of the Carolines, the Ladrones, and other groups to the northward, Lepers Islanders, Malicolos, Tanna men, besides half-castes, quadroons and octoroons of every shade and nationality, may be seen daily in the streets. Yet this wonderfully mixed population forms a most law-abiding community, among whom crimes of any magnitude are hardly known. I question if there is any township or village in the British Empire or beyond it, that has so slight a criminal record as Levuka, in much-abused Fiji.

The sanitary arrangements of Levuka are also well cared for, as an inspector is perpetually on the war-path after 'matter in the wrong place.'

According to a recent statistical return, the total white population of the group is 2000. There are only some 850 taxable males out of the above total, and Levuka is favoured with 300 of these, nearly 100 being married. There are in Levuka about 120 ladies; but of single young ladies, the number is only 30.

The cemetery of Levuka is at Draiba, about two miles to the south of the town, beautifully situated on the side of a hill. The walks are well kept, and the place has been planted with a very light green broad-leaved grass, presenting a marked contrast to the surrounding vegetation. Levuka is a healthy place, and plots of real estate at Draiba are not much in demand.

The Levuka cricket-ground lies to the north end of the town, close to a suburb called Vagadace (pronounced Vagadally), and is a good level bit of turf. The Saturday half-holiday is an established institution, and the scene on the cricket-ground on the afternoon of that day strikingly reminds the British traveller of 'home.' Looking seaward, he will find the bay dotted with the white sails of pleasure-crafts, racing, it may be, out of one entrance of the coral-reef and in at the other. The German becomes a naturalised British subject, and in time learns almost to forget the Fatherland—nay, as I know from personal experience in America, repudiates all connection with it; but John Bull is John Bull wherever he may be found. The average British pioneer colonist always reminds one of a commercial traveller; he is eternally pushing the claims and introducing the specialities of Messrs. Jno. Bull & Co.

And here a line in defence of gentlemen who used to be much maligned in dear stop-at-home Old England. I allude to the majority of the settlers whom I happened to come across, and I use the word 'gentlemen' advisedly. To many, both in Australia and the Mother Country, a Fijian colonist has meant nothing else than a runaway bankrupt from Australia or New Zealand, happy enough to have settled down years ago in a little-known archipelago which, if it did boast man-eaters, was equally able to glory in the non-existence of the principles of extradition. An editorial of mine, contributed to the *Fiji Times* towards the end of 1876, deals with this opinion in the following fashion:

'The people in England know nothing of us; the vast majority of them believe firmly that these islands were annexed by the Imperial Government because the cannibals residing here were a dangerous nuisance to the few semi-crazed settlers who, in defiance of everything practical, would paradoxically insist on courting death by living here; that not only were these colonists mad themselves, but almost as objectionable to the world's pacific relations as the cannibals with whom they so willingly took up their abode. The whites in Fiji were supposed to be the offscourings of the Australian colonies, men who, having failed by want of honesty, industry, or temperance in New Zealand or New South Wales, had obligingly come down to Fiji, there to add to immoderate gin-drinking a taste for slave-driving, which, with tropical effrontery, they called the labour trade; and as their proceedings in this exhilarating branch of commerce often required the interference of Her Majesty's war-ships, with possible inconvenience to their officers and crews, it was judged far better to take the whole thing over, annex these obnoxious islands as a Crown colony of a severe type, and so prevent the cannibals from eating the madmen, and the madmen from selling the cannibals.'

I need hardly add that the assumptions referred to are gratuitous libels. There was such a thing as 'blackbirding' or man-stealing for providing labour carried on by scoundrels of every nationality under heaven, and to a limited extent Fiji was for a time one of the numerous centres of their operations. But I do not hesitate to say that the great majority of the Fiji settlers never countenanced the trade, and only asked for labourers on fair terms. The colonists I met with were as a rule gentlemen by birth and education; and if one takes grasp of subject, general knowledge, and honest courtesy as a criterion of intellectual strength, a comparison might be established between a smoking-party of Fijian planters and an equal number of men in the smoking-room of a London club, and I fancy that the comparison would end favourably for Fiji.

In matters ecclesiastical Levuka is not behind the times. The best church is undoubtedly that of the Catholics, which possesses a peal of bells. The chief of the Roman missionaries, Father Bretheret, has been thirty-five years in the group, and is most deservedly loved by all, whether inside the 'pale' or out of it. Father Bretheret is one of the Marist order, and is, I believe, Vicar Apostolic of Fiji. The Catholics have not anything like the following of the Wesleyans, but if I remember aright, they count 9000 communicants. The number of the priests in the mission is ten. Father Bretheret is a good sailor, and anything but an indifferent boat-builder.

The Anglican Church boasts a neat chapel, attended by his Excellency, and served by the Rev. W. Floyd, M.A., who did good service during the measles epidemic. The Church of England has, however, no missionary establishment in the group, the only two Christian bodies possessing such, being the Catholics and Wesleyans.

According to a late return, the statistics of the Wesleyan body are as follows: Churches, etc., 841; European missionaries, 10; Native ministers, 48.

There are three medical men in Levuka, and a well-conducted hospital is located on an elevated plateau above the town, surrounded by the most exquisite foliage, and commanding an extensive sea view of great beauty.

The fourth estate is represented by the *Fiji Times* bi-weekly, and the *Fiji Argus* weekly; the former being in bitter opposition to the present *régime*, while the latter is more or less on the side of the Government. If a little more spirit was infused into the conduct of the latter paper it would do better. Apparently, its course of action hitherto has invariably been to let 'I dare not wait upon I would.' At the new political capital, Suva, a weekly *Times* is now issued. The *Royal Gazette* is published monthly, and at irregular intervals a native paper appears.

The Governor, Geo. W. des Vœux, Esq., C.M.G., is assisted in his labours by the Executive Council, consisting of the Colonial Secretary, the Hon. J. B. Thurston, C.M.G., Attorney and Receiver Generals, the Commissioner of Lands, and the Chief Justice. The Legislative Assembly consists of these gentlemen and a few of the prominent planters and merchants. Justice is represented by Sir J. Gorrie as Chief; while there is a chief police magistrate and registrar-general, and eight European stipendiary magistrates, who are scattered over the group of islands.

The group is divided into twelve provinces: Lau, Lomai Viti, Tai Levu, Rewa, Naitasiri, Nadroga, Ba, Yasawas, Ra, Kandavu, Bua and Macauta. Each of these has its *roko*, or chief, while there are eighty-two *bulis*, or sub-chiefs, who receive small salaries. The Armed Constabulary, soldiers in all but the name, number about one hundred, and are under the command of Englishmen. There is, in addition, a Levukan town and provincial civil police, while the *rokos* of each province maintain a sort of militia, more or less trained after the British model.

CHAPTER VII.

LIFE IN LEVUKA.

LIFE in Levuka is very pleasant to those to whom enjoyment is possible without the roar of a big city. A delightful climate, comfortable quarters, and good food, ought to make up a great part of man's terrestrial happiness, and these he can enjoy in the capital of Fiji.

I do not for one minute pretend that Carnarvon House, or the Levuka Hotel, rival European or American luxury; but they are clean and comfortable, and everything is done to make you happy. As regards food, a professional gourmet would turn up his scientific nose at a Levukan breakfast; but, at any rate, it suffices for the planters and merchants, who, in their crass ignorance, think a meal of eggs poached and boiled, bacon fried, or cured ham, chops and steaks, curries, and preserved salmon 'fixed' in half a dozen ways, tea and coffee, watercress and oranges, is good enough for them.

A day in a Levukan boarding-house may not be uninteresting to my readers. You are awakened about six a.m. by your 'boy' (or native servant) bringing the matutinal tea; and you put on a pair of light shoes or slippers, and start for the falls—although it should be added that all the hotels, etc., have excellent baths, shower and otherwise. A good quarter of a mile in rear of town and hospital is a most delightful waterfall, some 3 feet in breadth (I have seen it 4) by some 10 feet in height. This falls into a pool about 20 feet in circumference and 4 to 5 feet in depth. A cave of refuge lies to the rear of the waterfall, and it makes a capital bathing-place. Surrounded by the most exquisite tropical foliage, with views extending all down the Totoga valley, added to clear, and, for the tropics, ice-cold water, the bathing-hole of the southern Levukans has no parallel except in that paradise of bathing-places, Waitova, described by the late Commodore Goodenough as his ideal of a perfect bathing locality.

About 2 miles from the centre of the town are these falls of Waitova. They are approached by a gradual ascent through a dense mass of the most luxuriant vegetation, terminating in some extensive patches of taro, which the natives have shown skill in irrigating. Leaving these, you find a steeper ascent, and then skirt a rocky promontory, on the sides of which a few steps have been cut. Behind this rocky guardian is a large-sized and most magnificent pool, shallow as you approach it from the rock, but of great depth at the other end. It is surrounded on both sides by precipitous hills, clothed to their summits with the richest trees, plants, and flowers, and backed by a waterfall 25 feet in height. A series of smaller falls are below the pool to seawards. As in the bathing-hole of the Totoga creek, there is a cave immediately in rear of the fall, but of twice its size. In fact Waitova 'washing-place' is a superb pool and waterfall in the mountain-side, and the view down that glorious valley to the blue sea, bisected by the glittering coral reef, is surpassing in its beauty.

Waitova in the early sunlight—when its exquisite avenue is illumined by the morning rays, and the ever-varied undergrowth is disclosed by the same means—is a valley for a poet to sing of. As a matter of fact, the distance prevents most Levukans from reaching Waitova before breakfast. Business in the stores commences about nine, and goes on with little intermission till past five in the evening. Levukans may lounge about and gossip a good deal; but they do work, and work hard.

At the principal hotels and boarding-houses lunch is served about one, and consists of one or two warm dishes, including curries, cold meats, sardines, and other canned fish, and odds and ends, which make an appetising meal.

In the afternoon a siesta is often taken for an hour or so, which always agrees with the digestive organs. Dinner is served about 6 to 6.30, and is generally of the conventional type—soup and fish, *entrées* and joint, puddings or tart, and dessert. Considering that the boarding-rates in no case exceed £2 10s. per week (when I stayed at Carnarvon House the tariff was only £2 2s.), no one has much right to complain.

Spirits are retailed at sixpence per glass, while the same price is charged for a glass of the 'square gin' of Schiedam —the J.D.K.Z. brand—the favourite liquor of all Polynesians. Rum is now made in the colony, but little of it is consumed in Levuka. Perhaps it would be better if clarets and hocks were drank instead of the fiery compounds known as brandy, or in place even of the comparatively mild square gin; but from China to Peru the Anglo-Saxon is the same. He takes kindly to the stronger beverages, and a generation of Wilfrid Lawsons will never eradicate traditional preference. I think it is Mr. Buckmaster, in his admirable book on 'Schools of Cookery,' who remarks that until we better understand the culinary science, all hope of inducing Englishmen to confine themselves to those wines which go best with delicate dishes will be futile. In tropical countries, where the Spaniard has ruled, salads and delicious dishes of mixed vegetables are seen on the table as often as bread. In Fiji and other British colonies, as at home, the cook's imagination rarely soars beyond a curry and a hash; and for vegetables, we have the usual greens and potatoes.

As a rule, fowls and turkeys are very plentiful in Levuka; but sometimes there is a great scarcity of the latter. Fish is of the mullet order, but is not in very regular supply, and is obtained sometimes—O shade of Izaak Walton!—by means of dynamite. Good beef costs about ninepence, and mutton eightpence a pound, fowls about two shillings a pair, ducks (when to be had—market uncertain) about two shillings and sixpence, and turkeys from four shillings each. To the heathen Chinee, who to a small extent is represented in the group, is mainly due the credit of the successful introduction of European vegetables, for in my opinion a native yam, sustaining as it is, is after all a poor substitute for cabbage, and that mottled, soap-looking root, the taro, is to my taste anything but appetising. Lima beans, cabbage, radishes, watercress, spring onions, and lettuce, have all been cultivated with success. Potatoes are at present entirely imported from Auckland and the other colonies.

The one drawback to Fijian beef is that it is sometimes very tough, in consequence of being cooked the very day it is killed. The papaw (*Cerica papaya*) grows, however, luxuriantly all over the Pacific, and is a remedy for this. The juice is found to possess the property of rendering tough meat tender when boiled with it. If the unripe fruit be placed in the water in which the toughest meat is to be cooked, it is found to render it perfectly digestible, and the same results are observed if the meat be merely washed with the juice of the fruit. The thick white milky juice, when extracted from the unripe papaw, contains properties similar to those of pepsine; and it is possible that it may be susceptible of chemical preservation, and become a valuable preparation. Tough meat is not unknown in England, and surely the papaw could be canned and sent over here, even if no other mode of preservation is arrived at.

Among indigenous fruit and vegetables, tomatoes grow wild, but are smaller than the cultivated European variety; the fruit pronounced 'wee' has a sharp flavour, stringy flesh and a large stone in the centre; the moli-apple, also growing wild, gives a refreshing cleansing of the mouth; while the grenadilla, common to the West Indies, is also to be found in abundance. The pine-apple, limes and oranges, shaddocks, citron and sweet lemons, all grow wild, as do bananas, which are now being extensively exported. Pomegranates, gourds, and vegetable-marrows flourish abundantly, but the latter are not seen as often as they might be. Oranges of the most delicious flavour are to be had very cheap, sixpence purchasing a basket containing thirty to forty, while limes are to be had for the asking in most localities. The young leaves of the cocoa-nut tree make a most delicious salad if properly dressed; but all of us know who sends the cooks, and Fiji is no exception to the universal scope of that gentleman's operations.

Levuka is not much troubled with those pests, the mosquitoes, but still, nets are necessary at night. Sometimes so deliciously cool are the nights, that a light blanket can be borne in addition to the sheet. As regards dress, it must be remembered that Levuka is the metropolis, and what is quite good enough for the planter on his estate is hardly the thing for the capital. Suits of good white drill, of white flannel, or of thin serge, are the correct thing, while a sun-helmet (if possible of cork) is the best protection for the head. White canvas-shoes are generally warm, while a water-proof coat and a pair of leggings are indispensable. An umbrella is required both for sun and rain. Braces are seldom worn in Fiji, a broad waistband sash being generally adopted; and it is an undoubted precaution against stomachic diseases.

After what I have said as to the advanced state of social life in far-distant Fiji, it will not surprise my readers, I suppose, to learn that evening-dress of the 'complete waiter' order is *de rigueur*. The black 'stove-pipe' or chimney-pot hat is never seen in Coral Lands, though it is a fact that two prominent gentlemen of Levuka still wear its time-honoured shape in white. For my part, I was heartily glad to get rid of that modern monstrosity. I did hear, however, of one tall black hat, which was worn for a whole week on Levuka beach for a wager, and then crushed in. The bet was a farce—the sequel was a tragedy. The successful wearer having to all intents and purposes ruined the ghastly head-gear he had been sporting, filled it with cubes of very hard stone, and placed it a few feet from the path of those churchward-bound on a Sunday morning. Who could resist the temptation, recalling, perhaps, episodes of boyish life at home? With head erect and stately step advances the Hon. ———, a member of the Legislative Assembly. He sees the damaged abomination, hesitates, and then, taking a few steps, gives it one gigantic kick. He never went to church that morning, and complained for weeks after of very sore toes. A second victim immediately followed the speedy retreat of number one; and after practically laming two of the best-known Levukans, the wretched hat was pitched into the sea—a fate which I devoutly wish would be that of all its species.

On this day Fiji demonstrated her civilisation to the world. The '*Jamais!*' of M. Rouher was as nothing to the unalterable decision of sensible Levukans to never, *never* tolerate a black silk hat.

A leading London financier said to me the other day: 'Ah! Fiji—yes, Fiji; well, it has hardly got out of its laughing-stock days yet, has it? Cold missionary on the side-board, and cooked Christians always ready day or night.' The joke is an old one, and 'Polynesians' can now afford to laugh at it.

There is direct monthly communication by steam between Levuka and Auckland, New Zealand, Sydney and Melbourne; the English mail arriving in San Francisco and Auckland, and returning *viâ* Sydney and Suez. Two inter-insular steamers connect the islands of the group to leeward and windward, while there is talk of a monthly steamer to the neighbouring kingdom of Tonga, and another is proposed to be shortly put on the station between the commercial capital of Polynesia, Levuka and Samoa. There are regular steamers between the Rewa river in Viti Levu and Suva, the recently declared seat of Government. There are moreover regular lines of sailing-vessels to and from Auckland, New Zealand, and Sydney, as also to Samoa (Navigators' Islands), and all the out-lying archipelagos.

The first postage-stamps ever used in Polynesia were those of the *Fiji Times*, of the values of 1d., 3d., and 6d. Under King Cacobau's government regular perforated stamps were introduced, and good specimens of art they are. The stock not being exhausted at the cession, a V. R. has been simply printed in black lettering over the engraved C. R. and crown, and these are now the ordinary tokens of free postage in the group and far beyond. The value of these stamps, as issued by the late Government, were, I think, 1d., 3d., and 6d., although the British authorities have changed the value of some of the colours, which are respectively blue, green, and pink, by just printing a new price on them. A new shilling stamp with the Queen's head has just been issued. Letters reach Levuka in about fifty-five days from London, but usually take sixty days in getting home.

Before our annexation the coinage was all in dollars and cents, American and English money being taken equally, the latter at four shillings for one hundred cents. The first paper money was that issued by a private firm, Messrs. Brewer and Joske, of Suva, in connection with the Polynesian Land Company; but these notes were for very small sums.

King Cacobau's Government issued some beautifully executed notes for five and ten dollars, bearing the initials of his Majesty, with the crown and arms of Fiji, with a Fijian motto: '*Perevaka na kalouka Doka na tui*,' or, 'Fear God and Honour the King,' underneath. The 'supporters' were palm-trees.

The earliest effort to introduce financial facilities into the group was that of the Fiji Banking and Commercial Company, a society in close connection with the Bank of New Zealand. The charter of the former was dated August 19th, 1873, and was signed by King Cacobau and twelve native chiefs; also by Messrs. John B. Thurston, George A. Woods, Howard Clarkson, and Robert S. Swanston. This document provides that there shall be conveyed to the Company, free of cost, 10,000 acres of country lands at the Company's choice. 3000 acres of these were selected, and sold, with the other assets, to the Bank of New Zealand. The liquidators of the Fiji Banking Company are now endeavouring to get from the British Government the balance of 7000 acres, as they allege, still due to them. The British Government, however, do not write in what may be called a reassuring style, for in a comparatively recent letter the following passage occurs. It is from the Colonial Secretary of the Government of Fiji to the liquidators of the defunct Company: 'Her Majesty's Government and the Colonial Government entirely disclaim the slightest obligation to become responsible for the liabilities incurred, or to make good the engagements entered into by those who professed to administer the affairs of Fiji previous to its cession to Great Britain, and they are, therefore, unable to recognise the existence of any rights purporting to have been conferred by a charter which they do not admit to be in force.'

The Union Bank of Australia has a branch at Levuka as well as the Bank of New Zealand, while the Mortgage and Agency Company of Australasia, the first company formed exclusively to further the interests of Fiji, is established at the same place.

In regard to matters of commercial and social convenience, it should be mentioned that numerous fire, marine, and life insurance companies have agencies in Levuka, and do a good business. Fifty years ago its inhabitants would have insured the traveller's death at a very early date.

CHAPTER VIII.

RELIGION, PAST AND PRESENT.

In Fiji the traveller is face to face not only with the Anglo-Saxon, safe under the British flag, but with a Christian native population who have only just emerged from the most horrible forms of cannibalism. On all sides he will see traces of the ancient devil-worship, but he will also notice how the majority of the traditions of heathenism, though dying very hard, are fading away, while all that is good in the old system is being carefully adapted, so as to fit in with the Christianity now professed. Fiji has been the last stronghold of organised and systematic cannibalism, and though the history of the religion and customs of Fiji prior to the country's general acceptance of Wesleyan and Catholic teaching may be steeped in horrors, it will be of interest to the student in after years, who will marvel, in the presence of a Christian and industrious population, that they ever could have had such a ferociously bloodthirsty ancestry.

I make no apology, therefore, for dwelling at some length on the manners and customs of the Fijians of the 'good old times,' especially as, intermingled with Catholic and Wesleyan Christianity, much of the old leaven remains. My knowledge of the language is so imperfect, that it is impossible for me to say exactly how much still exists, though I judge that a few more years will see the end of every trace of devil-worship and its concomitants.

The Fijians will, I apprehend, never in our time grasp the spirit of our religion as we do, but marvellous progress has been made, and although it may be fashionable to sneer at missionaries and mission work, it is just as well now and then to judge by results, and give honour where honour is due. From a great experience of big cities in all parts of the world, I am a firm believer in the axiom that 'charity should begin at home,' but it need not necessarily end there; and, if I remember correctly, the Divine commission was to 'teach ALL nations.' Divided, as those who profess a common Christianity unhappily are, I cannot agree with perhaps the majority of the missionaries in the Southern Seas; but despite all differences of creed, I tender them the most respectful homage when I think what those men have done.

Missionaries may have traded, missionaries may have lived too luxurious lives, and perhaps there is no great approach among the majority to the spirit of sainted Francis Xavier; but is not the meanest native teacher (even if he professes a mutilated creed), who preaches the elements of the Sermon on the Mount, a thousand times better as an advanced guard of what we are pleased to call European civilisation, than any of the trading scoundrels, from whose infectious blackguardism Fiji is only just recovering? The day is happily past for these mission-haters, who have themselves for the most part gone to answer for their conduct to a higher authority than that of the Lord High Commissioner of Western Polynesia; but the fact remains that men of Anglo-Saxon lineage have been the curse of the Pacific, and have caused the deaths of such men as the Protestant Bishop Patteson and Commodore Goodenough. The uncontrolled Fiji labour-trade of former years may not have been exactly slavery, but the ruffians I have referred to (Her Majesty's Government's blue-books bear evidence of their infamy), not only carried on a regular slave-trade, but considered murder as one of its branches.

When I reflect on the perfect self-denial of the Marist Fathers, who have left their native land *for ever*, to spread in distant Polynesia the great truths of Christianity as taught by the one Church which speaks with the consciousness of claimed infallibility, I am lost in admiration. These men have no comfortable homes to repair to after a few years' labour under sunny skies; nor wife nor child to solace them during that labour. For them life is indeed a following of the Cross, which is sustained by the certainty that a crown will follow in God's good time. The labours of the servants of the Propaganda Fide are little known to the world, but they are registered by Him who knows His own. Barely supported, hardly thought of by the bulk of Europeans, the silent work of the French missionaries in Fiji goes on, and they care little for human praise or human blame. Though, as Mr. Litton Forbes says in 'Two Years in Fiji,' they are the most careful civilisers of any religious teachers in the South Seas; their business is a school for eternity, and when their life's class-time is over, they know they will reap their reward.

The Fijians have among them legends said to be handed down from time immemorial, which are strangely analogous to certain portions of Mosaic history. One is, that in ages past, the sea suddenly came right over the land (*Na Viti Levu*), drowning all inhabitants except a few who escaped in a large canoe, and others who at the time were gathering *yaka* * on a high peak not submerged. The canoe had been built on an inland height, though why there, and for what reason, their history sayeth not. When the inundation occurred, a number of men and women got into and launched it, several being crushed in the process. May there not be some connection between the old Fijian custom of launching a chief's canoe over human bodies, and the progress of the Hindoo Juggernaut car

* *Yaka* is a fibrous plant from which the most durable fishing-nets are made.

over its crushed victims? The tradition continues: the women and children who were gathering *yaka* were reduced to great straits, having only salt water to drink; but when they were at the last extremity, 'one' came to them and commanded them to follow him; they did so to a rock which he struck with his stick, and from which good water immediately flowed. The analogy with Moses and his rod here is obvious. When the flood subsided, there were but few persons left alive to re-people the land, and only such little animals as Fiji now has. I endeavoured to elicit an opinion as to who that 'one' who drew water from the stone was, but could obtain nothing definite, though it is evident that the individual must have been regarded as at least possessing supernatural power.

I do not know whether any other writer on Polynesia has noticed it, but I was informed by a 'beachcomber,' that in some of the islands of the Low Archipelago, there is a tradition of some of the ancestry of their people having gone over to or returned from a big land to the East—or more properly speaking, over West—*i.e.*, America. It is a fact that the skeletons found in the caverns of Kentucky and Tennessee are wrapped in feather cloaks, which was a custom of the Sandwich Islanders; while it is the opinion of most American antiquaries that the best-defined specimens of art among the antiquities of Ohio and Kentucky are of a decided Polynesian character. The difficulties of the sea-passage between the Eastern groups and South America is no greater than between the Sandwich and Society Islands, and yet the identity of the inhabitants of the latter places is undoubted.

Mr. Ellis, in his 'Polynesian Researches,' says:

'In the most remote and solitary islands occasionally discovered in recent years, such as Pitcairn's, on which the mutineers of the *Bounty* settled, and on Fannings Island, near Christmas Island, midway between the Society and the Sandwich Islands, although now desolate, relics of former inhabitants have been found. Pavements of floors, foundations of houses, and stone entrances have been discovered ; and stone adzes, or hatchets, have been found at some distance from the surface, exactly resembling those in use among the people of the North and South Pacific at the time of their discovery. These facts prove that the nations now inhabiting these and other islands have been in former times more widely extended than they are at present.'

There are, besides, many well-authenticated accounts of long voyages performed in native vessels by the inhabitants of both the North and South Pacific. In 1696 two canoes were driven from Ancarso to one of the Philippine Islands, a distance of eight hundred miles. Their occupants said they had run before the wind for seventy days, sailing from east to west. Thirty-five had embarked, but five died from the effects of privation and fatigue during the voyage, and one shortly after their arrival. In 1723 two canoes drifted from a remote distance to one of the Marian Islands. Captain Cook found in the island of Wateo Atiu inhabitants of Tahiti who had been driven by contrary winds in a canoe from some islands in the eastward unknown to the natives. In 1820 a canoe arrived at the island of Maurua from one of the Austral Group, which must have sailed some eight hundred miles. While recently, Mr. George Prescott, brother of the author of the 'Conquest of Mexico,' sailed from Tahiti to Samoa in a whale-boat, and, by his route, must have sailed some fifteen hundred miles ; and a certain Harry Williams, accompanied by some natives, went from Maldon Island to his own island of Mannihiki, a distance of five hundred miles, in a flat-bottomed punt.

The ancient religion of the Fijians is most difficult to trace, on account of the vagueness of their traditions, and the multiplicity of their gods. The relics of sacred trees and groves clearly point to a Druidical form of worship. These groves and trees, according to Dr. Seeman, were not worshipped as gods, but, as in the Odin religion of our ancestors, looked upon as places where certain gods had taken up their abode. There were sacred stones on the same footing; and one near Bau, the abode of a goddess, was reputed to give birth to a little stone whenever any woman of rank was confined in the Fijian capital. The large stone was taken away on the introduction of Christianity, but the numerous little offspring still remain in the once sacred spot to testify to the reality of Fijian mythology. The Fijian's *tarawau* does not seem to be regarded as a sacred tree in the Druidical light, but it was held to be the business of the dead to plant it, and was believed to grow not only in this world, but also in Naicobocobo, or the Fijian one beyond. Hence the saying: '*Sa laki tei tarawau ki Naicobocobo*'—'He has gone to plant *tarawau* at Naicobocobo;' that is to say, 'He is dead.'

The Fijians firmly believed in a future state, and thought that their time would be then spent in amusing themselves with canoes and arms, and all fruits were supposed to abound.

Serpent-worship existed among them. I have already referred to their tradition of the Deluge, and the means by which some of the progeny of the first man and woman, together with *Rokora*, the god of carpenters, and *Rokola*, his head workman, were rescued.

Benga, an island to the south of Viti Levu, is supposed to be the place where the eight survivors of this inundation landed, in virtue of which, and also of a tradition which relates that the *Ndengi*, or chief god, first made his appearance there, the chiefs of that place used to take precedence of all others.

Their account of the Creation is that all men are descended from the same parents. The first-born was the Fijian; but he misbehaved himself, and was black, with but little clothing. The next born was the Tongan, who was not quite so bad, and was consequently whiter, and received more clothing. *Papalagis*, or white men, were born last, but did not sin, and were therefore quite white, and had many clothes. The character attributed to some of the Fijian gods was not such as to exercise an elevating influence on their worshippers. For instance, a certain *Roko Bati-dua* is described as a man with wings on which are claws to catch victims with. *Kokola* had eight arms, which indicated his mechanical skill; *Matawalu* boasted eight eyes, denoting wisdom; *Ra Kambasanga* had two bodies, one male and one female, united like Siamese twins; *Kanusimana* used to spit miracles; *Naitono* was a leper. A god named *Ndanthina* was accused of stealing women of rank and beauty; while another, called *Batimona*, was named brain-eater. Another deity named *Ravuravu* was a murderer; while a rival, *Mainatavasari*, was 'fresh from slaughter.' Besides these, there were a host of gods and demi-gods, all supposed to have special functions and tutelary powers. The Fijians were never actual idolaters, though they believed that certain birds and fishes were the favoured abodes of their gods, and entitled therefore to especial veneration.

The priest, or *ambati*, was a most important personage, and no chief's establishment was complete without one. The office was generally hereditary. No priest would ever approach the gods unless he had received the customary presents, which generally consisted of a whale's tooth, or of native grog, *kava*. A great religious festival was held every November, lasting four days, during which the gods were invoked for a plentiful harvest, and other favours.

Formerly the rite of circumcision was performed on all youths. The ceremony as described by Mr. Williams, whose long residence and careful study of the natives qualified him to speak authoritatively, was as follows:—A party of from ten to twenty were circumcised at one time, the cutting instrument being a piece of split bamboo. After the operation the youths live together in some public building until they have recovered, their food being carried to them by women, who chanted the following ditty:

'*Memu wai o gori ka kula;*	'**This is your broth, sirs the circumcised;**
Au solia mai loaloa;	**I give it from the wilderness;**
Au solia na drau ni cevuga;	**I give the leaf of the cevuga,**
Memu wai o gori ka kula.'	**This is your broth, sirs the circumcised.'**

I am not aware whether the ceremony is continued at the present time, but the practice supports the theory of a Jewish origin for the nation.

The *soro* or peace-offering rites of the Fijians were complicated. There were different grades: firstly, there was the offering of a whale's tooth or club, which would avail for any offence, from stealing a yam to running away with a chief's wife; secondly, there was *soro* with a reed, more humiliating than number one, but far exceeded by that with a spear, which was offered with such an attitude of contrition and humiliation as to give the idea that the suppliant deserved to be transfixed with his spear. There was another *soro* which was connected with war, and as it meant cession of land or other property, it was the Fijian equivalent for the 'milliards' of civilised Europe. Then again, there was the *vesi dravu*, or *soro* with ashes, which was only used in cases involving life or lives. The offender's chief would cover his breast and arms with ashes, and with the most profound humiliation entreat for his life. How like the solemn ceremony with which the Catholic Church commences her forty days of penance.

When I was in Fiji this custom of *soro* was dying out. Both the Catholic and Protestant missionaries had discountenanced it for years, on the ground that it had been of late more used as a means of corruption than anything else. While there was much that was theoretically right and certainly interesting in this ritual of peace-offerings, we can hardly regret that it has been superseded by the freer forgiveness of the Christian's code. Whether the Fijians are as forgiving as their new religion requires, is another question.

CHAPTER IX.

FIJI IN CANNIBAL DAYS.

I CONFESS to a strong feeling of repugnance in approaching the subject of cannibalism. The only inducement to dwell on such an abominable custom, is the reflection that it is now a thing of the past (I believe even the Kai Colos have abandoned it); and it may be useful, now that Fiji is a Christian colony of the British Empire, to show what she was only a few years back, when cannibalism was one of her institutions.

In Wilkes's days (about 1840) prisoners were fattened for a feast, and then roasted alive; he thus describes the awful practice:

'When about to be sacrificed, the victims are compelled to sit upon the ground with their feet drawn under their thighs and their arms placed close beside them. In this position they are bound so tightly that they cannot move a joint. They are then placed in the oven upon hot stones, and covered with leaves and stones, and so roasted alive. When the body is cooked, it is taken from the oven and the face painted black, as is done by the natives on festal occasions. It is then carried to the *bure*, where it is offered to the gods, being afterwards cut and distributed to be eaten by the people.'

Women seldom ate of *bukalo* (or human flesh), and it was prohibited to certain of the priesthood. In some parts of the group, the natives, to procure this loathsome food, would frequently open graves. No other food was ever served with *bukalo*, and the ovens, forks and cooking utensils used for it were kept quite distinct. The Fijian cannibals were, however, inconsistent and whimsical, as the very people who would rob graves to get hold of *bukalo*, refused to eat the flesh of the porpoise, because it has ribs something like a man.

Some writers have supposed that the passion for revenge originated this horrible custom. It is certain that some chiefs kept the skulls of particular victims to be used as drinking-cups, thus reminding one of the Valhalla of the Scandinavians.

The names of some notorious cannibals at present remain in native tradition; but it is probable that these memories of evil days will be steadily discountenanced by the Christian missionaries. The greatest of these was *Ra Undreundre* of Raki-Raki. This gentleman was compared by the natives to a huge receptacle for turtle, so great was his love for and consumption of human flesh. The fork of this gourmet in horrors was given to a missionary in 1849 by his son, who made no secret of his father's dreadful propensity. He used to register the number of bodies he had eaten by stones, and though many had perhaps been removed, there remained in that year some eight hundred and seventy-two.

Of course I heard many stories of the 'bad old times,' but I will inflict few of them on my readers. The object of this book is to let stay-at-home Europeans know what earthly paradises there are in the Pacific awaiting civilised industry, care and capital; not to give a *réchauffée* of horrors that had better be forgotten. Mr. James Harding, whose gallantry both as a soldier and civilian I have already referred to, favoured me, when in Fiji, with an account of a long visit he made, just after annexation, to the cannibals he had beaten a few months previously. Some details of his narrative may be of value as showing to what depths the degradation of the human race can go, and also the marvellous change that has been effected in three short years.

In a battle that took place near the banks of a tributary of the Ba river in Viti Levu, between the Christians of the Bua district and the mountaineers, the former were hopelessly beaten, and it was noticed that the cannibals took no prisoners either for torture or for their feasts; their great object seeming to be to knock to pieces as many heads as possible. The Great Spirit (*Kalou rerere*) worshipped by them was supposed to feed on human brains, and the heathen were anxious to propitiate him with as much food as possible. After leaving this delectable spot (the river ran with provisions for the *Kalou rerere*), Mr. James Harding encountered a party of his late enemies, and told me that, after he had got through the eating and drinking, and the necessary formal speeches associated with those operations, they verbally fought the battles over again, and compared notes, some of which were written in very indelible ink. Instead of the wounds bearing a harvest of grudges he found them to be the very bond of good fellowship; and the most startling remarks were made with good-humoured *naïveté*. 'I don't suppose that you remembered seeing me at Naculi, for I had a big head then. I tried to shoot you, but you put a revolver bullet through my hand' (showing the wound). 'My brother shot you in the breast, and then you shot him with your *dakai lekaleka*' (little gun) 'between the eyes. I think that the Qaga men who were fighting with you ate him.' Then said another to J. H., 'We nearly caught you and another white man at Koroimuqo; you killed my uncle, but my cousin put a bullet through your shirt. We got one of the soldiers, a big red man, and we sent his body' (this with an air of virtuous self-denial) 'as a present to Wawabalavu, chief of Nibutautau, who ate the best joints of him.' Again, 'We heard before that you were a *vudivudi*' (one made impenetrable), 'but were not certain until that day at Naculi, when many of us tried hard to kill you. I was with the Nibutautau people in the ambuscade on the hill, and I killed one white man who had a long beard' (poor Gresham!) 'and wore dark trousers. It was always necessary for one side to run, and, as you whites wouldn't, of course we had to.'

During a ten days' detention with others of his quondam enemies, Mr. Harding told me he had long conversations upon divers subjects, and had to answer numberless questions quaint and pertinent. The principal were as to the relative values, advantages, and strengths of the past and present Governments, to which there was, of course, but one reply. And as to Her Majesty: 'Was the *Marama levu*, or great lady, really so anxious as was said for the welfare of the people? What was the name of my town? Ah yes! They had heard of London; it was an enormous city indeed. They had heard from a Fijian who had been there that the fowls all laid their eggs simultaneously early every morning, so that the ground between the houses was covered with them, and you could hardly hear anything for the cackling. Then at breakfast-time a *lali*' (drum) 'was beaten, and the cooks, with one accord, put all the frying-pans on the fires, when ensued a roaring like the loudest thunder until the *lali* sounded again, when they were all taken off at the same moment.' With every desire to extol the discipline and regular habits of our race this was too much, and, in the manner in which they related it, irresistibly funny. They showed a few clumsy sleight-of-hand tricks which were reciprocated, and described those performed by professed conjurors, explaining also the modes of operation. Then they drifted about amid a variety of topics as they were suggested by one another, or the queries of the audience. Steam power, electric telegraph, history of European civilisation, great battles, weapons, wild animals, fables, eclipses, meteorology, solar system, plurality of worlds, future existence, and so on. The perspicacity shown by these people was very marked, and, to my mind, promises much for their future if they be properly directed. If they did not understand any particular point, they asked intelligent questions until the matter was cleared to their comprehension, indicating, clearly, that they possess the capability to progress in learning.

While at *Na Drau*, the locality where the foregoing conversation took place, Mr. Harding observed the interior of a house called Sofatabua—the resting-place of the cannibal trophies of the tribe.

Besides human skulls and thigh bones, with clubs and spears inlaid with teeth, etc., the interior was thickly lined with tally-reeds numbering the victims. When ten men were killed by the tribe, a bundle of ten reeds would be made up and stuck within the roof of the house, while a solitary *bukalo* was recorded by a single reed, and so on. The four sides of the Sofatabua were equally adorned in this way, so, when those on one side were counted and found to exceed a thousand, it was easy to compute the whole terrible score as between four and five thousand. Among them were those representing the unfortunate Na Lotu people, who were the first mountaineers to accept (and suffer for) Christianity. All the hill tribes formed an offensive alliance, and attacked the Na Lotu stronghold on the range of that name, but without success, for they occupied a position impregnable in native warfare. Then the attacking allies sent word to them that they would relinquish the attempt as useless, and asked them to attend a feast to cement the reconciliation and amity. The poor wretches went, and, when utterly unprepared, were massacred almost to a man, the few who escaped doing so by lying still among the heap of dead bodies until nightfall enabled them to creep away unobserved. This done, the heathens, at their ease, slaughtered the unprotected women and children. During the Governmental wars were seen houses in every town decorated in the way described, with 'cannibal reeds;' and to this fact, in association with the sadly common infanticide and enforced celibacy among the lower *kaisis*, seems mainly attributable the startling contrast between the present number of inhabitants and the many evidences of the interior having been at a former period far more populously occupied than now.

On another occasion Mr. Harding asked his cannibal acquaintances why they used forks for human flesh only.

They replied that human flesh when cooked emitted in the dark a peculiar halo which, according to their description, resembles a phosphorescent lustre or magnetic flame. The utensils or saturated wrappers containing it, or the hands of anyone manipulating it, present the same appearance; and therefore it is that, being much afraid of this, they used the well-known 'cannibal forks.'

These cannibal forks are made of hard wood, and have

generally two or more prongs. I managed to get one, but they are becoming very scarce in Fiji. Mr. Harding told me that the topic of cannibalism once started, it fairly ran away with his coloured friends; the favourite joints, the rich yellow fat, the tender juicy meat, and the exquisite flavour, were so dilated on with only half-suppressed ferocity and longing—their eyes sparkling and teeth gleaming with horrible suggestiveness—that, dizzy and sick, he peremptorily changed the subject, and moved an adjournment into the cool evening air.

It is a fact that while cannibals would not touch ordinary meat in the least tainted, they would feast off *bukalo* in a most advanced stage of decomposition. In the northern part of Vanua Levu, I obtained some of the large dishes used for *bukalo* feasts.

Having on several occasions been present at *meke-mekes* (or dances) where a 'war' was acted, I distinctly remember the almost too faithful representation the natives gave of bloodthirsty ferocity when fighting. The savage glare of their eyes —the pearl-like teeth clenched with vindictive firmness—the piercing war-cries resounding through the still night air, while the clubs, as they rose and fell in mimic battle, kept perfect time with the weird music. This was a game got up to pass away the evening of a few idle *papalagis*. It seemed to me, as a novice, that it must be very like the reality; and having seen it, I can quite understand the terrible scenes which used to frequently occur in the men-eating days. The semi-military advance of the conquerors raising their cruel shouts—their faces expressive of a bloodthirsty anticipation of the cannibal feast to come—the clubbed corpse of the victim borne along tied to a pole—are easily realised by anyone who has seen a war-*meke*.

CHAPTER X.

FUNERALS IN TAVIUNI.

Many of the native superstitions curiously resemble some weaknesses of our own people. For instance, the howling of a dog at night is generally believed to betoken death; a cat purring around a man's feet, notwithstanding that it is frequently repulsed, gives rise to the same grim fear. Rats scratching around the grave of a woman are supposed to indicate that she had lived an unchaste life. I have heard something similar to this in portions of Southern Italy. The large shooting-stars were said to be gods, and the little ones the departing souls of humankind. Many people imagine that a great storm often accompanies the death of a great personage, and they instance the hurricane throughout Europe on the 3rd September, 1658, the day on which the soul of Oliver Cromwell went to his account, or the tempest which swept over St. Helena while the Head of the Grand Army was dying. The same thought is met with in Fiji, and Mr. Williams assures us that on one occasion being off the coast of Vanua Levu, he heard a single loud report like a clap of thunder, though the sky was cloudless. The natives told him that it was the noise of a spirit; they were near the place where the spirits plunged into the other world, and that a great chief had just died.

In the days before the bulk of the natives became Christians, there was no such thing as affection or care for the aged and infirm; and as the idea prevailed that in the future world a person's condition would be almost exactly that in which he died, the old used often to request their children to strangle them before they reached total infirmity or second childhood—

a behest which the younger were not slow in obeying. In fact, they did not always wait for it.

Of kindness to the sick no trace existed. In one part of the group they used to visit a famous tree when a person lay dangerously ill—if a branch had newly fallen, the patient would die; if a branch had been broken off, the patient's recovery was to be looked for. A troublesome patient used sometimes to be clubbed or even buried alive.

This summary way of saving doctors' bills was not, however, applied to chiefs, or men of position. When the hour of death approached, a chief would call his family together and instruct them as to what he wished to be done—his equivalent for our 'last will and testament.' A good deal of implacable revenge on his enemies was inculcated on these occasions, which the rising generation of cannibals used carefully to bear in mind.

Once dead, a chief's departure was announced by wailing and by the firing of muskets. The principal people of his province would then come to pay their respects, some of them bringing presents for a feast, or as offerings to the memory of the departed. The wailings at these ceremonials were (and are to this day) something of the Irish wake order. One of the choruses asks: 'Why did you die? Were you weary of us?' The body is then laid out, washed, and oiled. In the old days the ceremony of *loloku* commenced after the laying-out, which, in plain English, means that certain of the dead chief's relatives, wives, and attendants, were strangled that they might bear him company in the other world.

When Tanoa, the aged father of ex-King Cacobau, died, five of his wives were strangled, notwithstanding the protests of Sir Everard Home, who was then in the group in command of H.M.S. *Calliope*, and who lingered about the islands three months waiting for the old man's death, in order to prevent by force a perpetration of this barbarous rite. The old cannibal, however, lingered on, and the *Calliope* was forced to leave. Sir Everard would never permit a cannibal to touch his quarter-deck, and refused to give a passage to one of Cacobau's sons till he had been positively assured that the lad had never tasted human flesh.

The climate necessitates speedy interment, and early on the morning following the death of a chief his grave is dug. Two sextons, seated opposite each other, make three feints with their bamboo digging-sticks, and then commence business. The grave is seldom more than three feet deep, and mats are laid in it, in which the body—or, as frequently happened, the bodies—are wrapped. The sextons having performed their ablutions and purifications, return to partake of the funeral baked meats, supplied in the most extravagant profusion. Articles that were prized by the deceased are frequently buried with him, so that it often happens that a poor *kaisi* (or commoner) who in life could not obtain one mat, would be buried with four or six. Funeral reform, it may be noticed, is required as much in Fiji as at home. In some parts of the group I noticed a sort of mausoleum erected over the grave of a native chief. These resemble cairns more than anything else, and are very carefully made—they stand about six feet high, the gables being filled in with sinnet (a strong rope made from fibre of the husk of the cocoa-nut) wrought into different-sized squares and arranged diagonally.

To enable my readers fully to understand the change that has come over Fiji, I give Mr. Williams's account of the death and funeral of the Tui Cakau, king or prince of Somo-Somo, in Taviuni, of which he was an unwilling witness, and in glorious contrast, that of the funeral of his son, who was buried with all the rites of the Catholic Church, in the same place, thirty-four years later, *i.e.*, in April, 1879, which I condense from the *Field.*

'On being told on the morning of the 24th of August that the king was dead, and preparations were being made for his interment, I could scarcely credit the report. The ominous word *preparing* urged me to hasten, but my utmost speed failed to bring me to the king's house in time. It was evident that as far as concerned two women, I was too late. The effect of the scene was overwhelming. Scores of deliberate murderers, in the very act, surrounded me; yet there was no confusion and no noise, only an unearthly horrid stillness. Nature seemed to lend her aid to deepen the dread effect: there was not a breath stirring in the air, and the half-subdued light in the hall of death showed every object with unusual distinctness. All was motionless as sculpture, and a strange feeling came upon me, as though I myself was becoming a statue. To speak was impossible; I was unconscious that I breathed; and against my will I sank to the floor, assuming the cowering posture of those who were not actually engaged in murder. My arrival was during a hush, just at the crisis of death, and to that strange silence must be attributed my emotion; for I was but too familiar with murders of this kind. Occupying the centre of that large room were two groups on the floor; the middle figure of each group being held in a sitting posture by several females, and hidden by a large veil. On either side of each veiled figure were eight or ten strong men, one company hauling against the other on a white cord which was passed twice round the neck of the doomed one, who thus in a few minutes ceased to live. As my self-command was returning, the group farthest from me began to move; the men slackened their hold, and the attendant women removed the large covering, making it into a couch for the victim. As that veil was lifted, some of the men beheld the distorted features of a mother whom they had helped to murder, and smiled with satisfaction as the corpse was laid out for decoration. Convulsive struggles on the part of the other poor creature near me showed that she still lived. She was a stout woman, and some of the executioners jocosely invited those who sat near to have pity and help them. At length the women said, "She is cold."

'The fatal cord fell; and as the covering was raised, I saw dead the obedient wife and unwearied attendant of the old king. Leaving the women to adjust her hair, oil her body, cover her face with vermilion, and adorn her with flowers, I passed on to see the remains of the deceased Tui Cakau. To my astonishment, I found him alive! He was weak, but quite conscious, and whenever he coughed, placed his hand on his side as though in pain. Yet his chief wife and a male attendant were covering him with a thick coat of black powder, and tying round his arms and legs a number of white scarves, fastened in rosettes, with the long ends hanging down his sides. His head was turbaned in a scarlet handkerchief, secured by a chaplet of small white cowries, and he wore armlets of the same shells. On his neck was the ivory necklace, formed in long curved points. To complete his royal attire, according to Fijian idea, he had on a large new *masi*, or large *sulu*, the train being wrapped in a number of loose folds at his feet. No one seemed to display real grief, which gave way to show and ceremony. The whole tragedy had the air of cruel mockery. It was a masquerading of grim death, a decking as for the dance, of bodies which were meant for the grave. . . .

'I came to the young king to ask for the life of the women, but now it seemed my duty to demand that of his father. Yet, should I be successful, it would cause other murders on a future day. Perplexed in thought, with a deep gloom on my mind, feeling my blood curdle, and the "hair of my flesh to stand up," I approached the young king, whom I could only regard with abhorrence. He seemed greatly moved, put his arm round and embraced me, saying before I could speak: "See! the father of us two is dead." "Dead!" I exclaimed, in a tone of surprise—"dead! No!" "Yes," he answered; "his spirit is gone. You see his body move; but that it does unconsciously." Knowing that it would be useless to dispute the point, I went on to say the chief object of myself and my colleague was to beg him to "love us and prevent any more women from being strangled, as he could not by multiplying the dead render any benefit to his father." He replied, "There are only two, but they shall suffice. Were not you missionaries here, we would make an end of all the women sitting around." The queen, who pretended grief, cried: "Why is it that I am not strangled?" The king gave as a reason that there was no one present of sufficiently high rank to suffocate her.

'Preparations were made for removing the bodies, and we retired. In doing so, I noticed an interesting female, oiled, and dressed in a new *liku*, carrying a long bamboo, the top of which contained about a pint of water, which, as the bodies were carried out of one door, she poured on the threshold of another. The bodies of the women were placed on either end of a canoe, with the old king on the front deck attended by the queen and the *mata*, who with a fan kept the insects off him. The shell ornaments were then taken off his person, which was covered with cloth and mats, and the earth heaped upon him. He was heard to cough after a considerable quantity of earth had been thrown in the grave.

'A family on the opposite coast, Vanua Levu, enjoys the privilege of supplying a hale man to be buried with the king, that he may go before and hold the Fijian Cerberus. On the present occasion, no such man could be found, and the old chief was even sent to meet the dangers of the gloomy path without a club.

'Next day the *Kana-bogi*, or fasting till evening, commenced. This is observed during ten or twenty days. Many made themselves "bald for the dead," some by shearing the head only, others by cutting off whiskers and beard as well. Females burnt their bodies, and orders were given that one hundred fingers should be cut off; but only sixty were amputated, one woman losing her life in consequence. The fingers being each inserted in a split reed, were stuck along the eaves of the king's house. Toes are never taken off for this purpose. Some to express their grief merely make bare the crown of the head.

'During the mourning days for a chief, the young men shout, dance, and make a general uproar. Blindfolded lads try to hit a hanging vessel of water; if successful they are supposed to become great warriors. The common women are not allowed to eat flesh or fish; and the chief wife for three months following may not touch her own food with her hands. The coast for four miles was made *tabu*, so that no one might fish there; and the nuts for at least six miles made sacred.

'The following observances take place at stated intervals after the funeral rites: On the fourth day the *Vakavidiulo*, "jumping of maggots," a bitter lamentation, which consists of picturing to each other the corruption that has taken place in the body of the departed. On the fifth night is the *Vakadredre*, "causing to laugh," in which the friends of the dead are entertained with games and buffoonery, for the purpose of helping them to forget their grief.

'About the tenth day, the women arm themselves with cords, switches and whips, and ply these weapons freely upon all but the highest chiefs. The men never retaliate in earnest beyond throwing mud occasionally, and the custom is to endeavour to escape as quickly as possible.

'Funeral feasts are kept up by friends at a distance out of respect to the dead, and for the purpose of consoling the living; and even if the news does not reach the loving friend of the departed until a year has elapsed, the feast is still observed.

'Every canoe arriving at a place for the first time after the death of a great chief must show the *loloku* of the sail. A long *masi*, fixed to the mast-head or yard, is sometimes the *loloku*; or a whale's tooth is thrown from the mast-head, so as to fall into the water, when it is scrambled for by people from the shore. When the canoe gets nearer, both the sail and *masi* are thrown into the water.

'The final ceremony in honour of the departed chief is the *lawa-ni-mate*, or the accomplishing some unusually great or important work, such as the building of a canoe, the weaving of a bale of cloth, roll of matting, or the making of an immense ball of sennit, in memory of the dead, whose name is given to the finished work.

'In some parts a long line of women march in procession, each bearing a green basket of white sand to strew over the grave; one party chants in a loud tone *E-ui-e*, to which the other responds *E-yara*, and the effect is both solemn and agreeable.

'In the case of a chief drowned at sea, or slain and eaten by his enemies, the *loloku* is as carefully observed as if he had died naturally. This was the case when Ra Bithi, the pride of Somo-Somo, was lost at sea—seventeen of his wives were sacrificed. Again, after the news of the massacre of the Namena people in 1839, eighty women were strangled, to accompany the spirits of their murdered husbands.'

This took place in the Fiji of 1845. Let my readers observe what has been done in the interval:

'On April 19, 1879, Tui Cakau (pronounced Tui Thakow), one of the most powerful chiefs in the group, died. He had been on a visit to a neighbouring island, and on his return complained of not feeling well, lay down in his large house, and never rose again alive. An ingenious explanation of the cause of his death was given to me by a white man, who was his valet. He told me that after a talk with the widow of the chief, both had come to the conclusion that the amount of *kava* taken by him had so coated the inside of his stomach that when it cracked—from a cold caught while on this visit a few days before—he gave up the ghost. "You know," he added, "these people are very often right in matters of this sort, and they know a great deal about the insides of people; they used to be——" A pause. "Of course," I remarked, knowing he did not want to use the word "cannibals," being a dependent of the chief's household. I soon saw that they got the idea of the coating of the stomach from the bowls in which this *kava* drink is prepared. The bowl is made of wood, being a horizontal section of a large tree, slightly hollowed out on one side, and standing on three legs. After long use the inside of the bowl becomes coated with a whitish crust. I hope they did not think Tui Cakau had a wooden stomach, though he might have had, judging from the large amount of liquor other than *kava* that he used to drink. When a great chief dies, it is necessary that the king should be present at his funeral. On this occasion, to perform the last rites over his friend, son-in-law, and ally, King Cacobau (pronounced Thakombau) with his two sons, Abel and Joseph, embarked with us on board H.M.S. *Cormorant* to go to Taviuni. The grey-headed old king bore the journey well, lying on his cane couch-chair, and was accompanied by his chaplain and native police magistrate, besides other attendants.

'Leaving Levuka in the morning, we arrived at Taviuni at dusk, and lay a short distance from the shore, just abreast of the village or town of Somo-Somo. It was almost dark when we got there, and the first thing I heard was a succession of curious noises from the shore, which I discovered were produced by the wives of the late chief blowing large conch shells. These manifestations of regret were not conducive to the repose of Prince Joseph, King Cacobau's second son, who had received his education in Sydney, and spoke English well; he was obliged by etiquette to sleep on shore, in the house specially set apart for royalty.

'Next day I landed with two friends to see the town, and what we could of the island. The temperature was 86°, so we strolled leisurely about the village. The first house we entered was that of the late chief. It was a large barn, with four doors, remarkably well put together, and exquisitely thatched. The pillars supporting the sides were of cocoa-nut palms, and the rafters of bamboo; mats, made of rush or reed, lined the lower part of the walls, and large pieces of *tappa*, the native cloth, made by beating the bark of a tree, divided the building into two parts, in one of which was the chief in his coffin, bound up in innumerable mats; in the other his wife (a daughter of Cacobau) sitting on the ground fanning herself. She was a remarkably fine specimen of a Fijian, and, although she had been crying a good deal, looked really very nice. I was told that she had looked even better before her hair was cut off. This had only just been done as a sign of mourning. Every one in the village who had acknowledged Cakau as chief had cut his or her hair for the same reason.

'After leaving the chief's house, we walked through the

6—2

village, which is in the midst of a large cocoa-nut grove, and witnessed the preparations for the feast of the morrow. Groups of natives were scraping cocoa-nut to a powder, grating sugar-cane on old biscuit tin-boxes, killing pigs and preparing the holes in the ground in which to cook them, or cutting the fins off turtle to make them more adapted for cooking in the same method as the pigs. Yams, taro, bread-fruit, and plantains were in process of preparation. Troops of natives, in Indian file, carrying these viands, were making their way to the late chief's house to offer them to his widow, each tribe, both in this and the neighbouring islands, contributing its quota. Having arrived near the chief's house, the troop halts and forms a body; they then march *en masse* to within twenty yards of the door, and sit down on the grass in a circle with their donations before them. A member of the chief's household then comes out, and, after a few moments' consultation with the leader, re-enters and apprises the widow of the purport of their visit; he then conveys her gracious acceptance of the gifts to the party, who express their pleasure by clapping hands.

'Passing the house where royalty was put up during this ceremony, we saw that the piles of yams were assuming haystack dimensions, and the number of turtle was astonishing. At midday we landed our blue-jackets and marines abreast the ship, where all the chiefs, who had come to the funeral, were seated; they were then marched to the side of the house nearest to the grave, and lined the path from the house to that spot. Slowly the procession moved out. The Catholic priest, accompanied by black boys in red cassocks and white cottas, and bearing candles, led the way; after these came the coffin, borne by ten lusty natives, and followed by the widow alone; next Her Majesty's representative, the Lieutenant-Governor of

Fiji; then old King Cacobau and his retinue, followed by the chiefs in order of rank. Arriving at the spot which was chosen as a resting-place for the once most powerful chief in all Fiji, the service was read and the coffin was lowered into the grave and wrapped up in mats, with which it had been previously lined. Three rounds of blank cartridge were fired over the grave, and the procession moved homeward, followed by the landing-party to the bugle march. After this came more mourning with conch shells; the natives assembled to drink the *kava* and thence to the feast.

'Though the Fijians are large consumers of their peculiar foods at meals, they must not be considered gourmands at their feasts, for, though the preparations are on a large scale, the desire is not to eat so much as to have plenty if need be.'

CHAPTER XI.

FIJI LIFE, PAST AND PRESENT.

In olden days marriage among the Fijians was celebrated as it is now by religious rites, and a short *résumé* of the ceremonial may be interesting. A woman could not marry without the consent of her brother, even if she had obtained that of both parents. The assent of the latter was shown by their acceptance of the lover's presents. The daughters of chiefs were engaged at a very early age; but *bonâ-fide* courtships were common among all ranks. In Commodore Wilkes's account of his cruise in the Pacific, he describes a wedding: 'The *ambati*, or priest, having taken a seat, the bridegroom is placed on his right and the bride on his left. He then invokes the protection of the god or spirit upon the bride, after which he leads her to the bridegroom, and joins their hands with injunctions to love, honour and obey, and be faithful, and die with each other.' The allusion to the widow sacrifice excepted, the formula closely resembled ours, and it was followed by a wedding-breakfast, which probably was as indigestible a meal as obtains with us. I quote Commodore Wilkes's account, however, with 'all reserve,' as the great Fiji missionary Williams has stated that though blessings were invoked, the presence of a priest was not considered necessary.

In some cases of mutual attachment, the courtship is of a formal character. After the gentleman's presents have been accepted, the young lady is taken off to the house of the future husband's parents with her presents. The bridegroom's friends console her with trinkets, and this quasi-ceremony is called *vakamaca*, or the 'drying up of tears.' Then food is prepared by the man and taken to the bride's friends. Four days of probation follow, after which the girl bathes, and, accompanied by matrons, goes fishing and prepares what is caught, which with yams, taro, etc., form the wedding-feast. In some places this completes the ceremony; in others, the man goes away to build a house, while the woman repairs to her parents' house till this is finished.

The marriage of Ratu Joe, the youngest son of King Cacobau, in 1879, partook somewhat of the nature of an elopement, and was evidently a union of pure affection. The parents and friends of the young chief were anxious that he should wed the daughter of Tui Suva, a damsel of parentage equal to his own and having a liberal dowry of broad acres. The young lady herself was somewhat smitten with Joe, but he remained true to his first love, and being unduly pressed, he arranged a clandestine wedding with a bride of somewhat humble birth at the mission-house. The old king was at first very indignant at Joe's *mésalliance*, but eventually, like a sensible man, came round, and prepared a sumptuous feast for the propitiation of numerous friends and relatives.

Society in Fiji is divided into six recognised classes, in which there is much that resembles the system of caste. The grades are :

1. Kings and queens.
2. Chiefs of large islands.
3. Chiefs of towns and priests.
4. Distinguished warriors, chiefs of carpenters and chiefs of the turtle-fishers.
5. Common people.
6. Slaves by war.

Rank is hereditary, and descends through females.

In cannibal days the dignity of a chief was estimated by the number of his wives, which used to vary from ten to fifty, or even one hundred. Polygamy was as much an institution in Fiji as it is to this hour in Utah. The ex-King Cacobau for a long time resisted the exhortations of the missionaries to give up heathenism. His conversion to Christianity was much owing to the earnest entreaties of his favourite wife—Andi Lydia. On one occasion he got very angry with her, and said, 'You don't know at all what you are talking about. If I become a Christian, I may marry one of my other wives, not you.' She replied, 'I don't mind, so that you do become a Christian.'

Polygamy died hard in Fiji. A worthy Catholic priest told me in Taviuni that a certain nameless chief was by no means a bad sort of man, but now and again he would burst out into polygamy.

As regards the children now so well looked after and daily

attending school, they were in the cannibal times tersely addressed as 'rats,' and infanticide was as systematically practised as in a model baby-farm in civilised England, the unfortunate little girl-babies being generally the victims, as they could not in the after-time wield a club or poise a spear.

Solomon's maxim about the child and the rod is thoroughly appreciated all over Coral Lands, but in the old days of Fiji the instrument of correction was a good-sized truncheon of about the thickness of a broomstick.

Fijian sailors are a merry race; they generally sing while at their work, which they seem to regard very much in the light of a joke. To this day they are very superstitious, but in old times they had very curious customs, which differed from those of any other native races. Certain parts of the ocean were passed over in silence and with uncovered heads, through fear of the spirits of the deep, and they were particularly careful that no fragment of food fell into the water. The common tropic bird was the emblem of one of their gods, and the shark another; and should the one fly over their heads or the other swim past, they would utter a word of respect. A shark lying across their course was considered an evil omen, and was greatly feared.

The Fijians thoroughly understand consecration, and to this hour certain things are *tabu* or sacred; and on some of the canoes it was *tabu* to eat food in the hold, on another on the house and deck, on another on the platform over the house. Canoes have been known to be lost in a storm because their crews, instead of exerting themselves, have left their work to *soro*, or propitiate their gods by throwing over whales' teeth, or *angona* or *kava* root.

The Fijian sailors are now all Christians, and are taught, I do not doubt, by their pastors that the highest form of prayer is the performance of duty. In many parts of the Pacific, the whale's tooth is regarded as a propitiatory sacrifice, and at one time, on the death of a Fiji chief, two of these teeth were placed in his hands to throw at the tree which was supposed to stand on the road to the regions of the departed.

The Fijians are the most skilful boat-builders of all the inhabitants of Polynesia, and until comparatively recent times quite a brisk trade was done in this branch of industry. The larger kind of canoe is usually built double like the Calais-Douvres, braced together with a sort of extending upper-deck on which a small house is erected. The bottom of the canoe is formed of one single plank to which the sides are dovetailed, as well as being strengthened by lashings, and the joints are made watertight by gum. The depth of hold is generally about 6 feet, while they are frequently as long as 100 feet. When they cannot use the sails the natives propel the canoes by oars about 10 feet in length; and when rowing, they stand up to their work. In all canoes there are small hatchways with high combings at both ends, and when under way a man is continually employed in bailing out the water. The canoes of the *rokos* have immense white sails and royal streamers, and are much adorned with shells of the *cypræa ovula.* These crafts sail very fast, and have a beautiful appearance; but the picturesque is giving way to the practical in Fiji as elsewhere, as some of the chiefs have now small cutters of the English pattern, and I think it very unlikely that many more of the highest-class canoes will ever be built in the colony again.

These canoes are steered by an oar which, for the large ones, is about 20 feet long with an 8 feet blade and 16 inches wide, and which is very heavy. Their weight, however, is eased by means of a rope passed through the top of the blade, the other end being made fast to the middle beam of the deck. Rudderbands are attached to the handle of the oar, yet it requires two and sometimes three men to keep the canoe on her course. Nearly all these large canoes have an outrigger.

The general dimensions of the larger vessels rarely exceeds 100 feet by 20, but the measurements of one of the largest I saw were as follows:

	FEET.		FEET.
Length over all . . .	118	Length of mast . . .	68
Length of deck . . .	50	Length of yards . . .	90
Width	34		

The capacity of such a canoe is such that it will carry 100 native passengers and several tons of freight. The ordinary canoe is simply a 'dug-out,' with an outrigger, and these are common to the whole of the Pacific, and in fact, with the single exception of the Solomon Isles, are to be found from Ceylon in the west to the Marquesas in the east. I have had some little experience of short trips in canoes, and unromantic as it may seem, I infinitely prefer a coasting-steamer for inter-insular travel.

The Fijians and other islanders of the South Pacific are good sailors on European-rigged craft, and are capital divers and swimmers, as the following cutting from a Fiji newspaper testifies:

'A Tongan and his wife, the sole survivors of twenty-two who were lately capsized in a canoe near Totoya, arrived recently in Levuka. The man was severely bitten by a shark on the heel, and he and his wife, after being *a day and a half* in the water, reached Totoya. All the rest of their friends were eaten by sharks; but they managed to frighten off these ravenous monsters by constantly waving their *sulus* in the water. Though completely exhausted when they reached the shore, they seem now none the worse for their terrible swim.'

CHAPTER XII.

THE FIJIAN OF TO-DAY.

THE Fijians live under a community system—are divided into two *qalis*, which are redivided into *mataqalis*. Of these *qalis* or tribes there are about 140, and of *mataqalis* or families about 4000, residing in about 1220 towns or villages.

As already stated, the colony is politically divided into 13 provinces and 3 districts called *yasanas* (districts have not the distinction of being governed by a Roko Tui), 4 of which contain about 10,000 inhabitants each, 2 over 4000 each, and the remaining 3 under 2000 each. These numbers are very fairly proportioned to the extent of each province, so that the population is scattered with some degree of equality over the whole group. In fact in Fiji it may be truthfully said, that with the exception of some lands claimed but not occupied by white men, no large tract of country or island of importance is uninhabited.

The provinces are again subdivided into 139 districts called *tikina*, and these divisions, each of which is ruled by the hereditary chief of the rank of *buli*, generally contain one or more *qalis*, which were generally considered the unit of the wider political combinations in former times.

The chiefs and people are the hereditary owners (*ai taukei*) of the lands, and reside in towns and villages. Each town again contains one or more of the family divisions called *mataqali*, which may be considered the unit of tribal combinations. There is little doubt that they are originally the germ from which the *qali*, or tribe, has sprung; or perhaps, to make it clearer, *qali* is nothing more or less than an aggregation of families or *mataqali*. The family community, assumed to be of common lineage and descent, are the hereditary holders in common of the land, the *mataqali* is in fact the only true proprietary unit; and no matter the number of individuals or families within itself, it is the only true owner of the land, holding it for the present and future use of the community or brotherhood, whether they be full birthright members, or only strangers admitted to share in the benefits for a time, or adopted into it for good.

Each *mataqali* has a distinct name by which it is known, and which is not unfrequently the name of the principal allotment of its land, which belongs to its chief or head.

A Fijian's house consists of bamboo canes diagonally interlaced, fastened to cocoa-nut tree uprights, with a cocoa-nut log for a ridge-pole, and thickly thatched with dried cocoa-nut leaves. In many cases the thatch exceeds three feet in thickness. The ridge-pole generally extends for a foot or more on either side of the building, and some of the condemned cannibals in the war of 1876 made their exit from this world from the ridge-pole of native houses. The interior is not luxurious. The floor is covered with layers of straw and reed-mats, in the manufacture of which the natives show great skill. One end of the room is raised slightly for a sleeping quarter. A few kava bowls or dishes, mostly made out of solid pieces of wood and having four legs, lie around, while some oval taro or yam platters, also carved out of solid wood, with some cocoa-nut shells for drinking purposes, represent the furniture in the living part. The Fijian's pillow is a piece of timber, or more commonly bamboo, resting on two crutches of wood about four inches from the ground. On this apparently most uncomfortable receptacle for the head, the natives recline with pleasure and sleep with astonishing soundness. Their hair is always kept with great cleanliness and care, and they prevent it in this way from touching the ground.

At Suva, in Viti Levu, the house of a chieftainess is a gem in its way. Outside, the bamboos of which, like all other native houses, it is constructed are arranged in lozenge-shaped patterns; the thatched roof is nicely trimmed along the eaves; the inside walls are tapestried with native cloth; the beams and doorposts polished and ornamented with variously coloured sennit, or cocoa-fibre rope, and the floor is laid with fine white matting. The bed is raised about a foot from the floor, and enclosed by a mosquito curtain.

The people live a settled life, in towns of good and comfortable houses; they respect and follow agriculture; their social and political organisation is complex; they amass property, and have laws for its descent; their land-tenures are elaborate; they read, they write, and cipher. Women are usually respected, and are exempt from agricultural labour. There is a school in almost every village, and to the classical Fijian of Bau is added the English tongue. Some of their chiefs possess accounts at the bank, conduct correspondence, and generally exhibit capacities for a higher grade of civilisation. The Fijians, as I have said, all profess an at least nominal allegiance to Christianity; and that it has largely influenced the life and character of great masses of the population, the most sceptical cannot, I think, deny.

The political unit is the village. In every one of these is found a local chief, practically hereditary, but nominally appointed by the district council. He is assisted by a council of elders and certain executive officers, a magistrate, frequently the chief's brother, one or more constables to carry out his decisions, a town-crier (an hereditary and important officer), and a garden overseer. An uncertain number of villages—sometimes few, sometimes many—are grouped together under the *buli* of the district, who once a month assembles all his town chiefs, and discusses with them, in the Bose ni Tikina, or district council, the affairs of his own district. These district councils nominate the chiefs of towns, whom they may also suspend from office. They discuss and regulate all local matters, such as the cleansing and scavenging of villages, the management of animals belonging to the different communities, as distinguished from individual property, the keeping open and maintenance of roads and bridges, the control of public bathing-places. The council also superintends the payment, out of local rates, of the village constables. In a similar manner the *buli* districts are grouped under the headship of a greater chief, the Roko Tui, each of whom twice a year assembles the *bulis* of his province in the Bose vaka Yasana, or provincial council, where the local affairs of the province are discussed and settled, by which local rates are imposed, and to which each *buli* makes a detailed report of the condition of his own district.

This organisation is purely native, and of spontaneous growth. To it has now been added a meeting annually of the Roko Tuis and the Governor. This Bose vaka Turanga, or Great Council, is also attended by the native stipendiary magistrates, and by two *bulis* from each province, chosen by the Bose vaka Yasana. At it each Roko Tui in turn makes a detailed report of the state of his province, and suggestions are offered as to executive and legislative measures which it is thought desirable by those assembled that the Government should adopt. The suggestions made by the Bose vaka Turanga have received, and I think merited, the warm commendation of Her Majesty's

Government, on account of the good sense and practical capacity for affairs therein displayed.

There is no doubt that we should have been spared many bloody colonial wars if we had always followed the course which was adopted after mature consideration by Sir Arthur Gordon, on the advice of those who knew Fiji and the Fijians best, of encouraging the retention by the natives of their original political economy. Mr. Carew, the indefatigable Commissioner of Viti Levu, strongly urged this policy on the Government in October, 1875, and a summary of his letter to Sir Arthur Gordon will give a very clear insight into the feelings of the natives themselves in this matter, and also some of their social characteristics. He says in effect: English law is quite inapplicable to the exigencies of the native community, except to a certain extent in capital offences. The natives have a perfect dread of English law; they know nothing of it. We have no right whatever to tear down the whole system of native policy based on centuries of experience, and which they all understand, without being able to substitute anything comprehensible in its place. The natives insist on punishment for adultery. If unpunished, murder is generally the result. A native's wife is his cook, his gardener, his horse and cart, his water-carrier, his fish-provider, and the bearer of children to him to hand his name down to posterity. A native without at least one child is an object of pity to his tribe. If his wife leaves him to go with another man, he is totally undone. He is heart-broken, and regards himself on a level with a pig. His house is uncared-for—his food uncooked—his garden overgrown with weeds; he has to rely on the assistance of his friends; the elders of his own and the neighbouring tribes will cease to visit his house or to consult with him; he is a miserable creature: he is *guca*, or going down-hill.

Since Fiji has been annexed, the people have been ostensibly governed according to the principles of British law alone, but such has not been the case except in the law-courts of Levuka. In the provinces, so great was the Fijians' dread of the delays of British law, that not unfrequently they took the law into their own hands and executed summary justice. For instance, a particularly brutal murder was committed by a native. His chief said: 'Let us not send him to court to be tried in the white man's incomprehensible fashion, and then allowed to escape punishment; let us kill him at once,' and they did so. This district has been Christian for several years. The chief was a Government servant receiving Government pay. This chief came to an English gentleman a week after the execution and confessed the whole affair, but the *papalagi* wisely kept his counsel till it had blown over. There has been no crime since in that large district.

The dual system has worked well. For capital and very serious offences a native is tried before the supreme court; minor matters are settled by his chief, or if any difficulty occurs with that authority, by the local British magistrate. Some of the native laws are exceedingly severe, and in some places working on Sunday is an offence.

CHAPTER XIII.

MORE ABOUT THE FIJIAN OF TO-DAY.

WHEN Commodore Wilkes of the United States Navy visited the Fiji Group some years back, he landed a party of his blue-jackets, and put them through some light infantry drill. Inquiring of one of the chiefs present what he thought of the performance, the Fijian replied with that irony which is one of their marked characteristics when they care to assume it, 'The men *might* be very good warriors, but they waddled like ducks.'

The natives of Fiji are a fine race, of dark olive complexion, good physique, and fairly intelligent cast of countenance. The men perhaps average 5 feet 8 inches in height, while the *rokos* and some of the *bulis* exceed this standard. The women have sometimes pretty faces and undeniable figures when young, but their natural grace early disappears; for being simple Fijians, and ignorant of women's rights, they labour too much for their dusky lords, and the claims of Venus are merged in the demands for fish to fill the husband's larder. In youth both sexes have a superb carriage, and walk with the importance of a life-guardsman with his sweetheart.

No wonder therefore that the *roko* was struck with the rolling gait of the American sailors: a slouching Fijian would, I fancy, be soon sent to Coventry by his friends. The military class sometimes affect a ludicrously warlike adornment in the way of red ochre and black patches on the cheeks, reminding one forcibly of the very fierce-looking devils on the Chinese war-standards. But this piece of eccentricity is not so common as formerly. The civilians, in many cases, affect blue cheeks.

The natives of Fiji are emphatically agriculturists. Notwithstanding that some are called fishing tribes and others carpenter or building, yet even these cultivate more or less extensively. No greater mistake can be made than to suppose that they are not as a people very industrious cultivators of the soil. The idea of a race of lotus-eaters residing 'in summer isles of Eden set in purple spheres of sea,' is certainly not realised in our new colony, as it is a fact that few cases will be found of anyone, from a lad of twelve years up to an aged man, who has not his own plot of cultivation each year; and in some places even the women have their own particular gardens. How different is this prosaic record of facts from the commonly received accounts of writers whose experience of the great South Sea has been only one of pleasure or excitement! The articles the Fijians most largely produce are yams, bananas, *masi*—which has already been referred to—sugar-cane, arrowroot, tobacco, and *angona*, the root from which *kava* is manufactured. *Dalo* or *taro* is also extensively cultivated by the natives; there are two ways of treating this vegetable: one is planted on the dry land, and the other, and by far the most important, is grown in the water.

The implements of cultivation used by the Fijians consist of an axe and knife for cleaving purposes, and the universal digging-stick (*doko*), for dealing with the soil. Some Europeans have considered this *doko* to give a better cultivation than the plough; and it is certain that no foreign native yet introduced into Fiji can effectually compete with a Fijian in the use of his *doko*.

Whilst each individual attends to his plot or plots of cultivation, whatever they may be, yet in the spring or planting season they work in communities. Thus a whole town or village will be employed at one time in the garden of one individual. Commencing with a *mataqali*, they will go through the land of every individual until the whole of the inhabitants' gardens are complete. This common helping not unfrequently extends to the seed to be planted, as well as the digging and working of the soil; all that is required of the actual owner being that he furnish a plentiful supply of good provision for the day.

It should be added, that besides their individual gardens, the Fijians have also gardens in common, which may be cultivated, planted and kept in order, according to their extent and object, by a whole *mataqali*, a town or district.

It has always been urged by the chiefs and heads of families that their communal system of cultivation and work conserves their industrial habits, and tends to increase their wealth and comfort, comprehending as it does not only the cultivation of their food, the erection of their houses, the cutting and building of canoes (or what is more common now, the purchase of boats), the making of roads, or whatever else may be for the common good, but also placing within the reach of every individual food and a good house, no matter what his class or circumstances.

The manufacture of *malo* (native cloth), plaiting of mats, making of crockeryware, and other articles of domestic and household necessities, are chiefly confined to the women, and are also tribal specialities ; hence certain districts are noted for particular kinds of pottery, or for the quality of particular kinds of mats, baskets, etc., and the manufacture and printing of different kinds of *malo*, known by their special names, which indicate the tribe by which they are manufactured, or the island on which they are made.

Many thousands of mats are plaited every year, and the amount of native cloth prepared is enormous ; but it would be very difficult to give an accurate estimate of these native industries, either of the amount of cultivation or of the articles manufactured, which were formerly much more extensive than at present, but are said of late years to be reviving.

No Fijian considers that he has realised the idea of a householder (*ai taukei*) unless he has a supply in store on his *vata* more than sufficient for the everyday requirements of his family, dependents and wayfarers. Besides food, either housed or in the ground, he must have rolls of mats and native cloth, as well as other property in store for all contingencies, even to the shroud in which he will fold up his dead. Plenty to eat and plenty to give is the *beau idéal* of a Fijian, whether chief or commoner.

Though often judged by foreigners—perhaps at times with some truth—to be indolent and improvident, yet, taking into account the influences under which he lives, and the usages and customs to which he has been born and brought up, he is a useful member of society, and very well fitted for the place he is called upon to fill among his kith and kin.

The average Fijian is naturally docile and obedient, but you must thoroughly realise and act upon your power over him. If he doubts for a moment your ability to act or the verity of your word, his confidence in you is gone for ever; and in time of need, when you want his friendship or aid, he is likely enough to turn out a cruel and most treacherous enemy. Fairly dealt with, adding at the same time the exercise of the most unrelenting justice when occasion demands it, the Fijian is above the average of the Polynesian; but with him, as with other native races, maudlin sympathy on account of his race and colour is simply thrown away. If you promise to pay a 'boy' a dollar, you have to pay that dollar, or he will regard you as a thief for evermore. If you promise a boy punishment, you must punish him accordingly, or he will never again respect you. The Fijian is of a suspicious character, and any idea of trickery on the part of a stranger will bring out the worst traits of his man-eating ancestry. He is vain to a fault and very sensitive of ridicule, but has no objection to ridiculing others.

Very few of the natives talk English; but in Levuka and

the principal centres they understand it tolerably. If a European has acquired sufficient knowledge to follow their ordinary conversation, they have a trick of defeating him in his accomplishment by changing their dialects or slang phrases to others which he cannot understand. Gratitude expressed by words is unknown to them, and they have no equivalent for our 'thank you.' Ordinarily good-natured, they are as a rule kind to each other, but trivial tribal jealousies, as in Scotland and Ireland, militate against their better nature. As to Fijian truthfulness in general, it is out of my power to give a fair opinion, all my friends varied so much. I was, however, credibly informed that a *kaisi*, or commoner, will as a rule give evidence in court just as his chief wishes. If the *roko* saw a fact and says so, the *kaisi* saw it; if the *roko* heard a thing and says so, the *kaisi* heard it and will swear to it. I should hesitate, however, before describing the Fijians as in the main deliberately untruthful. In the Polynesian mind loyalty to the chief is virtue *par excellence.* The influence of the *rokos* may perhaps decline, but the action of the British authorities has been very wisely adverse to any too sudden changes, especially when due allowance has to be made for the innate conservatism of the Fijians. This insular Toryism is another of their peculiarities, and it is in no way more marked than in their punctilious observance of etiquette of all sorts. A mere *buli* or sub-chief rarely goes unattended by his spearmen and advanced guard. If you enter a native house or discussion forum, the conversation is directly stopped, and the junior member rises and in the most polite terms acquaints you of the subject under debate, so that you may, if willing, join in.

Hospitality is a virtue of the first-class, and the *papalagi*, or white man, is generally singled out for its exercise. Instead of the port, sherry, or spirits offered by the white man, the

Fijian has a very effective substitute in his *angona* root, the raw material of the 'Fiji cider,' which I tasted on arrival at Kandavu. A friend of mine who stayed a few weeks in the group, thus described his experience of ceremonial *kava* drinking. *Quant à moi*, I seem to have gone in for it from the commencement; and though I cannot say I like it, still I learned not to dislike it.

'Late in the evening we learned that Sir Arthur Gordon had arrived, and on the following morning we had the honour of an interview with him at the Bure. Here also we had a second interview with Cacobau, who had called to pay his respects to his Excellency. The occasion was interesting in many respects, but for strangers like us, who wanted to see as much of native life as possible, no small part of the interest consisted in the opportunity afforded us of witnessing "*kava* drink," a ceremony which appears to be a great social institution in Fiji. *Kava* is the name given to a liquor produced by chewing the root of a shrub called *angona*, and the ceremonious part of the preparation consists in chewing the root. The process is wearisome, and to one who witnesses it for the first time it cannot but be disgusting. A score or two of Cacobau's men squatted down on the floor, one of them with a large wooden bowl before him, and the dry root of the *angona* cut into small pieces. Putting a piece into his mouth, and reducing it by chewing to a soft pulpy state, he squirted the juice into the bowl; and so with piece after piece, until the bowl was nearly full. Pouring water into the bowl, he stirred the liquor about, and strained it with a fibrous sort of wisp till it was clear. While this chewing, squirting, and straining was going on, the fellows squatted around the chief performer, chanted an invocation, or something of that sort, in a droning way, and clapped their hands at the end of every stave. The liquor being cleared, one of the men dipped a cocoa-nut cup into the bowl, and presented it with bended knee to Cacobau, who drank it off at a gulp. The cup was replenished, and handed to the other chiefs present, until the great bowl was quite empty. A cupful was offered to the Governor, but he declined to drink. It was not in accordance with native etiquette, we were told, to offer it to anyone else. Perhaps we should have declined too had it been offered to us; but possibly there were some amongst us who might have liked to taste this native grog out of curiosity. It tastes, they say, like soap-suds seasoned with pepper. The natives are very fond of it, and even Englishmen get to like it, unpleasant though it be at first. Constant indulgence in the use of it tends to paralyse the lower limbs. The ceremony over, we had luncheon, and here it became evident that his cupful of native grog had not quite satisfied Cacobau's appetite, so amazingly did he polish off glass after glass of Bass's ale.'

Kava has certainly an exhilarating effect, and has this peculiarity over all other intoxicating drinks that I have ever heard of—it affects the legs first and head afterwards, the latter rarely. I have seen a Fijian so affected by *kava*, that he could not stand at all, while at the same time he was disputing with his master (a Taviuni planter) as to the current value of some King William the Fourth shillings.

The sale of alcoholic drink to the natives is forbidden by Government ordinance, but if they can get hold of any, there is no mistake about their delight.

The Fijian has a long memory, and bears a kindly recollection of those who treat him well, while his memory is just as tenacious of the alleged evil deeds of his enemies. With him procrastination has been simply reduced to a science, and the word *malua*, or in Queen's English, 'I'll think about that to-morrow,' is incessantly in his mouth. *Malua* is now an Anglicised word in the group, and over and over again, when waiting very patiently for something or other, I have sincerely regretted the demoralising influence of a tropical climate which has infected white men as well as natives with that do-nothing system of *malua*.

I forget which great foreign statesman it was who said, 'Never do to-day what you can put off till to-morrow.' If he had ever visited Fiji, its interesting inhabitants would have much improved on his well-known dictum. Their *malua* is, in the words of Shakespeare, an eternal 'to-morrow, and to-morrow, and to-morrow.' The sweetness of delay is all-in-all to them, and even the most accomplished representative of the 'Circumlocution Office,' in all its dilatoriness, would pale into insignificance before a Levuka day-labourer making up his mind whether he will accept a job or not.

The Fijian is an inveterate haggler. I have seen a native with some wretched live fowl or duck on his arm, come into Levuka quite early in the morning, and demand for hours a price twice as much as he knows he will ultimately get; he will haggle and haggle with you over that bird, till you send him off in disgust, and then perhaps late in the afternoon he will come back and take one shilling for what, at seven in the morning, he valued at two shillings. He has no idea of keeping a secret, and anything known to one 'boy' is known to his neighbours in an inconceivably short space of time. If you pay him a little more than he expects he immediately tells all his friends, and as likely as not shares the plunder with them. He often makes presents, but expects presents in return. A young man will not perhaps work well at home or near his friends, but will go away for a time, make a modest fortune, which he generally invests in useless boxes, butchers'-knives, necklaces, looking-glasses, and Jew's harps; and then he will return to the paternal domain, divide his purchases among his friends, and have a good spell of downright laziness, until his people get quite tired of him and make him go away and work again.

Some of the English-made handkerchiefs with comic pictures on them, illustrating the growth of civilisation in Fiji, are much appreciated by the natives, who are beginning to like a few articles of European clothing. While staying with my brother at his place in Savu Savu Bay, Vanua Levu (the second-largest island of the group), I managed to ruin a grey tweed waistcoat by pouring over it a quantity of sulphuric acid. My brother immediately remarked, 'Give it to Rowena' (his servant); 'he will glory in it.' I did so, and at dinner that evening Mr. Rowena entered the room, his face beaming with smiles, and arrayed in my damaged vest, half of which was a light grey, the other a brilliant yellow. He told my brother in confidence afterwards that he was now half a *papalagi*, or white man.

The natives work in Levuka as ordinary labourers at a shilling to eighteenpence a day, and it seemed to me that they took the most amazing pains not to overtire themselves. In the provinces they work much better, and, according to an anonymous pamphlet which I recently received from Levuka, native boys of twelve or thirteen can drive the engines of sugar-mills just as well as white men.

The characteristics of native life are much the same in Fiji as they are everywhere else. Its chief phenomena are irregular alternations of excessive labour and excessive repose, and so it will continue till the fitful and uncertain habits of the people are corrected. Freedom, to their mind, means freedom to do nothing at all. The ordinary natives cannot understand our working, and they are at a loss to comprehend why we should wish them to work.

'Having all these fine *wongas*' (ships) 'and clothes, and knowing all about engines and glass and the like, whatever makes you white people come over here, where we have so little to give you?' asked a minor chief of me one day.

However, my native aristocrat was very particular in getting the highest price for his cocoa-nuts, and relished J.D.K.Z. gin like a Dutchman. The Fijians are honest as a rule, but some of them are not so punctilious about stealing cocoa-nuts as they might be, and I heard of a few cases of shirts and pocket-handkerchiefs being 'borrowed' from back-yards—after sundown.

The Fijian is curious to a fault. He will stay and watch everything you do with astounding patience. Your dinner-table is to him an inexhaustible fund of interest, and he will stare with undiminished attention till every dish is disposed of and 'thanks' are returned. I remember on one occasion my brother's 'boy' asking him to whom he was writing, and on being informed, replied, 'Ah! give him my love,' a request which was complied with. The process of nailing was at one time a source of endless delight to the natives, but the rapid increase of ship and boat-building in the group has rather interfered with the pleasure of the business, as far as they are concerned.

In many cases very affectionate relations exist between the *papalagis*, or white men, and the Fijians, and some touching stories have been told of their self-devotion. A poor friend of mine was endeavouring to shorten the sail of his cutter, when he was washed over by a heavy sea. The boys who were with him jumped overboard, remained swimming about in the pitchy darkness for some hours, and were quite overcome with grief at the failure of their efforts to find him. It was pitiful to hear them reproach themselves for not having done more to save him. On the other hand, the awe in which the white man was once held has in great measure diminished. A *roko* told me that at one time the Fijians considered the whites gods or immortals; 'but since,' he added, 'we know you do die and go there'—pointing to Draiba, the Levukan Kensal Green—'now we know you are men like ourselves.' Like the aboriginal races of other countries, they first deemed all *papalagi* civilisation, arts, and sciences were the results of enchantment; and a staggering blow to their self-confidence was the appearance in Levuka Harbour of a steamer which entered without a stitch of canvas set or any smoke or steam escaping. A steamship is to them a 'fire-ship;' but their wonder as to the doings of the white men has almost entirely ceased. As a Taviuni friend once remarked to me, 'If you were to cut off your head and carry it under your arm the length of Levuka beach, and then fix it on again, you would hardly astonish the Fijians.' We are past wonder, as far as they are concerned.

The Fijian is naturally cleanly; he is constantly bathing; but after he has got himself thoroughly clean he somewhat inconsistently anoints his body with cocoa-nut oil, with a not over-pleasant result in warm weather.

I found out this cocoa-nut oil fashion of the Fijians in a very practical way. I was landing in Levuka one day from a small boat, but the tide did not enable us to come up to the little pier, which ran out from the shore. Not caring altogether to chance the stones and bits of coral with bare feet, I accepted my boatman's offer of his broad shoulders. I was dressed in spotless white drill, and when I landed, I had to change all I had on.

CHAPTER XIV.

MEKE-MEKES.

DANCING is one of the chief amusements of the Fijians, and is taught by professionals; and this is also the case in nearly all the islands in the South Pacific. Games of a school-boy order, like hide-and-seek, hare-and-hounds blind-man's-buff, and ducks-and-drakes, are all known and appreciated by native adults. The natives are also fond of swinging, and a game called *lavo*, which consists of pitching the fruit of the *walai* (*Mimosa scandens*); the fruit is flat and circular, and somewhat resembles honey in appearance. Another game indulged in resembles our pastime of skittles, stones being substituted for the wooden pins. It is said that skilful players can pitch their stone with their back towards the skittles. Wrestling is a favourite amusement, and sometimes the Fijians make it a very rough game indeed. One of their most skilful games is the *veivasa ni moli*, which consists of suspending an orange or lemon, and trying to pierce it with a spear when it is in motion. To a certain extent this resembles the old English game of quintain.

Dressing the hair of the chiefs is a very serious business—so serious indeed that the occupation of a chief's barber is almost a sacred appointment. They are tabooed from doing anything else, and I understood were not even allowed to feed themselves. A chief's coiffure often takes several hours in preparation. It is first saturated with oil, and then blackened with the charred kernels of the candle-nut or *lauci*. The more the barber succeeds in distending the hair, the greater the dignity he attains, while the happy possessor of a well-frizzed and fancifully extended head of hair is looked upon with envy and admiration. A chief's hair is enveloped in a sort of turban reserved solely for men of his rank, and in former times a commoner who wore this head-dress would have been put to death in a very summary manner.

The hair of boys is usually cropped close, but on attaining the dignity of manhood, they can indulge their fancy to an extent only limited by the hair they possess.

In addition to the fanciful shapes which the hair is made to assume, colour in streaks or patches is freely added.

The women, especially when young and unmarried, wear their hair long, in its natural state, and on gay and festive occasions decorate it with flowers. After marriage such adornment is considered unnecessary or imprudent, and a short crop or 'frizz' takes the place of flowing locks. Those women who may be verging on baldness have recourse to 'wigs,' in the making of which the native barbers have attained an amount of skill which would rival that of the young men at Truefitt's. Occasionally women have their hair dressed in the same style as men, though not to the same extent in size. Certainly the coiffure of a chief was fearfully and wonderfully made. Mr. Williams states that he has measured some that were 3 feet 10 inches in circumference, and one masterpiece measured 5 feet. A coating of jet black powder is thrown over all, interspersed with stripes or patches of vermilion. Chiefs and priests used occasionally to wear a frontlet of small scarlet feathers fixed on a palm-leaf, with a long black comb or tortoise-shell 'scratcher' projecting from behind the ear.

Ear ornaments are used by both sexes; they are not mere pendants, but are passed horizontally through the lobe of the ear, which is greatly distended for that purpose, the size of the 'boring' varying from the thickness of the finger to that of the wrist. A white cowrie is sometimes inserted in the opening. Some of the more ambitious have the opening distended so as to admit a ring of 10 inches in circumference.

The natives display great taste in adorning themselves with natural shrubs, vines, dried grasses, and flowers made into wreaths, necklaces, or scarves worn over one shoulder.

Tattooing proper, however, is confined to the women, and to those parts that are covered by the *liku* or dress. The women also have their fingers interlined, for the admiration of the chiefs to whom they may have to hand food. The old and middle-aged women used to have patches of blue at the corners of the mouth, some say in order to notify that the woman has been a mother; scandal occasionally attributes it to vanity, in order to hide wrinkles and conceal the ravages of age.

The tattooing process often takes months to complete, and is a painful and tedious operation, only submitted to from mingled reasons of vanity and fear. The tattooing is performed with an instrument called a 'tooth,' which consists of four or five teeth inserted in a light handle. The pattern is cut into the flesh with this instrument, and the colours rendered permanent by means of a pigment composed of charcoal and candle-nut oil.

The custom of tattooing was instituted in accordance with an ordinance of their God Ndengei, and a neglect of this custom would entail punishment in the future state.

In Fiji, the practice of tattooing is confined to the women; but in Tonga the practice is reversed, the men only are subjected to this decoration. The Fijians say that this peculiarity of the Tongans arose from a blunder on the part of a Tongan chief who was chanting a well-known formula, 'Tattoo the women, and not the men;' his foot stumbled, and, hardly knowing what he did, he altered the refrain to 'Tattoo the men, and not the women.'

The softness and flow of the Fijian language will at once strike the traveller. It is evidently a branch of the Polynesian-Malay or Oceanic type. I made no great study of it, as I generally travelled in the company of English-speaking settlers or half-castes, who were thoroughly at home with our tongue. Of course, for a planter it is absolutely necessary to pick up something of Fijian, though I met with many who, at any rate two years since, knew little more than I did.

In many respects it is a very full language, inasmuch as there are distinctive names for every shrub and plant which grows; there are names for the various kinds of yams, of which the natives enumerate fifty; and there are Fijian words which are capable of affording expression to the most delicate subtleties of thought. There are very many dialects; in fact, the Fijian of the leeward groups can only make himself understood with some little difficulty in Vanua Levu or other of the windward islands. It is said there are seven distinct dialects, the most classic being that of Bau, into which the Testaments and prayer-books of the missionaries have been translated.

There is a good grammar and dictionary published, and I should say it is not at all a difficult language to pick up. The vowels are pronounced as in Italian, and the sound of *m* always comes before *b*, and the *c* is pronounced as the exact equivalent of our *th*, so difficult for the continental foreigner to acquire. The *n* has always *d* before it, and *g* has the sound of *ng*. It seemed to me a great pity that the missionaries did not base their labours more phonetically. For instance, the correct pronunciation of the word Bau (the native capital) is really *Mbaw.* Again, there is a pleasant suburb to the north of Levuka, where the cricket-matches come off, written Vagadace; it is pronounced *Vagadally.* 'What is that?' is in Fijian *A cava ogo,* and is pronounced *athava ongo.* Could not the words have been spelt as pronounced? It may be added that the group is called Viti in the leeward, and Fiji in the windward islands.

The manufacture of the club is a serious matter, the shapes of these instruments being as varied as the tastes of the owners. Most of them are made at home, and frequently the club of a Fijian aristocrat will have occupied months of patient toil. In some the shape is imparted whilst the tree is growing. A chief's club is carefully inlaid with ivory, adorned with human teeth and elaborate carving. A similar diversity and elaboration of carving and decoration is shown also in their spear-heads and handles.

Bows are made of the pendent shoots of the mangrove-tree; the arrows used for killing fish have several barbed points. The manufacture of fancy dishes and bowls forms an important branch of industry, and the natives display great ingenuity in carving and shaping these articles. Formerly, the making of cannibal forks was a somewhat extensive industry, but it has of late years happily declined; and, like everything else in this nineteenth century, even cannibal relics are getting vulgarised, and, so to speak, adulterated; and the honest 'beachcomber' of the Fiji provinces is not at all above manufacturing relics for Levuka, Sydney, or 'home.' The trade in 'curios' is a very important one all over the Pacific, and there are several shops in Levuka devoted almost entirely to their sale. Curios fetch bigger prices at Levuka than they do in London; and the enterprising traveller who thinks he can make a 'good thing' of a 'spec' in clubs, spears, and whales' teeth, will be bitterly disappointed when he receives his account of sales, or interviews personally the leading London dealers. The Fijian processional swords struck me as being particularly handsome. While in Fiji I became possessed of a Springfield (U.S.) flint musket most beautifully inlaid all over the stock and butt with human bones in stars and other designs. This was greatly prized by the cannibals, and was taken by the Government troops in the Viti Levu war of 1876.

Conch-shell trumpets are very popular, and a most dreadful noise is made with them. Indeed, it struck me that our Polynesian fellow-subjects are fond of noise of any sort. The firing of guns gives them inexpressible pleasure; but their champion din is a *meke-meke* with empty kerosene cans, which they get from the whites. A combination of all the German bands in London playing different tunes, and an 'obstructive' parliament of tile-prowling cats, would give something like an idea of the fiendish noise produced by conch-shells, *lalis*, kerosene tins, and the natives' own sweet shrieking. Some of the Fijian 'boys' are not very considerate as to the time they select for this dreadful infliction. One Christmas time, I remember, they commenced their orgy about eleven o'clock at night. The police soon put a stop to it, however—another proof of the superior civilisation of Fiji. In London, the torture of the sick and dying by a ghastly version of *Adeste Fideles*, as rendered by the 'waits,' is not only tolerated, it is almost approved.

The natives have, however, good ears for music, and sing very nicely. Both in the Catholic and in the Wesleyan churches they sing a great number of hymns or litanies during the service, and the perfect time of the people's voices, rising and falling according to the beating of the *lali* in a *meke-meke*, is one of its most marked characteristics.

Some of the natives are rather fond of practical jokes, often of a very advanced order, and they evidently relish making a *lia lia*, or fool of a neighbour, by sending him on a bootless errand. We are a very superior people, no doubt; but I have heard of very foolish journeys accomplished in England on the 1st of April. Sometimes, if on particularly good terms with a *papalagi*, a Fijian will actually try a bit of fun with him—sometimes more than fun, as the following anecdote of the experience of a friend will show:

As he was sitting, somewhat late one night, on an old *lali* which had witnessed, and drummed the accompaniment to, many a terrible scene, he suddenly saw advancing towards him from the old Sofatabua house *a glowing human head*. A moment's stare of amazement and then all the horrors of the thing, the locality, and the previous conversation overwhelmed him with a terror indescribable. His scalp became, he said, an ill-fitting cap, his skin was goose-fleshed into little hillocks, his heart gave one great bound into his throat, whence it sank lead-like into his shoes, and then (just when the awful fear was becoming an active madness which said that it or he must be annihilated) a boy's voice within the head asked: 'Sa vinaka?' ('Is it good?') What a relief it was! And how thankful he felt that the apparition had spoken in time to save itself from harm! The mischievous young monkey had collected a quantity of luminous fungus leaves, which he had stuck thickly over his face so as to illuminate it.

One of the prettiest Fijian spectacles I ever saw was a grand *meke-meke* or ceremonial dance. Early in the morning it was very amusing to see the country people streaming into the native village, their countenances glowing with anticipated pleasure. They carried their smart dancing-dresses tied up in bundles; some had their faces already painted, and their hair done up in *tappa* in the oddest way possible. All the time the *lalis* (native wooden drums) were making a great row in the square, and when all the people were assembled, we sat down under a canopy of mats which had been put up to screen us from the sun.

First came the school-children in single file, and coiled themselves up in the centre of the square. Each child as it passed halted, and read a verse from a Testament. Then they unwound themselves, and came up in the same fashion with their writing on slates. Then came a dance called the *meke.* They retired a little, divided into bands, and then came forward in a sort of dance, turning first to one side and then the other, moving in the most perfect time, and chanting as they came. All their movements were graceful, and the way in which the tune, if one can so call it, was first of all sung by those in front, and then taken up, a third lower, by those behind, was very effective. When they had come close enough, on a signal they all sat down and began a geography lesson. The native teacher called out the name of a country, as 'Peritania' (Britain), and one of the children in a lower minor key began to chant 'Peritania sa matanitu' ('Britain is a kingdom'). Then a third higher some other words, saying where Britain is, etc., and then, with a swaying motion of their bodies and a rhythmical clapping of hands, sometimes beating the ground, sometimes pointing on one side, sometimes the other, and sometimes joining hands overhead, they all joined in a chant descriptive of the extent, government, etc., of the British Empire; in fact, it was elementary geography turned into a rather pretty song. In this way they went through nearly all the countries in Europe. After which, singing 'God save the Queen' in English, the school-children left the ground dancing.

Then came the event of the day, the great State *meke*. The first was the 'Flying Fox Dance.' From the half-hidden roads leading out of the corners of the square came two bands of men dressed in *likus* (a sort of kilt) of green and coloured banana leaves. These *likus* were beautifully made, the leaves lying very thick one above another, and reaching below their knees. The men were very fine specimens of humanity; some had their faces blackened or painted black and red, and their heads done up in the most elaborate way with white *tappa*. Garlands of flowers and leaves hung round their necks, and they had garters and armlets of bright-coloured leaves on their arms and legs. To describe the dance as it deserves to be described, is impossible. There must have been over two hundred men and about sixty children taking part in it. The two parties approached each other in the usual *meke* form, an odd mixture of march and dance, and after various evolutions, every man threw away the huge palm-leaf fan which he carried in his hand. This was the end of the first act.

In the next part the flying foxes proceeded to rob a banana-tree. A pole was set up in the middle of the square, and on the top of it a banana plant, with a bunch of artificial fruit made of husked cocoa-nuts full of oil. The two bands advanced, and seemed to consult, and then messengers were sent out from either party, to see, I suppose, that all was safe. They went flying round the square with their arms stretched out, making a noise like a flying fox. With a great deal of dancing the main body approached the tree, and one of them climbed up, whilst the little flying foxes circled round, and finally clustered under the tree, crying with delight at the sight of the fruit. The fox in the tree hung by his legs and flapped his arms, when another climbed after him, and they bit and scratched and squalled just as big bats do, and the first comer was turned out. The whole dance lasted about half an hour, and between each figure there was a slight pause. The time was wonderful—every swish of their *likus* was in unison, and they were most clever in adapting themselves to any inequality in the ground. There was a musical accompaniment of native drums and hollow bamboos, played by about twenty gaily-dressed old gentlemen.

Next came a 'Club Dance.' The square was surrounded, except on one side, where stood the great church, by plantations of bananas and bread-fruit; so that one saw nothing of the preparations or formation, and heard the chant of the dancers before they came in from the different paths. From either side advanced a party, each about eighty strong, marching three abreast, armed with short spears made of bamboo, cut into fantastic shapes at the end, or with the shafts painted or covered with a matting of reeds. As the two parties approached each other—very slowly—they chanted, and swung their bodies from side to side, thrusting and parrying with their spears, which were held overhead; every hand and every foot moving exactly together. When about twelve yards from each other, each body wheeled away from us, and we saw advancing between them from some distance another body of men, of about the same strength as both the others, but twelve abreast, and armed with clubs. This *meke*, in which over three hundred men were dancing, was wild and picturesque, and the men fine, well-made fellows, all chiefs or men of high birth. The dresses in this dance were even more brilliant than in the last. Each man had a *liku* of strips of *pandanus* leaf, dyed black, yellow, and red in strips. Their bodies and faces were elaborately painted black and red, and their heads were done up in folds of very fine *tappa*, white or brown, or in some cases (what I had never seen before) of a bright blue. They had sashes of white *tappa*, in thick folds, terminating sometimes in streamers, and sometimes in a long train, not allowed to touch the ground, but looped up again into the sash. Each man in the front rank of the larger body had a splendidly-made breastplate of ivory and pearl-shell. Many had a good-sized whale's tooth hung round their necks—rather an effective ornament—and armlets, garters, and bracelets of shells, ivory, or black water-weed, according to his fancy.

The next dance was the most graceful of all. It was called 'The Waves of the Sea,' and represented the sea coming up on the reef. The dresses of the men were much the same as in the last; but there were also a number of children in bright *likus*, and with garlands of leaves and flowers. First of all they formed into a long line; then, breaking the line, danced forward, ten or twelve at a time, for a few steps, bending down their bodies and spreading out their hands, as the little shoots from a wave run up on the beach, wave after wave rolled in, and then at the end of the long line ran round, first a few at a time, some falling back again; then more and more, as the tide runs up on the shore-side of the reef, and nothing but a small island of coral is left. The band kept up a sound like the roar of the surf; and as the tide rose and the waves began to meet and battle over the little island the dancers threw their arms over their heads as they met, and their white *tappa*-covered heads shook as they bounded into the air, like the spray of the breaking surf. The people sitting round screamed with delight. The idea of the dance was decidedly artistic, and was most artistically carried out.

The Fijians of old were first-class potters for a savage race, but the art is rapidly dying out. The three-legged iron pot of the Birmingham district has killed the native industry. I saw very few specimens, and these were in the hands of Europeans, and greatly prized as 'curios.' The natives had well-designed globular drinking-vessels, earthen arrowroot-pans, dye-bowls, and fish-pots. A friend told me that he saw on one occasion an earthen pot capable of holding a hogshead, and which had four apertures to facilitate its being filled or opened. The ordinary earthen cooking vessels contained from five to ten gallons. The Fijians employed red and blue clay, tempered with sand, and although the means at their disposal for manufacture must have been of the rudest character, yet the work they turned out had as true an outline as if made with a wheel. Pottery work was entirely confined to the women of sailors' a few puffs, and fishermen's families.

Both sexes avail themselves of the solace of tobacco, and their style of indulging in it is pre-eminently social. A cigarette, being lighted, is passed from one to the other, each one taking and handing it to his neighbour.

The half-castes are great in pipes, and many of the labourers about the plantations indulge in the common clay pipe of British or colonial manufacture.

CHAPTER XV.

BRITISH NATIVE POLICY--FIAT JUSTITIA.

THE foregoing chapters will, I hope, have convinced the reader that Fiji has possessed for centuries laws, customs, rights, and obligations which, unlike any other system to be found in Western Polynesia, bound the Fijians together as a homogeneous people. In dealing with such a race, only half escaped from barbarism, and clinging with savage conservatism to the traditions of their ancestry, great judgment was required to accomplish the ends sought by Her Majesty's Government: *i.e.*, the provision of necessary funds to defray the expenses of the colony; and the inculcation of habits of industry, in a manner which the natives would understand and appreciate. There can be no doubt that the Fijian Government have solved this problem very successfully, notwithstanding an opposition on the part of some of the whites which has been virulent in the extreme.

The same 'lying spirit' which was abroad when disappointed place-hunters had the wickedness to tell suffering natives that the measles epidemic was introduced by the British Government to extirpate their race, has prompted the hostility with which the policy of Sir Arthur Gordon and his able coadjutor, the Hon. John Thurston, on the subject of native taxation, has been attacked by a small section of the white settlers. Some of these gentlemen are perhaps now regretting the course they have adopted. It is amusing to find that the cry is now, not that the British Government want to exterminate the blacks, but that Sir Arthur Gordon and Mr. Thurston want to turn out the white settlers. The best answer to the grumblers is the financial success of the policy. From every point of view the matter is one of importance, and I think a *résumé* of the question as put by his Excellency and his minister will demonstrate the wisdom of their course.

In a colony like Fiji, where the natives form ninety-nine per cent. of the population, it is self-evident that as they cause a large portion of administrative expenditure, they must contribute to defray its expenses. The question was, how should this contribution be obtained — by money, or in kind? In semi-civilised regions or countries like India or China, where the science of political economy is almost unknown, the system of payment in kind largely prevails. This mode of paying taxes is doubtless a bad one, for experience teaches that public revenue derived from such a source usually suffers so much from the mismanagement and peculation of the collectors, that little of what is contributed by the people ever finds its way into the treasury.

For these and many other reasons the collecting of the public revenue in money is to be preferred. It may however occur that countries exist, the people of which tenaciously adhere to the antiquated customs of their race; and where, as they have no money, they must either pay in produce or not at all.

Fiji is certainly one of these places. Its people have no money among themselves, and the European trading and planting population (under 900 persons) is too small to provide the bulk of them with work or any other means of gaining money. There can be no doubt also that, if it were possible to collect revenue in money, the same objection would be taken as is made above to the levying of taxes in kind. In a young colony like Fiji, with a large native population, the collection of revenue must in a great measure be entrusted to native chiefs. There are two temptations which many Fijian chiefs find it difficult to withstand: one is that of getting into debt with traders; the other is that of looking upon taxes paid to them by their tribe, on account of the Government, as in part a sort of 'benevolence' to themselves. The facility with which they can accumulate debt upon debt, together with the constant pressure of petty creditors, is the primary cause of their appropriating public money to their own uses. 'This tendency to accept credit,' observes a late writer, 'is a state of things which occurs in every part of the world in which men of superior race freely trade with men of a lower race. It extends trade no doubt for a time, but it demoralises the natives, checks true civilisation, and does not lead to any permanent increase in the wealth of the country, so that the European Government of such a country must be carried on at a loss. The custom of Fijians is to pay their taxes in produce or service, and the custom only requires to be properly defined and settled, in order to produce a fair amount of revenue at a moderate cost of collection.

To use Mr. Thurston's own words:

'The characteristics of native life in Fiji are much the same as they are everywhere. Its chief phenomena are irregular alternations of excessive labour and excessive repose—and so it will continue until the fitful and uncertain habits of the people are corrected. This measure is not calculated to interfere with the freedom of trade in any way, but its tendency is to promote those habits of steady industry that can alone develop faculties which are requisite to the exercise of an actual, instead of a nominal, freedom in business.'

The strongest part of Mr. Thurston's address, in my opinion, is where he dwells on the habits of industry which a tax in kind would teach the native race. Certainly no place better illustrates the final consequence of commerce depending upon mere natural productions than those parts of Brazil and Peru watered by the Amazon and its affluents. The forest there formerly abounded with resins, oils, balsams, gums, textile plants, and medicinal plants. At the present day few or none of these things are to be found except under cultivation. Those sources of wealth planted by nature, and which had been neglected by man, had ceased to exist. To reap, man must sow. The British Government had accepted the sovereignty of the Fiji Group, and in doing so, had accepted the responsibility of caring for all its inhabitants, white or coloured. The British Government has a higher mission than to augment the fortunes of people who, born in the United Kingdom, settle in every part of the world. It has very serious duties towards the inferior races owning its sway, and the laws that apply to other possessions must affect Fiji with equal force. The Fijian knew nothing of the capabilities of his native soil: he was susceptible to instruction, but there was no one to teach him. If properly taught, he could grow coffee and tobacco, and plant sugar-cane with the same ease as he attended to his taro-beds, or cultivated his yams.

Supplied with the proper materials and carefully taught, the Fijian would advance steadily towards a higher civilisation, increase his own wealth and that of his country, and accomplish all this in his own fashion.

If the main object of the British Government had been to supply cheap labour for the settlers, perhaps the best plan would have been to impose a heavy poll-tax, and get the money from the Europeans; but this would have constituted slavery under the guise of 'labour;' and it would sooner or later end in the destruction of the natives.

As Sir Arthur Gordon happily put it in his lecture, the Fijian has more affinity with the acute and cultivated Hindoo or Cingalese than the wandering and naked savages of the Australian bush. The Fijian has not, it is true, the arts, culture, literature, and luxury of Eastern civilisation; but he has in many ways advanced beyond the ruder stages of savage life, and possesses those receptive powers which fit him for a far higher social and intellectual life. The preservation and advancement of these people has been rightly considered by the Governor and his advisers as among their most pressing and important duties.

Mr. Thurston demonstrated the serious responsibility which the guardians of a native race like the Fijians incurred, and went on to prove that the substitution of a tax in kind for payment in money would result in the Fijians becoming planters and producers, instead of being merely collectors for the white men. These are his words:

'I have already said that the system of demanding the native tax in money, which has so many advocates, can lead to no permanent good to the colony, and I will endeavour to explain why, as it is one of the strongest reasons for this measure. The reason is that the native does not produce anything. I use the words—the produce and the producer—in their highest, and not in their lower or more restricted sense. I do not call the man who catches fish, or who searches the woods for gum-resins or dye-woods, a producer. He is a mere collector, a poacher upon nature's preserves. I call that man a producer who, by his personal exertion and industry, causes two blades of grass to grow where only one grew before, or who replaces rank grasses by fields of waving wheat. It is to produce in this sense that I should like to see the Fijian instructed. It is upon certain, and not upon uncertain, industry I submit that the revenues of this colony should depend.

'The Fijian, then, does not produce anything beyond a few yams and taro for the use of himself and family. The Fijian simply sells to the trader so much of the natural productions of his forests or seas as he can with some little labour collect. Of these productions, even when collected, he is by no means careful, and he takes no measures to increase or even maintain the strength of these natural reserves. They have a limit, therefore, which is not very difficult to define. Is the revenue to depend upon this uncertain and unintelligent state of affairs? The Fijian is no more a producer than the native of the Indian seas who dives for pearl-shell until he has exhausted the bed, or the half-bred Indian of South America who destroys whole forests to obtain india-rubber or cinchona bark. And what has been the result in all parts of the world, whether civilised or uncivilised, when there has been a constant demand for any natural production, and no foresight has been exercised to maintain the supply? We know that if the supply is not increased in exact ratio to the demand, harder work, worse pecuniary results, misery, and sometimes famine, follow. As Roko Tui Ra said lately at Draiba, "Of *bêche-de-mer* there will soon be none, for the drying-houses encompass the whole land." But how are they going to make the supply overtake or keep up with the demand? The natives cannot sow or plant *bêche-de-mer* as they do cotton or coffee seed. It will be the same with pearl, tortoise-shell, and other things upon which the natives, until lately, entirely depended to provide their money-tax and their little luxuries bought from traders. The supply will become smaller by degrees and beautifully less, or I am very much mistaken.

'A few years ago Scottish fishermen got but three-and-sixpence per hundred for their haddocks, and earned a decent livelihood; they now obtain twelve shillings and sixpence, but work harder and obtain a bare subsistence. The same thing may be said of oyster-beds. Constant demand has caused the exhaustion of what were once natural reserves. Men have cut away their supplies without a thought for the future, much in the same manner as we are, or, I hope I may say, as we were, doing here.'

The Fijian is now growing coffee, sugar-cane, cocoa, vanilla,

Pandanus utilis for making bags (the *Vacoa* of Mauritius), and mango, in addition to the following articles which have been up to the present time the leading items of produce brought in by them: these are copra (or the dried kernel of the cocoa-nut), cotton, candle-nuts, tobacco, and maize; while *bêche-de-mer*, a sea-slug, and a delicacy much appreciated by the Chinese, is also accepted.

The produce thus paid by the natives is put up to public tender, and the highest is accepted in each article, and to the successful tenderer all the produce delivered or collected in discharge of the tax is transferred on its receipt by the Government. The *modus operandi* of the system is thus described by Sir Arthur Gordon:

'The amount of the assessment fixed, and the prices offered for various articles of produce by the successful tenderer or tenderers, are intimated to the Roko Tui or native governor of each province.

'The apportionment of the shares to be borne by each district in the province, and the selection of the article or articles of produce to be contributed, are then made, nominally and according to law, by a board appointed under the Ordinance, but practically by the *Bose vaka Yasana*, or provincial council, which, as I have previously explained, consists of chiefs of districts, styled "*bulis*," under the presidency of the Roko Tui, frequently, though not always, aided by the presence of the Governor's commissioner.

'The next stage is the apportionment of the tax of each district by the *Bose ni Tikina*, or district council, consisting of the town chiefs of the district, under the presidency of the *buli*. By this body the share of each several township in the district is determined.

'Lastly, the individual share of produce to be contributed

or work done by each family in each village is settled by the town chief, aided by the elders of the township.

'The mode in which the articles are raised is left to the people themselves to determine, and the methods adopted have been very various. In some places each village has grown its own tax produce along with what it grew for sale or domestic use; in others, several villages have combined to grow their produce in one large plantation. These latter are what, by those who wish to discredit the scheme, are called "Government gardens;" but, in fact, no such gardens exist. The soil and the produce both belong to the people themselves.

'This machinery recognises the primitive community system, on which all political and social institutions in Fiji are based, and which, even in the matter of taxation, I found to be still in use as regarded the rates for local purposes, such as payment of schoolmasters and village police, which, quite irrespectively of the Government (and, as some would say, illegally), were imposed by the provincial councils by a species of voluntary assessment.

'This species of taxation is, consequently, familiar to the natives, and thoroughly understood by them; a fact which causes the pressure of the impost to be more lightly felt than it would be if demanded directly from the individual by the Government. It moreover renders the natives themselves, to a very large extent, active and responsible agents in the collection of revenue.

'Both of these are, I need hardly say, points of very considerable importance.

'But these were not the only results which the system was aimed to effect, nor are they the only objects which have been attained by its adoption.

'As was anticipated by the framers of the Ordinance,

the cultivation of articles of export by the natives has been largely promoted.'

Competition among the merchants being as keen in Levuka as it is everywhere else, the Government manages to get a very good price for the native taxes, and any surplus beyond the assessment of the district is of course returned to the Fijian producers. In the year 1878 the amount of tax produce sent in as taxes, exceeded the assessment to the value of two thousand pounds, and this has been sold for the benefit of the contributors. In 1879, one province alone had five hundred pounds returned to it, but the full statistics have not yet reached this country. Of course there may be harsh and overbearing *bulis* and *rokos*, but to *rokos* and *bulis* the Fijians have for centuries been accustomed, and it is evidently the duty of the Government that these officers should be very carefully looked after by white magistrates. As regards the natives, notwithstanding the efforts that have been made to prejudice them against the tax in kind, I believe that the majority infinitely prefer it to a money-tax.

'A few days before I left Fiji a native of great intelligence spoke to me of the efforts of certain whites to excite a prejudice against the Government. He spoke bitterly of the mischief which might be done by these intrigues, and added: "We Fijians are great fools, and there are many of us who are likely to be gulled; but, after all, we are not such fools as to have lost all memory of the time when these gentlemen, who are now so solicitous for our welfare and our rights, had all things in their own hands; and you may take it for granted that most of the ignorant villagers who answer '*E dina šaka*' ('Quite true, sir') when it is suggested to them that they are oppressed, are perfectly aware that a money-tax would cost them double labour, and laugh secretly, though respect leads them to yield a seeming assent to a white man's assertion."

'The statement that the payment of a tax in cash would require double labour is, though startling, perfectly true. Taking the article copra, for example, it will be found that the mean or average price offered by the traders to Government in 1877 was £10 10s. 6d. per ton (2240 lb.). The average prices given by local traders to natives at the time was £5 per ton; and, as payment was generally made in articles sold at a large profit, even that value can only be regarded as nominal.

'It follows, therefore, that if the native under the present system had to pay ten shillings worth of copra annually by way of taxes, he would have to provide 106 lb. weight of that article only; but if he had to pay ten shillings in money, he would have to sell 224 lb. weight to the trader in order to raise the amount of money required.

'I do not suppose that the people of Fiji, more than people in other parts of the world, *like* taxation in any form; but, as a general rule, they are quite aware of the advantage to them of the present system, as contrasted with that of which it takes the place; and that they have, at all events, thriven under it, not half an eye is required to perceive. Everywhere the increased areas of cultivation, the enlarged towns, the good new houses, the well-kept roads, the cheerful and healthy-looking population, present the strongest possible contrast to the aspect of the country in 1875. This was fully admitted to me, not long before I left Fiji, by a leading planter, who said that nobody who had eyes in his head could deny that the natives were very much better off than they were three years previously; but he added (and there was much significance in the admission) that this was by no means an advantage to the planter, whose difficulties in obtaining labour were thereby materially increased.'

It is true that for a time the native taxation scheme did interfere, to a certain extent, with the supply of Fijian labour for white men's estates; but the temporary inconvenience was caused by the Government as much in the planters' interests as that of the Fijians and other natives.

Some 6000 Polynesian labourers (from other groups outside Fiji) had been working on Fiji estates, and their time of service had expired. The Government, anxious to establish the fair fame of Fiji in the islands where these people came from, determined that, in accordance with the terms of their agreement, they should be returned to their homes.

The whole of the labour trade of the colony is in the hands of the Government. The labourers are engaged for three years at a time, at three pounds per adult per annum, payable to the Immigration Department, plus about twelve pounds to cover the cost of passage to Fiji and their return home. Boys are engaged at half these rates. Food and clothing bring up the cost of the labourer to the planter to about ten pounds per annum.

This supply is supplemented by the native Fijians, the younger of whom are always willing to work for the planters at similar wages; but the law limits their engagements to one year at a time. These men are of great service, as they can be engaged for a few weeks or months only when required.

Compare these wages with those paid to the Chinamen in the Sandwich Islands or in the British West Indies, and it will be seen what advantages the Fiji planter possesses, especially as the Fijian or Polynesian is in every way the superior of the coolie. Coolies to a limited extent have been introduced from India; but the planters wisely prefer the Polynesians, who contemptuously describe our Eastern fellow-subjects as 'rats.'

I venture to suggest whether it would not be a good plan to institute additional payment for time-work, as adopted on the sugar-estates of Demerara. Perhaps the most interesting fact observable at the present time is that the natives of Fiji are becoming very large producers; the value of the articles paid by them in the form of taxes only, reached in 1879 the respectable figure of £22,514, or, in produce, 300 tons cotton, 1100 tons copra, 180 tons of candle-nuts, 30 tons of minor products, and 30,000 bushels of maize.

So much for the Native Taxation Scheme. I am no blind partisan, but justice necessitated no faltering comments on such a topic as the native policy of the British Government. *Liberavi animam meam.*

CHAPTER XVI.

ZOOLOGY AND BOTANY OF FIJI.

As I have previously said, Fiji has one enemy, the mosquito, and he is no despicable foe. In some parts of the group he is simply a supreme nuisance—though no worse in Fiji than in other places that I have visited. The bites of these gentry, scratched by the finger-nail, turn into troublesome sores; but these, with healthy constitutions, soon heal. The natives seem, however, very indifferent to them, and let crowds of black flies feed upon the open wound, utterly regardless of what to a white man would be the most exquisite torture. They say the flies take the poison out.

In some of the islands a favourite way of self-adornment is to slash the arms and legs with broken glass, the scars coming out as crosses or the like. Children are often treated in this way, and sometimes injure themselves on their own account. The natives of the Southern Seas certainly do not feel pain as we do.

The native medicine-men used to study the art of killing as well as curing. The flora of Fiji abounds with poisonous plants, but the knowledge of their properties is confined to a few families of the native professional men. The latter are looked upon with a certain amount of fear, and are generally attached to the person of a chief as body-guards and ministers of his vengeance. They used to be seen, says Mr. Litton Forbes, lounging one day in the neighbourhood of some village—on the next they disappeared. Soon afterwards the chief or some other head-man drooped, and died suddenly under unusual circumstances. No inquiries were made and no questions asked, but perhaps within a week or two the dead man's wife would join the harem of the superior chief. The prudent said little on such occasions, lest a similar fate should befall themselves.

As regards some of the medicinal plants, they are perhaps more difficult to find out than the poisonous ones used for illegal purposes. Those who profess to be acquainted with their properties—often women, and answering to our herbalists—cannot be tempted by any presents to disclose secrets which prove to them a lucrative source of income for life. It is only the virtues of commonly known plants that a casual inquirer has any chance of learning. The leaves of the *kura* (*Morinda citrifolia*, Linn.), a middle-sized tree, with shining leaves and white flowers, not unlike those of the coffee shrub, are heated by passing them over flame, and their juice squeezed into ulcers, whilst the leaves themselves are put on the wound as a kind of bandage. The bark of the *danidani* (*Panax fruticosum*, Linn.), a shrub about 8 feet high, and cultivated near the native houses on account of its deeply-cut, ornamental foliage, is scraped off, and its juice taken as a remedy for *macake*, the thrush, ulcerated tongue or throat. The properties of the sarsaparilla as a means of purifying the blood are well known. The creeper is found throughout the group, especially on land that has at one time been cleared, and might be gathered in quantities if there were any demand for it. In the London market, it would at present be unsaleable. It belongs to that section of sarsaparillas distinguished by pharmacologists as the 'non-mealy,' the most valued representative of which is the Jamaica species. Moreover, it has no 'beard' or little rootlets. The natives of Ovalau, Viti Levu, and Vanua Levu name it *kadragi* and *wa-rusi;* those of Kadavu, *ra-kau-wa*, literally, 'the woody-creeper.' Dr. Seeman met with it years ago in the Hawaiian Group; it is said to be also common in the Samoan and Tongan Groups, and prepared sarsaparilla occasionally imported to the two last-mentioned has found no market, the indigenous being preferred to the foreign production. Curious to add, in Fiji it is not, as with us, the *rhizome* that is used, but the leaves, which are chewed, put in water, and strained through fibre, like the *angona* or *kava* (*Piper methysticum*, Forst.), before being taken. Strong purgative properties reside in the *vasa* or *rewa* (*Cerbera lactaria*, Ham.), a sea-side tree, 25 feet high, with soft wood, smooth shining leaves, and white, scented flowers, used for necklaces by the natives. The aromatic leaves of the *laca* (*Plectranthus Forsteri*, Benth.), a weed abounding in cultivated places, and having purple bracts supporting pale blue flowers, cure, it is said, 'bad eyes' and headaches on being brought in contact with the affected parts. It is also recommended for coughs and colds, in common with an acanthaceone herb, inhabiting swamps (*Adenosma triflora*, Mus.), which shares its aromatic properties. The people of Somo-Somo declare that the leaves of the *vulokaka* (*Viter trifoliata*, Linn.), with which their beach is thickly lined, when reduced to a pulp by chewing, are employed by them for stuffing hollow teeth. The leaves and bark of another sea-side shrub, the *sinu mataiavi* (*Wikstræmia Indica*, C. A. Meyer), are employed for coughs, the bark alone for sores.

The Fijians are also very clever in performing operations with the rudest instruments, in many cases difficult amputations being effected with nothing better than the edge of a broken glass bottle.

A medicine which is of common repute is the oil of the *dilo-nut*, which, with its kernel, is about the size of a walnut. The oil of this nut, properly extracted, is a most marvellous remedy for sprains and rheumatism. Captain A. R. Winckler, late of the bark *The Goolwa*, informed me that on his return voyage from Levuka and Loma-Loma, Fiji, to London, several of his men were struck down by rheumatism and rheumatic fever; but, by careful treatment and external application of *dilo-nut* oil, he soon rendered them fit for duty. This evidence might be indefinitely enlarged, as the cures in Polynesia by the oil of the *dilo-nut* are among the common topics of conversation.

The fruits of the *Calophyllum inophyllum*, the *dilo-nut* of Fiji, runs a medical description, were imported from the Mauritius under the name of 'oil seeds.' They consist of the hard woody endocarp, about the size of an English oak-gall, nearly globular, with a small projecting point at one end, and contain a yellowish-white oily kernel. According to the official report of the products in the Indian Museum, the seeds yield sixty per cent. of a fragrant green oil, fluid at ordinary temperatures, but beginning to solidify when cooled below 50° Fahr. In India it is used as a lamp oil, and also as an outward application for rheumatism. Although apparently unknown in the commerce of this country in 1847-8, nearly 4000 gallons of the oil were exported from Madras to Ceylon and the Straits Settlements. The tree yielding these seeds bears handsome white fragrant flowers, and it may not be out of place here to remark that there is a wide field for experiment among the native plants of India for those interested in perfumery. The following note from Seeman's '*Flora Vitiensis,*' will show how highly the oil obtained from these nuts is esteemed in Fiji, as well as the method of extraction: The most valuable oil produced in Fiji is that extracted from the seeds of this tree, the *dilo* of the natives, the tamarind of Eastern Polynesia, and the *cashumpa* of India. It is the bitter oil or *woondel* of Indian commerce. The natives use it for polishing arms and greasing their bodies when cocoa-nut oil is not at hand. But the great reputation this oil enjoys throughout Polynesia and the East Indies rests upon its medicinal properties as a liniment in rheumatism, pains in the joints, and bruises. Its efficacy in this respect can hardly be exaggerated, and recommends it to the attention of European practitioners. The oil is kept by the Fijians in gourd flasks, and, there being only a limited quantity made, I was charged about sixpence per pint for it, paid in calico and cutlery. The tree is one of the most common littoral plants in the group; its round fruits, mixed with the square ones of *Barringtonia speciosa*, the pine-cone-like ones of the sago palm, and the flat seeds of the *walai* (*Entada scandens*, Benth.), densely cover the sandy beaches. *Dilo* oil never congeals in the lowest temperature of the Fijis, as cocoa-nut oil does during the cool season. It is of a greenish tinge, and very little of it will impart its hue to a whole cask of cocoa-nut oil. Its commercial value is only partially known in the Fijis, and was found out accidentally. Amongst the contributions in cocoa-nut oil which the natives furnish towards the support of the Wesleyan missions, some *dilo* oil had been poured, which, on arriving at Sydney, was rejected by the broker, who purchased the other oil, on account of its greenish tinge and strange appearance. On being shown to others, a chemist, recognising it as the bitter oil of India, purchased it at the rate of £60 per ton; and he must have made a good profit on it, as the article fetches £90 a ton. In order to extract the oil, the round fruit is allowed to drop in its outer fleshy covering, and rot on the ground. The remaining portion, consisting of a shell, somewhat of the consistency of that of a hen's egg, and enclosing the kernel, is baked on hot stones in the same way that Polynesian meat and vegetables are. The shell is then broken, and the kernels pounded between stones. If the quantity be small, the macerated mass is placed in the fibres of the *vau* (*Hibiscus tiliaceus* and *tricuspis*), and forced by the hand to yield up its oily contents; if large, a rude level press is constructed by placing a boom horizontally between two cocoa-nut trees, and appending to this perpendicularly the fibres of the *vau*. After the macerated kernels have been placed in the midst, a pole is made fast to the lower end of the fibres, and two men, taking hold of its end, twist the contrivance round and round, till the oil, collecting into a wooden bowl placed underneath, has been extracted. Of course the pressure thus brought to bear upon the pounded kernels is not sufficiently great to express the whole of the oil, and there is still much waste. Ipecacuanha, with senna, was introduced into the island years ago by the Catholic missionaries, and both grow wild all over the low lands. Another remarkable remedy has recently been introduced from Fiji, and is now well known under the name of '*Tonga.*' A friend of mine discovered that a certain mixture of native medicines wonderfully relieved him from neuralgia, and after successfully curing himself, he sent the preparation over to a firm of manufacturing chemists in England, Messrs. Allen and Hanburys, who named it '*Tonga,*' and physicians have declared it to possess the qualities my friend claims for it.

All Polynesia is in fact a great drug-producing country, but so reticent are the natives, that it is difficult even on the spot to ascertain the exact truth in regard to drug plants. It may be stated in this regard that the native way of preparing medicine is to break or cut up the herbs to be used into very small pieces, and then to tie them in a piece of grass cloth and to soak the packet in a drinking vessel of water for a while, and so make an infusion which is then drunk as a dose.

Nearly all the animals now thriving are of imported origin. There are about a hundred varieties of the lizard, some of them very beautifully marked, and the centipede flourishes too much to be altogether agreeable. There is a lizard which inhabits trees (*Choroscartes fasciatus*); it is of a beautiful green colour, and about two feet in length. There are snakes in nearly all the islands, averaging three feet in length, but they are perfectly harmless.

Birds are plentiful, and many varieties, both of the edible and ornamental kinds, exist, the principal being the wild-duck, pigeon, teal, bittern, hawk, owl, and various kinds of paroquets of great beauty and richness of plumage. There are two varieties of wild-duck, the red and black, or the *Ngandamu* and *Nga loa*, as the natives designate them. The former is comparatively rare; the latter is not so wild, and affords good sport. One species of paroquet, the *Conphilus solitarius*, was formerly in great demand by the traders on account of its lovely plumage, and so highly prized was it by the natives of the Friendly Islands, that it was a not uncommon occurrence for them to barter their wives and daughters in exchange for these birds.

When I was in Fiji, a gentleman named Klinesmith, an American citizen of German extraction, was engaged there by the great Pacific house of Godeffroy and Co. of Hamburg, for the purpose of collecting objects for their museum, and not long since he obtained an Albino parrot, one of the common parrots of Fiji, which being destitute of the requisite colouring matter to develop his plumage, remains a brilliant yellow.

Fish are good both in quantity and quality. Dr. Macdonald enumerates twenty-three varieties, of which eleven are fresh-water kinds. Amongst others there is a species of fresh-water shark, which infests some parts of the river Rewa to an unpleasant extent. This species, however, does not attack the natives of the Bau district, although it is not so considerate to other specimens of humanity. The salt-water sharks, which abound, number nine varieties, and are much dreaded by the natives. Many of the edible fish attain a great size, some having been caught which measured five feet in length and three in girth. A large species of fish known as the *wailangi*, is caught at Navuso.

A Fijian tradition thus accounts for the flatness of the sole: one, Davilai, was the leader of singing amongst the fishes, a sort of chorus-master, I suppose; and on one occasion when the members of his band were assembled for a select harmonic meeting, this Davilai obstinately refused to lead off, or oblige the company even by a single stave, whereupon, in revenge for such a slight, the other fishes trod him under foot until he became literally as flat as a flounder, or his own voice, and that flatness of shape has continued in the family ever since. Hence the natives say when anyone refuses to oblige the company with a song, 'Here is Mr. Davilai!'

I mentioned the general absence of fresh fish at Levukan dinner-tables. There are many varieties in addition to the mullet, of which the golden-tailed variety is the most common—the silver fish, the *sanki* (some of which weigh as much as 8 lb. each); the *sievala*, the flying-fish; the *gard* (so esteemed in Sydney), the pike, a species of skate; the *schnapper*, and john-dory, while some authorities add the sole and *singaree*. The fishing is by hand-nets, and of the most primitive description.

Shrimps and prawns are caught all over Fiji, and in parts of Viti Levu; in the estuaries of the big rivers, the Rewa, Sigatoka, and Ba, a description of *écrevisse* is found, fairly edible, though I never hear of Bisque soup being attempted. Lobsters in some parts of the group are plentiful at times. In many of the lesser islands a species of land-crab is found, called *agavule*, which has strong pugnacious proclivities. It is a fact that they will climb the most lofty palms in search of cocoa-nuts, from which they succeed in extracting the contents.

The shore abounds with a large variety of beautiful shells, the most prized and valuable being the orange cowrie (*Cypra aurantium*), which is used largely for ornamental purposes by the natives. There is a good supply of several kinds of oysters, and a prospect of remunerative pearl-fishing in the adjacent seas.

There are three varieties of turtle, including the aldermanic favourite, which yields the celebrated 'green fat,' and the other variety which supplies the shells. Five or six varieties of sea-slugs are dried and sent *viâ* Sydney to China, for the delectation of the Celestials.

Horses were introduced in the year 1851, and were the cause of a panic among the natives when they first beheld them with their riders. The advent of these quadrupeds caused as much astonishment as that of a centaur would do here.

The existing animals all being imported, their names in the Fijian language indicate to the traveller the nationality of the people to whom the introduction is due.* For instance, a horse is to them *orsee;* a dog, *coolie* (evidently from collie); an ox or cow, *bule-ma-kau,* pronounced *bulemacow;* while a sheep is simply *scepi,* the *h* being unpronounceable by the Fijians. I give the sounds of the words from memory, and as to spelling rely much on the forbearance of Fijian scholars.

CHAPTER XVII.

A VERY SUGGESTIVE CHAPTER.

SIR ARTHUR GORDON, in his lecture on Fiji, delivered before the Royal Colonial Institute, said:

'I believe Fiji to be an admirable field for the investment of large capital. . . . After a careful investigation extending over more than a year, it has been reported to me by most competent and most cautious scientific authority, that the

* I am told, by the way, that in parts of Japan the name of a dog is 'comeer,' the repeated admonition of 'come here' by Englishmen and others having got the animal the name.

annual value of the agricultural exports of the colony, when its powers of production have been fully developed, will probably exceed *ten millions sterling.*'

These are weighty words, coming from the Governor of a Crown Colony of Great Britain.

Of the agricultural wealth of Fiji, and in fact of Polynesia generally, it is impossible to speak too highly. Cotton, the cocoa-nut tree, candle-nuts (*Aleurites triloba*), cinnamon bark, turmeric, croton plant, tapioca, twenty-five varieties of plantains, yams, taro, limes, shaddocks, oranges, pine-apples, lemons, bananas, ginger, nutmegs, annatto, sugar-cane, all grow wild; india-rubber is found all over the island of Vanua Levu. By some, great importance has been attached to the dye barks, while Fiji timber has found a home in the large pianoforte manufactory of Messrs. Jno. Brinsmead & Sons.

The tabulated statements of exports in the Appendix speak for themselves, but they also demonstrate that the trade of Fiji is entirely in its infancy. In 1880 the imports of the group amounted to £185,740, as against £142,000 in 1879, while the exports had attained the respectable total value of £229,902. The most significant advance of late has been in sugar. From a value of £3245, it has risen to £20,920 in 1880; while again 7265 tons of copra were exported in 1880, as against 4089 tons in 1879. The principal items of import are drapery, hardware, and machinery.

Fiji is mostly known to the world by the superior quality of her 'sea island cotton,' which gained gold medals at Philadelphia in 1876, and at Paris in 1878; but, owing to the comparatively low prices ruling now in the English markets, a great number of the planters have entirely discontinued its cultivation. Perhaps the best houses who still adhere to cotton-planting are the Messrs. Ryder, of Mango; Messrs.

Hennings, of Loma; and Messrs. M'Evoy, of Chichia. Large sums of money were made in Fiji by cotton-planting in 1870 and 1871, owing to the abnormal prices obtained in London; but the money was spent as fast as made, and when the reaction came, it found Fiji planters with mortgaged lands and a ruined industry. The early planters of the group seem to have believed only in cotton, and never thought of anything else; the men who will make fortunes in the future out of Fiji will be wiser if they carefully avoid this cardinal error. The kidney variety of cotton grows well, and is being cultivated extensively by the natives. Over 5000 acres are now under cotton cultivation.

There can be no doubt that it would be more profitable to cultivate the sugar-cane in many places than to continue to grow cotton; as nearly all the cotton land is well adapted for the growth of the cane, yielding sugar to at least the value of £60 and upwards per acre for a yearly crop. However, cotton will certainly grow well on the hill-sides in the driest parts of Viti Levu, where coffee is not sure of success. When cotton lost all its attractiveness, the manufacture of copra, or the dried kernel of the cocoa-nut, took its place, and copra is at present the leading article of export in the group.

The process of the manufacture of copra is of the simplest kind. The best is that which is dried whole in the nut. For this purpose nothing is necessary but a large house, or shed, in which to stack the nuts. They must be placed upon a floor, or stage, to prevent them from touching the ground, or else they will not dry, but grow. The husk must not be removed, otherwise the eye in the end would be attacked by the *kalulu*, a sort of cockroach, for the sake of the water they contain; and the air being admitted to the interior, the kernel would at once begin to decay. If unpeeled and kept off the ground, in three months the water has disappeared and the kernel has become of a consistency like leather, in which state it will keep for ever, undergoing no change from the effects of climate, damp, or from any other cause.

The best copra makes the clearest and the sweetest oil, and does not diminish in weight by evaporation. When thoroughly dry, which is easily found out by shaking the nut, the husk is stripped off, the shell is broken, and the kernel cut into pieces, so as to prevent its taking up too much room.

The other system is that of drying the nuts in the sun, which, if pursued carefully, makes good copra, although never equal to that which has been dried in the shade, for the reason that in the former case the water which the nut contains is evaporated suddenly, and so not always effectually; in the latter, gradually and perfectly. The usual practice is to skin the nuts, break them in two halves, throw out the water, and lay the broken pieces out on the coral beach to dry. This, in fine weather, will occupy about three days; but they must be taken in or covered up at night, and in case of a shower of rain, immediately protected from it, as copra which has been rained upon will not keep, but always turns mouldy after a time, and will infect and spoil all the rest with which it may come in contact. Another singular fact in connection with this process—and for which it is not very easy to account—is as follows: It frequently happens that a long spell of cloudy or damp weather takes place at a time when a quantity of copra is being sun-dried. To counteract the mischief created by the damp, it has been the practice of very many to make fires under stages, and so complete—as they supposed—the drying process by artificial heat. In such a case the copra invariably breeds animalculæ, which within a few months will entirely consume it, and spreading to any other sound stock which may be stored in its neighbourhood, will destroy that in like manner.

One willing labourer can perform in one day, of six hours, all the work of gathering, carrying together, peeling, and breaking four hundred cocoa-nuts; and as they are ripe at all times of the year, there is no season of enforced idleness, but the work may go on continuously.

Along the margin of the sea, in a bed of little else than coraline sand, the cocoa-nut tree grows to perfection; on the uplands also, as long as it is within the influence of the sea-breeze, it produces only a little less prolifically. Each tree in full bearing should produce about one hundred nuts per annum: about six thousand nuts make one ton of copra. The same number of nuts yield one ton and a fraction of fibre. The average number of trees to an acre is eighty, and they should be planted about 25 to 35 feet apart, according to the quality of the soil, exposure to wind, or the rainfall of the district. The trees commence to bear at five years old, if well attended to, and should be in full bearing from the seventh to the tenth year. Taking, therefore, the yield of nuts at six thousand per acre, the copra and fibre together should give a good annual return. At present a great deal of the valuable fibre is simply thrown away. Copra is worth from £13 to £16 per ton in London, and a trifle more in Hamburg, while good cocoa-nut fibre fetches an equal sum. From copra is made the celebrated lubricator, cocoa-nut oil, while its refuse goes to enrich cattle food. Nuts can be purchased from the natives at about 20s. per thousand. In 1880 over 16,000 acres were under cocoa-nut cultivation. If proper machinery for manipulating the fibre were introduced, the present annual loss to the colony of something like £50,000 would be saved. The foregoing facts speak for themselves, and show what fortunes from the cocoa-nut tree alone are to be made in Fiji.

Young plantations of the tree made by natives and whites are rising on all sides, but there is great room for extension. The cocoa-nut tree does not succeed well in many parts of Viti Levu, and where it does grow on that island it bears comparatively few nuts. This is owing to the ravages of a small caterpillar, which attaches itself to the underside of the leaves and eats their softer parts. The consequence is that the leaves are unable to perform the functions assigned to them, and the tree is thereby weakened and unable to bear fruit, if it be not killed outright by the attacks of the insect. The action of this caterpillar has been noticed on the cocoa-nut trees growing in other islands of the group; but it is probable that outside Viti Levu birds or some antagonistic insect keep it in check. The whole subject demands inquiry, and it is very likely that if this were given, a means would be discovered of destroying the insect altogether, or greatly diminishing the mischief done. If such were the case, the cocoa-nut tree could be planted all over Viti Levu. The Australian laughing jackass is a formidable foe of this insect; and these birds are now being imported into the group.

Apart from this island the fertility of this tree is somewhat wonderful. The nut begins to grow in a few months after it is planted; in about five or six years the stem is 7 or 8 feet high, and the tree begins to bear. It continues to grow and bear for fifty or sixty years, or perhaps longer. While the plants are young they require fencing to keep pigs and goats from getting at them, but after the crown has reached a few feet from the ground, the plants require no further care. Everybody knows the cocoa-nut tree leaf, but there is a curious provision of nature to protect the nuts against the violence of the strong winds, which is not so familiar to Europeans. A remarkably fine strong fibrous matting, attached to the bark under the bottom of the stalk, extends half-way round the trunk, and reaches perhaps 2 or 3 feet up the leaf, acting like a bracing of network to each side of the stalk, which keeps it steadily fixed to the trunk. While the leaves are young, this substance is remarkably white, transparent, and as fine in texture as silver paper. As the leaf increases in size, and the matting is exposed to the air, it becomes coarser and stronger, assuming a yellowish colour. I write mainly from memory, and forget the native name for this curious substance, but I think it is *aoa*. There is a kind of seam along the centre exactly under the stem of the leaf, from both sides of which long and tough fibres about the size of a bristle regularly diverge in an oblique direction. Sometimes there appear to be two layers of fibres, which cross each other, and the whole is cemented with a still finer fibrous and adhesive substance. The length and evenness of the threads and fibres, the regular manner in which they cross at oblique angles, the extent of surface and the thickness of the piece, with the singular manner in which the fibres are attached to each other, cause this curious substance woven in the loom of nature to present a remarkable resemblance to cloth spun and woven by man's ingenuity. The Fijians use this matting for various purposes, chiefly for making bags. In the Society Islands, jackets, coats, and even shirts were made of it in years gone by.

The flowers of the cocoa-nut tree are small and white. The fruit does not, as a rule, come to perfection in less than twelve months after the blossoms have fallen. A branch will sometimes contain twenty or thirty nuts, or even more, and there are often six, seven, or eight branches to a tree. The tough fibrous husk is about 2 inches in thickness, and this torn away, and the eyes of the nut pierced, you get at the milk as it is called; and when the nut is not quite ripe, this will be found to measure a pint or a pint and a half. The milk is perfectly clear, and in taste combines acidity and sweetness equal to the finest lemonade. It is deliciously cold, but to drink much of it is bad for most Europeans. The mixture of a little good brandy or gin with it is a first-class corrective.

In a few weeks after the nut has reached its full size, a soft white pulp, remarkably delicate and sweet, resembling in appearance and consistence the white of a slightly-boiled egg, is formed around the inside of the shell. If allowed to hang two or three months longer on the tree, the outside skin becomes yellow and brown; the skin hardens, the kernel increases to an inch or an inch and a quarter in thickness, and the milk is reduced to about half a pint.

One of the most extraordinary facts in natural history is the reproduction of the cocoa-nut tree by itself; and although this may be an oft-told tale, an account of it should, I think, not be omitted from a work treating of the land of cocoa-nuts as well as coral. If the nut be kept long after it is fully ripe, a white, sweet, spongy substance is formed in the inside, originating at the inner end of the germ which is enclosed in the kernel immediately opposite one of the three apertures in the sharpest end of the shell, which is opposite to that where the stalk is united to the husk. This fibrous sponge ultimately absorbs the water and fills the concavity, dissolving the hard kernel, and combining it with its own substance, so that the shell, instead of containing a kernel and milk, encloses only a soft cellular substance. While this marvellous process is going on within the nut, a single bud or shoot of a white colour, but hard texture, forces its way through one of the holes or 'eyes' of the shell, perforates the tough fibrous husk, and after rising some inches, begins to unfold its pale green leaves to the light and air; at this time also two thick white fibres, originating in the same point, push away the stoppers or coverings from the other two holes in the shell, pierce the husk in an opposite direction, and finally penetrate the ground. If allowed to remain, the shell which no knife would cut, and which a saw would hardly divide, is burst by an expansive power generated within itself. The husk and shell gradually decay, and forming a light manure, facilitate the growth of the young plant, which gradually strikes its roots deeper, elevates its stalk and expands its leaves, until it becomes a lofty, fruitful, and graceful tree.

> 'The Indians' nut alone
> Is clothing, meat and trencher, drink and can,
> Boat, cable, sail, and needle all in one,'

says George Herbert.

The real wealth, however, of the group lies in the sugar-cane. Among the more important products of the Fijian group the cultivation of the sugar-cane holds a prominent place. Every visitor (even from countries in which the sugar-cane is almost the only plant cultivated) cannot fail to be struck with the size, healthy appearance, and rapidity of growth of the sugar-cane in Fiji. These remarks do not extend only to the 'pet' canes of the Fijians, which are to be found growing near the houses in every native town, but also to the canes in the settlers' plantations as well as to those planted by the Fijians for thatch.

The wild canes (*vicos*) of these islands are the subject of admiration to the cane-grower. They suggest to him interesting ideas with regard to the parentage of the sugar-cane, which undoubtedly originated in the islands of the South Sea, where from time immemorial it has been cultivated by the inhabitants for various purposes, and carried to the islands and countries in the eastern part of tropical Asia by their inhabitants when on migratory or piratical excursions. An experienced cane-grower would at once pronounce the so-called 'China cane' an imported *vico*, were he equally well acquainted with both. To him the varieties of the latter present all the various colours and habits of the varieties of the cultivated sugar-cane; but it yet remains for a careful botanical examination and comparison of the flowers of both to prove whether the *vico* of Fiji is a species of the genus *Saccharum* or not. The climate of Fiji is by its nature well adapted for growing the sugar-cane, and so is the soil. This is in most places rich alluvium on the banks of the rivers, loam on gentle slopes or hillocks, volcanic soil of the richest description, and at the bases of low hills, *débris* brought down by innumerable agencies from the sides of the mountains.

The cane lands are to be found in all parts of the group; in the far interior of Viti Levu, as well as at the mouths and on the banks of the Rewa, Sigatoka, and other rivers; in many localities of Vanua Levu, Taviuni, Rabi, etc., and even in Ovalau and some of the other smaller, though in this respect not less important, islands. The extent and richness of these lands, in conjunction with a climate extremely favourable for growing and maturing the sugar-cane, make all well-wishers of Fiji long for the time when sugar will be manufactured there and exported by the hundred thousand tons, and to the value of millions of pounds sterling.

Before such results are brought about, the capitalist or sugar-maker will see that it will tend to his advantage to encourage the planter to grow sugar-cane, and the planter will see that it will be to his profit to have a cane-mill near his property. The steam and common plough will be extensively used, as well as the grubber, drill, hoe, and harrow, on rich alluvial flats. The pick, spade, or Indian hoe will be in request on hilly land to put down a cane top until it will grow. All mechanical contrivances, as well as hand labour, will be needed to till the soil, and manures to renew its fertility. The canes will be cut at the proper season of the year instead of all the year through, as at present. This practice is really a waste of products, which expediency can scarcely excuse. About one-half of the canes are crushed when the density of their juice is at the lowest, and therefore yields a minimum amount of sugar. The canes are cut at the end of the warm weather instead of at its commencement; the warm, wet season is the natural time of the year for the canes growing, and the cold one for maturing them for the crop in September, October, November, and perhaps December. When cut in March or April the ratoon canes are made to grow in cold dry weather, when they will grow least, and to ripen during the hot, moist weather of December, January, February, and March, when they will naturally grow most and ripen least. Such practice is *hors saison*, and the want of success and small returns are not surprising. By cutting the canes during the months above mentioned, namely, September to December, the ratoons grow in the proper season, *i.e.* the warm and wet one, and the canes ripen during the cold one. The crop is made when the density of the juice is at its highest, and the canes yield the most sugar.

It may be said that the best kind of cane to grow is the one which yields a maximum quantity of sugar and gives a minimum amount of work in cutting, carting, crushing, and making sugar out of its juice. At the same time such a cane must be hardy and healthy, grow rapidly, ratoon freely and often, and be well suited to the climate of the locality in which the plantation may be situated. Many of the canes grown in Fiji possess these latter qualifications, and appear to be short of the former ones ; in a word, they give a maximum amount of work in cutting, etc., and yield a minimum quantity of the sugar. The desired result is not the greatest weight of cane which an acre of land will produce, but the greatest amount of sugar per acre which the cane will yield. On several estates in the Sandwich Islands, I have seen six tons (over 12,000 lb.) taken per acre per annum from large tracts of sugar land—that is to say, from plant canes—ratoons yielding sometimes as much as three or four tons. For virgin land like Fiji it would, I think, be safe to take two and a half tons, or say 5000 lb. per acre, as an average. At the present time about 3000 acres are under sugar-cane cultivation.

According to the estimate of an expert, a sugar-mill capable of turning out seven to eight tons of sugar per day of twelve hours, would give fifty tons per week, or allowing the factory to be actually at work for twenty weeks in the year, say a crop of 1000 tons of sugar per annum. The cost of the plant here, my informant says, is £7500, and he puts £7500 for freight, insurance, and all expenses till it is ready for working ; an unnecessarily high figure, in my opinion, as £5000 would be ample. Under this head the cost of cane per ton of sugar may be taken at about £10 per ton, skilled and other labour at £4 per cent., fuel 1 per cent., and interest and depreciation at 20 per cent. The market value of sugar in Fiji is £25 per ton, so there is on an expenditure of £15,000 a clear credit to the right side of profit and loss of £7500 per annum. I do not wonder now at the princely houses which some of the sugar aristocracy boast in every city of their choice. By last accounts some 3000 acres were under sugar cultivation. This acreage of sugar shows a marked increase on the preceding years; but perhaps the most 'suggestive' thing in connection with the growth of the sugar industry in Fiji is the action of the Colonial Sugar Refining Company of New South Wales, whose factory on the Rewa river, in Viti Levu, has already developed into an important township. The following particulars of the resources and enterprise of this highly successful corporation will be read with interest by all who care to appreciate the future that certainly awaits the Mauritius of the Antipodes. If these things are done in the early days of Fiji, what will the record of the not very remote future amount to?

The Colonial Sugar Refining Company have at the present time invested in plant, buildings, steamers, punts, and land in connection with their business in New South Wales and Fiji about £650,000, of which sum only about £50,000 represents the cost of the land held by them. They employ during the sugar season in the former colony between 1000 and 1200 men, but no Chinese or coloured labourers, and during the remainder of the year 400 or 500 men. In Fiji they have now about 90 white men, and 400 to 500 coloured labourers. In the refinery, in Sydney, they work at present about 500 tons of sugar per week. Their sugar-mills on the Clarence, Richmond, and Tweed rivers, five in all, are capable of producing 14,000 tons of sugar in the season of five months. The Fiji factory will be equal to producing 6500 tons of sugar in a season of five months. To give some idea of the plan, it may be mentioned that the Company have between fifty and sixty steam boilers of large size at work ashore, besides many others of small power; and afloat they have two ocean steamers, six paddle-tugs and two more building, one screw-tug building, eight steam launches and four more building, eight large lighters and four more building, seventy-five cane punts (each of 50 tons capacity) and fifty more building; also a floating dock for overhauling the river craft, capable of docking a vessel 140 feet long. One distillery is worked in connection with the mills; this is capable of producing about 5000 gallons of spirit a week, but has not of late been worked to its full capacity. Very little of the rum made is sold in the colony, as it is needed for supplying export orders. All the mills are worked on the central factory system; that is, the canes are grown by farmers in the neighbourhood and purchased by the Company at a fixed rate per ton for a term of years.

In Fiji there is a large extent of land which, from a variety of causes, is better adapted for growing coffee than any other tropical product. The greater portion of this land lies in the interior of Viti Levu, Vanua Levu, Taviuni, some portions of Rabi, Ovalau, etc. These islands contain large areas of incomparably fine coffee land, and enjoy a climate which is at once healthy and well adapted for the growth of the coffee-tree plant, or bush. Next to cane-growing, that of coffee will in future years claim the largest share of attention. Coffee will be second to nothing except sugar, in value; its export value should ultimately reach to about a million and a half or to two millions sterling. The plants of coffee seen in the interior of Viti Levu, Vanua Levu, and Taviuni were remarkably healthy-looking. On several estates the last coffee crops were estimated at 8 cwt. per acre.

The Government has sent large supplies of coffee seed into the interior of Viti Levu to form coffee gardens for the natives. Coffee has been tried during the last ten or eleven years in several islands of the group; however, it is only within the last two or three years that much attention has been given to its culture. Several plantations have been formed, and land for others is now being cleared. It would be a wise precaution not to plant coffee in places which face the trade winds, and receive its full force unbroken, and directly from the sea, without well protecting the plants by dense plantations of hardy trees and shrubs. Very nearly 2000 acres were under coffee early in 1880.

The soil and climate of some parts of Fiji are well fitted for growing cocoa (*Theobroma cacao*).

There were till recently very few plants of cocoa in Fiji, and none of them have arrived at the fruit-bearing age. It will most likely be some time before any extensive plantations of it are made in Fiji. Mr. Thurston introduced into the colony during the year 1878 over 1000 cacao trees, which were all doing well when I last heard from Levuka.

Cocoa is a subject demanding particular attention from the Government of a country whose wealth lies solely in its agricultural products. The more varied these are, the less will be the danger of distress from a season of low prices or failure. About fifty plants of each of the best varieties of the *theobroma* cultivated in South America and the West Indies would in a few years yield sufficient young plants to stock Fiji. These young plants might be sold at a low price to pay expense of rearing and introduction, and in a new colony like Fiji would be of the greatest importance. The same might be said of many other kinds of plants, the introduction of which would be a benefit to the community. Experiments in cultivation could be tried with advantage if a botanical garden were established in the colony.

Next in importance to a large introduction of *theobroma* would be that of tea and cinchona. The soil and climate of some parts of the interior of Viti Levu, more especially of the mountains at the sources of the principal rivers, are well qualified for the culture of these plants. Roughly estimated, the extent of country in which tea and cinchona could be successfully cultivated is not less than 100 square miles, and a joint-stock company has just been started in Levuka for tea cultivation on a somewhat extensive scale on the island of Taviuni.

Mr. Thurston recently also planted 800 cinnamon trees, and some dozens of cloves and vanilla, while *Pandanus utilis*, for making sugar-bags, was introduced in thousands, besides mango, lychee, pomelo, and other fruit trees.

Tobacco also grows well in Fiji; but the want of knowledge in the preparation of its leaves for the market is the main reason why it is not more extensively planted. This difficulty could easily be overcome.

The above may be termed the principal articles of tropical produce which will succeed in Fiji, and there remain only those of secondary importance to be alluded to, viz., rice, Indian corn, arrowroot, and tapioca. The arrowroot and tapioca manufactured are of excellent quality. Rice no doubt could be extensively grown in Fiji. Many places seem fitted by nature for its cultivation. The clove, ginger, cinnamon, nutmeg, allspice, pepper, camphor, and vanilla will also grow successfully, but to cultivate them with any degree of success, the cultivator should possess considerable experience. Many of the settlers in Fiji have little or no knowledge of the culture required by different sorts of tropical produce. Being the first in the colony, they have been groping in the dark. To say that all have succeeded in applying theories derived from books would be incorrect; nevertheless, some have done so, and are now on a fair way to competency, if not to fortune.

Among fruits which would be likely to succeed in the parts of this colony which enjoy a temperate climate, the peach and the strawberry may be mentioned. The orange tribe thrives magnificently in all parts of the group, the oranges of Namosi being especially excellent.

Bananas and pine-apples of good quality abound everywhere. The former are grown extensively in Fiji as an article of food. To say that the mango, sour-sop and sweet-sop, custard-apple, *cherimoyer*, *rambutan*, *lychee*, tamarind, among other tropical fruits, and perhaps the *mangosteen* and *durian*, will grow in Fiji is a truism. Fiji is now extensively exporting tropical fruit, especially bananas, to the markets of Australia and New Zealand. Situated within the tropics, Fiji is only eight days' steaming from Sydney and three from Auckland, where the demands for her produce are extensive and increasing. From the bountiful nature of the soil and the favourable climate, she will successfully compete in these markets with all rivals, not excepting the tropical portions of Australia. It is to Australasia Fiji has to look for a market for most of her tropical products, and not to those of Europe, from which she is too far distant. It will be a long time before her produce overstocks the markets of Australia and New Zealand, and when that time comes, if it ever should come, it will be easier for the colony to send her surplus coffee, etc., to the Western States of America than to Europe. All that Fiji at present requires for the development of her resources is capital, and men skilled in tropical agriculture ;—by this I mean men who understand the growth of the sugar-cane, the making of sugar, the growth of coffee, tea, etc., and the preparation of these for market.

In what may be termed sylvan wealth, Fiji is also rich. But the quantity of useful timber is not so abundant as it would at first appear to the inexperienced. However, there is a sufficient quantity of home-grown timber to meet the home demand for years to come, even were the importation of timber to cease. The Government have passed laws for the protection of trees and forest reserves, in order to preserve a sufficient supply of timber for future generations, and are working these forest reserves for the benefit of the community; thus preventing an indiscriminate destruction of forests, so that the country may not be parched by droughts one season and desolated by floods the next. This ordinance will tend also to preserve the present healthiness of climate for which Fiji is famed. Mr. Horne suggests that the Government should plant trees in the north-western portion of Viti Levu, and Macauta in Vanua Levu, to restore the climatic conditions from the want of which they grievously suffer. This matter is far too important to the community to be left in the hands of private individuals, though of course Government should not plant and preserve timber to compete with private enterprise. It is necessary for climatic reasons that the Government should plant and preserve trees, and, when these reach maturity, to see that they are not allowed to waste and rot. On the other hand, it is the interest of the community to see that the products of the Government preserves are properly utilised, and that the Forest Department is made self-supporting.

First in point of value among the sylvan riches of Fiji is sandalwood, now very scarce owing to indiscriminate cuttings; so much so, that what remains will only serve as a nucleus from which seeds can be obtained for the extension of this much-prized forest product.

Among timber-trees of the colony the foremost is *vesi* (*Afzelia bijuga*), which yields a useful and durable timber; it is now very scarce. Next is the *dilo* (*Calophyllum inophyllum*), valuable not only on account of its timber, but also for gum resin, which exudes from the bark when the tree is wounded, and for the oil which can be extracted from its seed. Good timber, the produce of this tree, is also very scarce.

Next in order are *damanu* and *vaivai* (*Calophyllum spectabile*, *C. burmanni*, *Serianthes myradenia*, and *S. Vitiensis*), which yield excellent durable timber fit for any purpose. *Dakua* (*Dammara Vitiensis*), besides yielding a timber which is better than any kind of pine, and even more easily worked, gives a valuable gum resin. The timber which the *Dakua*, *salusalu*, *Kau solo*, *Ko tabua*, *Lewininini* and *Kausia* (all different species of *Podocarpus*) produce is as valuable as the best pine. The climate and soil of Fiji would favour the growth of teak, sal, mahogany, ebony, sisson, rosewood, gutta-percha, caoutchouc, ratans, etc. —in fact, any product of the tropical forests would succeed in Fiji, and ought to be introduced and naturalised.

Besides timber-yielding trees of more or less value peculiar to the country, Fiji also possesses several trees which yield caoutchouc of good quality. These, although by no means scarce, are at present too far apart for the juice to be profitably collected. But if brought together, as they would be in a forest reserve, the juice could be easily collected at stated periods, and made a mercantile commodity.

The country abounds with plantains, of which the natives distinguish about twenty-five sorts. According to Seeman, the 'Soaqua,' a wild variety which grows in all the valleys, a few hundred feet above the level of the sea, is the *Musa troglodytarum*, the plant from which, says Sir John Bowring, in his work on the Philippine Islands, Manilla hemp is obtained. There is also a cultivated variety, named Vundi Vula, or white plantain, which, I think, is the *Musa textilis* of botanists. This variety yields a fine, bright, and strong Manilla hemp. Samples sent to Sydney were valued at from £35 to £40 per ton delivered there. The hemp is obtained from the stem or trunk of the plant. The fibre, obtained from the petioles of the leaves, is so fine that it is said the finest muslins may be made from it. The preparation of these fibres by hand is both a long and difficult process; and, in order to export them in any quantities, machinery must be imported. It is very probable that, with a little alteration, the machinery used in New Zealand for cleaning *Phormium tenax* might be adopted here for Manilla hemp. If the thick laminæ, of which the plantain stem is composed, were crushed between smooth or fluted rollers, the hard outer epidermis would be broken up, and the cellulose—of which there is a large quantity—might be got rid of by washing and beating. In the preparation of an article like this the services of women and children might be very largely engaged.

The fibre also of the *yaka*, the pine-apple, and the aloe might be treated very much in the same way as New Zealand hemp. One variety of the arum is said to yield a very valuable fibre, and I am inclined to think there are many plants of a similar character not as yet generally known to settlers. Water privileges, to use an American term, are numerous in every district. An overshot water-wheel, made of durable hard wood, fitted with ironwork ready for erection, can be laid down in Levuka at a cost of from £70 to £100, according to size. 'Devils' for preparing cocoa-nut fibre can be procured at about £50 each, or if contracted for in any number, perhaps for less. Machines for preparing Manilla fibre would cost about £25 each in Auckland. If erected in suitable places, I believe these machines would rapidly repay the expenditure incurred for their purchase, as the coir or cocoa-nut fibre now thrown away would then be all saved. Natives could soon learn to work the machinery when driven by a water-wheel, which is a simple and steady power. At Rambi, Lauthala, and

Wakaya, the imported labourers have been taught to manage machinery running at a rapid rate, and driven by steam-power.

Candle-nuts grow wild over all the group. By squeezing the nuts in the hand, the oil exudes, and this is equal to rape-seed oil in value, *i.e.*, from £30 to £35 per ton. The great difficulty has been in separating the nut from the kernel, but with proper machinery this would be soon obviated; at present the shells are simply crushed by the natives witl stones, and the kernels shipped in bulk to England or Germany These nuts possess very remarkable medicinal powers if eater freely, and are not unpleasant to the taste.

Maize is being constantly exported to Australia and New Zealand, while Fiji rum is making for itself a home in the latter colony.

Cattle and horses all thrive well, and there are now 360 horses, 5000 cattle, and 4700 sheep in the group, besides 50,000 pigs; and Fijian wool is now a regular article of export.

In regard to *bêche-de-mer*, or 'sea-slug,' considered by the Chinese such a delicacy, I have been frequently assured that upon the north coast of Viti and Vanua Levu, and at some places in the Windward Group, particularly Fulanga, any active Fijian can in two nights catch sufficient 'fish' to fill when dried, a three-bushel bag. The value of such a bagfı would be from twenty-five to forty shillings, according t variety, and the perfection with which it is cured. At presen this trade is almost entirely in the hands of Chinamen, whc employ quite a fleet of small boats. *Bêche-de-mer*, like turtles, are among the Fijians 'royal fish.' They used only to be caught by command of the Supreme Chief.

More than thirty years ago £16,000 worth of *bêche-de-mer* was taken away by one trader at the rate of £3000 worth per annum, and all from the north coasts of Vanua and Viti

Levu. Until lately the reefs have not been fished, excepting in an irregular and indifferent way. The native wars which raged between the tribes of the north coasts of the above-named islands for the ten or fifteen years preceding 1863-4, and from which they have never recovered, made them poor and indolent. Their family power and relationship was weakened, and in some instances destroyed, and no one chief has until recently been established as a ruler.

The Fijian Government has determined to put a stop to indiscriminate *bêche-de-mer* fishing all the year round, and by a recent ordinance, licenses for this fishing will be granted for such times, and under such limitations, as the Governor may direct.

CHAPTER XVIII.

MORE HINTS FOR CAPITALISTS.

THE long list of Fijian products and industries is not yet exhausted, and I learn that the efforts made to introduce the angora goat into the group, and to make it profitable in a commercial sense, have been attended with the success which they deserved. Five years ago, the Honourable R. B. Leefe undertook the introduction of the angora goat on his estate at the Nananas on the Ra Coast. He commenced with seventy does and two pure bucks, the number of the latter being increased from time to time as occasion required. The flock in June, 1879, consisted of one hundred common does and four pure bucks, seven hundred first and second cross does, besides a flock of wethers two hundred and fifty strong. Mr. Leefe expected an increase during the month of June last year of fifteen hundred kids, a proportion of which will be third-cross. In the month of May, Mr. Leefe sheared one hundred and sixty yearlings second-cross does and wethers, in addition to four bucks. The former gave about one pound, the latter five pounds, of hair each. From the length and fineness of the clip taken from those sheared, it may be confidently anticipated that the third-cross will very nearly, and the fourth-cross will fully, equal pure hair. The report upon that already sent to market (London, I believe, but I am not quite certain) was, 'Well grown, fine, silky, and almost equal to the best Turkish.' It fetched as much as three shillings per pound. The animals browse during the day, but are yarded every night, and the does give an unusual quantity of milk, while the angora-crossed wethers supply a meat much more tender than mutton, partaking in fact more of the character of venison. When it is considered that these most profitable animals will live and thrive where sheep would starve, the inducement to make their breeding a matter of regular and general enterprise seems to be exceptionally great in the Fiji Group.

As a further exemplification of what Fiji can accomplish, I will just mention the articles that Messrs. Ryder Brothers, of Mango, and the Rambi Plantation Company, exhibited at the Sydney World's Fair. Messrs. Ryder Brothers sent Sea Island cotton, Sea Island cotton in seed, cotton seed, Mocha coffee, plantation coffee, copra prepared in two different ways, tapioca, maize (or Indian corn), dried bananas, and lime-juice. Captain Hill's company showed four different samples of the cocoa-fibre industry—coir bristle, fine coir fibre, finest straw-coloured coir, and curled straw-coloured coir. One *dholl* of each were sent, as also two bottles of the finest cocoa-nut oil. The foregoing facts will show what, even in its infantile state, the colony of Fiji can export. But everything depends on the introduction of capital, with the right sort of men. What Fiji requires is, in fact, an aristocracy of planters, who will add to a very natural desire to create a competence, a keen sense of responsibility to all around, whether white or coloured. The day is past when the British adventurer could claim, because he is an adventurer, a sympathy often denied to his more suffering compatriots at home. Even now, people must go out to Fiji as pioneers, and prepare to 'rough it;' but, in fairness, it must be added that the 'roughing it' of 1882 is a totally different thing from what it was in 1871. A man must be of a peculiarly disagreeable and discontented nature who would not soon reconcile himself to the very few drawbacks of Fiji. As a 'new chum' he can learn a great deal, but as a 'new chum' he will have to be content to be taught. Fiji is not like the Australasian colonies, it is the exact counterpart of the West Indies and the Mauritius.

The sort of men who can turn their hand to anything, who are 'roughs' one day, gentlemen the other, are not required in our new Crown colony. The irrepressible working man is always more or less to be congratulated—especially at the approach of a general election; but I should do myself no credit by counselling his immediate emigration to Fiji; as a general rule he is not wanted, and, unless I am very much mistaken, is not likely to be wanted. For the surplus population of Britain's working class the dependencies of the empire that most assimilate in climate to that of the mother country (like those of Australasia and South Africa and Canada) are the natural goals; but Fiji, with all its wealth, offers no such field. Then, again, there is another class which are wanted even less than the 'horny-handed son of toil,' and that is the commercial clerk whose sole recommendations are that he has an irreproachable character, wears in England the universal black coat, and can read, write and cipher with dexterity. The commercial clerk, unless fitted by nature for something very different, is a drug in most markets: he is a nuisance in Fiji. What that colony requires is a steady influx of clear-sighted men, not opposed to work, not obdurate where learning is concerned—men who have at command the sum of at least some three or four hundred pounds, and who are willing to learn, work, and wait. Of course it would be better if the capital were larger; but the true well-wisher of Fiji would not look so closely to the balance in the bank-book as to the character of the man in whose possession it is. I am inclined to think that there is no colony of the British Empire where a young man, coupling a reasonable amount of brains with a moderate capital, can so easily secure a competence as in Fiji. Of course hard work, steady perseverance, undaunted courage, and firm hope, must be the leading features of intending emigrants. If they have not these qualities—coupled, I may add, with the needful cash—they had better stay away. Neither in New Zealand nor Fiji are fortunes to be picked up by those who, like many leaving the port of London, seem to think that a millionnaire is to be made by the loan of a spade; and, as I am writing about a new member of that earth-hungry institution, the British Empire, I feel it incumbent on me to say very plainly what class of emigrants it wants.

There are several ways of reaching the group. The mail routes are those of the Peninsular and Oriental Company viâ Suez to Sydney, and the Pacific Mail Company's line from San Francisco to Auckland, and thence by steamer to Levuka.

The fine steamers of the Peninsular and Oriental Line now start from Tilbury every fourteen days, and the traveller by the famous line which boasts the motto *Quis separabit*, will have plenty of opportunity of studying men and things at any rate to a small extent in Egypt, Arabia, Ceylon, and the Australasian colonies of Western Australia, South Australia, Victoria, and New South Wales. The fares by this eastern route to Sydney are £70 first class, and £45 second.

Those who want to combine great luxury, rapid travelling, and economy, will unquestionably find the steamers of the Orient Line the best means of reaching Sydney. These steamers leave London every fourteen days, going alternately viâ the Canal, calling at Naples, and viâ Cape of Good Hope, calling at Cape Town. They carry first, second and third class passengers, the saloon fares being from 50 to 70 guineas; the second class 35 to 40 guineas, and the third from 15 to 20 guineas. The Orient liners have often beaten the mails both viâ 'Frisco and Galle, and it is little short of a scandal that they are not long ago in receipt of adequate payment for their postal services. To give some idea of the luxury of travel by one of these boats, it may be mentioned that their new steamer the *Austral* (whose displacement is no less than 9500 tons) is lighted throughout by electricity, and bath-rooms are set apart for each class of passengers, and for the firemen and crew.

Messrs. Chas. Bethell and Co., London, have recently started a direct line of sailing vessels to the colony, and the fares by these vessels are £40 first class, £25 second class, and £16 third class.

The sailing clippers of the London Line to Fiji leave the Thames about every six weeks, and usually have comfortable passenger accommodation, besides carrying cargo at moderate rates of freight. Fiji is certainly a perfect sanatorium for weak-lunged people, and I should think nothing would tend more to prolong a consumptive life than a stay in the group for a few months, going to and fro in a sailing vessel of the direct line. Of the wonderful effects of the Fijian climate on diseases of this class, I can speak from a varied experience.

In most of these ships it is necessary to fit out your own cabin; but a wise man will so select his 'fixings' that, instead of their being unsaleable rubbish when he reaches Levuka, they will be of great use in furnishing. The washstand, etc., which are so useful on shipboard, should continue to be of value in Taviuni and Viti Levu. The furniture, for instance, which folds into very small spaces, is just the thing for the islands. As regards an outfit, I would say, do not overdo it, the stores in Levuka being not only well stocked, but very reasonable in price. Plenty of white and coloured shirts, some white drill and flannel suits, with others of thin blue serge, are indispensable; and, of course, a sun helmet or two are needful. White canvas shoes are also good things to take; and a waterproof coat and pair of leggings are, as I have said, necessary.

For night wear I consider *pyjamas* infinitely superior to any other attire, and the intending settler should supply himself with a fair stock of these articles. To do the thing luxuriously, a South American hammock should be taken. A night in the veranda in one of these hammocks is one of the glories of existence in Fiji. A camphor-wood box for keeping one's clothes in is an absolute necessity, and I think they can be had cheaper in England than in the colony. There *are* such things as mosquitoes and cockroaches in Fiji, and you must have curtains to guard against the first, and camphor or camphor-wood boxes to prevent the very hungry incursions of the latter. Patent medicines are somewhat dear in Fiji, and planters are often separated from medical men by considerable distances. A few simple remedies, easily understood and easily prepared, are very useful to have; but I never heard of any serious cases of illness among the planters. There were a few attacks of mild dysentery, brought on mainly by ill-considered devotion to 'Three Star' brandy; or 'biliousness,' produced from much the same cause. For the latter we used Eno's Fruit Salt, which is a valuable medicine for the tropics. The favourite remedy of Dr. Macgregor, of Levuka, was, when you could get them, to suck half a dozen oranges before breakfast; and with most people this acts as a charm. Water-cress is to be had in various parts of the group; as everyone knows, it has a reputation for purifying the blood, and this is a useful hint to new arrivals, who will more or less be subject to attacks of those troublesome pests, the mosquitoes. As I have said, if the marks which these gentry leave are scratched or irritated, very nasty sores supervene; but these are easily curable by attention—constant application of cold water, with a simple ointment easily made up by either of the Levuka chemists. It is needless to remark that the very necessary tub in England is a *sine quâ non* in tropical Fiji, and many of the settlers bathe twice or even thrice a day. Nearly all the estates are bountifully blessed with that glorious luxury in a hot climate—cool, clear-running, fresh water. Nobody bathes in the sea.

A few more practical hints may not be out of place, and these are intended mainly for those who may be induced to try Dame Fortune's favour where, in my opinion, she smiles most encouragingly on those possessing, as I have said, 'brains and money.'

Levuka is a very small place, and, like all small places, is given to gossip—shall I say scandal? Therefore the new-comer should not believe all he hears; he must judge for himself. He will be made (unless things have very happily altered since 1877) the recipient of stories which he had better listen to and forget as soon as he has heard. He will, unless I am very much mistaken, be invited to take sides in some political dispute about the Governor, the Legislative Council, or the like; but if, as I suppose, his main object is to make an honest living, he will first cast about him for the *modus vivendi*, and, if he deems it right to speak, he can after some little experience do so with effect. If the intending settler has first-class letters of introduction, he will be in no lack of friends in that most hospitable of capitals, Levuka; but I cannot help fancying that a policy of reasonable reserve—at any rate for the first few weeks—is best fitted for a man about to venture much, perhaps his all, in a comparatively unknown colony. I should decidedly recommend him to put up at either the Levuka Hotel or a first-class boarding-house, and look around, carefully keeping his own counsel. He will, if he keeps his ears as well as eyes open, hear much, and should learn a little. If he concludes to venture on real estate, with a view to planting, he will doubtless hear of many sites that will suit him; but if at all in doubt, he cannot do better than consult Mr. Charles W. Drury, whose knowledge of this subject may be relied on. In mentioning Mr. Drury's name, I only allude to one out of a very numerous body whose advice, based on years of Fiji experience, is equally valuable; but Mr. Drury has made real estate his special business.

The progress of Fiji has been somewhat retarded by the unavoidable delay in adjudicating upon and adjusting the claims of European settlers to their lands obtained prior to its cession to Great Britain, which must be sifted thoroughly before Crown grants are issued.

Land can be obtained from the Government by intending settlers. The upset price is:

	£	s.	d.	
For first-class Land	2	0	0	per acre
,, second ,, ,,	1	0	0	,, ,,
,, third ,, ,,	0	15	0	,, ,,

I shall deal with the subject of the titles for land in the subsequent chapter.

There are many people in Fiji holding big estates with thorough knowledge of their requirements, who would, I feel convinced, gladly make terms with energetic young men from the mother country possessing a command of ready cash to a small extent, and who are willing to work. Here is an opening for those who would naturally shrink from the responsibility of running a big plantation unaided. Sugar, coffee, and tobacco—quite independently of copra—will be the great sources of wealth for Fiji in the future, and it is advisable that men who intend to go out should know something of the grammar of tropical and semi-tropical agriculture.

Angus Mackay's 'Semi-tropical Agriculturist' is one of the best books on this subject; but, after all, book knowledge is worth very little. Still, in the case of Fiji a little knowledge should not be a dangerous thing—it should be the stepping-stone to practical wisdom. In many cases it would be far better for a young fellow anxious to get on in Fiji to give his time gratuitously for a term on an established plantation, and learn a great deal, than attempt too much at first. Paying for board and lodging at the rate of £2 a week for a few months, even if a premium is demanded in addition, is better than experimenting with the land of which he knows nothing, and products of which he knows less.

Nearly every planter that I know in Fiji has had to pay very heavily for his experience, and it is not likely that this hard-earned knowledge should be communicated gratuitously; still, good terms are to be made even by those possessed of small capital, coupled, of course, with willingness to work. Before concluding this chapter, I will just quote from a letter I received from one of the senior members of the Legislative Council of Fiji, who is at present residing at Sydney.

'Fiji is,' he says, 'in a sounder position than any of the colonies; land has increased in value greatly since you were there, capital is wanted to develop the sugar and coffee industries; and with capital and brains, I believe that there is a better prospect for a man in Fiji than any other place I know, and I speak from a thorough knowledge of the country. Labour is arriving in abundance from Polynesia . . . Sugar and coffee are going to be the great industries of Fiji.'

CHAPTER XIX.

LAND TITLES.

THE difficulties which have in other colonies beset the path of the early settler by reason of the insecurity of his land title are not met with in Fiji, and those who may think of acting practically on my hints for capitalists will assuredly read with interest the following account of how land is held by European colonists in Fiji.

The white settlers who have proved the *bona fides* of their claims receive a grant from the Crown, which thenceforward becomes the basis of the title. This is issued in duplicate under the seal of the colony, one copy being retained for registration, and the other delivered to the grantee. A plan of the land by the Crown Surveyor of the Colony is delineated on the grant. All the mortgages and encumbrances on the land are also entered thereon by the Registrar of Titles, so that the grant not only shows who is the grantee, but also the condition of the land as regards indebtedness. When a grantee sells he must use the form of transfer provided by the Real Property Ordinance, 1876, printed copies of which are publicly sold, and which may easily be filled up by any intelligent person. If a solicitor be employed his remuneration is regulated according to a moderate scale of charges contained in a schedule to the Ordinance, and the fee thus allowed covers all professional work in connection with the transfer. The transfer is, in its turn, registered by handing in a duplicate for the purpose, and the Registrar of Titles then issues a Certificate of Title, which is practically a renewed Crown grant to the purchaser, with all the mortgages and encumbrances marked thereon, as in the case of the original Crown grant.

A new Certificate of Title is granted as often as the property is transferred, so that the title consists of one deed simply, and is always kept clear and distinct, without any accumulation of papers and deeds so puzzling to non-professional persons, and so fruitful a source of expense in lawyer's charges and otherwise. It is provided that the original grants and all Certificates of Title granted upon transfer are indefeasible. An exact reproduction of the title is kept in the volumes of the Registrar of Titles, and the Registrar has ample powers to deal with any of the ordinary accidents which may occur in regard to documents. Where any question of importance arises—for example, whether a particular caveat or mortgage should be inscribed first—the Registrar of Titles has power to refer, in a summary way, to the Supreme Court, and the Court, after hearing parties, can give directions.

The whole system of land titles is based upon registration, so that the transfer or mortgage only becomes effective when registered. In place, therefore, of the transfer conveying the property when signed and delivered, as would be the case in England, the transfer is rather the warrant to the Registrar to change the title to the new name. Again, in order that there may be no mistake as to the time when a document concerning land, whether mortgage, transfer, or encumbrance, is handed in, a book is kept called the Presentation Book, in which all documents are entered the moment they are presented for registration. The hour and minute of presentation is at once inserted in the appropriate column, and that date, so fixed, is the date of registration which is thereafter marked on the deeds, and rules the rights of parties.

The only property in land which is recognised by the law is that of fee simple, so that the whole of the perplexing conveyancing law of England in regard to limited and conditional fees and fees in tail is inapplicable to the colony. When a proprietor desires to make a provision for his wife and children he may set forth his wishes, for example, in a trust deed, which may be registered as such in the Register of Deeds, but any provision to affect the land must be made according to the forms in the Real Property Ordinance, and the purposes of the trust are not allowed to encumber the title to land or the registry of titles. If the proprietor should desire to limit his own right in the land to a life-rent, and to transfer the estate to the trustees for the purposes of the deed or settlement, he must create an encumbrance of his own life-rent, and execute a transfer to the trustees of the fee simple. A Certificate of Title will then issue to the trustees as proprietors of the fee simple until they in their turn transfer, with the life-rent of the proprietor marked on the Certificate of Title as an encumbrance. The title will thus be kept clear even in those cases where proprietors wish to tie up their own hands from dealing with their own property, but which can only be done to a limited extent, as there must always be a living proprietor in fee simple entitled to deal with the land subject to the mortgages and encumbrances.

A mortgage is defined to be a pledge of the real property for the purposes of security only. If the money borrowed be not paid, the mortgagee—the holder of the pledge—may, after sufficient intimation of his intention, apply to the court to order a sale. Precautions are taken to prevent the property being sacrificed at a moment inopportune for sales of land. The mortgagee cannot enter into possession of the property in the old way, for the purpose of holding and working it by means of his own capital, and then long years afterwards be called by the mortgager to file his accounts and re-deliver the lands. This system of the neighbouring colonies, so prolific of embittered law-suits, is inconsistent both with the only idea of property in land which is recognised in Fijian law, viz., that of fee simple, or with that of a forfeited pledge, which, if forfeited, ought to be sold under regulations. The mortgagee in the case of an entry upon the lands would not be proprietor in fee simple, and thus the clearness and simplicity of title on the register, which has been the aim of the Real Property Ordinance, would be interfered with by one person being the virtual proprietor for a time, and another the legal and registered proprietor.

When the land which has been given in pledge is sold, the Court distributes the price among the mortgagees and encumbrances according to the order of their priority, handing over the balance, if any, to the mortgager. The purchaser obtains a title by the issue of a new Certificate of Title by the Registrar in his favour, purged of all previous mortgages and encumbrances. Thus again is the title kept clear, and the value of the landed property in the hands of the purchaser by so much enhanced, which, in turn, ensures the highest market price being obtained for the property on its sale.

Leases are treated as encumbrances, and to be valid must be registered if they are for more than one year's duration. As encumbrances they are entered on the title, so that when a proprietor of land applies to a banker or capitalist for an advance, he shows his Crown grant, or Certificate of Title, upon which is entered all the mortgages affecting the land, all the encumbrances of every kind, such as provisions for children, and all the leases. The banker may not be unwilling to make the advance desired, and if it be for a temporary purpose only, for which it is not considered necessary to draw out a mortgage, the title may be deposited as an equitable mortgage. This may be protected by a caveat entered on the register, which prevents all dealing with the land to the prejudice of the holder of the equitable mortgage. The land may be sold for the sum found to be due under the advance when judgment has been obtained, but within a shorter space of time than where there is no equitable mortgage.

It will thus be seen that the European titles to land in Fiji are absolutely secure, each Crown grant or Certificate of Title upon transfer, which is in effect a new grant from the Crown, being indefeasible, and that everything has been done which experience of the systems adopted in other countries rendered possible to keep the title from confusion, to make mortgages secure, and to enable money advanced upon land to be at command for re-payment, without the lender subjecting himself to onerous responsibilities, or the land being itself rendered unsaleable and out of the circle of credit, by the title being weighted with uncleared encumbrances, from which no one could derive any possible benefit.

CHAPTER XX.

A SAMPLE OF POLYNESIAN WANDERINGS.

AND now for some of my personal experience outside Polynesia's far-famed capital. I had learned all that was to be learned about exports and imports. I had interviewed the oldest inhabitants and listened very attentively to all that they had to say, and I started on my first cruise with the following sentences ringing in my ears: 'Go and judge for yourself now you know a little about it, and you will find that if British capital was judiciously invested in the group, there would not be a more prosperous colony under the British or under any other flag.'

I elected to visit the second-largest island of the group—that of Vanua Levu (or Big Land), and a very nice journey we had there. Our only means of communication was a 14-ton schooner—nearly full of cargo, and five passengers besides. From Levuka to Daku post-office in Savu Savu Bay is about 90 miles' sailing, and we had something like a 30-hour sail. Our commissariat was of the most deplorable kind, consisting chiefly of strips of sun-dried something called beef, and yams. Who does not recollect in Mark Twain's 'Innocents Abroad' how the associated friends all agreed in saying 'I pass,' as the greasy Turkish cook offered to each the already dog-licked sausage-meat? Well, 'I passed' with a vengeance, when my brother, who had very considerately offered to show me some of the beauties of Coral Lands, suggested that 'there was my meal.' New to that part of the Pacific I was not new to travel, and had fortunately provided myself with a cask of bottled Bass and some canned meat *pro bono publico*, and great was the κῦδος I obtained when these were produced.

Our crew consisted of some three or four natives, with a half-caste mate and a European captain. After a night on deck (there were cockroaches below!) and drifting all the morning and afternoon, we leisurely rounded Savu Savu Point, and I soon learnt something of the proportions of one of the finest bays I have ever entered. The bay of Savu Savu lies to the south-east of Vanua Levu, and is about 18 miles long, in a straight line drawn from north-east to south-west, and has a coast line between the points of over 40 miles. For 8 miles the north-east corner of the bay is land-locked on all sides save the west, and has a magnificent anchorage for ships of the largest class close in shore. Opposite this anchorage are some splendid tracts of level land, just suitable to the requirements of a growing town. The entrance to the bay is a fine passage, exceeding 3 miles in breadth. A chain of hills, following the coast line, stretches nearly round the bay. These hills are from 700 to 3000 feet in height; while Mount Thurston, to the north-east of Savu Savu Bay, is judged approximately to be at least 4160 feet high; and a belt of level country, ranging in breadth from 1 to 5 miles, lies between them and the sea.

Like nearly all the land in Fiji, the soil is of the most fertile description. Near the beach it is of a light loamy character, increasing in richness as the hills are approached. Vegetation of the most luxuriant type, as usual in all Coral Lands, stretches down to the sandy beach. It is now some little time since I first saw Savu Savu Bay, but the impression its wondrous beauty made upon me is unforgotten; I think the intense silence all around struck me even more than the beauty of the place. Once landed by the little dingy belonging to our inter-insular packet (the *Mary*), we were hospitably received by her owner, Captain Barrack, now a member of the Legislative Council.

The loan of a boat and its stowage with divers and sundry packages completed our business at Captain Barrack's, and towards seven in the evening the Fiji 'boys' we had engaged were steadily pulling 7 miles across the bay for the northern shore, where at Vu-ni-wai-Levu my brother had chosen to fight for existence, and replace, perhaps in the distant future, money not lost by *him* in that luckless struggle of 'Stars and Bars' against 'Stars and Stripes.' He had been extremely unfortunate, for he had only a few months previously been burnt out of house and home, and a two-roomed wooden house facing the sea was all he could offer me, but a very happy home it was.

Vu-ni-wai-Levu did not boast of the luxury of the Palace Hotel, San Francisco, or of the comforts of the Junior Carlton; but the hospitable partners (for I cannot forget Dick Heyward) did their best, and for a reasonable man is not that enough? Copra-making is the firm's chief business. The want of capital has prevented Messrs. Heyward and Cooper from doing much more than make a hard-earned living out of their land, still they hope on, hope ever, and for the humblest pioneer the tide will turn at last. Here, taking it altogether, I fared sumptuously every day. Of fowl hot and fowl cold and fowl curried, we had plenty, and good they were; while goat's flesh is not a contemptible substitute for Welsh mutton. Fish we did not have, except in the shape of the universal sardine; pork was in abundance, and tomatoes were to be had for the trouble of going into the bush. The Fijian pork and poultry ought to have a refined flavour, for though pigs are not at present, as Sydney Smith advised, fed on geranium-blossoms to improve the colour of the future ham, all animals in Fiji eat the meat of the cocoa-nut, and fowls are especially greedy over the grated variety.

It is needless to dwell further on Vu-ni-wai Levu. To say that the scenery all around is exquisite, is to say it is in Fiji—to describe the loveliness of the banks of the Drek, the river which runs into the sea close to the estate, would require a volume of word-painting, and then be hardly understood.

Miss Gordon Cumming, the gifted sister of the famous lion-hunter, has made some very good sketches of the beautiful scenery of Savu Savu Bay, which will give the public some idea of its charm.

From Vu-ni-wai-Levu to the nearest white man's estate, that

of Wai-Wai, is a four-mile march, and *en route* I had plenty of opportunity of studying native life, denuded of the semi-civilisation of Levuka. The Drek-ni-wai (or river Drek) had first to be crossed, and a very rapid stream it is at its mouth, requiring great care in its passage. Once safe across, in an anything but safe dingy, we were welcomed by a thoroughly representative Anglo-Polynesian, who occupies a Fiji-built house on the right of the river's mouth. Mr. Bath was one of those waifs and strays of the Pacific who are in themselves a class totally distinct from every other kind of settler. Bath was, I understand, a sailor in the mercantile marine, and a native of Wiltshire; but many years ago he settled in Savu Savu Bay, Fiji, married a native wife, and lives to a great extent a native life. He seemed perfectly happy, and was surrounded by a numerous progeny. I do not think I shall offend Mr. Bath by calling him an original beachcomber—a settler who settles to make the best of everything in the Polynesian world. These men constitute a strange race; and are to be found from Christmas Island in the North Pacific to the Kermadec Group in the South. They have abandoned a great deal of European knowledge, and have acquired a good deal of native *je ne sais quoi:* they are, in fact, connecting links between the aggressive Anglo-Saxon with his sugar and coffee-planting schemes, and the apparently indolent aborigine, whose only thought is how to kill time with the least trouble and most pleasure. No comparison is possible between the beachcombing pioneers of the Pacific and the early settlers in any other part of the world. There is a poetry about these men (a rough class of poetry, it is true) which one finds it very difficult to convey in words. Some of them have possessed a fair amount of education, and at one time were Europeans in tastes and habits; but once among the islands, Polynesian life was too attractive for them.

The freedom of the South Pacific, combined with its glorious climate, seemed to satisfy some undefined craving, and they refused again to abandon their perfect independence for the trammels of civilisation. To slightly alter the well-known lines of Tennyson:

'They have burst each bond of habit,
They have wandered far away,
From island unto island,
At the gateways of the day.'

Mr. Bath, in spite of his Fijian proclivities, had not forgotten all his European tastes. He admired the flavour of the Bourbon whisky in my flask, and the 'square gin' he tendered us was above suspicion.

Mr. Bath's family seemed healthy, and the children were well-made and shapely, some of them fast becoming men and women; but my experience of the half-caste race, at any rate in Fiji, has, generally speaking, not impressed me in their favour. Curious love-stories are told of many a wandering beachcomber's hopeless pursuit after some pretty Fiji girl. The Fijians are as a rule chaste, and differ materially in this respect from many of the South Pacific islanders. Some years ago when Mr. Thurston was British consul in the group, a Rewa river settler came to him for a marriage license, as he had fallen in love with and had been accepted by some dusky beauty in his own locality. The papers were granted, and one-legged Tommy (he had lost an understanding in action as a sailor) went his way rejoicing. A few weeks after the Queen's representative had congratulated the maimed mariner, business took Mr. Thurston up the Rewa river, and at the stem of his boat flew the consular flag. On approaching the domain of Tommy with the one leg, the boat was loudly hailed by that gentleman, and after some little parley H.B.M. Consul consented to go ashore.

'What's the matter now, Tommy?' he inquired.

'Oh!' said the sailor, his voice broken with suppressed emotion, 'she won't have me, sir.'

'Well, how can I help that?' was the reply. 'You English people think your consuls can do anything for you—make your fortunes, and settle your love affairs. This is really out of my province altogether.'

'Come and see her—do, sir,' implored the lover; and with his usual good-nature Mr. Thurston consented, and interviewed the Fijian belle as she lazily lay on a bed of mats, gently touching her delicately-shaped feet with a long fan she carried in her hand. One-legged Tommy addressed her passionately in her native tongue with all the Oriental imagery of the Fijians. She made no answer. At last, being somewhat sharply interrogated by Mr. Thurston, she scornfully replied that if she married at all, 'she would prefer a man with two legs.'

Swiftly changing his language from the softest and most classical Fiji to the most unmitigated Billingsgate, Tommy 'rounded on' the recent object of his affections, and with a host of unnecessary expletives, asked: 'If she married a man for his legs, why did she not marry a d——d centipede, and have done with it?'

There is a tolerable road between Vu-ni-wai Levu and Wai-Wai, and several minor streams have to be crossed. The first cocoa-nut tree log bridge I went over was, to put it very mildly, a surprise. We are not all Blondins; a single log placed some feet above the level of a rapidly-running stream caused in my case some unheroic fears as to my probable fate if I fell over. However, confidence was soon gained, but in crossing these very primitive bridges I very much prefer bare feet to the most perfect-fitting boots; there is a grip of the naked foot which leather does not possess. A good many cocoa-nut trees fringe the beach of this part of Savu Savu Bay coast, and you pass through many native plantations of maize and other products. Two considerable native villages—or towns, as they are called—exist between the mouth of the Drek-ni-wai and Wai-Wai. Some of the interiors of the native huts are adorned with clubs and spears, but these were conspicuous by their absence in Savu Savu Bay, where 'curios' seem very scarce.

On this march I had the pleasure of being introduced to the district *roko*, named Tovi-Tovi, who presented me with a club or two, and a very fine walking-stick (for which kindness, of course, he immediately went into debt at my brother's little store, as I afterwards found out). Like Mr. Bath, his rokoship appreciated whisky, and said it was *vinaka sara* (very good). This gentleman had recently been in trouble with the authorities, as his insular eccentricity had so far led him astray as to cause one of his wife's feet to be nearly burnt of, for which he deservedly suffered severe punishment.

Late in the evening, I arrived at the house of Mr. Edward Chippindall, a retired lieutenant of the Royal Navy, and owning unquestionably one of the finest sites in Savu Savu Bay. His house is situated on a commanding plateau, backed by a steep hill, down which flows a cool mountain stream, making an excellent bathing-place in the rear. It contains four good-sized bedrooms and a large well-ventilated parlour. Round the house is the inevitable veranda, with a shelving lawn in front leading to the edge of the plateau, from which a steep path descends to the low-lying land reaching to the shores of the bay, which are fringed by plantations of cocoa-nuts. During my visit Mr. Chippindall was irrigating the lowlands for the better growth of the sugar-cane, while the uplands were being planted with coffee-trees.

A man's library is an index to his mind. Wai-Wai could not boast of a big library, but the books scattered about were characteristic. There were copies of the *Sugar-Cane*, a magazine devoted to the interests of sugar-planters, and numerous works on tropical agriculture. An odd number of the *Field* showed that interest in manly sports which an Englishman never abandons. A few books of travel and reference, with a sprinkling of novels (Walter Scott, Thackeray, and Dickens were especially prominent), and a well-worn Church of England Prayer Book completed the list. The furniture was Spartan in its simplicity, but I have found it possible to be exceedingly comfortable without any more æsthetic surroundings than tables and chairs. The house was built of Savu Savu Bay wood, by a Savu Savu settler, Mr. Dods, of Valaga, and is a substantial affair, the roof being thatched with dried cocoa-nut leaves, and perfectly water-tight.

A line of hearty recognition is due to the kindness received at Wai-Wai, and the gloriously free and easy Christmas-time spent there. One of the jovial party there assembled, Mr. Black, our host's manager and overseer, has since been drowned in endeavouring to reach the bay from Levuka in an open boat, so there is a tinge of melancholy over my recollections of Wai-Wai. What chiefly impressed me in the Fijian planters with whom I became acquainted was their goodness of heart and intense genuineness. Hospitality is hardly the word to describe their kindness. It seemed more like the traditional habits of the Scottish and Irish peasantry, by whom a man is welcomed because he is a man. The settlers' knowledge of men and things is very comprehensive; as a rule, they thoroughly understand the politics not only of the mother country (and home is very dear to them), but of the United States and the provinces of Australasia. The Imperial feeling is naturally very strong, and although *Punch* treated the idea as a joke, it would be quite possible to raise several regiments of six-foot Fijians, officered by military or naval settlers in the group, for service in any part of the empire.

While I was in the Pacific the loyal Maoris of New Zealand were intensely disgusted that they were not allowed to accompany the Indian troops to Cyprus. We have Colonel Whitmore's report that the men came forward in thousands to volunteer. The 'gentlemen of England who live at home at ease' can but faintly picture the enthusiastic love for their mother country felt by colonists, and the strength of the link which binds the majority of our native fellow-subjects to the Queen—the *Marama Levu*, or 'great lady,' as they call her in Fiji.

CHAPTER XXI.

A LITTLE 'BLOW'—AND SOME LIGHT FROM THE CANDLE-NUT AND OTHER THINGS.

THROUGHOUT Polynesia the summer months are the rainy ones, and while in Savu Savu Bay we had plenty of evidence that when it likes, 'the rain it raineth every day.' There is moreover about the summer season a damp heat, which naturally has its drawbacks, although infinitely more endurable than a muggy day in London, or a Pacific fog in San Francisco. The months of December, January, February, and March are those in which 'blows,' as hurricanes are locally termed, may be expected; and hurricanes of great violence do occasionally visit the South Sea Islands, though they are insignificant in comparison with the cyclones which sweep over the West Indies, such, for instance, as that which destroyed the mail steamship *Rhone*, and a whole fleet of merchantmen at St. Thomas, in the autumn of 1867. Houses have existed in Levuka for years, which under a similar visitation would have been blown miles out to sea. The little dread the residents have of a 'blow' is shown by the fact that a few fathoms of light chain added to the roof of a weather-board shanty is considered sufficient precaution.

Savu Savu Bay is more sheltered than Levuka, though storms of violence have reached its shores; on one occasion my luckless brother's house and all that he had was blown into the sea. However, I have the strongest doubts, from personal investigation, whether my brother's 'residence' would have stood a 'strong wind' on any English or Scottish upland. I have seen powerful men knocked down by a 'gale' at Hastings, and know something of a 'strong breeze' off the 'Three Kings' to the north of New Zealand; and if some of my Polynesian friends had been in Sussex on the one occasion, or in the powerful 3000-ton American steamer on the other, they would have staked their lives that both were 'hurricanes.' Unquestionably there are certain unmistakable natural indications of the approach of a 'blow,' and as nearly every white settler claims to be weather-wise, the incessant prophecies one hears as to 'blows' are really alarming. 'A blow' is certain for 'to-morrow' or 'the day after,' or 'this week;' or else 'they are having it hot in some other part of the group.' One would almost think the wish was father to the thought, though a strong wind may be the ruin of many a planter's hopes as regards cocoa-nut and other crops. Thunder-storms of some severity, accompanied with vivid lightning, are not uncommon in January and the early part of February. I witnessed several of these, but very little damage was done; and I believe there are few cases on record of human life having been destroyed by lightning. It may be that the cocoa-nut trees act as conductors, but I gained very scanty information on this head.

To return to Wai-Wai. We got up about five a.m., according to the custom of planters in every quarter of the globe, and having had a good dip under the glorious waterfall at the bathing-hole already referred to, complied with other Fijian customs by having a quiet 'nip,' and lighting our ante-breakfast pipes.

F. C. Burnand, in one of his books, describing his voyage to Antwerp on board the *Baron Osy*, says he felt inclined to swear purposelessly, and dance a hornpipe; why, he could not tell, except that he felt himself a 'jovial tar' on the ocean wave. It is just the same thing on Polynesian plantations. The genius of the place seems to impregnate your being, and you get up at inconceivable hours, indulge in little nips, and smoke pipes before breakfast, as if these customs had been the ritual of your life. We strolled out on the plateau; the cocoa-nut trees on the beach were sighing sad music to the accompaniment of a light morning breeze; the sunbeams were just glistening on the coral reef miles away to our right front, and playing amidst the luxuriant and many-tinted vegetation around. In addition to sylvan music, sunlit coral reefs, and tropical verdure, we revelled in a panorama of beauty. To our left the bay spread out for 15 miles, broken here and there by jutting headlands, which in themselves were botanical gardens, while the southern shore, terminating slightly to our left front, was visible for miles, with the exquisite little island of Nawi nestling in its farthest corner. To our right the bay extended for an equal distance, though in much bolder proportions. We could well distinguish the entrance to this noble land-locked harbour, the points of Savu Savu and Kombelau, and between them and beyond, to our right and to our left, lay the plain of liquid azure, broken only where the waves murmured on the coral reef, or far-distant islets studded the horizon. Waitova Falls I had thought surpassingly beautiful, but this scene exceeded my tropical dreams, and I said so. My brother, who had been chatting with one of the native labourers for some time, remarked, without noticing my eulogium, that he should not be at all surprised if we had 'a blow' to-day, and Chippindall, Donald Smith, and poor Black agreed with him. Familiarity had bred contempt, and the planters were thinking not of natural beauty, but of copra, sugar, coffee, and tobacco; so away we went down a steep path to the low-lying lands where the sugar-cane was growing to perfection, and extensive irrigation works were in progress, and after a lengthened ramble over the estate, we returned to a planter's breakfast with planters' appetites.

Later in the day, taking a quiet siesta after lunch, I woke about three p.m. to find that the sky, bay, and all around had changed as if by magic. There was a restless movement of the trees, and a curious lull in natural sounds, mingled with the lurid glow and indescribable oppressiveness that foretells a storm. We were all up in no time. 'It's coming,' said one. 'It's not much of a blow,' said another. 'A passing storm,' predicted a third. The bay was in a moment a sea of 'white horses,' and with fierce fury did they leap over the coral patches near Kombelau Point. Darker grew the sky as the rain came down in a deluge—the distant cocoa-nut trees bent their lofty trunks, while their leaves spread wildly out before the strong wind. Far away to the south, which Wai-Wai faces, the blue outline of an island was lit up by lightning, while a distant peal of thunder was heard.

A few minutes later the wind dropped, the sea grew calm, the cocoa-nut trees raised their heads, the clouds broke, and the warm sun was peeping out. I ventured to remark that it was a grand sight from my host's lofty veranda, but was it a 'blow'?

'Not exactly a champion one for these latitudes, but quite as much as we want,' was my brother's business-like reply.

I have had several so-called 'blows' in various parts of the Pacific, but I never experienced one much worse than that I have attempted to describe. The records of the Southern Seas, however, and also the underwriters' ledgers, have a different tale to tell; happily Fiji has for many years been exceptionally free from any very serious visitation.

Dinner at Wai-Wai during my visit took place at the hour most convenient for the majority. Our host was not particular—the comfort of his visitors seemed all in all to him, and there was something so thoroughly hearty in our Wai-Wai welcome, something so thoroughly representative of the customs that obtain among more recent arrivals of the pushing Anglo-Saxon race in that unexplored field of wealth, the South Pacific, that I make no apology for dwelling on my reception at Mr. Chippindall's—and *ex uno disce omnes.* Mark Twain tells us that his youthful diary consisted for months of monotonous repetitions of 'Got up, washed, and went to bed.' After a time Mark found this dry reading, and discontinued his diary. If I were to dwell on every hospitable reception, and recapitulate all the details of personal travel, I should become as dull as the youthful journalist, and a few personal reminiscences must serve as types of the rest.

A good meal is a wonderful sweetener of this life of ours.

Dickens struck a familiar key when he made Mr. Pickwick's lawyer say: 'I wonder what the foreman of the jury had for breakfast?' A badly cooked meal, badly served, and worse digested, is a wretched preparation for work or pleasure of any sort, and I don't believe that the evening after 'the blow' at Wai-Wai would have been found either instructive or amusing had not all of us dined well.

We had soup and turkey, goat cutlets and salads, curry and pine-apples. To our good appetites it was a feast worthy of Lucullus; after which we sauntered into the veranda.

The moon was full, and the bay shone under its rays like burnished silver, to which the dark foliage of the opposite coast formed a most effective contrast. The Fijian is said to be hopelessly insensible to the beauties of the surrounding scenery, and he would barter all the loveliness of his group for an extra dish of yams. As in the case of *malua*, the Anglo-Saxon has been decidedly influenced by the Fijian in this particular. Throughout the whole of the Pacific, if you remark to any settler on the beauty of the scenery, he generally stares as if you were a weak-minded fellow, who ought to be relegated out of the busy world.

Intermixed with Polynesian yarns (no Pacific settler can be five minutes in your company without some particularly good story being told), the conversation at Wai-Wai was very interesting, and sometimes scientific. I learned that evening a great deal about candle-nuts (*Aleurites triloba*, or more correctly, *Aleurites molucanna*). They are the fruit of the *Lauci* tree, which is one of considerable size, and conspicuous in the Oceanic forests from the fine white powder which covers its leaves and young shoots, but which is easily rubbed off. As the fruit matures, the shell hardens and becomes covered with a chalky sort of coat, and the kernel closely adheres to the shell. Each nut weighs about 160 or 170 grains. The adherence of the nut to the hard shell has been the difficulty in dealing commercially with the candle-nut, as at present there is no effective machine for separating them, and each nut has to be shelled separately, of course at great expense to the planter or merchant. They are called candle-nuts because in Fiji, Hawaiian Islands, and Tahiti the kernels, threaded on a split bit of cane or mid-rib of a palm leaf, are occasionally used as a substitute for candles, and in some places they use them when fishing at night. From burnt shells they make a rude sort of lamp-black, which in Tahiti is used for tattooing, and in Fiji for putting on 'war paint,' and printing patterns on *tappa*, or native cloth. In some parts of Fiji, as soon as a baby is born the nurse rushes to the tree, gathers a fresh fruit, and squeezes the oil into the infant's throat to enable it to announce its arrival more effectually.

These nuts are common not only in the Pacific but in Central America, India, the islands of the Indian Ocean and Amboyna (one of the Moluccas). They are eatable, but are said to intoxicate if taken in any quantity. The taste is like that of a walnuty almond, and they are strongly aperient. By twenty horse-power pressure sixty per cent. of oil can be extracted, and this is said to be equal to the very finest rape.

From maize and candle-nuts and coffee-growing we drifted back to story-telling, and one of poor Mr. Black's yarns was 'The Battle of the Beach,' which I translate from his characteristic local idiom :

About a year before annexation, the King's residence at Nasova was approached by a mob of whites with a petition, or rather a demand, for the consideration of his Majesty. Mr. Woods was informing the spokesman of the crowd that the paper would be received, but must not be read out in public, when some thoughtless fool in the European assemblage fired a revolver. The 'Royal Guards,' under the command of English officers, quickly advanced, and drove the unhappy demonstrators right along the beach. Such a stampede of Europeans had never before been seen in the Southern Seas. With their fixed bayonets at the charge, the native soldiery made the pace, and kept it up. Some of the stories of this absurd *fiasco* of a deputation will live for ever in tradition. One gallant gentleman, finding that his brother had longer legs and better lungs than he had, and would soon get shelter in the town, cried out excitedly, as he was being rapidly outstripped, 'Tell mother that I died a Christian, and the key of the safe is in my right-hand drawer.' Another is of the unfortunate new-comer, whose knowledge of Fijian extended to only one word, '*vinaka*' or 'good,' and finding the bayonets of the troops in unpleasant proximity to his person, exclaimed repeatedly, '*Vinaka, vinaka!*' whereupon the soldiers increased their attentions, to his manifest terror. However, no harm was done. It speaks volumes for the discipline of the military force and the character of Messrs. Woods and Thurston that Levuka was not that day the scene of a sanguinary struggle.

'I think you Fiji fellows were rather fond of agitating,' I said.

'We wanted annexation and we got it,' was Black's comment. 'Did you ever hear the nigger sort of annexation doggerel which was sung in procession up and down Levuka beach in 1873? The chorus went:

'"Oh my! Glory! Hallelujah!
Fiji is a happy land!
But on England we rely,
And old Cacobau defy,
And we'll all join the annexation band."

'The fellow who said "I care nothing who makes the laws of a country, let me make its ballads," would form rather a poor estimate of Fiji, I'm afraid,' remarked our host. 'Parsons, of the police force, came out with a song once describing annexation. You all know *wonga* means a boat or yacht. Well, this is how Parsons put old King Cacobau's claims:

' "Now this is what the King said to the Commodore,
In the presence of the Fiji chiefs at T'tonga,
If your Queen she wants these islands make it right with me before,
A thousand pounds per annum and a *wonga*." '

'Shall we sail up the bay to-morrow as far as Valaga, and give the Dods and Pillans a look in?' asked Mr. Chippindall.

'By all means,' was the chorus of replies.

'Well, we'll have to start early, as I have got a *meke-meke* for you fellows in the evening, and we may have to be pulled back all the way.'

'There's going to be some cricket at Valaga next week, and we'll all have to go,' broke in Cooper *lailai;* in other words, smaller Cooper, my brother. 'It won't be elevens though, as there are not fifteen white men in the bay.'

'The beds are all ready—mosquito-curtains and all. It's getting quite late, and a trifle chilly; let us turn in.'

We followed this advice, knocked the ashes from our pipes, and so ended our evening at Wai-Wai.

CHAPTER XXII.

SAVU SAVU TO TAVIUNI.

Mr. Pillans and the kindly Dods offered us a hearty welcome, but for any amount of hospitality we were prepared. The former gentleman possessed (he has left Fiji now, to educate his large family) a weather-board house, of the bungalow character, while that of the Dods—father, mother, and sons—is of the log order, and, to my mind, more substantial, though of course not so imposing. After an early lunch was disposed of, most of the party, reinforced by two of the younger Messrs. Dods and Mr. Thomas P. Elphinston, departed to practise for the cricket-match, while Black and myself went to inspect some native yam plantations.

The yam is the staple article of food in the South Pacific. The shape of the root is usually long and round, and the substance fibrous, but remarkably farinaceous and sweet. It is generally of a dark brown colour, and has a rough sort of skin. The slopes of the inferior hills and the sunny banks sometimes met with in the valleys are the best places for its growth. Small terraces are formed one above the other, covered with a mixture of rich earth and decayed leaves. The roots intended for planting are kept by themselves in baskets till they begin to sprout; a yam is then taken, and each eye or sprout cut off, with a part of the outside of the root about an inch long and a quarter of an inch thick attached to it, and these are put in a place to dry, the remainder of the yam being baked or boiled and eaten. When the detached pieces are sufficiently dry, they are carefully put in the ground with the sprouts uppermost, a small portion of dried leaves is laid upon each, and the whole lightly covered with mould. When the roots begin to swell the cultivators keep them covered to about an inch with rich light earth. Yams can be preserved longer out of the ground than any other Polynesian root, and thus make excellent sea stock. The average price in Levuka for yams is from £3 to £4 a ton.

I have already mentioned the *taro*, on the cultivation of

which the natives bestow a great deal of attention. This has a large solid tuberous root of an oblong shape, sometimes 9 to 12 inches in length, and 5 or 6 in diameter. The plant has no stalk; the broad heart-shaped leaves rise from the upper end of the root, and the flower is contained in a sort of sheath. There are several varieties, but I do not know their names. Taro is best cultivated in marshy spots. It is generally baked, the rind or skin being carefully scraped with a knife. The roots are solid, and have the appearance of mottled soap. They are farinaceous and nutritive, but I don't like them; they may, from a scientific point of view, be the nearest approach to the potato, but if so, the nearest seemed to me to be very far off.

Speaking generally, there is no comparison in my opinion between the fruits and vegetables of temperate latitudes and those of the tropics. I confessedly prefer the potatoes, cabbages, and asparagus, the apples, pears, and strawberries of England or America, to all the pine-apples, bananas, grenadillos, yams, taro, and bread-fruit of lovely Polynesia. The exceptions I make are the lime and the orange. These are delicious. A fresh-gathered lime squeezed into a tumbler of water, with a little sugar added, makes a most refreshing drink.

Use is second nature, and some of my friends were wont to declare that they preferred yams and taro to the best potato. I said nothing, but used to think of Reynard and the grapes. Potatoes will not grow in the South Sea Islands, as far as I know, and for outlying settlers to import them from Levuka, where they are sent from New Zealand, would be expensive. It should be said that the cultivation of grapes has been attempted in Fiji, but with very partial success. I know that a trial shipment was made, but have not heard the result.

Leaving the yam plantation, we wandered down to the beach again. Many of the trees have their branches extending right over the water, and the parasites from them drooping down to its surface form an exquisite floral veil through which the sea can be seen.

Some of the woods near Valaga contain trees which yield very valuable dye barks—at least they are so considered by the natives. I have not heard of any serious attempt to try them in England; but the effort would cost little, and might be worth the trouble. I heard of four varieties. The bark of the *kura* root contains a powerful crimson dye; the bark itself is yellow, but the natives develope the other colour by the addition of lime or ashes. Mr. James Harding, who wrote to me from Navesi in Viti Levu on the same subject, says that he believes the wood as well as the bark of the *kura* root contains dye. The natives get a purplish colour from *nageti*, the bark of the trunk of a tree, by mixing it with the juice of a species of uneatable lemon. *Tiri* is a purple dye obtained by the same means. *Doga* is a third purple dye; but this variety yields less colouring matter. Of these barks there is a practically inexhaustible supply in the group.

After a very pleasant and instructive day we were pulled back to Wai-Wai, reaching there in time for another bountiful meal. It had been arranged that we were to spend a day or so at Valaga for the cricket-match, in which *nolens volens* I was to take a part. Mr. Elphinston and two of the Messrs. Dods returned with us in the boat, and joined the Wai-Wai party, which now numbered eight white men—an assembly unprecedented in the annals of Savu Savu Bay.

After dinner we had the usual discussions in the veranda whilst awaiting the expected *meke-meke*. The Eastern Question, the Presidential election, the whereabouts of 'Bully Hayes' (a celebrated nineteenth-century pirate of the Pacific), the price of copra, the dense ignorance concerning Fiji which prevailed at home, were the topics under review. Stories of life and adventure all the world over were told by everybody; some pathetic, some amusing, and all marked by a strong flavour of American humour.

The moon was shining brightly as a weird-looking procession approached the steps of the veranda. There was a *lali* party of four, forming a group by themselves. The people for the *meke-meke* numbered about forty men and women, and after they had respectfully squatted for a short time, Black gave a signal, and the entertainment commenced. The *lali* man beat time with his *lali* stick; the three sombre-looking musicians commenced a low sighing sort of chant, something like a mixture of Gregorian with the strange Oriental music one hears in Russian churches. The men took one side, the women the other; sometimes they were bending double; sometimes going one way, sometimes another; but all in the most perfect time, and chanting to the tune of the instrumentalist and his assistants. Anon they would rise, and pass round the chanting four in single file, and would at once break off into a *ballet d'action*, representing the news of a Government order reaching the mountains, and the consequent discussion, war, peace, setting sail in a native canoe, a chase, etc., all accompanied by the low, and anything but monotonous, sing-song which rose and fell as the sentiment of the scene depicted might require.

The *meke* lasted some time (the Fijians seem never to tire of this amusement), and new *sulus* and other little presents having been given by Mr. Chippindall, the *papalagi* were left to contemplate the moonlit bay, and to discuss things in general.

It has been my wish in these personal recollections to give my readers some little insight into the interior economy of a Fiji planter's existence; an extract from a letter of mine home will further explain how apostolic was our daily life:

'I really don't know where a large proportion of our guests would have been but for my stock of trousers and shirts. Everybody goes about from house to house without baggage of any sort, gets soaked through by rain, fording streams, or at sea, and then comes down on his host for clothes. Walter (my brother) and Dick Heyward are both wearing other people's coats and my understandings. Donald has on a portion of my Bordeaux suit and a shirt of the Dods', while Black's rig is, I believe, representative of every settler in the bay. Such a possessing of all things in common I never saw yet.'

In my Polynesian wanderings, miles from Wai-Wai or Savu Savu Bay, I soon got used to this 'primitive Christianity.'

A visitor is always expected to give a helping hand when required, and this expectation is invariably complied with. One fellow will superintend a gang of labour, another will assist in the kitchen, a third will see that some bush is cleared, or a cargo of produce for the interinsular packet is properly loaded in the plantation boat. There is active healthy employment for anybody and everybody. I am writing of course of pioneer days, and of a bachelor establishment. The time is approaching, and more rapidly than most people think, when planting in Fiji will be on the same level as it is in the West Indies and Ceylon, when perhaps railways will exist for produce transportation and personal travel, and telegraphic cables (perhaps telephones) extend from island to island. The nineteenth century moves apace, and the advanced guard of the all-conquering Anglo-Saxon is on British soil in the archipelago of Fiji.

The cricket-match at Valaga duly came off. I never was much of a player, but having made a decent score in the first innings, I asked Mr. Dods, senior, a most charming old gentleman, to see me do the same in the second. Pride invariably precedes a fall, and the first ball I received gracefully interfered with the perpendicular of my middle wicket, and I then remembered with satisfaction that I had told my companions I was no hand at cricket.

A day or so later I paid a visit to the hot springs which bubble up on the other side of the bay. A native woman was very contentedly boiling a chicken over them. In the appendix to this volume I give a chemical analysis of this water, obtained for me by my friend, Mr. Henry Bowmam.

A few days later I quitted Savu Savu Bay and made for Koro, an island which gives its name to the sea lying between the windward island and Ovalau. Here I was hospitably entertained by Mr. Chalmers, who has a comfortable house in a most lovely situation, similar in many respects to Wai-Wai. He had, at the time I write, a large flourishing arrowroot plantation, and was a regular exporter of that flour to Australia and New Zealand. Mr. Chalmers is now a resident of Levuka, and a member of the Legislative Council, a *locum tenens* for my friend the Hon. J. C. Smith.

Taviuni has been called the 'garden of Fiji,' and well deserves the name; but where almost every island is a garden, it is difficult to say which is the most perfect. To my mind some of the coast walks in the island of Koro are the most beautiful in the wide Pacific. In no other island did I notice such a continuation of exquisite creepers, forming a lattice-work of floral beauty through which could be seen the blue sea, and in no other island did I see such perfect flower-gardens cultivated by man.

Mr. Chalmers is fortunate in having an accomplished wife and a charming family. Their home-life is wisely divided between study and play, and I have never seen more happy, healthy faces than those I met in distant Koro. One of the pleasantest of my Pacific experiences is a rather wild game of romp which I indulged in round the big trees on Mr. Chalmers's lawn. The climate of the Pacific may be enervating to some white people. I confess I could have wished it more so for children, when I was over and over again run to earth by my youthful friends.

Arrowroot flourishes best near the sea, in a light soil and dry situation. It is indigenous to the islands of the South Pacific; but when cultivated a single root uncut is planted, a number of tuberous bulbs about the size of large new potatoes, are found at the extremities of fibres proceeding from this root. The leaves are light green and deeply indented; they are not attached to one common stem, the stalk of each distinct leaf proceeding from the root. The stalk bearing the flower rises in a single shaft, resembling the berries of the potato. To the shape and size of the reed, or shaft bearing the flower, the arrowroot is probably indebted for its name. When the leaves from the stalk dry or decay, the roots are dug up and washed. The rind is then scraped off, and the root goes through a variety of grating and sifting processes to fit it for market. Koro can boast of several fine cotton plantations, but these are not so numerous as in former days, when cotton formed the staple of the group, and Taviuni was a garden by cultivation as well as by nature.

Taviuni is about 25 miles long, with a coast-line of about 60 miles. It is in shape one vast mountain, gradually rising to a central ridge of over 3000 feet. Heavy clouds generally hide its summit, where a considerable lake is situated about 3 miles long by 1½ mile wide, pouring through an outlet to the west a stream which, after dashing and foaming along its narrow bed, glides quietly through the native principal town, called Somo Somo, which at one time was the name given to the island, furnishing it with a good supply of fresh water. The bed of this lake is supposed to be the crater of an extinct volcano. A tolerable road extends about 7 miles across the island at its southern end from Vuna Point, where there is a flourishing store, and several very comfortable residences, including a ladies' school, and a good hotel, called the 'Masonic.' A road has, I understand, now been completed from the north to the south of the island. At Selia Levu is one of the most important plantations of the group.

As you approach the end of the road on the west side of Taviuni, a fine view is afforded of Mr. Hunter's extensive plantation, consisting of a clearing of about 400 acres, nearly 300 of which are under sugar-cane. A ride for about a mile through this valuable crop, brings the visitor to the snug little residence of the proprietor; and another half mile lands the visitor at the sugar factory. Both within and without the mill a busy scene presents itself. Outside, the place is kept alive by the continual arrival of dray-loads of the rich juicy cane, drawn by teams of oxen, under the care of the black grinning native, who cracks his whip with all the *aplomb* of the Australian bushman. Now and again the shrill steam whistle echoes over the plantation to hurry up the teamsters, a warning that the mill is running short of cane. From the principal entrance one passes through the drying and packing-room, which contained some 30 tons of manufactured sugar at the time I was there; out of it a passage leads to the main portion of the manufactory. Some forty or fifty labourers are continually employed in the mill, and what with the whirr of the machinery, the revolution of wheels, and the escape of steam, the scene presented is that of a hive of industry.

On the north side of the road, about 3 miles from Vuna, are situated Messrs. Smith and Aitchison's plantations, each having 10 acres of coffee. Both these small patches of coffee have been tended with the greatest care. Each shrub or tree has been carefully staked, and not a weed is to be seen. The trees are covered with berries.

Within a mile square at Vuna there are numerous herds of cattle, belonging to Mr. James M'Connell, one of the most enterprising and successful merchants in the group, and other gentlemen; while there are several flocks of sheep of about 100 each, belonging to the same gentlemen. On the plantation of Mr. Moore there are a considerable number of cocoa-nuts bearing, which are to be manufactured into copra; and an area of some 100 acres of young nuts, which are not yet available. At Holmhurst is Mr. Billyard's plantation, a most valuable property, and in view of its position in every way suitable for the erection of a large central mill. This property consists of about 1000 acres of the finest land in one and the same block in Fiji, and is surrounded by 3000 or 4000 acres of equally good land, on a slight gradient, leading to the homestead. With the exception of 20 or 30 acres under maize, and well-kept paddocks for the stock, operations are stayed, awaiting the advent of a mill; Mr. Billyard being naturally unwilling to sacrifice his property to cocoa-nuts.

At the northern end of the island is a prettily located little township called Wairiki, which boasts a good-sized Catholic church, with schools attached, and a really excellent store, kept by the Messrs. McKissack, whose kindness to the shipwrecked crew of an unfortunate San Francisco schooner, which sailed under my late firm's flag, I wish gratefully to record.

Some few miles past Wairiki is the extensive plantation of Mr. Peckham, who has more than 700 acres planted with cocoa-nuts, while his cattle, feeding in pastures like those of England, thrive splendidly. A neighbouring island has been planted by this gentleman with coffee-trees, specimens of whose produce have realised high prices in the City of the Golden Gate.

To furnish a sort of directory to Fiji plantations is not my object; it is rather to give such samples of them as will enable readers faintly to realise what is doing in one of the fairest provinces of the British Empire. Possibly I should only weary those I want to interest in Coral Lands by long accounts of the great trading station of the Messrs. Hennings at Loma Loma, with the exquisite scenery which surrounds it; of cotton plantations in Chichia, or of the grand sugar-cane fields which border the noble Rewa, in Viti Levu. On the last-named island a volume could be written; and the same may be said of each of the clusters of groups constituting the Colony of Fiji. But they would bear a marked resemblance to Mark Twain's diary—an 'iteration' which would almost necessitate an occasional expletive. We live in the busy, practical nineteenth century. The salient features of a country once known, the details are soon filled in by those interested. If my outline is fairly accurate, I shall rest content.

If Wai-Wai is a representative planter's bachelor home, so is Mango Island the model of a cotton estate.

CHAPTER XXIII.

MANGO AND MANGO COTTON.

I PREFACE this reference to Mango by a personal acknowledgment. To Mr. Rupert Ryder—one of the most active partners in the firm of brothers who lately owned the island now transferred to the Mango Island Company (which has a capital of £100,000)—I am indebted for recent information of the progress of the estate; information received in fact while writing. Of his courteous hospitality I will not speak, except that you could expect nothing else of him or his family.

Mango Island, lying about 14 miles south of Vanua Balavu, was purchased in 1863 by one of the brothers Ryder from the great Fiji house of the Messrs. Hennings, who still own more than 60,000 acres in Fiji. In 1864 the pioneer Mr. Ryder was joined by two of his brothers; cotton planting was determined on, and the estate has been 'run' with that end in view for more than fifteen years, and is in fact the longest established concern in the group, others which preceded it having ceased to exist.

The island is nearly round, and enclosed almost entirely by a coral reef, the circle being completed by an excellent roadstead harbour, protected from the prevailing S.E. trade-winds, and properly buoyed. This has been visited by several men-of-war. Like all the islands embraced in Coral Lands, it is of volcanic origin. The coast-line is formed of high hills, while the interior is a basin with a formation like the flattened crater of an extinct volcano. Seven hundred acres of the finest Sea Island cotton are now under cultivation. The land selected by the Messrs. Ryder for this purpose was the heavily-timbered level land in the centre of the island, which was to be had to any extent, as the area of Mango exceeds 8000 acres.

Nothing has been more discouraging for Fiji planters than the terrible fall in the price of Sea Island cotton. In 1869 it fetched 4s. 4d. per lb. in the English market; and in 1870, owing to the closing of numerous French factories (where it was largely used in the manufacture of certain classes of silk), in consequence of the war with Prussia, it fell to 1s. 4d. per lb. Its present price is about 1s. 8d. The seed used by the Messrs. Ryder came originally from the Southern States of America, the cotton of which the Mango grain has beaten, both in Philadelphia and Paris. The trees are planted in straight rows about 7 feet by 7 feet apart, and viewed from a slight elevation, have a very regular and highly cultivated appearance. They are perennial. Picking begins about five months after planting, generally in July, and lasts until September, after which another crop forms, which is generally picked up to the end of February. The month of March being regarded as the middle of the 'hurricane' season, the system is adopted of then pruning the cotton-trees, so as to prevent any serious damage if 'a blow' were to occur.

The company employ over three hundred labourers on the plantation, hitherto introduced under the Government regulations, in vessels belonging to the late firm, from the New Hebrides Group, which lies 600 miles to the westward of Fiji. Now, however, that the Government have taken the introduction of Polynesian labour almost entirely into their own hands, my Mango friends rely on the Nasovan authorities—paying the rates of wage already described. The crop of the two pickings referred to is on an average about 800 lb. of cotton in the seed to the acre. The Mango ginning establishment is an extensive one. Six cotton-gins are driven by a powerful steam-engine, and these give about 1 lb. of clean cotton to 4 of seed cotton, or as the bales weigh about 400 lb., half a bale of clean cotton to the acre annually: the return from the estate for the year ending September, 1879, being just 350 bales of clean Sea Island cotton.

Notwithstanding the wonderful success indicated by these figures, the company does not confine itself to their Gold-Medal cotton. Some 700 acres of the island are devoted to coffee-planting, there being now 150 acres of superior coffee coming into bearing. Altogether there are 1100 acres under cultivation in Mango, as a good deal of space is reserved for a crop of maize; and there are also plantations of bread-fruit, bananas, and other food for 'labour,' while the careful cultivation of limes is another marked feature of Mango.

Sheep and cattle thrive well on the island, and since I was in Fiji, Angora goats have been introduced, of which there is a flock of more than 300, so that a good export of Mango hair may be looked for. Goats' hair does not exhaust the products of well-cared-for Mango: the vast amphitheatre of the interior is studded with cocoa-nuts, which at present yield some 120 tons of copra per annum, and should furnish an equivalent quantity of fibre. The seed of the Sea Island cotton is also exported by the Mango Island Company in common with other cotton settlers. For the introduction of this small branch of Pacific exports I take some little credit, as it was formerly entirely wasted. In Mincing Lane, as I have said, it fetches from £7 to £9 a ton. What becomes of it after it reaches my broker friends I do not know exactly, but I have heard that its product returns to Fiji as the 'finest Lucca oil.'

Mango is splendidly watered, and its scenery is perfect, even for Fiji. The almost land-locked lagoon is one of the gems of Coral Lands.

Mr. Rupert Ryder was one of the members of the interim government formed pending the acceptance of the group by the British Empire, and was, until lately, a member of the Legislative Council. He and his brothers are in their way little princes. They have successfully turned a doubtful venture into a great success.

CHAPTER XXIV.

THE REWA.—LET FIJI FLOURISH.

A FEW hours spent in the interinsular steamer brings the traveller from Levuka to Laucala Bay, and rounding Suva Point he enters the noble harbour of Suva. A ridge of hills, averaging about 500 feet high, and covered with the densest undergrowth, bisects the peninsula. Three rivers, the Veisere, Lina, and Tamavua, enter the bay, and now Suva is made the capital of the group, the water supply will have to come from the last-named river. At present Suva is deplorably off for good fresh water, in which respect Levuka offers a most favourable contrast.

The population of Suva from the latest returns has only increased to a little more than 200, but already it boasts a good hotel kept by the famous Fijian restaurateur, Mr. W. T. Sturt, who formerly kept the principal hotel at Levuka. A great deal of the Rewa sugar is exported, and if the local mosquitoes were also shipped in anything like proper quantities, the steamer *Suva* would confer a double blessing on the place. For mosquitoes and sand-flies Suva has no rival in the group, and until more buildings are erected in Suva these pests will continue.

A road is in progress from Suva to Naitasiri, but when I left the group but little was constructed. The country in the interior after leaving the Rewa is generally a succession of bush-covered hills. Between Na Ato and Viti Levu Bay on the northern shore of 'big Fiji' is a beautiful grassy basin of large extent, with some clumps of fine trees. In fact, this is a magnificent pasturage country. A well-wooded fringe of fine land borders the bay at its extremity, while steep cliffs and ridges hem in its sides. The district of Raki-Raki is remarkably fertile, and there are several flourishing plantations of pea-nuts, much appreciated by the youth of America, and which are now regularly exported from Fiji to Australia and New Zealand.

It is said that the finest salad-oil can be made from these pea-nuts, which grow most prolifically in the island. Tobacco does remarkably well in this part of Viti Levu. The finest tobacco plantation in Fiji that I know is that of Mr. Leveney; but I learn that on the north-west of the island at Ba, a Mr. Roberts, who has had some experience in the cultivation and curing of the weed in Missouri, is distancing all competitors. As in the case of every other product of this wondrous group, tobacco-growing is in its merest infancy. The Ba valley is superbly rich, and only waits for the tiller and the reaper. The great feature of Viti Levu is, however, the noble Rewa, or *Wai Levu*, 'great-water,' the largest river in the islands, and navigable for 91 miles. It empties itself into the sea by four mouths, and the deltas are fertile and cultivated. One of these deltas is traversed by a canal which saves a distance of 21 miles between Rewa and Bau, and also a considerable distance between the latter place and the main channel of the river. The canal is 2 miles long and 60 feet wide, and admits of the passage of the largest canoes. It is traditionally reported that this canal was originally constructed for military purposes. Looking at the primitive means which these natives had for the accomplishment of such an undertaking, viz., staves to loosen the earth, their hands for shovels, and baskets in lieu of barrows and carts, this channel must be looked upon as a masterpiece of barbaric engineering and patient toil. It seems, in fact, to be a reminiscence of the civilisation of a long bygone time.

The Rewa receives the waters of the Wai Manu at Navuso, about 12 miles from its mouth, and this tributary is navigable for about 10 miles. It takes its rise in the neighbourhood of Mamosi, and flows through a thickly-populated district. Thus the inland navigation by means of these two streams is equal to about 100 miles.

Whilst I am on this subject I cannot do better than quote a description of Rewa scenery, given by Mr. Macdonald some years ago:

'The scenery is very beautiful on account of the great diversity of the surface and richness of the forests. The distant mountains peeped now and again between the slopes of the hills, or when we gained an elevation, stood up boldly against the horizon. From an elevated spot the surrounding country presented the most charming aspect, enlivened by a narrow strip of the sea, with the islands of Ovalau, Wakaya, Mbatiki, Nairai, and Nyau spread upon its bosom. The forests in the district are exceedingly dense, and stored with valuable timber. The sedimentary rocks, composing the heights of *Koroi*, abound in foraminifera. Fossil casts of animal and vegetable structures were everywhere to be seen, so case-hardened apparently by a superficial layer of oxide of iron, that their forms stand out in bold relief on the large slabs of rock. The whole district is full of interest to the geologist, who may examine the layers of an ancient marine bed now elevated about 400 feet above the level of the sea; and abutting against mountain masses of breccia and conglomerate, consisting of fragments of close-grained primary lavas, cemented together by minute detritus of the same materials.

'At Navuso, the junction of the Wai Manu, the banks of the Rewa exhibit a rich ferruginous sandy basis, with a fine alluvial surface 4 to 5 feet in depth. The river runs at first nearly due north from Navuso to Kasavu, a distance of about 3 miles; then winds suddenly westward, Bau lying to the north-east. The banks on the right hand then passed rather abruptly into rude hilly country. Continuing our course from Navuso, we noticed a few beautiful Niusawa trees (a species of *areca*) growing on the point opposite Nakandi, and every reach onwards from this exhibited more loveliness and picturesque effect. Naitasiri opened when we rounded a richly-wooded point of the river, called Wai-ni-Kumi, literally 'Water of the Beard.' A superstition connected with it exists among the people, that beardless boys may expedite the growth of their beard by bathing the chin in the water dripping from the rocks. The latter were of a sedimentary formation, presenting a nearly vertical face, over which a small stream of water was rushing down. This stream might possibly then be much augmented after heavy rains; but it is the only approach to a waterfall occurring in the district. Rich foliage, embowered with creeping plants, beauteous trees, ferns, and *Niu Sawa* trees everywhere met the eye. All the intervening spaces, but more especially the immediate banks of the river, are covered with tall grass and humbler herbage. The river gradually narrows from Wai-ni-Kumi towards Naitasiri, but widens out again at the latter place, the left bank in particular rising to a considerable height.'

After following the course of the river for about 10 miles through the heart of the country in a N.N.W. direction, Mr. Macdonald proceeds:

'Here the vegetation was more beautiful than anything it is possible to conceive. There is a particularly remarkable species of *flagilaria*, with a stem of about 4 inches in circumference, scaling the tallest trees by means of its prehensile leaves. Having left this place, we proceeded up the river to Vakandua, a rather small but well-inhabited town, most beautifully situated on elevated land, and surrounded by river and forest scenery. Proceeding up the river, past the town of Nondo-Yavu-na-ta-Thaki, the scenery is most charmingly mountainous, with occasional rapids and shallows. Then Na-Seivau, famous for its hot springs, which form splendid natural baths, is reached, and the voyage is continued as far as Namosi, which lies on the right bank of the Wai Ndnia, in the luxuriant valley of Ono Bulcanga, which trends nearly east and west between rugged and lofty mountains. The sublimity of this scenery cannot be faithfully described.'

All round the islands of Viti Levu and Vanua Levu there are rich tracts of land, waiting the advent of men who will utilise them. I annex a description of an estate on the former island, near Ba, which I wrote when in the group; I fear the concluding remarks are true to this day:

'The estate comprises about 1000 acres, of which 400 acres are rich arable soil, easily worked. The remainder is composed of fine grazing land. The plantation has a sea-frontage and a good anchorage for vessels of 50 tons, and has the additional convenience of easy land carriage, there being a decline from the most inland part of the plantation to the beach. An ever-flowing stream runs through the centre of the land, and could be applied for irrigating purposes during dry seasons at a very small outlay. There are at present under cultivation about 100 acres, 80 acres of which are now producing sugar-cane of a very superior character, and the remainder is employed in the cultivation of tobacco, tapioca, maize, yams, and sweet potatoes. The sugar industry is at a complete standstill for want of the proper machinery.'

There is no place on earth of which it can be more truthfully said, 'If you tickle it with a hoe, it will laugh with a harvest,' than Fiji. The colony smiles most encouragingly, in spite of past neglect and the comparative poverty of its settlers. What it will do when benefited by some of the hoarded wealth of these islands, Mr. Home, of the Mauritius, has told us. That gentleman is no sanguine dreamer, and an annual export return of ten millions sterling is the only estimate we can anticipate of the Fiji of the future, when her powers of production have been fully developed.

Fiji, now that her tide has turned, has, I firmly believe, an era of unparalleled prosperity opening before her; and though I have no doubt on this subject, I have done my utmost to keep within the limits of hard facts, while with all sincerity I adapt the Glasgow motto to the colony—'Let Fiji flourish.'

CHAPTER XXV.

THE SAMOAN OR NAVIGATORS' ISLANDS.

SOME 630 miles to the north-east of Levuka is the Samoan or Navigators' Group of islands, second only in importance to the Fiji Archipelago in the whole of Western Polynesia. Except by occasional war-ships, there is no steam communication between Levuka and Samoa, so one has to content one's self with the uncertain voyage of an ordinary sailing-vessel. It was my good fortune to avail myself of the *Bhering*, Captain Brown, and I have pleasant memories of my week's voyage in his company. Captain Brown was a representative English sailor in true courtesy and kindliness of heart, to which he added a *bonhomie* peculiarly his own. Like all true Anglo-Polynesians, he had an inexhaustible stock of yarns, and many of these were recounted to very attentive listeners, as we lazily stretched ourselves under the awning aft to avoid a mid-day sun, or after a substantial dinner, watched the stars light up one by one the dark blue heavens above us.

The *Bhering* landed her passengers at Apia, the capital of Samoa, which is situated on the north side of the island of Upolu; but before speaking of that town, I will give a short description of the principal islands in the group.

The Navigators are situated between 169° 24′ and 172° 50′ west longitude, and between the parallels of 13° 30′ and 14° 30′ south latitude, the group being 265 miles long. There are ten inhabited islands, extending from Ta'u, the easternmost, to Savaii the most western island, viz, Ta'u Olosenga, Of'u, Aunu'u, Tutuila, Nutele, Manono, Upolu, Apolima, and Savaii. The native population may be estimated at about 34,000 to 35,000. In 1863 the native population was 35,097, and in 1874, 34,265. In 1839 Commander Wilkes visited and surveyed the group, and he states it to contain 1650 square miles, divided as follows:

	MILES.		MILES.
Savaii . . .	700	Apolima . . .	7
Upolu . . .	560	Manu'a and Ta'u . .	100
Tutuila and Aunu'u .	240	Olosenga . . .	24
Manono . . .	9	Of'u . . .	10

I have not heard that the group has been surveyed since Wilkes's time. Savaii is nearly 50 miles in length, by

20 in breadth. It has never been so populous or important as the other islands, and its inhabitants were the last to become Christians. It has a low shore with a gradually rising slope to the centre, where there are a few extinct craters to be seen. A lofty peak in the middle of the island is generally invisible through clouds. This is the highest land in the group, and according to Commander Wilkes, certainly exceeds 4000 feet. Mr. Whitmee states that he has ascended a peak in the centre of Savaii, which he measured with an aneroid, and found to be 4760 feet high. Water is comparatively scarce in some parts of Savaii, owing to the porous nature of the rock (*vesicular lava*) of which it is composed, but this applies only to a small portion, the greater part being the best watered of any of the islands. Near the shore, there are numerous springs of good fresh water. The coral reef is broken to the west and south. The soil, composed of decomposed volcanic rock and vegetable mould, is very fertile.

A curious ceremony occasionally takes place in Savaii in connection with the betrothal of any Samoan lady of rank to a chief, the leading feature of which is that the virtue of the bride-elect is publicly placed beyond a doubt in the presence of the bridegroom. I need not add that this practice has been most zealously opposed by the missionaries, Catholic and Protestant, though the conservative Samoans, like my friend the Taviuni chief, will now and again break out for the 'old paths.'

Ten miles to the eastward of Savaii is the island of Upolu. It is about 40 miles long and 13 broad. A main ridge extends from east to west, broken here and there into sharp peaks. Small ridges and gradual slopes run down to a low shore, which is encircled by a coral reef, interrupted at intervals by convenient entrances. At Apia the reef extends across a good-sized bay, which affords a harbour for ships of very large tonnage.

Olosenga is a very rocky island, about 1500 feet in height, and precipitous on every side. The principal village is situated on a strip of land in front of this precipice. It was $2\frac{1}{2}$ miles from the eastern point of this island that the subaqueous eruption of 1866 took place, which is mentioned in an earlier chapter. Olosenga is 2 miles to the west of Upolu, and is encircled by a reef. One of the features of Olosenga is a precipice 1200 feet in height.

Manono is nearly triangular in shape, and less than 5 miles in circumference. It has a mountain a few hundred feet in height, from which a splendid panoramic view of Upolu and Savaii can be obtained. Its population may be set down at about a thousand.

Tutuila is the easternmost and smallest of the three principal islands, with a length of 17 miles and a width of 5. The land is mountainous, forming here and there lofty peaks, the highest of which—Matafae—is 2327 feet above sea-level, and forms an admirable landmark for the excellent harbour of Pango-Pango. I will describe it in the words of Captain Wakeman, who was sent by Mr. W. H. Webb of New York (who at one time ran the San Francisco and Sydney mail boats) to report on its advantages as a coaling depôt :

'At daylight I found myself in the most perfect land-locked harbour that exists in the Pacific Ocean. In approaching this harbour from the south, either by night or day, the mariner has unmistakable landmarks to conduct him into port —on the port-hand, a high-peaked conical mountain 2327 feet high ; and on the starboard-hand, a flat-topped mountain 1470 feet in height. These landmarks can never be mistaken by the mariner. The entrance to the harbour is three-quarters of a mile in width between Tower Rock on the port-side, and Breaker Point on the starboard-hand, with soundings of 36 fathoms. A little more than 1 mile from Breaker Point on the starboard-hand to Goat Island on the port-hand we open out the inner harbour, which extends 1 mile west at a breadth of 3000 feet abreast of Goat Island, to 1100 feet at the head of the bay. Carrying soundings from 18 fathoms to 6 fathoms at the head of the bay, the reefs which skirt the shores are from 300 feet to 500 feet wide, and almost awash at low sea. They have at their edge from 4 fathoms to 5, 6, and 8, and deeper in the middle of the harbour. The hills rise abruptly round this bay from 800 to 1000 feet in height. They are covered from base to summit with a luxuriant growth of evergreen foliage; the little valleys which nestle at their bases, and the narrow belt of land which skirts the shore, is densely covered with cocoa-nut groves, bread-fruit, banana, orange, pine-apple, lime-trees, and a variety of tropical plants. The different streams of fresh water which pour into the placid waters of the bay, dotted with canoes, some of which are capable of carrying three hundred people, complete a most interesting picture. The island of Tutuila is 17 miles in length by 5 in breadth. There is nothing to prevent a steamer, night or day, from proceeding to her wharf. About half-way from Breaker Point to Goat Island, and near mid-channel, is Whale Rock, with 8 feet of water over it at low sea. It has a circumference of about 50 feet, and breaks frequently. A buoy obviates danger. The services of a pilot can never be required by anyone who has visited this port before, as the trade-winds from east-south-east carry a vessel from near Breaker Point with a free sheet on a north-north-west course into the harbour.'

A friend of mine, who was resident in this place twenty-two

years, says that he never knew of a longer detention than nine days to any ships in that time, and of but one gale, which came from the eastward, and unroofed a wing of his kitchen. The trade-winds are frequently liable to haul from east-south-east to east-north-east, giving a ship a chance to get out with a leading wind. At the different quarters of the moon the tide rises 4½ feet. The temperature was 82°, and the water 78° during our stay. The passing showers of rain keep the ground moist and the air fairly cool.

Pango-Pango harbour is distant from the following places as under:

	MILES.		MILES.
Auckland, N.Z. . .	1577	New Caledonia . .	1445
Vavau, Friendly Islands .	380	Sydney . . .	2410
Levuka, Fiji . .	630	Melbourne . .	2864
Tongatabu . .	475	Honolulu . . .	2283
Tahiti . . .	1250		

The climate of the Samoan Group is mild and agreeable, though in the wet season it rains there a great deal more than in Fiji, and perhaps more than in any other part of the Pacific, especially in Pango-Pango and Apia. The temperature generally ranges from 70° to 80°, but, as in Fiji, there is a constant sea-breeze. The average for two years only has been found to be 80°. The south-east trades blow steadily from April to October, being strongest in June and July. From November to March westerly winds frequently blow, but not for any length of time.

A 'blow' may be looked for in January, but it often happens that a year passes without a gale of any severity. February is as a rule fine, but a very severe 'blow' occurred in the February of 1865, when a barque was wrecked in the harbour of Apia, and the island of Manono laid almost bare as the effect of the hurricane. March is considered the most boisterous month in the year, though there are frequent exceptions to the rule. Rain falls copiously from December to March. June and July are the coolest, and September and October the hottest months; but there is really little variation of temperature. The 'blows' which do so much damage to the unencircled groups of the Pacific, rarely affect Samoa. Thus in 1840 there was a severe gale, but nothing approaching to a hurricane. In 1850 a 'hurricane' did occur, and two ships and a schooner were wrecked at Apia; and for fifteen years afterwards the islands were entirely free from anything worse than strong gales. Sometimes these are very local; for instance, in the January of 1870 a veritable cyclone passed over Tutuila, but did not touch the other islands.

The number of European or American residents may be set down at about 300; the great majority of whom are British subjects: but the States and Germany are well represented.

There are few diseases indigenous to Samoa, which is one of the healthiest places on earth. European ladies have better health in Samoa than even in Fiji, where (perhaps only at Levuka) they suffer occasionally from lassitude. The children of white parents are robust, rosy, and vigorous.

The only drawback which the Samoan Group possesses is the presence of elephantiasis, from which disease the foreign residents are not exempt. It is confined almost entirely to settlers of twelve years and upwards. Quinine is said to be an excellent remedy for it.

Elephantiasis is most prevalent in low-lying districts. In the little island of Aunu'u the inhabitants are entirely free from this scourge. Excessive *kava*-drinking aggravates it, and it may be safely said that, with the exception of elephantiasis and its incipient febrile symptoms, all the few diseases which obtain in the Pacific are due in great measure to over-indulgence in intoxicating stimulants of inferior manufacture, or to the native grog. Dysentery is a common sequel to excess in this regard, and for whites, the late Dr. Mayo told me Dr. Collis-Browne's Chlorodyne is a preventive of serious consequences. I know it cured a fellow-traveller of mine.

I do not know any part of the world where the malformations caused by elephantiasis assume such tremendous proportions as in Samoa. Dr. Turner is, I understand, engaged in a work on this topic, and he is well qualified for the task, having successfully operated on some of his suffering neighbours during his long residence in the islands. Some photographs I have seen of recent severe cases would task the credulity of anyone who had not been face to face with the reality.

On the other hand, the temperature of the islands is so mild, considering that it is within 15° of the equator, that Europeans are, as in Fiji, at all seasons of the year able to perform outdoor work without damage to their constitution. The great age to which some of the 'beachcombers' have arrived is a clear proof of the suitability of the climate to the European constitution, in addition to the fact that smiths, carpenters, timber-cutters, and men engaged in hard outdoor labour, pursue their daily tasks with perfect health. Wood-sawyers, English and American, toil in their saw-pits all day without shade of any kind, and never complain of the temperature. These men at any rate show little of the so-called enervating influences of Polynesia.

Flies and mosquitoes are as troublesome in Samoa as in Fiji. I fancy they are worse in Apia than even at Suva; but when wider clearings are made in the dense vegetation that everywhere surrounds the towns and villages, they will in all probability disappear to a great extent, as they have disappeared from Levuka.

CHAPTER XXVI.

LIFE IN SAMOA.

THE Samoan race is immensely superior to the average Fijian. The natives are tall, handsome men, of a light brown colour, many of them not being so dark as some Italians or Spaniards. They are docile, truthful, hospitable, and very lively; and in conversation among themselves, or in their dealings with foreigners, they are exceedingly courteous. They have different styles of salutation corresponding with the social rank of the person addressed. For instance, in addressing the chiefs or distinguished strangers, they use the expression *Lau Afio*, or your Majesty. In speaking to chiefs of lower rank, they address them as *Lau Susunga*, as we would use the words, your Lordship. To chiefs of yet lower degree, the term *Ali Atala* is used; and to common people the salutation is *Sau* in the singular, or *Omai* in the plural, simply meaning, 'You have arrived,' or 'You are here.' I think the language of Samoa is the most musical I ever heard, and the easiest to acquire: each syllable contains one or more vowels, and some have no consonants at all. *M* is understood before *b*, *n* before *d* and *g*, *c* and *t* are identical in pronunciation and are used indiscriminately. The language is quite different from the Fijian 'lingo;' and while a Fijian has no word to express 'Thank you,' or 'Good-morning,' or 'Good-night,' the Samoan language abounds in kindly expressions. The Fijian, when you part at night to retire to rest, says *Sa moce* ('Go to bed'). The Samoan says *Ka Lofa* ('My love'). In Fijian 'Bring me some water,' is *Kautomai na wai;* in Samoan, *Omai sa vai.* Differing from the Fijians, the men as a rule only tattoo; not on their faces, as is the case with the Maories, but on their bodies from the waist to the knee, which are entirely black for the most part, except where relieved by some gracefully executed stripes and patterns. Of these they are very proud. At a little distance you would think they wore black knee-breeches. The clothing of both sexes is, as in Fiji, a piece of calico or native cloth wound round the waist and reaching to the knees. The women generally adopt a pair of coloured handkerchiefs for their breasts and shoulders. Many of the girls and women wear the elegant *sacque*, a garment plaited at the neck and trailing a little behind. Some adhere to the *lava-lava*, or waist-cloth, which is made of a fathom of cotton print, generally of a gaudy pattern, twisted round the body from waist to below the knee; and on Sundays and holydays they wear a pinafore elaborately got up with satin and lace. The chieftesses wear in addition to this, grass mats of beautifully fine texture, hand made, and almost priceless in value. All carry the inevitable fly-flap and fan. When at work on plantations, or in the bush, or fishing, they wear a kilt of the long, handsome leaves of the *Ti* (*Dracæna terminalis —Cordyline*). If there is one thing in which the Samoans take pride, it is their mats; and they are really fine specimens of art; in fact, they esteem these mats more highly than any article of European manufacture, and the older they are, the more they are regarded. Some of them have names known all over the group. The oldest is called *Moe-e-fui-fui*, or being interpreted, 'The mat that slept among the creepers.' It got this title from its being hidden away for years among the creeping convolvulus that grows wild along the sea-shore. It is known to be two hundred years old, as the names of its owners during that long time can be traced down. The possession of one of these old mats gives the owner great power over families and land; in fact, it is a title-deed to rank and money. It is no matter if the mat is tattered and worn out; its antiquity is its value, and $500 would be scornfully refused for some of the most cherished of these hereditaments.

The Samoans, like the Fijians, spend much time in dressing their hair, which, by the aid of lime, they get to a reddish hue; and both men and women wear flowers in their hair, often blossoms of the beautiful scarlet *hybiscus*, which is generally to be found growing near their houses.

In common with other races whom nature has blessed with such an abundant supply of food growing wild at their very doors, they are not intuitively inclined for hard work, but I should certainly not describe them, considering their happy circumstances, as a lazy people. Their houses are usually circular in shape, with conical roofs, supported in the centre by two or three stout posts, and open all round, but fitted with narrow mats made of cocoa-nut leaves, which are strung together like venetian blinds, and can be let down in stormy or rainy weather, and at night.

The Samoans have five different kinds of canoes: the *Alia*, or large double canoes, some of which are capable of carrying two or even three hundred men; the *Taumualua*, from 30 to 50 feet long (these are fashioned after our whale boats); the fishing-canoes with an outrigger; and the *Soatau*, or dug-out canoe, with an outrigger, which will hold five or six people; and lastly the *Paopao*, or very small dug-out canoe, for one person.

The natives of Samoa were never by disposition cruel or fond of shedding blood; on the contrary, all their traditions contain evidence of most excellent and merciful laws, such as the providing of sanctuaries or places of refuge where a man could be secure from the vengeance of those whom he might have offended, and there was an institution of public reconciliation (a great improvement on the peace-offerings of the Fijians), whereby the life of a man could be saved even if justly forfeited in consequence of some evil deed. Moreover, in all their wars non-combatants have been respected; a curious incident could be mentioned in support of this. When there was a brush with the natives and the sailors of H.M.S. *Barracouta*, a Lieutenant was walking with naval *sang froid* in an open space at Mulinuu whilst the firing was going on. The writer said to the *Admiral* Sotomi, who had a command in the defending party, when this was related to him, 'Why didn't you fire at the lieutenant?' He replied, 'He didn't fire at *us*, so why should we want to hit *him?* We only aimed at those sailors who aimed at *us*.' Infirm persons, children, and women were never slaughtered as in Fiji. The Samoans have never been cannibals, rarely human sacrificers, or idolaters, and perhaps the readiness with which they have embraced Christianity and the extraordinary aptitude some of them seem to possess for a religious life—witness the Samoan Sisters of the Catholic Church, as well as the numerous native teachers of the Protestant mission—is due to their admirable conduct for many years.

In nearly every respect the Samoan is a totally different being from the Fijian, and the difference is all on the right side. Treachery is no part of their nature. Women are treated with the greatest respect, and children are regarded with an affection that almost amounts to extravagance.

Naturally a peace-loving and generous people, the civil wars that have been devastating their beautiful island for years have been mainly not of their own seeking. They have been generally thrust on them by foreign adventurers, whose proceedings should long ago have necessitated the armed interference of civilised powers. It is a disgrace to this age of boasted 'material progress' that the only material advancement the Samoans have made since their first acquaintance with civilised man, some sixty years ago, is their improved knowledge of rifles and gunpowder, with which the civilised traders have been careful to supply them at—of course—a reasonable profit. According to the opinion of men who have forgotten more about the South Pacific than I have ever learnt, the Samoans are the best-conducted of all the people of that region, except those of the Hervey, Austral and Union Groups, who may be considered quite abnormal people, insomuch as until visited by white men they were altogether destitute of weapons of offence.

None of the Samoans have as yet been taken away in labour vessels, as they have the strongest objection to leave their own islands, and would not of free will engage themselves as labourers. In fact, the cotton-growers and other planters in Samoa have to rely on imported labour mostly from the Line Islands, or from Niuè or Savage Island, or the New Hebrides. The former men are much darker in colour and vastly inferior in physique to the Samoans, who very naturally look down upon them. The Niuè men, on the contrary, are of a better class, and usually adopt European costume. Like the Fijians and Tongans, the Samoans have a princely carriage, and the chiefs are usually a good deal over six feet in height, and superbly limbed. A few have beards, but the majority cannot boast that ornament.

Eloquence seems to be a natural gift with Samoans, and the speeches of their orators are often replete with well-chosen metaphors. But under these flowing periods runs a vein of strong common sense and logical argument. The orator is a most important individual, for at the *fonos*, or political meetings, stalking majestically to the front, he stands leaning on a staff about six feet long, with his fly-flap over his shoulder, and pours forth a perfect torrent of eloquence for hours.

In many respects parts of the Samoan Group are even more fertile than Fiji. Cotton succeeds well, and has run wild in all the sea-coast lands; but this is all of the kidney variety, and it thus prevents the Sea Island cotton from being propagated to advantage, as the bees and other insects carrying the pollen of the wild-cotton flowers inoculate that of the Sea Island, and cause it to become coarse. Large tracts of sugar-cane and maize are cultivated by the Germans, who have also planted coffee and rice of a kind enormously prolific, which is grown upon the elevated plateaux without irrigation, it being of a species not requiring to be flooded at any time. The seed is said to have come from South America, but I am not certain as to this. Vegetables and cereals of the temperate zone do better in Samoa than in Fiji, and the Catholic missionaries have been very successful in their cultivation. Cabbages, cauliflowers, peas, beans, carrots, asparagus, cucumbers, and melons of every kind, with all the pot-herbs of Europe, are to be seen growing luxuriantly in the gardens of the Catholic clergy. Potatoes, as in Fiji, turn to *komotès* (or watery) in the second season in the low lands, and onions do not exceed grape-shot in size, though there is reason to believe that both these vegetables would grow very well upon the level summits of the high mountain lands. Barley, and the various kinds of millet, produce abundant crops, and English grass mixed with clover takes ready hold of the ground, and spreads rapidly. The products, however, more especially suited to the climate and local conditions of Samoa are cotton, coffee, sugar, tamarinds, tobacco, indigo, vanilla, rice, cinnamon (a tree analogous to which is a native of Samoa), nutmegs, ginger, arrowroot, and the various oil-producing trees. Tea and cinchona would undoubtedly do well in Samoa.

For the cultivation of the two last, no climate or country presents more favourable conditions. There is no reason why Englishmen, having once conquered the popular prejudice that tea cannot be successfully cultivated or manufactured by Europeans, or outside certain localities, should not enter upon this industry in the great islands of the Pacific, especially as the amount of labour required is so small in comparison with that necessary for the cultivation and preparation of coffee, sugar, cotton, or tobacco.

Tea adapts itself to various temperatures in a manner impossible to coffee, is extremely hardy, and bears a crop which defies rains or hurricanes; it luxuriates on high and sloping grounds, especially those of ancient forest where the giant trees are allowed at intervals to remain, affording a shade in which it delights. It is, of all products, one of the most suited to the woodlands of Samoa. The seed could be easily procured from China, and if gathered at the fitting season, and packed in damp sand or sugar, would arrive in good germinating condition. The tea-shrub yields its first paying crop in the third year from the planting of the seed. For the plantation labour, the services of Polynesians are suitable, and easily procurable. The skilled workmen required for the manipulation of the leaf are to be met with in Hawaii, or can be obtained from China, and at a low rate of remuneration.

All the long list of Fiji plants applies to Samoa, which has in addition some trees with very fragrant blossoms that might be used for the preparation of scents: notably the datura tree, which grows to the height of an ordinary cottage, and which is completely covered in the season by lovely cream-white flowers with yellow petals, which are used by the women as bouquet-holders, and which emit an almost too powerful perfume resembling that of the hyacinth.

Cattle thrive well in Samoa, as in Fiji, and many of the natives possess horses on which they ride about from town to town.

The following jottings of the memoranda of my short residence in Samoa will perhaps add a personal interest to the preceding particulars.

I had seen something of the exquisite beauty of the scenery of the South Pacific islands before my visit to Samoa, but certainly I was not prepared for the glorious sight that met my eyes as I entered the harbour of Apia. The Bay of Naples, lovely as it is, cannot in my humble opinion be compared with it. The harbour of Apia, Samoa, is a vast semicircular expanse of the purest blue water—water so transparent that you can look over the ship's side and distinctly see the variegated colours of the coral grottoes fathoms below, and notice the bright-hued fish darting here and there in shoals. Protecting this smooth-water anchorage is the coral reef, which stretches from point to point, with just a break large enough to allow ships to enter with comparative ease. On this reef the surf breaks often as high as the foreyard. On one side is the hilly headland of Mulinunu, on the other the sandy point of Matautu. As I entered, the bay was alive with dug-outs and outriggers, manned or 'womanned' as the case might be. As a background, there is the white coralline sand of the beach, fringed with the stately cocoa palms, while the coo of the pigeon and the all but too powerful aromatic scents of many flowers compel the acquiescence of the other senses to the dogma of that of vision, that this place is Nature at her best, God's creation in its earthly perfection.

The Bay of Apia is divided by the outfall of two rivers into three parts, the centre of which is the town of Apia, which consists of a long straggling street on the beach, but with houses on both sides. On higher ground is the Catholic Cathedral, and bishop's and clergy houses, a capital hotel called the Pacific Stores, the British Consulate establishment, and the Wesleyan chapel. At Mulinunu there are the offices of the American and German Consulates, a few stores, and a ship-building yard, while at Matautu are the stores of Messrs. Godeffroy, some minor stores, and a native village, which, charmingly ensconced in a grove of the cocoa palms, and sheltered by breadfruit trees, oranges, limes, and bananas, boasts the residence of the native Governor of the district, Patioli, and until lately his sister, the Samoan belle, Coé-o-le-Sasa o le Tuanasaga, the richest and perhaps the prettiest girl in the islands, though it should in justice be stated there is no lack of female beauty among the Samoans. Coé is now married to the chief Malietoa.

One feels quickly at home in the Navigators' Islands, much more so, in fact, than in any other group it has been my lot to visit. The Samoans are gentle and friendly to a degree, and as you pass along the street you are greeted with the kindly expression, in the soft idiom of the native language, 'My love to you!' After making the acquaintance of the estimable Catholic bishop, and lunching with him on a substantial meal of eggs and vegetables (it was a day of abstinence), I accompanied Monseigneur Elloz to the top of a hill behind the town, where I inspected the Mission School and College, and was astonished at the perfect order of the scholars, as well as their marked proficiency in some very advanced stages of the art of knowledge. If the view from Wai-Wai, in Savu Savu Bay, was beautiful, what shall I say—how shall I describe that gem of South Sea beauty which met my eyes as I looked seaward from this Samoan outpost of the Holy See? Surrounding us on all sides, and descending to the snow-white beach, was the dense mass of evergreen foliage, varied here and there with the yellow, red, and white of scented flowers. The blue sea was just laving the outward edge of the coralline sand, and beating with fury against the coral breakwater beyond, and from that it spread as far as the wistful eye could reach. I sat down, and revelling in that living dream of Paradise, I reflected on a certain passage of Holy Writ which says, 'Eye hath not seen, nor ear heard, nor hath it entered into the heart of man to conceive' what that celestial glory is, which is promised for the just, when time has given place to eternity.

A few days later I was invited by my friend Patioli to a *kava* feast, and after a good gallop, in company with himself, his charming sister, the British Consul (who is, I regret to say, now no more), and a few other friends, including a gallant naval officer, we adjourned to his house. We, the Europeans, were seated on a pile of mats at one end of the house, and all round, a little below us, were some twenty chiefs. A large wooden bowl standing on four legs was brought in, and ceremoniously placed in front of the princess and one of her cousins, who then took small pieces of the root, which a lad had carefully sliced, and after rinsing their mouths and fingers with a little water, thoroughly masticated (shall I say *ruminated?*) a few mouthfuls of the root, and delicately placed the lumps, each about the size of a walnut, into the bowl, which was then almost filled with water. This was well mixed, and the fibre deftly strained away with a bunch of the long fibres of the inner bark of the hybiscus. A half cocoa-nut shell was then filled by a dexterous twist and squeeze of the bunch of fibre, and handed to us each in turn, as our names were mentioned, with great ceremony.

Each one emptied the shell at a single draught (it is rude to sip it), everyone clapped their hands and shouted '*O mārā!*' The *kava* had just the same flavour as that I tasted in Fiji, except perhaps that the Apia *kava* had a distinct flavour of horseradish as well as soap and water. Afterwards we partook of dinner, which consisted of at least fifty different dishes placed on the floor. Soup, fish, fowl, pork, snails, grubs, cooked and uncooked entrails of fish, formed the extensive *menu*, which, however, only afforded me one or two dishes to my taste. The most entertaining feature of the repast was the vagaries of the old magnate upon whom devolved the duty of explaining to us the different viands, and the manner of partaking of them. The mode of his procedure was thus: taking an enormous bite out of a piece of raw pork, or a handful of grubs, he would hand the remainder with an insinuating gesture to the European guest nearest to him, who would first regard it with a horrified gaze, and then with a bland smile give it to his neighbour, with the muttered remark, 'I pass.' This reckless course was conscientiously adhered to throughout the repast by the old fellow, and we were agreeably surprised to find that he appeared next day to be none the worse for his labours. His digestive powers must be remarkable. Had he died in the cause I would have been compelled to say, 'He did his duty well.'

After the meal we went out and enjoyed our pipes and *siluies*—a kind of cigarette made by wrapping a little tobacco in a piece of banana leaf, and of which the girl who makes it takes the preliminary suck to light and *sweeten*—and then we returned to see a native dance which had been arranged for our special amusement. This was performed in the centre of the hut by several girls, Miss—I beg her pardon, Her Royal Highness—Coé being one, and consisted of several *pas fan-*

tastiques, the native company sitting round and beating time with their hands, whilst some of the girls kept up a most melodious tune in capital time. When this performance was over, there were some songs sung in chorus by the young ladies, who seemed to thoroughly enjoy themselves. I do not know what they were about, for at *that* time I did not know a word of the language; but I fancy they were humorous and broadly personal, for there was much laughter, and I cannot help thinking that *we* were the subjects of it. Then a pack of cards was produced, and the natives played a very curious game, which Coé very kindly tried to teach me; but I fear she found me a very stupid pupil, and my mistakes caused a great deal of fun, and I found I had very soon *gambled* away all my tobacco. I was then escorted to my boat by most of the company, and I came to the conclusion that of all the good-tempered, harmless, childlike people I have ever had the good fortune to meet, the Samoans bear the palm.

A few days later the Catholics were keeping the feast of Easter, and it was certainly very strange to listen (in what the great majority of English people would consider one of the 'cannibal islands) to the soft voices of some hundred of the natives joining in the grand old hymn of paschal time, '*O filii et filiæ.*'

Though it will be seen by what I have said that the Samoans are in a comparatively very advanced stage of civilisation, it would be rash to counsel Englishmen or others to invest money in land there until the group obtains the protection of the British flag. That a large majority of the natives would enthusiastically welcome annexation, and that sooner or later it will be forced by British immigration from Fiji on the Imperial Government, I have not the least doubt.

CHAPTER XXVII.

GODEFFROY AND CO., THE SOUTH SEA KINGS.

The firm of Godeffroy of Hamburg has been in existence for about a century. Until about 1857 they maintained a fleet of vessels, many of which traded in the Indian Sea, under the direction of an agent established at Cochin, while others made regular voyages to the Spanish main, Valparaiso being their rendezvous. At Cochin they maintained a large cocoa-nut oil-pressing establishment. At Valparaiso their captains took instructions from a general agent, whose subordinates resided at Coquimbo, Valdivia, Takuano, Guayaquil, San José de Guatemala, and elsewhere. Their trade was chiefly in saltpetre, copper, and cochineal.

At this time it was usual for Tahitian traders to dispose of their produce at Valparaiso, and to return to the Society Islands with cargoes of flour for the use of the French garrison. The attention of Mr. Anselm, the local agent of Messrs. Godeffroy, was attracted to their operations, and he decided on visiting the islands. When there, he at once saw the great profits made by Messrs. Hort Brothers and Mr. John Brander, both in cocoa-nut oil and pearl-shell, and he established an agency in the Tuamotu Group. Messrs. Hort and Brander had separately branch establishments in the Samoan Archipelago, which they used as an intermediate station between Tahiti and Sydney. Anselm, following their example, removed there, and, under instructions from his principals in Hamburg, made it the headquarters of their operations in the Pacific. Mr. Anselm was lost at sea, but the establishment he founded flourished and soon assumed large proportions. To use Mr.

Sterndale's words: 'By the exercise of tact, and a show of liberality among the natives, he and his successor, Mr. Theodore Weber, in great measure swallowed up the trade of the Samoan Group, and in a manner thrust both Hort and Brander off their own ground.'

In 1872 the establishment of the Godeffroys at Apia consisted of a superintendent, a cashier, eleven clerks, a harbour-master, two engineers, ten carpenters, two coopers, four plantation managers, a surgeon, and a land-surveyor. These were the permanent establishment, and were all Europeans, and, naturally enough, mostly Germans. In addition there were numerous supernumeraries of all nationalities, among whom may be counted half-breeds, Portuguese, and Chinamen. They generally employed, as plantation labourers, about 400 Polynesians, imported from the Savage and Line Islands. Their property at that time, and it has immensely increased since then, comprised a commodious harbour, a building-yard for small vessels, three plantations containing an aggregate of about 400 acres under cultivation, and something like 25,000 acres of purchased land, of which it may be truthfully said that the greater proportion is not to be surpassed in fertility in any part of the tropics. Mr. Sterndale says: 'It was bought at a low rate, not upon an average exceeding 75 cents per acre, and paid for chiefly in ammunition, arms, or such articles of barter as are most in vogue among semi-barbarous people.' In September, 1879, about 4500 acres were under cotton cultivation, and 1000 Polynesian labourers were employed.

The land consists chiefly of alluvial valleys of astonishing richness and elevated plateaux of fertile volcanic soil, covered in many large tracts with valuable timber. Large streams intersect the estates, and these are not only made available for floating down logs, but afford water-power for driving mills.

One-third of the estate comprises ancient cultivations abandoned in consequence of civil wars.

During the progress of these internecine disturbances, Messrs. Godeffroy possessed exceptional advantages in dealing with the natives, as they had a manufactory of arms at Liége, in Belgium (the 'Birmingham of the Netherlands'), by means of which they could supply the instruments of fraternal murder—or war, if the term is to be preferred—at a cheap rate, with a 'reasonable profit.'

Messrs. Godeffroy gradually abandoned the Tuamotus, and other islands claimed as dependencies of France, partly for the reason that about 1867, mother-of-pearl commanded an unusually low price; but more in consequence of their determination to strike out new channels for themselves. With this view they pushed their agencies southward to the Friendly Archipelago, including Nieuè or Savage Island, Fortuna and Wallis Island, northward throughout the whole range of the Kingsmills and the isles in their vicinity, that is to say, the Tokalau, Ellis, and Gilbert Groups. Then they approached the Marshall Group, and so got to the Carolines, and as far as Yap, a great island at the entrance of the Luzon Sea, where they purchased 3000 acres of land, and established a large depôt, intended to be an intermediate station between their trading-post at Samoa and their old-established agencies at Cochin and China. A glance at a chart of the Pacific will show the extent of their operations, Samoa being in 169° W., and Yap, one of the Pelew Islands, in 134° 21′ E. In fact, they had an agent in every productive island inhabited by natives sufficiently well-disposed to permit a white man to reside among them.

In 1873, the Godeffroys maintained agents in the following islands to the north of the Samoan Group:

The Union Group (or Tokelau), which consists of three islands, Takafao, Nukunono, and Oatafu.

The Ellis Group, Nukufetau, which is the property of Messrs. Godeffroy, they having purchased it from the natives. It has an excellent harbour, and is the only island of the archipelago, extending between the Navigators and the Carolines, which contains any deposit of pearl oyster; but the quality is very inferior, the shell being small, and the pearls of little value.

Oaitapu and St. Augustine.

The Tarawau or Gilbert Group, commonly spoken of as the Kingsmills; Arorai, Tamana, Peru, Onotoa, Nukunau, Tapetuia Nonoiti, Maiana, Tarawa, Apiang, Marakei, Makiu, and Puturitari. This includes all the Kingsmills, with the exception of Apemama, Kuria, and Aranuka, which belonged to the King Tem Baiteke, who for years would not allow any Europeans to settle on his islands. While in the Pacific I heard that the great Hamburg monopoly had an agent there, but of this I am doubtful.

In the Marshall Group: Ebon, Jaluit, Namerick, Mille, and Awe.

In the Carolines: Strong Island, Ascension, and Yap, and also in the Palaos or Pelew Group.

And in Western Polynesia, in New Britain and New Ireland, and also in the New Hebrides.

We have so far traced the scope of the operations of this gigantic establishment before the flash-in-the-pan prosperity of Berlin tempted them to speculations which had such unfavourable results. Let me now quote from the New Zealand blue-book (printed, by authority, at Wellington in 1874) the statements of their employé, Mr. Sterndale, explaining what was their *modus operandi*. These are Mr. Sterndale's words:

One remarkable circumstance in respect to the operations of this famous mercantile house, and to which their great success may in some degree be attributed, is that they pay as a rule very low wages, but liberal commissions. Thus masters of ships belonging to them, and ranging from 500 to 1000 tons, receive no more than $25 per month on voyages which extend from one to three years out and home; but over and above this, they receive 3 per cent. on the net profits of the venture . . . The profits on their European goods are very great, insomuch as a strict regulation exists among them all that to no person whatsoever, including the servants of the firm, are they permitted to sell any article of trade at less than 100 per cent. advance on the cost price, exclusive of freight and commission. The manager for Messrs. Godeffroy, in the choice of his employés on the various isles of the Pacific, takes little account of nationality; many of his agents in the outlying groups are English or American, as are most of the mariners who have run wild in these seas during past years, and so got a thorough knowledge of the native language and habits. Theodore Weber is a very shrewd man of the world, although young, and the great development of the Godeffroy house is largely owing to his enterprise. He had but three questions usually to put to a man who sought employment of him: 'Can you speak the language?' 'Can you live among the natives without quarrelling with them?' 'Can you keep your mouth shut?' *i.e.*, concerning your masters' business when you meet with white men. To a man who can return satisfactory answers to these queries, Godeffroy never refuses employment. He gets the means of transport to those isles upon which he is to be at home; everything necessary to build a stone house, and a stock-of-trade to put into it. They pay no salaries; they simply trust a man with so much goods, and expect of him, within a reasonable time, so much produce at a fixed rate. There is another point upon which they lay great weight: 'Have a woman of your own, no matter what island you take her from; for a trader without a wife is in eternal hot water.' Lastly, they impose the condition: 'Give no assistance to missionaries either by word or deed (beyond what is demanded of you by common humanity); but wheresoever you may find them, use your best influence with the natives to obstruct and exclude them.' It would occupy too much space for me to explain the reasons of this last condition; it is enough to say, that it has originated on very simple grounds. Throughout the Pacific for the past twenty-five years, there has been a constant struggle for the mastery between missionaries and merchants, each being intensely jealous of the influence over native affairs obtained by the other. Merchants make the greatest profits out of savages, for the reason that savages are content to sell their produce for blue beads, tomahawks and tobacco. When these savages are brought under the influence of the missionaries, they are instructed to demand payment in piece goods wherewith to clothe themselves, and in coin for the purpose of subscribing to the funds of the missionary societies. This reduces the profits of the merchants, who bitterly resent such interference. Moreover, the English missionaries were for years the grand opponents of the Messrs. Godeffroy in the matter of Bolivian coin, and although the firm came off victors, they have never forgotten or forgiven their ancient antagonists.

Another singular feature of the Godeffroy system, so essentially peculiar in many respects, was the sending of their vessels to sea from their headquarters at Samoa with sealed orders, so that no one on board knew positively where they were bound for, until in a certain latitude the master opened his instructions in the presence of his mate. Furthermore, they shipped no man as mate who was not fully competent to fulfil the duties of captain in case of need, and they did not insure their ships. It has been a matter of conjecture with many what could have been the object of Messrs. Godeffroy in purchasing such a vast tract of land as Samoa. I have enjoyed peculiar facilities for knowing their exact intentions. Very much of their land is so elevated as to possess a mild temperature well suited to the European constitution. It consists of fertile plateaux, anciently inhabited and cultivated. Their idea was to subdivide it among German emigrants, to whom they would lease it in small lots with the option of purchase, Godeffroy to provide means of transport and all necessaries to begin with. It was proposed that the settlers should cultivate corn, coffee, tobacco, cinchona, and other produce which had been scientifically and successfully experimented upon, while the low lands in the vicinity of the sea-beach were to be devoted to the growth of cocoa, palms, sugar-cane, rice, jute, etc., by the labour of Chinese, who were intended to be brought over in families and established as tenants on a small scale, so as to do away entirely with the idea of servitude. The Franco-German war prevented the realisation of this scheme at the time intended. The results, there can be no doubt, would have been very great and certainly beneficial to Messrs. Godeffroy, tho white settlers, and the influence of the German Empire. It is to be hoped that the idea, which they have been compelled to abandon, may be acted on by our own countrymen at no distant date.

The Government of the then North German Confederation regarded the matter with paternal interest, and several personal interviews and a voluminous correspondence passed between the senior partner of the house of Godeffroy and Herr (now Prince) von Bismarck, who had been great friends in youth, and who did not hesitate to lend his aid in furthering this new field for German advancement. The matter had not been long under discussion, when the approval of the Prussian authorities took a practical shape. Plans, prepared upon the ground by a surveyor of the locality intended for a settlement, were laid before the Government of Berlin; a programme of the course of colonisation to be adopted was drawn up; extraordinary powers were given to the German Consul at Samoa; grants of arms of precision from the Royal arsenals were made for the protection of the settlement, and the *Hertha* (the first, it is said, of the continental ironclads of Europe to pass through the Suez Canal) received orders to proceed from China to Samoa, to settle all disputes between the Germans and the chiefs of that group, and by a judicious display of power to prepare the way for the first detachment of military settlers, who were to leave Hamburg as soon as her commander should have submitted his report.

At the same time the Messrs. Godeffroy had completed arrangements with their representative in Valparaiso to ship to Samoa a number of mules and their Chilian drivers, for the purpose of opening a regular communication between the north and south coasts of Upolu, over the great central dividing range. Orders were also given to the manager at Cochin to despatch several Chinese families who had resided for many years at that place in the employment of the Hamburg house, in order to systematically commence upon the Samoan land the cultivation of rice and other Oriental products.

This was a well-conceived project, but owing to the march of events in Europe it collapsed before it was put into operation. The *Hertha* was countermanded in the Indian Sea, France having declared war against Germany. Hamburg was ruinously blockaded by the French fleet. Messrs. Godeffroy, with all their business knowledge and amateur statesmanship, severely felt the effects of the war and the blockade from which not even the patronage of the man of blood and iron could extricate them. By giving his powerful support to the well-conceived plan of a South Sea Island Company with an Imperial guarantee, Bismarck did his utmost for the firm, but by a majority of sixteen the Berlin Reichstag refused to set Humpty Dumpty up again.

CHAPTER XXVIII.

THE CAREER OF 'BULLY HAYES.'

ONE of the most respected of the inhabitants of Apia is Mrs. Hayes, the widow of the notorious 'Bully Hayes,' perhaps the last of the pirates of the Pacific. No sketch of Coral Lands would approach completeness if it did not give some account of this man's exploits, as for more than twenty years he was the terror of all honest men in that wide region. His first appearance at the islands of Hawaii was in 1858, when he and his first officer were put ashore from the ship *Orestes.* Hayes was at that time accompanied by his wife. In all his travels he used to be accompanied by a female companion of some kind or other, whom he picked up and dropped as the fancy took him. He left Honolulu in the early part of 1859 for San Francisco, and some two months afterwards he appeared at Kahului, on Maui, in command of a brig, bound to New Caledonia, and while negotiating for a load of cattle, he was taken in charge by the late Mr. Treadway, then sheriff of Maui, for violating the revenue laws in entering a closed port. The captain was highly indignant with his first officer for telling him that it was not necessary to enter at the Lahaina

Custom House, and treated the sheriff with distinguished consideration, invited him to dinner, and requested him to pilot the vessel to Lahaina. Mr. Treadway blandly consented; the brig was got under way, but when clear of the land, the captain, dropping his suavity, informed him that his destination was New Caledonia, and that he could have a passage there for a consideration, or he could go ashore in his boat which was alongside. The sheriff had no alternative; and he was compelled to leave, and witness his late prisoner triumphantly shaping his course for the setting sun.

The next mail from the coast brought the necessary papers to the United States Consul, authorising him to arrest Captain Hayes, and seize the brig. It appears that he had landed in San Francisco with a capital of fifty dollars, which he had borrowed when in Honolulu of the Rev. Dr. Damon. With this money for a basis of credit he bought the brig, fitted her for sea, shipped a crew, and set sail, paying for nothing but his water. This vessel was sunk off Wallace's Island, where part of the crew landed by means of a raft, while Hayes with his passengers made their way in the boat to the Navigators' Islands.

He then disappeared for some time, but finally was heard of at Batavia in charge of a barque chartered for Europe with a load of coffee. The Dutch East India Company, however, becoming acquainted with some of his past history, was glad to pay him the charter-money and get the coffee ashore again.

His next voyage was from Hong Kong to Melbourne, with a load of Chinese passengers. After being out for some time, he was informed by a ship which he spoke that he would have to pay fifty dollars per head on the Chinamen before he could land them. He kept on the even tenour of his way, however, until he arrived off Melbourne, when he choked both his pumps, started all his fresh water, and set his colours half-mast, union down, as if in sore distress. Two steamers soon came to his assistance and offered to tow him into port; but the captain's humanity overcame all selfish feelings, and he replied, 'Save these people, and let the ship sink. If she is afloat when you return we will try and get her in.' The Chinamen were landed, the steamers paying the head-money according to the laws of Victoria; but when they returned for Hayes, he was not to be found. His next cargo of Chinese were landed without trouble, as he had them all made British subjects previous to starting.

'Bully Hayes' was then lost sight of again, no one being able to learn anything of his doings or whereabouts, except that he occasionally dawned upon Tahiti like a comet, and disappeared as mysteriously as he came. Presently he commenced his career as a trader among the South Sea Islands, and after raiding and robbing stations for a couple of years, he was found under arrest at Upolu, in charge of the British Consul. Just then the renowned Captain Ben Pease arrived in the brig *Leonora*. Captain Hayes's chronometers required rating, and he obtained permission to take them on board the *Leonora* for that purpose. Next morning the brig was gone, with Hayes as a passenger, and shortly after turned up at Shanghai. Before she had been ten days in port Pease was in prison, and Hayes was owner of the brig. He fitted her for sea, as usual only paying one bill, which, in this case, was for a spare mainyard, and set off down the China coast, levying black-mail on its villages for means to carry out his speculations in the Pacific.

In Saigon, Hayes was chartered to take a cargo of rice to Hong Kong and way ports. At one of these by-ports the owner went ashore to make a sale of rice, while Hayes kept the vessel outside to save expense. The owner turned one corner of a street and the first officer the other, the latter immediately going back on board the ship, which left, leaving the owner to wonder what it all meant. Bankok was soon reached, and the cargo of rice sold at a good figure. The *Leonora* was newly coppered, and a complete outfit taken on board for the Pacific trade. The mail steamer entered the port with the owner of the rice on board, as Hayes was leaving. This gentleman had never met Hayes but once when he chartered the vessel.

We next hear of the U.S.S. *Naragansett*, Captain Meade, as being engaged in searching for Hayes, who was found at Upolu, arrested, and taken on board the man-of-war, where he had no difficulty in winning the hearts of both men and officers, and after three days' detention he was liberated, there being no evidence against him, and all being firmly convinced that he was a much-injured and most worthy man. Insinuating to Captain Meade that he was in want of some sails, he was supplied with all he required, and the gentlemanly pirate departed with the best wishes of captain and officers.

How he stole the schooner *Giovanni Apiani* is worth recording. She belonged to a Frenchman whom Hayes met at one of the islands in the South Pacific, and with whom he made a bargain for an interest in the schooner, in consideration of a certain sum of money and a share in some of the stations belonging to Hayes. One fine day, as they were sailing smoothly past an island, whose beauties the Frenchman was admiring, he was gently touched behind the ear, and as he turned his head a blow between the eyes 'put him to sleep,' as he subsequently expressed it, to wake on shore, with the schooner out of sight. In a moment of inconsistent faith in human nature Hayes entrusted Captain Pinkham with the schooner, and he never saw her again.

After the loss of another brig at Strong's Island, Hayes changed his tactics, and actually succeeded in persuading the missionaries that he was converted from the error of his ways. How he got possession of the schooner which took him thence to Guam I do not know; but after his arrival there he was captured while bathing, and it was generally believed that his romantic career had come to an end, but he resumed the religious *rôle*, this time as a Catholic, and bamboozled the clergy of Manilla as effectually as he had the American missionaries.

The Spanish authorities had sufficient evidence to garotte twenty men, but Bully Hayes was equal to the occasion; and whether aided or not by a mistaken interest of the clergy in their new and most promising convert, he managed to escape, and turned up at San Francisco, where he succeeded in stealing a schooner called the *Lotus* (I know he paid twelve and a half dollars for water, but for nothing else), and in this vessel he was cruising when I was in the Pacific.

Captain Hayes was a handsome man of above the middle height, with a long brown beard always in perfect order. He had a charming manner, dressed always in perfection of taste, and could cut a confiding friend's throat or scuttle his ship with a grace which, at any rate in the Pacific, was unequalled.

Hayes honoured Fiji with an occasional visit, but got somewhat shy of Levuka after the group became annexed to Great Britain. A friend of mine, who resides at Fiji's capital, told me the following characteristic anecdote of him: The Captain was in harbour with his schooner, and wanting a good supply of stores for a long cruise, gave a heavy order to my friend.

This was immediately executed, and goods and account were sent aboard. Next morning, when payment was looked for, his schooner was doing her utmost, under a depressing want of wind, to put as much distance as possible between her keel and Ovalau.

A round sum being at stake, my friend determined on a stern-chase; the native 'boys' pulled pluckily, and the schooner was overhauled. Captain Hayes, bland as ever, was most courteous.

'In what way could he serve the Levuka party? Any parcels or letters to take? Delighted, to be sure; but it was fortunate for them that the wind was so light, as by this time he ought to have been well out of the group.'

Somewhat dumbfounded at this reception, and hardly caring to drink the proffered 'nip,' my friend delicately hinted at his firm's transaction with the gallant skipper. The captain grew indignant.

'*Whose* account?' He was told.

'Paid yesterday,' was the response.

The merchant implied in return that he regretted such was not the case.

'Send for So-and-so.' He appeared.

'What's this I hear? Messrs. So-and-So's account not paid. You had my money and instructions; and you knew we left at daybreak.' Then the captain gave his purser a lecture in the choicest invective of the Southern Seas. Apologising to the merchant and his clerk for thus losing his temper, he explained that his drunken scoundrel of a subordinate had had the exact money wrapped up in the bill, and he would have to find it. In a few minutes the purser returned with the amount, as Hayes had stated, and the Levukans left the schooner, reflecting perhaps on the sin of harbouring unfounded suspicion against the innocent victim of a servant's negligence.

This worthy died what may be called a natural death, as he was, very deservedly perhaps, knocked on the head by an officer he had brutally ill-treated. The gossip of the Pacific credits him with many murders, especially of women.

CHAPTER XXIX.

PEARL FISHING AND 'BEACHCOMBERS.'

THERE can be no doubt that if the innumerable low coral islands scattered all over the face of the South Sea, and only occasionally visited by chance traders, were in the Eastern Hemisphere instead of the Pacific, they would long ago have had their great intrinsic value turned to profitable account by the commercial races of the world. One has only to reflect on the endless disputes between the great Powers interested in the coral banks of Messina, the amber dredging-grounds of the Baltic Coast, or the cod-fisheries of Newfoundland, and then to consider the unheeded wealth of Polynesia, to gauge the indifference with which the world regards it even now.

No exploring parties are required, the exploration has been accomplished over and over again. The question is, who in the future shall benefit by it? In this regard I do not intend to refer to the countless products I have mentioned in speaking of Fiji, Samoa, or Tonga. I deal only with pearl-fishing, and *bêche-de-mer*, as I have had exceptional opportunities of ascertaining the condition and mode of conducting these important industries.

All Australian colonists have heard of the extraordinary profits made some years ago by men like Captain Cadell and other pearl-fishers on the coast of North Australia. The same shell exists in vast quantities in various localities of the South Pacific under more favourable conditions, inasmuch as the divers are obtainable on the spot or in the neighbourhood, with the additional advantage that the food they require is produced spontaneously on the scene of their labours. For many years past, in the Pacific, men accustomed to the shell trade have been in the habit of collecting shell and disposing of it to such vessels as might chance to visit them, at prices ranging from £12 to £20 per ton, and considered themselves well paid, whereas the prices obtained in the London market have varied from £80 to £150, or even more.

It has been said that the South Sea shell is inferior to that obtained on the coasts of North Australia, Manilla, or Ceylon. This, however, is not really the case; but it is quite true that years ago Tahitian, the name by which South Sea shell is usually known, became greatly depreciated in the European market, in consequence of the merchants of that place having foolishly persisted in cleaning the shell before shipment. To accomplish this object the more readily, the traders used to throw them out on the sandy beach of the island where they were obtained, and let them lie for a day or two in the hot sun; the effect of which was that all the rough edges, knots, and coral lumps which were attached to them cracked off and left them smooth, but at the same time denuded of the splendid natural lustre they would have retained had they been placed under cover immediately the living fish were removed from them. The Manilla fishers were always aware of this fact, and profited by their knowledge; in consequence of which their shell has for years past commanded a very high price, and is, as I write, quoted at £100 a ton. The bulk of the Manilla shell is moreover obtained from the Pacific, that is to say, from Hogoleu, Lugunor, and other great islands of the Caroline Group, and is the same oyster which is found over the whole Pacific on all islands possessing the conditions necessary for its existence.

What pearl deposits are worth in other parts of the world may be gathered from the fact that according to returns published by the Indian Government, the value of a pearl bank in the Straits of Manaar (to the north of Ceylon), of 2 miles in circumference, with a depth of 7 fathoms or thereabouts, is estimated at from £35,000 to £40,000, subject to the royalty demanded by the authorities. The shell lies thick there, more so than is usual in the Pacific; but when we consider that in the latter case many lagoons are to be found, from 12 to 20 miles in diameter, wherein, so far as the shoal water extends, it is not possible to look over the side of the boat without seeing shell on the bottom ready for collection, and with neither dues, royalties, nor purchase-money to pay, it is very obvious that the profits to be made in the Pacific would equal or exceed those made in the Indian Sea.

In the atolls of the Low Archipelago there are numerous pearl-fisheries, the lagoons of which are in themselves beautiful beyond description.

They are generally shallow, though in some places they exhibit vast hollows, with an apparent depth of 50 or more fathoms. Their appearance is most extraordinary and beautiful, the water, from the absence of the *débris* of streams or any kind of alluvium (from the fact of the land being entirely composed of coral rock and gravel), exhibits so surpassing a transparency that an object the size of a man's hand may in calm weather be distinctly seen at a depth of 10 fathoms.

The aspect of the bottom is that of a wilderness of marine vegetation of the most wonderful forms and gorgeous colours, seeming in some places to be spread over the surface of sloping hills, in others to be growing out from the sides of tall pillars or towers pierced with vast caves, in which the refracted beams of the sunshine cause the water to glow with the colours of the opal, and the innumerable species of zoophytes clinging to the rocks to glisten like gems; while between the huge caverned masses are wide spaces floored with sand, perfectly level, and white as snow, upon which the great green mounds covered with coral trees throw fantastic shadows, so that in leaning over the side of a canoe and contemplating these very remarkable appearances one cannot escape being reminded of the fabled grove of Aladdin, or of that garden which Don Quixote imagined himself to have seen in the grotto of Montesinos, 'El mas bello ameno y deleytoso que puede criar la naturaleza' ('The most beautiful and delightful that nature can create'). Amongst all this are to be seen great multitudes of fishes of the most extraordinary shapes and hues—gold, and purple, and violet, and scarlet, jet black, mottled, and every shade of green.

In some of the enclosed lagoons of the Tuamotus, all the fish without exception are poisonous. There are many sharks, but, as a rule, they are harmless to man, their natural food being abundant; at any rate, the pearl-fishers take no heed of them. Their most disagreeable enemy is the *veki* or great squid. This creature, who possesses the wonderful faculty of being able, within five minutes, to change himself into fifty different forms, each more hideous than the last, is fortunately of a very retiring disposition and decidedly timid, otherwise he would constitute a most dangerous antagonist. He stretches out his long arms, and seizes whatever comes within his grasp. But his most objectionable practice is that of vomiting a quantity of inky fluid when disturbed, which renders the surrounding water intensely dark, so that the diver who chances to encounter him under some overhanging shelf or coral cave, may become bewildered in the gloom, and lose his way to the surface, or strike against the rocks. Fortunately, in the lagoons these offensive creatures are very small and incapable of much mischief; but in the deep sea outside the coral-reefs they grow to enormous size, and in exposed fisheries like that of Panama, they are a source of great dread to the Americans and Europeans, who invariably dive in armour.

From what I have seen, heard, and read, I have come to the conclusion that the pearl-fishing of the South Pacific is more free from accident than any other occupation connected with the sea. Of course it can only be successfully practised by persons of experience; the divers must be amphibious—born to it; the directors and overseers men acquainted with their language, habits, and wants.

The question must have occurred to many readers: How are the pearl-oysters propagated in the coral lagoons?

Two islands of apparently precisely the same character, as far as natural formation, outflow and influx of the tide, depth of water, etc., are concerned, may be found within a few miles of one another (as is frequently the case), yet the lagoon of the one swarms with pearl-oysters, while in that of the other not one has ever been found. It will be said, 'Why not transplant them as breeders do oysters?' This has been tried, not only in our time, but generations ago, without any success, by the aborigines, to whom pearl-shell has always been most valuable, not only for ornament, but because, for very many most necessary purposes, it supplies to them the use of metals

--as for the making of dishes, spoons, fish-hooks, knives, and a variety of implements; consequently in islands where it was not indigenous, they were most anxious to obtain it, and with that view made repeated attempts to introduce it into their own lakes, by carefully transporting the young shells attached to pieces of rock from one island to another, keeping them all the time in pure sea-water; but they never succeeded. Moreover, there is no tradition of the pearl-oyster having once existed in a place, and having become extinct; consequently there is some condition necessary to its growth with which we are unacquainted.

There is no variety in the species, but very much difference in the size and thickness to which it attains in divers localities, as also in the production of pearls of value. For some of these peculiarities there is a way of accounting. The pearl-oyster of the Pacific dislikes sand, and will not live upon it, or grow to its full size in its immediate vicinity—that is to say, in a tide-wave, or where the sand pollutes the water. In still lagoons, where the sand lies at a depth and is never moved, the pearl-shell grows well on the rocks which rise out of it. But this fish most delights in the great caves and hollows of the clean-growing coral, where the waters are limpid, and altogether free from such extraneous atoms as might irritate and annoy it. In such situations it grows to a great size (sometimes as much as eighteen inches in diameter). These huge bivalves frequently attach themselves to the roofs of caverns, sometimes a dozen being linked together by the strong fibrous threads whereby they make themselves fast: a rich prize for the diver, who is obliged to separate them with his knife, and from their exceeding weight to make more than one plunge before securing the whole of the congeries. As a general rule, in well-fed and clean-grown fish such as these, pearls are seldom to be met with. When that is the case, however, they are usually of considerable value, being large, well-formed and pure.

The oysters which produce the greatest number of pearls are thick and stunted, having a scabby and deformed appearance. There is a colour about their cable (or attachment whereby they hold on to the rock) unmistakable to an experienced fisher; so much so, that such a man could with safety lay a wager to pick out from a boat-load of unopened oysters at least 75 per cent. of those which contained pearls, upon most cursory examination. There can be no doubt whatever that the production of pearls is in most cases the result of some disease or inconvenience suffered by the fish. Instances are occasionally met with in which oysters in an apparent state of perfect health and large growth contain pearls, but then usually only one, and that large, round, and beautiful. On the other hand, in some distorted and shabby-looking shells, one will find, at times, twenty or more pearls (there have been instances of a hundred), small, shapeless, and of no value. Some have supposed that the irritation caused by the presence of parasites in the shape of small red crabs and lobsters which infest the pearl-oyster, and give it very much annoyance, are the cause of the existence of pearls. But I do not think such is the case, as these creatures are most numerous in large, clean, and healthy shells, where there are no pearls.

Pearls of great value are not often found in the Pacific lagoons, although in some localities they are to be obtained in sufficient quantities to pay for the expenses of getting up the shell. A very great number of the most valuable pearls in the Pacific fisheries have been and still are lost on account of the fishers allowing their diving women to open the shells, which they do between their knees, and in the act the loose pearls immediately slip out with the water and slime which the shell contains, and are irrevocably lost. As is well-known, these are much more valúable than those pearls lodged in the usual way in the muscle.

In some of the lagoon islands, the natives used to hoard pearls for superstitious purposes, and in many of their villages there was a house built and set apart for the keeping of their gods, or for what answered the purpose of such. In this house it was customary to make offerings of the largest of everything they found, as well as whatsoever was new and strange to them. Thus the largest cocoa-nut, crab-fish of any kind, shell or pearl, were made sacred, and hung up in this building. Small articles, such as little pearls, teeth of dead men, teeth and claws of animals, were enclosed in bags and carefully put away. These houses were in fact a sort of museum, where everything rare and curious had been preserved from generation to generation; but when the beachcombers came to settle among them, and offered gin and gunpowder for pearls, their faith in these interesting collections began to slacken, and they sold many of their finest pearls for a mere song. This is how it is that large-sized pearls are not so common in the Pacific as they used to be some twenty or thirty years back.

Many of the pearl robbers, for such they were, lost their lives in this trade, others became almost as notorious as 'Bully Hayes.' One man, a certain Captain Rugg, made a practice of cruising around the Tuamotus, and wheresoever he found a quantity of shell ready for shipment, he used to seize it by armed force.

This pirate met his just reward; having had the assurance to fire into the *Dolphin*, an American vessel of war, to which he had declined to render an account of himself, he was chased by the *Porpoise*, one of the same squadron, into the North Pacific, and there sunk with all his crew.

Up to the present time it may be safely estimated that the Tuamotu Group has yielded to traders of various nations not less than 25,000 tons of pearl-shell, representing, at the lowest rates which have ruled in Europe since the trade attracted any great attention, at least £1,000,000. The Tuamotu fisheries are frequently described in the Pacific, and by people who ought to know better, as exhausted. This is not true, although the quantity now obtainable there does not probably exceed 200 tons per annum. The reason is very obvious: the pearl-oyster takes seven years to come to maturity, and the fisheries have had no rest for more than thirty years. As they are exceedingly prolific, if allowed reasonable time to recruit they would soon recover their former flourishing condition. There are numerous other pearl islands besides the Tuamotus, which have never been visited by fishers, or have lain dormant for a great number of years; but I studied the pearl industries of that particular group, and it may be taken as representative of the rest.

I have already referred to the cable or muscle by which the pearl-oyster binds itself to the rock. This apparatus has the look of a large tassel, consisting of an infinite number of slender filaments, each about the thickness of a pack-thread. It springs from the body of the fish, and passes through an orifice between the shells immediately next the hinge. During life its colour is iridescent, changing from dark green to a golden bronze, exhibiting while in motion various prismatic hues. It fastens itself to the rugged coral rock with so tenacious a hold as frequently to require the utmost strength of a powerful man to tear it away.

It seems incredible that under these circumstances the creature should move from place to place, yet it is a fact that it does; and I know that under the influences of certain causes these bivalves are in the habit of migrating *en masse* from one coral shelf to another in the immediate neighbourhood. This is notably an effect of sudden change of temperature, or a scarcity of the animalculæ on which it feeds.

When pearl-oysters grow singly it has been noticed there are very few pearls; where crowded together or jammed into crevices of rocks, the reverse is the case. This may have some connection with want of liberty to move about, whereby it is possible they become diseased. However unlikely their migratory powers may appear from the aspect of the shell and the apparently immovable manner in which they attach themselves to the stone, I will give a proof, on first-class authority, which all experienced fishers will recognise as conclusive. Young pearl-oysters are usually found in vast multitudes packed closely together. Several bushels of them will frequently be attached to a single stone, filling up all hollows in a compact mass. It is perfectly evident that they cannot continue to grow that way, but as they increase in size they must loosen themselves and migrate elsewhere. It is certain that an oyster the size of a sixpence is as firmly bound to the stone, in proportion to its strength, as is one the size of a soup-plate; and if the small ones have the power to move, so have the large ones.

I have long been of opinion that the pearl-oyster of the coral lagoons is not spawned altogether within the lagoon, but chiefly in the deep sea outside, for the reason that if any man will go between the months of December and March (which seems in the Pacific to be the breeding season for many marine creatures), and stand upon the outer edge of a flat reef, on the windward side of any pearl lagoon, when the tide is making, he will observe the water to be everywhere full of young pearl-oysters no bigger than his finger-nail, and others much less, all floating in towards the still water of the lagoon, where having arrived they sink to the bottom and settle down for life. Again, when the tide is going out they are not seen to return to the ocean with it; neither if a man will go and watch upon the lee reef will he find any of them being carried over there. This has proved to me that the savages tell the truth—though the white men are not willing to believe them —when they say that if a diver could get down and work under the breaker on the outside of the coral reef he would find there even more shell than is to be found in the lagoon.

Wherever sea water becomes stagnant in the Pacific lagoons, a sort of marine centipede makes its appearance, which enters and soon devours the oyster.

In the Pacific all oysters are opened by the knife, which, if carefully performed, is the best plan. The best instrument for this purpose is a common table-knife of good steel, ground thin till the blade is flexible, and fitted into a good stout handle. A skilful operator will open a ton of shells in an ordinary day's work, and not miss the pearls if there be any. It cannot be done rapidly without frequently cutting the hands (sometimes severely), as the edges are as sharp as glass. But men working for themselves with a prospect of considerable gain do not mind such accidents. The excitement is something akin to gold-mining. White men, if they can avoid it, will never let valuable shells be opened by any other hands than their own, as the natives are sure to steal the pearls if they have the chance, and are so skilful in concealing them that detection is almost impossible.

When the shells are landed it is the custom of the 'boss' fisherman to sort them into two piles; those he supposes to contain pearls to be opened by himself, and the rest by the natives. In hard times it is usual for the men to eat the fish, but they are coarse, rank, and disagreeable, although perfectly wholesome. The pearls are usually lodged in the strong muscle of the fish, out of which the cable, as I have called it, springs; this is about the thickness of that part of a man's hand which is next to the thumb. The flesh being semi-transparent, the pearls are easily detected from their brightness, which refracts the light.

If it were in the power of a man to sift the bottom of one of the Pacific pearl-oyster banks he would be certain to obtain an enormous treasure, inasmuch as oysters after their seventh year produce most largely, then die and discharge their contents. It may be said literally of all localities where this valued bivalve exists—

'There are jewels rich and rare
In the caverns of the deep.'

The pearl and pearl-shell fisheries of the Tuamotus date practically from the time when the merchants of Valparaiso found out that the Catholic missionaries in the Gambier Islands had obtained several valuable parcels of pearls. They immediately despatched vessels to obtain some, and though they failed, so far as pearls themselves were concerned, they discovered that pearl-shell or mother-of-pearl was easily obtainable and extremely profitable; and so the trade has continued, with the usual fluctuations of fashion and market, down to the present day. Messrs. Godeffroy on one occasion shipped to Europe in one parcel pearls to the value of £4000, the product of a few months' collection among the Tuamotus. Beachcombers also, who had been daring enough to land upon remote lagoon isles and had managed to escape the cannibals, frequently used to realise large sums of money by the sale of parcels of these gems. Thus a certain man Bird was well known to have made more than £1000 in this way, a great part of which was found in his chest by his wives after he himself had been very summarily disposed of by his own men. Another gentleman of the beachcombing persuasion, named Henry Williams, of Manihiki, amassed silver coin enough to fill a powder-keg; and on one occasion having had quite as much as was bad for him of 'chain-lightning gin,' he broke up his keg with an axe, scattering the contents on the sand, and telling the savages among whom he lived to take as much as they wanted. The savages were of course equal to the occasion, and carried the dollars home to their houses, exclaiming: '*Aué! aué!* the white man has gone mad, and broken the barrel in which he kept his gods.'

Fine calm weather is of course most favourable to pearl-fishing, but not indispensable, as the amphibious natives of some groups seek the shell by swimming with their heads below the surface of the water; and having discovered it, inhale a good draught of air, and then go down and fetch up as many as they can readily lay hold of. Polynesian divers do not use any stones to immerse themselves, or any apparatus to close the nostrils, as do the Cingalese. They will stay under water about three minutes, sometimes longer, and can bring up shell from 20 fathoms deep. They want some extra inducement to go down to that depth, and of course they cannot persevere long; but Penrhyn islanders, Tuamotans, or Rapa men can do it if they like. The shells found at that depth are of enormous size, as much as 18 inches in diameter, so that a pair when opened out by the hinge will measure a yard across. This kind of pearl-diving is very difficult, and the heat of the sun, aggravated by its radiation from the still waters of the lagoons, is very excessive. On many islands women are more skilful at this work than men; and being accustomed from early life to supply cockles and clams to the 'lords of the creation,' they are the better divers.

Taking all expenses into consideration, it may be said that the cost of raising shell amounts to between £5 and £6 a ton. Some of the old fisheries are now abandoned. It is quite a mistake to suppose, however, they are valueless; the best of the shell is in the deep water, and in the great coral caverns underneath the exhausted shelves. Properly led and kindly treated, the natives will attempt the greater depths, and this is a very important point to notice. Moreover the shallow water of lately worked fisheries is skirted by sandy bogs, and in the neighbourhood of these, as I have said, the fish will not live. Pearl-oysters are like sponges—certain conditions are necessary to their development. In some localities, however, supplying apparently their requirements, they are not found at all.

I believe the magnificent necklace of pearls belonging to the Empress Eugénie, and lately sold by Mr. Edwin Streeter of Bond Street, came from the Tuamotus, and was obtained by the Messrs. Stewart of Tahiti.

A friend of mine says that in the lagoons of the Fanning Group, a short description of which will be found further on, there exists a species of large clam, called in the Pacific the *paahua* or *tridachua.* There are two kinds: one grows chiefly on the solid coral, and does not attain to so great a size as the other, which is found not only on the hard reef, but bound to loose rocks, or lodged upon the sandy bottom. This attains extraordinary proportions. It is in some cases, especially near the Equator, so large as to weigh several hundredweight. This is the kind of shell sometimes used in gardens for the basins of fountains. Some years ago, I was told on good authority, there was a trade in this kind of shell, and that it was collected for shipment in the Samoan Group and elsewhere, for what purpose was not known; though I have heard it was for the making of what is called in India *cowrie chunam*, a mixture of pulverised shells and cement, which is used in that country for the coating of columns in the interior of houses, giving them an appearance as though made of ivory. The trade has died out, but Mr. Sterndale's report calls attention to the fact that these shells contain pearls of exceeding value. He says:

'The first time which I remember to have noticed one of these gems as being of any possible value, was upon seeing one in the possession of a Raratongan, who had brought it from Fanning Island (of which more anon), and I purchased it for a lump of tobacco. It afterwards was sold to the surgeon of the ship for £10. The surgeon gave it to his wife in Australia, after having refused the offer of £25 made to him by a jeweller in Sydney. Its size was about that of a pea; it was round upon one side, on the other slightly flattened. Its lustre was crystalline; in the centre appeared a luminous point, from which radiated innumerable bright rays distinctly defined. On another occasion a pearl of this kind was shown me by a trader, who asked my opinion concerning its value. He had bought it from a savage of the Kingsmills for 4 fathoms of cotton print. I told him to the best of my belief it could not be worth less than $1000, which I would have been very willing to have given him for it. It was not globular, but somewhat of the shape of a convex magnifying lens, perfectly symmetrical, and without a fault; its diameter was considerably more than half an inch, and its thickness about two-thirds of the measure. It showed the same kind of luminous point in the centre as the one I have already described, with the same radiations. I do not know' what became of it. In the larger *paahua* these pearls are found in the body of the fish (as they are in the true pearl-oyster); they are very common, so much so that in some places, such as the coral lagoons near the Equator, a man may collect a hundred or more out of a day's fishing; but they are generally of irregular shapes, and perfectly opaque, like bone. Such as are well-formed and of sufficient lustre to be called gems are rare; but are nevertheless to be met with occasionally of so great a size as to induce the belief that if the search for them were systematically pursued, the fishers would stand a very good chance of making a fortune. I have never known anyone to fish for these shells for the sake of their pearls; but from those *paahuas* which we were in the habit of eating, I have seen some extracted of good shape, quite opaque, and of the appearance of bone, and as large as a Snider bullet. I have seen others again milky or semi-transparent, or like a dirty white opal, without any play of colours, but sometimes a little brilliancy at one end.'

There is another kind of shell in this latitude which produces pearls of fine quality, but generally not of great size. The largest I have seen are about the size of a pea; they are perfectly round and of golden colour, and very lustrous. The shell is similar to that of the oyster; the underside is always firmly amalgamated with the rock, so as to form part of it, and cannot be broken off; the upper valve is like a lid, with a very strong hinge. These shells are not found in clusters, but detached, which causes them to be somewhat scarce.

So much for the pearl-oyster fishing of the Pacific—in which two good friends of mine are now actively engaged.

I have alluded over and over again to the 'beachcombers' of Coral Lands. The veteran 'beachcombers' are those who have devoted themselves more or less to the pearl-fisheries. They are hardy, healthy, powerful, and bronzed. They have the strength to lift a kedge-anchor, and to carry a load of perhaps 200 cocoa-nuts out of the forest in the heat of a noonday sun, they climb trees like apes, and can dive almost as well as the natives with whom they live, they wear no shoes, but go at all times barefooted on beaches of sharp gravel and reefs of prickly coral. Some of these men have as many as twenty children with huge frames and gipsy countenances. Their intellect is of a low order, and their morals very lax; but it is quite possible they may improve as they multiply, and they are multiplying very rapidly. At any rate the developement of Polynesia will have to deal sooner or later with these men, and a powerful controlling influence of a high order once established in the Pacific, the beachcombers would either act as very useful pioneers (under rigid discipline) or be soon improved off the face of the earth. I confess I have little sympathy with many of these gentry, however romantic may be their histories or Crusoe-like their lives. The future of Polynesia, in a moral and commercial sense, seems to me to be a very important business problem with which sentiment has little or nothing to do.

'Pretty writing,' comparing beachcombers to lotus-eaters, or dwelling as some people have done exclusively on the poetical side that does unquestionably attach to their existence, is, to my mind, beside the mark. The civilisation they introduce is usually of the square-gin and musket order, which tends to destroy fine races of savages instead of assisting them to approach our level. There are, as I know, some noble exceptions, but I have a very shrewd opinion that the majority of these 'traders' have views as to the deplorable results, from a 'business' point of view, of the introduction of

Christianity; and it was on account of some of these people that a Lord High Commissioner of Western Polynesia was appointed. If the Anglo-Saxon race is prepared to accept the responsibility that undoubtedly belongs to it in the Southern Seas, beachcombing, as beachcombing has been understood for years, will be a thing of the past. It was the 'mean whites' of the Southern States who ill-treated the negroes when they had the chance, and then stirred up the negroes to rebel against their masters. The beachcombers of the South Pacific are, taking them as a class, of a superior order to the almost extinct American caste referred to; but they will have to rise with the rise of Polynesia, or seek some other 'islands at the gateways of the day.' Face to face with an organisation having a higher end than mere money-making, and backed by the imperial power of Britain, the vast majority of the beachcombers would, I feel convinced, accept the situation, serve themselves and advance their nationality and race. The majority of these men are of British stock, some of them with good yeomen's blood in their veins, but they could not be persuaded by any human inducement to return to the old world. One of them at Samoa used to say:

'Sir, I wouldn't go back to Britain now if you would give me £1000 a year; yet I will say that when I came here first, more than fifty years ago, I had a fashion of sitting on the stones by the seaside of a night, and crying to myself for the home and friends I should never see again. I know better now, and have done so many a year.'

When Commodore Wilkes's exploring expedition visited the Navigators' Isles our friend went on board the *Porpoise*, dressed in savage mats, and begged the captain to take him away.

'I don't want any men,' was the answer; 'but what countryman are you?'

'A Scotchman,' was the reply.

'Well, then,' replied the Yankee, 'I guess I pity you more than a little. I cannot take you away, but here's a sheath-knife and a plug of James River cavendish, of which I make you a present; had you been an American, I would have had you tied up to the gangway and have given you a dozen with the cat-o'-nine-tails.'

The Scot did not understand what he could have been guilty of to deserve this punishment, and asked the American to explain.

'Because,' retorted the commander, 'had you been a citizen of the United States I should have counted you a disgrace to humanity for letting yourself run wild among a lot of scalping savages; but seeing you are a Britisher, and there is not room enough for you all in your over-crowded country, I pity you from the bottom of my soul—I dew.'

There are extraordinary industries as well as extraordinary men in Coral Lands. A chapter is certainly due to *bêche-de-mer.*

CHAPTER XXX.

WHAT BÊCHE-DE-MER IS, HOW IT IS CAUGHT, AND WHAT IS DONE WITH IT.

ALL the lagoon islands of the Coral Seas are famous for the production of *bêche-de-mer*, a kind of sea-snail, which is one of the most important articles of commerce obtained in the Pacific.

Bêche-de-mer, called by the Chinese *Tripang*, by the Polynesians in the South Sea *Rodi*, and in the Caroline Group *Menika*, is that species of mollusc classed as the *Holothurides.* It has the appearance of a great slug or leech, and like most other marine animals of the same type, lives by suction, and upon microscopic animalculæ. Its anatomical structure is simple. It has the form of an elongated sac, of a gristly consistence, traversed internally by strong muscles; the rest consists of intestines, which are perfectly transparent, and, on close examination, appear to contain nothing but water and sand—of the latter a very large proportion, although what part so indigestible a substance can play in the economy of its organism may be known to the creature itself, but certainly is a puzzle to me. When disturbed it swells itself up very considerably, and takes in a great quantity of water, which much increases its size. It is so elastic, that if slung by the middle across a pole it will, by its own weight, stretch to several times its normal length.

The mouth of the *bêche-de-mer* is triangular, with three teeth like those of a leech. It has no appearance of eyes. Its powers of locomotion are limited, so much so, that one could not perceive it move except by observing its relative distance from any neighbouring object. Its normal condition is that of repose; perhaps it is a very harmless creature, but its degree of usefulness when alive seems very circumscribed. It has few enemies, with the exception of the turtle, which only molests it in the days of its youth, and at certain seasons of the year. Crawling along the mossy coral of the snow-white bottom of the lagoon, it leads a curious sort of life of passive enjoyment, which, as far as I could ever make out, seems to consist in taking water and sand in at one end, and squirting it out at the other.

There are four kinds of *bêche-de-mer*—the grey, the black, the red, and the leopard. The grey kind is the most valuable, but it is only found where the hawk's-bill turtle is found; that is to say, not much to windward (eastward) of the 180th meridian. It reaches usually when at maturity to about 18 inches long, and somewhat less in circumference. The colour is a slatey grey, and it is distinguished from the other species by having upon either side a row of little protuberances like teats. It frequents the flat reef and the sandy bottom of shallow lagoons. The black *bêche-de-mer* lives only on clean sandy bottoms, at a depth from knee-deep at low-water down to 10 fathoms. It grows large, sometimes as long as 30 inches, and as thick as a man's leg. On the back and sides it is jet black, smooth and bright like enamelled leather; the underside is a bluish, slatey grey. When very old it becomes encrusted with small shells. The red kind is the smallest, and of least value; it seldom attains more than a foot in length, usually less. It lives upon the coral reef, in the greatest profusion towards the outer edge, where the surf is continuously breaking. In this respect it differs essentially from the beach kind, which delights in quiet waters and smooth sand, and will not live either near noisy waves or on rough coral rocks. The leopard kind grows as large as the largest of the black; it is of an olive-green colour, variegated with green spots, surrounded by an orange-coloured rim, hence its name. It has another peculiarity: all *bêche-de-mer* are harmless when laid hold of but this one. When touched it ejects a quantity of slender filaments, something like white cotton lamp-wick; it can produce several hanks of it, so to speak. It is glutinous, and whatever it touches, it attaches itself to it in the most tenacious manner.* This would not signify if it were merely

* It is probably furnished with the same adhesive apparatus peculiar to the anemones of our own shores—each tentacle of which is equipped with myriads of minute javelins which are darted out the instant anything comes within their touch, each javelin being connected to the tentacle by a fine thread.

satisfied with sticking fast, but wherever it clings it burns like a blister; and upon any part of the human skin produces immediate and painful inflammation. Yet this hideous slug is worth in China from £80 to £100 a ton. The other varieties of this remarkable inhabitant of the deep content themselves with squirting out the water from their intestines. From their way of living, one would expect this to be perfectly harmless, but, like the similar discharge of a toad, if a drop of this liquid enters the human eye, it produces a sensation as if of contact with red-hot coal, resulting in a violent and dangerous inflammation. If inoculated into any abrasion of the skin, the consequences are still more serious. Cases are known in the Pacific of men very nearly losing their eyesight and suffering weeks of pain through this cause. It has been generally supposed that this mollusc is of slow growth. The *bêche-de-mer* fishers that I met are of a contrary opinion. The slugs will increase from 1 inch in length to nearly 9 inches in almost less than three months. They have other peculiarities besides these I have enumerated. For instance, they are not found everywhere upon a coral reef or lagoon bottom, but in great patches, which proves the *bêche-de-mer* to be a gregarious and sociable animal. They undoubtedly possess also a certain degree of intelligence which is evident from existing facts, but which seems very hard to explain. These creatures, as far as we know, have no eyes, and yet have some means of communicating with each other, and a very exact knowledge of one another's proximity. Often, for instance, fishers, after having discovered in any place a greater multitude of these slugs than it was possible at once to carry home to the curing-houses, would lay them down separately far apart from one another, with the intent of coming for them on the morrow. When they did so, they would find them all in batches as they were originally discovered. Again, if a fisher stripped all the visible *bêche-de-mer* from a coral reef, in stormy weather, after the wind's subsidence, the place would be found as thickly crowded with these molluscs as it had been before the storm. From this I concluded that they had shifted their quarters during the bad weather to crevices in the coral.

The wealthy classes of China exhibit such a remarkable fondness for the gelatinous flesh (if flesh it may be called) of this fish, that they are willing to pay very high prices for the luxury. There are especial reasons very powerful indeed with the Mongolian mind for this curious fancy of theirs for *bêche-de-mer.*

For centuries past Chinese mariners have frequented the coasts of the Indian Archipelago, New Guinea, and New Holland, and it was from this reason that the northern shores of that great island were as well known to them before the days of Marco Polo as they are to ourselves at the present time. When Captain Flinders was engaged in the first exploration of that locality, he encountered in one of the harbours a fleet of vessels which he first supposed to be pirates. On closer examination they turned out to be Chinese tripang-fishers, with whom he became very friendly. He received some valuable information from their intelligent commodore, and was shown by him a chart showing the principal features of the coast, and their relative positions to New Guinea and Timor. There can be no doubt that it was from this source that the Dutch navigators of former days derived the information which directed them to the discovery of New Holland, and set the Spaniards speculating upon the precise locality of that land which they were the first to call Australia.

As regards maritime enterprise in the Coral Seas, no traffic has ever done more towards the progress of discovery than the tripang trade of China, not even excepting the whale-fishery. The whale-men generally do but find islands, while the *bêche-de-mer* fishers land and live upon them until their cargoes are completed, and thus are enabled to supply information not otherwise obtainable.

I have stated that the price of *bêche-de-mer* in the markets ranges from £60 to £80 or even £100 a ton; these fluctuations are not altogether owing to the laws of supply and demand. There is always a great demand for tripang, and the difference in price has generally occurred from the quality of this stimulating delicacy. Of course this is a circumstance over which the fishers have little or no control; but John Chinaman will never pay £80 a ton for tripang which is not of a most luxurious description.

Bêche-de-mer fishing is one of the favourite avocations of the better class of Pacific wanderers, who, if permanent residents on any of its countless islands, would be called beachcombers. They are usually rough and wild fellows, but very hospitable and generous, dividing their profits as a rule very much to the satisfaction of the Polynesians with whom they work in concert. It may be noted that a thoroughly mean and sordid man can never get on with the islanders. As the natives divide their little gains among their friends, so when a *papalagi* goes into a sort of partnership with them, they expect him to be equally open-handed. These men are usually poor, but possess great power among the savage tribes. It is a common practice with them to build small craft with the assistance of the natives, and in this sort of vessel to cruise from one desert island to another, carrying cocoa-nuts for provender, and eking out the rest of their subsistence by means of fish, turtle, and sea-birds' eggs. When they reach an atoll which produces *bêche-de-mer* in anything like abundance, they will settle down there for a few months, or it may be a year or two, and cure and store it up until some passing vessel chances to call and purchase it. If no ship calls, they will fill their little craft with as much as she can carry, and set sail for some larger island where there is a trading station, and bargain for a vessel to come down and fetch the remainder. I have heard many a curious story about these strange nineteenth-century voluntary Crusoes. The scene of one of the best of these was in the Kingsmill Group, where a friend of mine had a conversation with a man of this kind, relative to the best way of cooking a crayfish.

'We,' said he, 'are used to cooking them in an oven of hot stones, but *white* men mostly like them boiled in a pot.'

It was evident that his mind was in somewhat of a fog as to whether he had himself any claim to be reckoned among the sons of Japhet. Another dates from the island of Manuai, where a *bêche-de-mer* fisherman asked him to read a certain paper for him.

'Were you never taught to read?' inquired my friend.

'Oh yes,' he replied. 'I had a good schooling once, but it's so long ago that I don't know English from Dutch when it's wrote down.'

This man's son (who spoke good English) remarked that he should like very much to be able to read. My friend, with a prophetic vision of a school board for Coral Lands, and a shilling in the pound rate, rejoined:

'Don't you try to know too much; knowledge is only a lot of bother.'

'Oh,' said the lad, 'but I should like to read the Bible; there's good stories in it, 'specially that part about the pirates.'

'Indeed, you must be mistaken; there's no such thing in the Bible.'

'Oh yes,' continued the son; 'don't you remember where Robinson Crusoe gets taken by the Turkish pirate?'

My friend told me he laughed very much, but was quite unable to convince the boy of his mistake. He further said that a seaman who had been cast away upon his father's island used to read the tale aloud to them from a large book; 'and I know,' added he conclusively, 'that this book was a Bible, for it was nearly half as big as a brandy-case.'

Besides these semi-barbarous adventurers, there are many shipmasters and merchants who have been long used to sail vessels, from thirty to one hundred tons, chiefly out of the ports of Tahiti, Honolulu, Guam (where Hayes came to grief), or Manilla, in quest of *bêche-de-mer*, whose practice it is to frequent such lagoon atolls as it is possible to anchor within. There they lie up for months until their cargo is complete. They land their trypots and other requisites, build some palm-leaf huts for lodging their men, and a smoke-house for the curing of the fish, and have usually a good time of it. The labour of collecting and drying the fish is performed partly by their crews—commonly Polynesian natives—with the exception of the mate and perhaps a trading-master and interpreter. To these are added aborigines if the island is inhabited, or natives they bring with them if it is deserted. Women are in great requisition on these expeditions, they being well up to the work, willing and good tempered, and much more easily controlled than men. Traders who have much experience of this pursuit universally admit the desirability of engaging an equal number of women to that of the men concerned in the enterprise. A neglect of this arrangement has, in many instances, led to serious quarrels.

There can be no doubt this sort of life has a charm which dwellers in the Babel of civilisation might be at a loss to comprehend. *Bêche-de-mer* fishing has not often been an experience of my own, but it is a grand break-away for a time from the daily routine of office, library, or plantation.

To spend one's days in a rock-bound haven where the waters are eternally at rest, no matter what storms may raise the sea which rolls outside the coral barrier; to run about barefoot upon silvery sands, where the cool sea-breeze all the year round conquers the sultriness of the tropic sunshine; to paddle about on the still waters of a calm lagoon, whose limpid waves display beneath them an infinity of strange and beautiful forms; to sleep softly and to dream sweetly, sung to rest by the ceaseless sounding of the distant sea and rustling of the night wind among the feathery palms; to know nothing of what is going on in the outer world, and to care as little; to have no ideas beyond those included within the horizon of vision; to climb to the summit of some lofty tree and to see at one glance all which constitutes for ourselves the material universe—is indeed to revel in nature, and nature as she only exists in Coral Lands.

There is this advantage in *bêche-de-mer* fishing, that upon the great desert reefs, where it most abounds, the fishers never need be idle. In calm weather they gather the red kind off the top of the reef, just inside the foam of the breakers; in stormy times they dive for the black species inside the lagoon. From its size and colour it is plainly visible to a depth of at least 10 fathoms, even when the water is much ruffled by the wind—the more so, as it lives only on the smooth, sandy white bottom. The material required for the prosecution of this business is of the most simple character—merely a boat, a few axes to cut building materials and firewood, a supply of long knives for all hands, and, in some cases, two or three of the great cast-iron boilers (or trypots), such as are used on board whale-ships, and forks with many prongs, of the same sort as gold-diggers use, and buckets. The preliminary operation is to build two houses—one for the curing of the fish, which is done by smoking, and the other for storage. These are rude sheds of palm-leaves, closed round on all sides with mats of coarse material. The thatch must be watertight, for though salt water does no harm to cured *bêche-de-mer*, rain-water entirely destroys its value. The smoke-house is built of an oblong shape, and has inside it two sets of stages made of thin sticks, fastened horizontally to a strong framework. A narrow passage is left between these, and underneath are two drains dug in the ground, wherein to make fires to create smoke. The terms upon which the labourers are engaged for *bêche-de-mer* fishing depend on the circumstances of the case.

The natives, though unable to read or write, or understand English, have a great liking for written agreements, and although the white men who draw these up alone can comprehend them, it must in fairness be stated that as a rule the conditions are faithfully fulfilled on both sides. The islanders are fond of giving a sobriquet to any white man with whom they engage in business, and the following is a verbatim copy of a *bêche-de-mer* fishery treaty:

'*We, men and women of Nukunivano, whose marks are put at the bottom of this paper, agree to go with the Captain Longbeard to the Island of Gannet Cay, and to fish for bêche-de-mer, and to fish for six moons; and to be paid, each man or woman, fourteen fathoms of calico, or twenty-one plugs of tobacco per moon, or other things as we like, such as knives and needles, at the value as we have before agreed; and at the end of six moons to be returned to our homes, if the wind should be fair for us to come back at that time. The chief, whose name is Dogfish, shall superintend the work. The Captain Longbeard shall tell the Chief Dogfish what the people are to do, and*

Dogfish shall tell the people. The Captain Longbeard shall not beat any of the people. The people shall not fight among themselves, but if there be any quarrel among them, they shall refer it to the Captain Longbeard and to the Chief Dogfish. If any one of the people die, that which is due to him or her shall be entrusted to the Chief Dogfish, to be given to his or her family. The Captain Longbeard shall supply to all the people for nothing, lines and fish-hooks, that they may catch themselves food. All food and fresh water shall be taken charge of and fairly divided by the Chief Dogfish. Twenty-eight days shall count for one moon; out of each moon shall be four days' rest—that is to say, the people shall work six days, and on the seventh day they shall do no work. They shall not lie to the Chief Dogfish, or be lazy, sulky, or dissatisfied. There is no more to say.'

Here follow the names of the people, with their marks, each against his or her own. As a rule they thoroughly enjoy an expedition of this sort; they live together like one family, and part good friends. People must know something of these natives before they can appreciate their good dispositions and realise the fearful injury some of our race have done them. A New Zealand colonist, who spent some time in the islands, thus remarks, and he can be truthfully endorsed by all well-meaning whites who have visited the Pacific:

'The poor barbarians are good-tempered, generous even to folly, and ready at any time to encounter the most deadly perils in the service of white men who treat them with kindness and liberality. Very many there are of us who have been indebted for our lives to their lovingkindness and unselfish bravery

'"Through days of danger and ways of fear,"

starving among desert cays, lost upon lonely seas, running with a rag of sail before furious winds, tossed in the foam of breakers where the sharks are jostling one another. Talking not long ago to a gentleman who has a morbid antipathy to Maoris, of whatsoever tribe and lineage, and would have them exterminated as noxious vermin, I remarked: "Be assured, my friend, had you known as many kind women and brave men as I have in the islands of the great South Sea, you would not wish to see them civilised off the face of the earth."'

Let us take, as a sample of such expeditions, a day's *bêche-de-mer* fishing on some desert island like Gaspa Rico.

Beginning with the dark hour just before the dawn, the stars light up the still surface of the lagoon, and under the dark shadows of the towering palms and banyans twinkle numerous points of light, the lamps of great glow-worms and luminous grubs. The great land-crab of the desert makes a noise like repeated blows with a pickaxe, for he is breaking a cocoa-nut for his morning meal. When the grey dawn glimmers in the east, the sea-birds flap their wings; and as the light increases, they fly away over the sea to windward—windward because they know full well that when they return home heavily laden with fish for their young ones, they will be glad of a fair wind. The natives bathe in the lagoon, and then a fish-breakfast of all sorts—including fat cockles and gannets' eggs, and perhaps a great turtle baked in his armour, and huge land-crabs and roasted nuts—is disposed of. Next the men collect their gear, knives and baskets, fish-spears and lines, and gourds of water. And the day quickly passes in light labour near the coral shoal, laughing and skylarking as only Coral Islanders can, while they gather the shiny tripang or spear other fish among the stones. Early in the afternoon they will return to their little camp, where some will clean and cook the *bêche-de-mer*, while others will prepare the evening meal; after which they make large wood fires, and lying on their spread-out mats, they will tell endless stories of phantom ships, ghosts and goblins, impossible adventures and voyages to wonderful islands very far away; and perhaps the happy day will end with a *meke-meke*—a dance on the smooth white sand by the light of the broad, bright moon.

And this is how the people of the Chief Dogfish would work out their six moons for the Captain Longbeard; that is to say, if the Chief Dogfish is loved and trusted by his people, and the Captain Longbeard not one of those insufferable white scoundrels who have been the scourge of the Pacific. It is true terrible tragedies have taken place among parties engaged in this pursuit, but in the majority of cases throughout those islands inhabited by the copper-coloured races of Polynesians, the preponderance of the blame has been on the side of the white man, and in most instances other men's wives have been at the bottom of the mischief. Again, it has frequently happened that Europeans—it is almost an insult to ourselves to describe them as such—destitute of the commonest principles of honour or humanity, have hired these simple island folk, and when the work was done have left them in strange places, or sold them for slaves.

The best way of collecting *bêche-de-mer* from the coral reefs is to make a little flat-bottomed punt of boards, or a small canoe dug out of a hollow log. There is a species of banyan-tree called *buka*, found on all the *bêche-de-mer* islands, the wood of which is soft and buoyant, and is very suitable for this purpose. This makes an excellent mode of conveyance, as the fisher trails it behind him with a rope, as he walks along the reef, and throws the slugs into it as fast as he can pick them up, and when the punt is loaded, tows it away to the edge of the deeper water, where he discharges his cargo into the larger boats which are used in the fishery. When the usual quantity of slug has been collected, the large boat is steered for home, and on the way the boat's crew employ themselves in gutting the fish. This is done by splitting up the whole length of the underside of the creature with a sharp knife over the gunwale, so that the intestines fall into the sea. When the boats arrive at the landing-place, the fish must be taken ashore, and cooked immediately, for a special reason. It is a remarkable peculiarity of this creature, that if a number of them be placed together, as long as they retain life they can be separated, although by reason of their plasticity they adapt their form to that of any other substance with which they may be in contact after having been taken out of the water; but shortly after their intestines are removed, they lose all resemblance to their original form, and amalgamate into an undistinguishable and indivisible glutinous mass of the appearance and consistency of birdlime, of which no use can be made, as it adheres to everything with the tenacity of glue.

There are several ways of preparing *bêche-de-mer* for curing. The most primitive is to steam it in a native's oven of hot stone. This is made by scooping out a large hole in the earth, in which the fire is made of small wood piled on its ends, cocoa-nut husks, etc. Over this the stones are heaped, intermixed with more wood and husks. Hard stones are preferred when they are to be got, as they hold the heat better than coral, and do not become calcined. When they are thoroughly hot they are spread out over the bottom of the hole, the fish is laid upon them as close as it will lie, and covered up, first with large green leaves, and then with palm mats, and finally with a mound of earth. This is the orthodox Polynesian method of cooking everything, and this description of a *bêche-de-mer* oven will suffice for all the kitchens in Coral Lands.

After the slug has been in the oven about an hour, it is removed to the smoke-house. The steaming process has in the meantime considerably altered its appearance; its size is reduced, and it is no longer slimy. It looks like a piece of cowheel or bacon-rind of a dark colour. It is usual at this stage to spread out each separate slug by means of spanners, or little bits of stick, inserted transversely into the under side, which have the effect of keeping it flat and preventing it from curling up during the curing process, so that it dries up more rapidly and completely. It is then laid upon the drying stages already described, and fires are lighted underneath it of damp and sappy wood, in order to produce a dense and pungent smoke. By this plan the *bêche-de-mer*, if a strong smoke be kept up, will cook effectually in forty-eight hours, or at the outside in three days. It must be turned at least once. Some people take out the teeth, but this is wholly unnecessary, as they dry up to the consistency of chalk, and do not in any way affect the value of good *bêche-de-mer*. Another method of preparation is by boiling it in the great trypots which are used by the whale-fishers. It is boiled twice in salt water, about ten minutes each time. This is the more expeditious way of cooking, but it necessitates a longer smoking, as it will not cure thoroughly after it in less than eight days, and after all never resists the damp so well as that which has been steamed in the oven. A third and most effective system is to put the *bêche-de-mer* into a hogshead, or close box, into which a steam-pipe is introduced from a boiler. This is a very expeditious plan, and most to be recommended. When sufficiently smoke-dried, the fish is packed into strong baskets of *nikau* (or palm leaves). These are not stitched up to the time of shipment, for the reason that it is desirable to occasionally spread it out and give it the advantage of a scorching sun, as its preservation depends entirely on its being thoroughly dried. When properly cured it should be of the consistency of sole-leather, and unless this result is obtained it is the most precarious kind of merchandise to deal in. The ultimate destiny of most *bêche-de-mer* being the Chinese market, which involves long transport, unless perfectly cured it can never reach the end of its voyage without becoming greatly depreciated, and sometimes destroyed altogether by decomposition. Whole cargoes have been thrown away into the sea on the Chinese coasts from this cause, which only arises from ignorance or negligence. It is not only quite possible, but with due care perfectly easy, to preserve *bêche-de-mer* in such a manner that it will keep without injury, not only for a long voyage to China, but for all time. If it is cured thoroughly, *bêche-de-mer* should rattle like a bag of walnuts. If it be shipped in wet weather, or in a vessel with leaky decks, the best plan is to put it into iron tanks, each holding some 300 lb., plastering the lid with white lead. It will then be secure from decay as long as the iron is not penetrated by the atmosphere, which at any rate would not be for some years. If this strange sea-slug be not divested of its juices, or if subjected to damp, or wetted with fresh water, it speedily dissolves itself into a glutinous fluid of an appearance like molasses, to which is added the pleasant odour of decayed eggs.

There is frequently to be met with among *bêche-de-mer* a marine animal of a very singular aspect. It is called by the natives of Tokolau *taumata*, or 'skull-cap.' It is about the size of a man's head, or perhaps a little larger. Its shape may be thus described. If you take a square piece of paper and double down the corners in such a manner that the points meet in the middle, that will represent it very nearly, excepting that the form of the animal is more rounded. The under side where the foldings take place lies flat upon the rock or sand; the upper is concave, and of a reddish-brown colour, so that it looks like a loaf of bread. It is of a gristly consistence, and covered with small warts. It has no appearance of eyes, or power of locomotion, so far as one can discern, and therefore seems to represent one of the lowest forms of animal life. The *bêche-de-mer*, blind and helpless as he is, may be regarded as an intelligent animal in comparison. This *taumata* appears to live on suction. When taken out of the water it can exist for a considerable time, if not too much exposed to the hot sun. It is never eaten. The islanders turn it into a skull-cap, or species of helmet, which they manage by cutting round the under side and scooping out the inside. When dry it becomes as hard as bone. *Bêche-de-mer* fishers sometimes cut these creatures into strips and cure them with their proper *bêche-de-mer*, a smart practice which has the effect of depreciating the correct article in the markets of the Celestial Empire.

CHAPTER XXXI.

TURTLE AND SPONGE FISHING.

TURTLE-SHELL is another of the valuable products of the Pacific. There are throughout the isles of the great Coral Sea certain laws (varying in detail according to local circumstances) in connection with turtle-fishing. In a majority of the groups whoever sees the turtle first (man or woman) claims the shell. This is valuable to the natives quite apart from the dollars or trade offered by the chance white trader. Articles of domestic use and grotesque ornaments are made of it. Long strips of it cover the seams of their canoes, and of the thickest portion they make ear-rings, finger-rings, bracelets and fish-hooks, spoons and knives. These latter are made from the blade-bones of the turtle, and though clumsy in form are quite as effective for any ordinary purpose as steel knives. They require to be very seldom sharpened, and have an edge which it would not be wise to run a finger carelessly along.

When a turtle is caught, be it large or small, the flesh is divided among the whole of the inhabitants of the village to which the captors belong, so that in many cases a very small piece comes to the share of each individual. The weight of a full-grown turtle is usually about 450 lb., but sometimes they weigh as much as 700 lb. They are profitable to fish for not only on account of the shell, but for the oil which they contain, of which a good-sized one will give 10 gallons. The trade-price is usually about $1 per gallon.

The natives relish the flesh greatly, and eat it either cooked or raw. It is very much like indifferent beef, and as I have said, the turtle-steaks of the South Pacific are about as disagreeable a dish as I have ever encountered; but everyone has his taste, and perhaps some people like it.

The scientific way of killing a turtle among the islanders, is to strike it on the back of the head with a club; a bundle of dry leaves is then ignited and passed over the shell, so as to loosen the plates, which are pulled off; the under part of the shell is then split from the upper, and the meat is cut up.

In some islands, as used to be the case in Fiji, all turtles are claimed by the king or local chief. In that case, the plates being removed from his back, the animal is put whole into an oven of hot stones and baked. When there are not sufficient in the royal circle to consume the whole carcase at one meal, the residue is preserved in a very ingenious manner.

The turtle is baked with its back downwards; the hollow

of the shell is filled with melted fat or oil which is baled out and taken care of. The meat which is intended to be preserved is cut into pieces of about the size of a man's fist. These are put into cocoa-nut shells, and the oil poured in until the shell is nearly filled; the mouth is closed, and a green leaf tied over it: it is then put away until wanted, when it is again put into an oven and made hot. In this manner turtle-steaks can be preserved for an indefinite time without fear of spoiling.

I am afraid I have reversed the wise counsel of Mrs. Glasse, and have been saying how turtles are cooked and preserved before telling my readers how they are caught. I will endeavour to supply the deficiency.

The best plan is to watch for turtle at night. If taken during the day, they are generally surprised asleep on the surface of the water. On these occasions, when the turtle is discovered, it is usual for a few persons to go out to it in a canoe and paddle noiselessly alongside, when they lift it on board before it is aware what is going on. They very rarely even attempt to bite, and are perfectly harmless except while floundering about, when they can give a severe blow with their flippers. If a turtle is too heavy for the party, they harpoon it.

During the breeding-season turtles are very careless of their safety, and do not try to escape the presence of man. When several turtles are in this state, a proportionate number of men having approached them from a canoe, will jump overboard and lay hold of them thus: the man gets on the back of the turtle, and takes hold with his hands of the front of the shell just behind the neck. This prevents it from 'sounding,' that is to say, going down headforemost, as a turtle will always do when alarmed if not prevented by the weight of a man on its back. He is now quite helpless, as he has no idea of getting rid of his rider except by diving, and he allows himself to be steered in any direction his captors may choose. Thus he is soon brought alongside the canoe, and hoisted into it without resistance. This seems a very simple bit of sport, but it requires great care. A turtle in water can cut a naked man very dangerously with his flippers, and he must never be taken hold of by his tail. If he is, he will immediately fold his tail to his body, whereby he will hold the man's hand as tight as though it were in a vice, and drag him down to the bottom of the sea. Turtles never visit the inside lagoons of islands, unless the entrance is wide and the tide flows freely. They do not like stagnant or warm water, but delight in the fresh spray that dashes on an outer reef. They relish *bêche-de-mer* as much as a Chinaman, and in search of these slugs they will frequent the shallow water at the top of the reef. At these times, wherever the male or bull turtle is found, the female is not far away.

By far the greater number of turtle are taken on shore on low sandy beaches (as at Vu-ni-wai Levu), where they resort to lay their eggs during the night. Full moon is always a favourite time with them. The female goes on shore, and the male lies out beyond the breakers and watches for his mate. She lands with the high-tide, and returns to sea with the next flood, so she remains ashore several hours. If overtaken by daylight before high water, she will go out to the reef and lie still there waiting for the tide to come in. Thus detained, they are often captured by the natives, as they never attempt to move, even when trodden upon by men searching for other fish.

When the turtle lands to lay, she goes well up the beach, above high-water mark, frequently under the shadow of trees, and there scratches out a great circular hollow, throwing out the sand with her flippers. As the creature turns herself round and round in the hole it becomes smooth within, like a basin, and about sufficiently deep for the turtle to sink below the level of the surrounding sand. Then in the midddle of this pit she digs out a small perpendicular cavity, about the depth of a man's arm, and therein deposits her eggs to the number of over a hundred, and filling up the whole excavation, returns to sea. Thus, though a man may easily find the track of a turtle, it takes great experience to discover the eggs. Native fishers on bright moonlight nights walk round the beach after high-tide and look for the signs of turtle, as the animal leaves a broad track on the sand.

If the fisher finds the tracks of a turtle on the sand, but should not succeed in catching it, he will generally know whether the turtle has been lately on shore there before; if there are no signs of a previous visit, he will look out again for it on the ninth night from that time, and if it does not come then, on the eighteenth, for if no accident has occurred to it in the meantime it will assuredly return at one of these periods, exactly at the same spot, or not more than a cable's length to leeward—never to windward. If it should not come back on the eighteenth night from its first appearance, it will never return any more, at least until the following year.

It struck me as curious that an animal of so stupid an appearance should display so marvellous an instinct in the observance of times and seasons. Moreover, the female turtle are very clever in the concealment of their eggs. If they perceive a man in the neighbourhood, instead of instantly rushing away, with the certainty of capture, they will lie concealed for hours, as though in hope that he may depart without perceiving them.

If escape by this ruse is evidently impossible, by the advance of one of the lords of the creation, they start for the sea beach at a most astonishing rate, and then they are almost always caught by turning them on their backs. To the uninitiated in this strange business it would appear hardly feasible for a single man running in heavy sand after an animal weighing three or four hundred pounds to turn it over on its back; yet knack in this matter, like many others, overcomes the apparently impossible.

The manner of a turtle's locomotion on dry land when interfered with is to wriggle by sudden jerks from side to side, making short strokes with its flippers. The fisher takes quick notice of the cant, and turns him over at the right moment with ease. There can be no doubt that the most humane way of despatching them is by a sharp axe, but even in that case they will move about for some little time after; and unless the head is taken off close to the base of the skull, it will not altogether die until decomposition sets in.

The eggs of the turtle are perfectly round and rather smaller than a billiard ball, and without shell, the outer covering being like parchment. The natives eat them, and I tried on several occasions to follow their example. I have determined never to try again. A turtle killed by my brother in Savu Savu Bay contained more than 300 eggs, but turtles rarely lay more than half they have at a time. When the young are hatched, which takes place in a month, they are about the size of a large crown piece, perfectly formed, and ready to start on their battle of life, many of them being quickly gobbled up by birds of prey, or the great land-crab to which I have referred.

Among other profitable industries the collection of sponges is not the least important. It is said that the sponges of the

Pacific are inferior to those of the Levant or Red Sea. It may be so, but sponges are occasionally met with in the Pacific as large and well-shaped, and apparently as soft, as any to be found in the London market.

To fish for sponges with success requires a good deal of practice, as they are very difficult to recognise in the water when in a live state. They grow on the coral, and very much in the crevices of it, and are not by any means conspicuous, as they look like a part of the stone. When removed they are heavy, slimy, hard, and as black as tar. The best of them are in the form of a mushroom, and they are found from the size of a man's fist up to 2 feet in diameter. They usually lie within the lagoons in water of a depth from 1 to 10 fathoms. They are inhabited by animalculæ, which in the process of cleaning are decomposed and washed away. In order to effect this object on a sandy beach where the tide ebbs and flows, a number of forked sticks are driven into the sand, and upon them are fastened slender poles as a sort of framework; from these, sponges are suspended by strings, in such a manner that when the tide is in the sponges are floating in it; when it is not they are exposed to the wind and sun. In the latter case the animalculæ die and decay, and by alternate scorchings and washings, the sponge becomes cleaned and bleached as well as softened, in consequence of the removal of the glutinous creatures which had inhabited it. When prepared in this manner the usual way of barter in the islands where they are chiefly obtained is four large sponges for one yard of calico. Sponges are much improved by washing them in hot fresh water strongly impregnated with the *alkali* of wood-ashes.

CHAPTER XXXII.

A GLIMPSE OF TONGAN HISTORY.

HAVING dwelt at length on some of the natural productions of the islands, I must now come back more strictly to my tour through the Coral Lands themselves. Fiji and Samoa have already been treated of; I now come to Tonga. According to Mariner the Tongans did not deserve the name Cook gave them, that of the Friendly Islanders; he says that the chiefs intended to treacherously massacre Cook and his company, but the scheme came to nothing on account of differences among themselves as to how their amiable designs should be carried out.

It is probable that the Tongans, always a daring, ambitious, and piratical people, were compelled to keep in check their natural desire to kill the confiding white men, and get possession of the weapons and other useful things which they coveted, in order to increase their power. In referring to Fiji and Samoa, I have pointed out the influence of these people in both groups. Maafu's history and the cause of the rise of the Malietoa family in Samoa are evidences of the 'pushing' tendency of the Tongans; in fact, they have been well called the Anglo-Saxons of the South Pacific.

The Tongan Archipelago is composed of at least a hundred islands and islets, comprised between 18° and 20° S. lat., and 174° and 179° W. long. The three principal islands of Tongatabu, Vavau and Eoa, are alone of any extent, each ranging from 15 to 20 miles in length. Six others, namely, Late, Tofua, Kao, Numuka, Lefuga, and Haano, are from 5 to 7 miles in extent. The rest are much smaller. Many of them are in fact only banks of sand and coral, covered with some tufts of trees. Tofua, Kao, and Late are sufficiently high to be distinguished 15 or 20 leagues off at sea. Eoa, Namuka, and Vavau are of a moderate height; Tongatabu and the rest are all very low—in fact, the highest point at the capital is only 100 feet above high-water level. I have heard a great many estimates of the population; but I do not think I am very far wrong in guessing it at about 30,000.

Tongatabu is in the form of an irregular crescent, whose convexity faces the south, and the concavity the north, deeply indented by a lagoon of 5 miles broad and 3 miles deep. Immense reefs of coral extend 6 or 8 miles off the island on all its north part, and form different channels, with a useful road for any ship that anchors there. Many islets are situated among these coral reefs, the greater number being covered with trees. Eoa lies to the south-east of Tongatabu, a channel of some 9 miles separating them. It is about 600 feet in height, rocky and barren, and has few inhabitants. The principal island of the Namuka Group is rather low, and has a salt-water lake in its centre, without communication with the sea. This extraordinary lake is about a mile and a half broad. To the north and east of Namuka, the sea is sprinkled with a vast number of islands, which lie scattered around at unequal distances. Most of them are entirely clothed with trees of all sorts, including the cocoa-nut palms and flowering shrubs, and each presents the appearance of a beautiful garden placed in the sea.

The Hapai, Lifuka, and Kotoo Groups call for no special remark. Tofoa, an active and volcanic island to the north-west of Kotoo, in lat. 19° 45′ S., long. 175° 3′ W., is about 2800 feet high. A remarkable lake, as in Taviuni, is said to exist upon it, from which the natives bring small black volcanic pebbles, which are greatly prized, to cover the graves of their friends. This island is covered with trees to its summit, and is about 5 miles in diameter.

One of the most frequented of the groups is that of Vavau, which lies 70 miles to the north of the Hapai Group. Late Island has a peak about 1800 feet high in the centre of the island, which at one time was a volcano. It is from 6 to 7 miles in circumference.

After this summary of the geography of the Tongan Group I can proceed to other matters. The Tongans, like the Fijians and Samoans, have had, from time immemorial, a civilisation of their own. They have more moral stamina, energy, and self-reliance than any other existing race in the Pacific. Had they been acquainted earlier with the use of metals, there can be no doubt that they would have subdued all Polynesia.

When Captain Cook was in the islands, the habits of war were little known to the natives; the only quarrels in which they had at that time engaged had been among the inhabitants of the Fijis. They visited that group for the purpose of getting sandal-wood, and to join the fighting Fijians for their own ends. From the latter they gained a knowledge of improved spears, and bows, and arrows. In Captain Cook's time, this warlike spirit of the Tongans was confined to the young men, who adopted a maxim they attributed to Fiji, that war and strife were the noble employments of men, and ease and pleasure only suitable for the weak and effeminate. Thus, some years after Captain Cook's visit, a certain Tui Hala Fatai set sail with his followers, about 250 in number, for the Fijian island of Lakemba, and first joined one party, then another, robbing, plundering, and murdering the natives, and doing all things necessary to maintain the pomp and ceremonial observance of the precepts of 'glorious war' as they understood it. Not content with 'washing their spears' (as the Zulus have it) with the blood of the unfortunate Fijians, who had fighting enough of their own without the gratuitous assistance of the Tongans, these enterprising gentry took to quarrelling among themselves on Fiji soil. For two years and a half they seem to have had, according to their notions of manly employment, 'a thoroughly good time.' Whether the Fijians appreciated their visitors and their ways is another question. At any rate, the dislike of the Tongans manifested by the Fijians to this day is very easily accounted for. These interesting filibusters returned to Tonga, but not in their own canoes, those of the Fijians being, as I have said, much better. So, very considerately, they made the Fijians a present of the clumsy vessels in which they had emigrated, and, as exchange is no robbery, took some new and fast-sailing Fiji-built canoes in return.

I am giving a very condensed account of what I know about these remarkable people, but I cannot resist saying that, in view of some of their proceedings, I rather regret having mentioned the fact that they are sometimes dubbed the Anglo-Saxons of the South Pacific.

On his arrival, Hala Fatai found that a certain Togo Ahu, who had long since been King of Tonga, had made himself as disagreeable as possible to his subjects. On one occasion, for instance, he gave orders ('Divine right to rule wrong' was a Tongan tradition, and the orders were instantly obeyed) that twelve of his cooks, who were always in waiting at the public ceremony of his kava-drinking, should have their left arms amputated, to gratify his vanity by distinguishing them from other men not occupying so enviable a rank.

A chief of the name of Tubu Neuha and his brother, called Finoo (I am by no means certain of the correct spelling), indignant at the eccentric surgical operations of their king, determined to depose him. They 'deposed' him in a characteristic Tongan fashion.

One evening Tubu Neuha and Finoo, attended by several of their followers, waited on Togo Ahu, as was now and then customary, to pay their respects to him by presents of kava-root (*angona*), cloth, a pig, and several baskets of yams; they then retired. This served as a plausible reason for their being that night in the neighbourhood of the king's house. About midnight they again repaired to his house with their followers, whom they placed around it as watchful guards, ready to despatch all who might attempt to escape from the place: of these Finoo took the command, while Tubu Neuha entered, armed with his axe, and burning with a thirst for blood. As he passed along on either side by the wives and favourite mistresses of the king, the matchless beauties of Tonga, perfumed with the aroma of sandal-wood and bearing around their necks wreaths of the freshest flowers, the sanguinary chief might have wept over their fate; but the freedom of his country was at stake, and the opportunity was not to be lost. He sought the mat on which his destined victim lay buried in profound sleep; stood over him for a moment, then, resolving that his victim should know from whom he received his death, he struck him upon the face with his hand. Togo Ahu started up, and hearing only the words,

''Tis I, Tubu Neuha, that strike!' was by a tremendous blow felled to the ground, never to rise again.

The loyalists rose *en masse;* a battle ensued, and the regicides were repulsed, when Hala Fatai and his Fiji party appeared on the scene and sided with Finoo. Another desperate engagement took place: it lasted three hours, and it is said that Tubu Neuha alone slew on that day (well remembered by tradition here in Tonga) forty royalists with his own hand. This time the rebels were completely victorious, but at the cost of some of their bravest men, and they had to retire to the Hapai Group, of which Finoo was declared king, and after installing Tubu Neuha as Viceroy of Vavau (the flight of whose chief to Samoa gave rise to the Tongan disturbances already referred to), returned to Tongatabu to complete his triumph.

In the end Finoo succeeded in making himself master of the greater part of the group, behaved somewhat treacherously to his brother, Tubu Neuha, and eventually shared the government of the group with his assassin, one Tubu Toa, a natural son of the late king. The assassination of Neuha was as dramatic as that of the old king; and the son of the man who had been killed by Tubu Neuha, after having struck the body of his father's murderer several times, thus addressed it:

'The time of vengeance is come! Thou hast been long enough the chief of Vavau, living in ease and luxury, thou murderer of my father! I would have acted long ago if I could have depended on others to second me; not that I feared death by making thee my enemy, but the vengeance of my chief, Tubu Toa, was first to be satisfied, and it was a duty. I was bound by duty to the spirit of my father to preserve my life as long as possible, that I might have the satisfaction of seeing thee thus lying dead.'

Finoo resided chiefly at Vavau, while Tubu Toa reigned at Tonga; thus the country was divided between them. Shortly before his own death, Finoo's daughter, six or seven years old, fell ill, and ultimately died; and to give some little idea of the religion of these people not many years before the introduction of Christianity, I extract the following from Mariner's account of his visit to Tonga in the early part of this century (the year would be about 1808). The little girl had been removed from her father's house to another inside a fencing consecrated to Talie Tabu, the patron god of the kings of Tonga.

'Almost every morning a hog was killed, dressed, and presented before the house as an offering to the god, that he might spare the girl's life for the sake of Finoo.' The divinity was thus invoked: 'Here thou seest assembled Finoo and his chiefs, and the principal *matabooles* of thy favoured land: thou seest them humbled before thee. We pray thee not to be merciless, but spare the life of the woman for the sake of her father, who has always been attentive to every religious ceremony; but if thy anger is justly excited by some crime or misdemeanour committed by any other of us who are here assembled, we entreat thee to inflict on the guilty one the punishment he merits, and not to let go thy vengeance on one who was born but as yesterday. For our own parts, what other object have we in life but to serve Finoo? But if his family is afflicted, we are all afflicted, innocent as well as guilty. How canst thou be merciless? Dost thou not see here Finoo? And is not Afoo here, who descended from ancient Tonga chiefs, now in Bolotoo (or paradise)? And is not Fotoo here, and did he not descend from Moumoua, formerly king (or Tua) of Tonga? And is not A'lo here, and Nine'apo, and Too'bo?—then why art thou merciless? Have regard then for Finoo, and save the life of his daughter!'

The funeral ceremonies of this child were remarkable, in that they were followed by signs of rejoicing instead of mourning, with the purpose, Mariner thinks, of insulting the god who had robbed Finoo of his dearly loved one. After the body had been laid out and washed with oil and water, it was anointed with sandal-wood and oil, and then wrapped in 14 or 15 yards of fine East India muslin, which had belonged to the officers of the wrecked English ship which brought

Mariner to Tonga. It was next laid in a large cedar chest, and over the body were strewn wreaths of bright flowers. The corpse lay in state for twenty days, after which it was deposited inside a house at the top of the grave, where the grieving father could always gaze at it. Combats of men and women, with the usual extravagant banquets of kava-drinking, wound up the first attempt at funeral reform in Tonga, for though the wives were rarely strangled at great persons' deaths, as in Fiji, there was as a rule any quantity of demonstrative howling; and mutilations of arms, fingers, and toes were very common.

Finoo being taken ill himself shortly after the funeral, one of his illegitimate children was strangled as a sacrifice to the gods; but all in vain. He followed his little daughter after the lapse of a few days.

The ceremonies at his obsequies were of the usual South Pacific character. The chiefs paraded up and down with a wild and agitated step, spinning and whirling the club about, striking themselves with the edge of it two or three times violently upon the top and back of the head (the natives of Coral Lands know very well how to avoid the chief arteries), and then suddenly stopping, looking steadfastly at the instrument spattered with blood, and exclaiming:

'Alas, my club! who could have supposed that you would have done this kind office for me, and enabled me thus to evince a testimony of my respect for Finoo? Never, no, never, can you tear open the brains of his enemies! Alas! what a great and mighty warrior has fallen! O Finoo! cease to suspect my loyalty! be convinced of my fidelity! But what absurdity am I talking? If I had appeared treacherous in your sight, I should have met the fate of those numerous warriors who have fallen victims to your just revenge, but do not think, Finoo, that I reproach you: no, I wish only to convince you of my innocence, for who that has thoughts of harming his chiefs shall grow white-headed like me? O cruel gods! to deprive us of our father, of our only hope, for whom alone we wished to live! We have, indeed, other chiefs; but they are only chiefs in rank, and not like you, alas, great and mighty in war!'

Finoo was reckless and ambitious, a born ruler of men. Mariner says he would frequently burst out in speeches like the following:

'Oh that the gods would make me King of England! There is not an island in the whole world, however small, but what I would then subject to my power. The King of England does not deserve the dominions he enjoys; possessed of so many great ships, why does he suffer such petty islands as those of Tonga continually to insult his people with acts of treachery? Were I he, would I send tamely to *ask* for yams and pigs? No! I would come down with the front of battle, and with the thunder of Botolane' (a Tongan name for the noise of the cannon). 'I would show who was to be the chief. None but men of enterprising spirits should be in possession of guns. Let such rule the earth, and be those their vassals who can bear to submit to such insults unrevenged.'

Finoo would never listen to the arguments in favour of Christianity. He said its precepts would interfere with his absolute despotism. The first missionaries who landed in Tonga were all killed by the natives, the majority by order of the king, in consequence of an English runaway convict, who had settled in the island, having quarrelled with them over an iron pot, denouncing them to the natives as witch-doctors, and having introduced a mortality, then raging, for their own ends.

This mission-hating murderer was as fine a specimen of the advanced anti-clerical party as I have ever heard of.

In the days of heathen Tonga, great importance was attached to the invocation of the gods and the inspiration of the priests. The night previous to the consultation of the oracle, the chief ordered his cooks to kill and prepare a hog, and procure a basket of yams, and two bunches of ripe plantains. These things being got ready, the next morning they were carried to the place where the priest resided. The chiefs and *mataboolеs* clothed themselves in mats, and repaired to the place where the priest was to be found; if at a house, the priest seated himself just within the eaves (the Tongan houses resemble the Samoan in being open all round, about 4 feet from the ground); if at a distance from a dwelling, he seated himself on any convenient spot of ground, with the *mataboolеs* on either hand, so as to form a sort of a circle. In this space, at the bottom of the circle, sat the man who prepared the *kava*, the root being previously chewed by the cooks, attendants, and others who sat behind him; behind these again sat the chiefs among the people. The chiefs occupied this retired and humble station on account of the sacredness of the occasion, conceiving that such modest demeanour must be acceptable to the gods.

As soon as they were all seated, the priest was considered inspired, the god being supposed to exist within him, and speak through him from that minute. He sat for a considerable time in silence, with his hands clasped before him; his eyes were cast down, and he remained perfectly still. During the time that the victuals were being shared out, and the *kava* prepared, the *mataboolеs* sometimes used to begin to consult him; sometimes he would answer them, at other times not. In any case, he used to remain with his eyes cast down.

Frequently he would not answer a word till the repast was finished and the *kava* also. When he did speak, he would begin in a very low and unnatural voice, which used gradually to rise to its natural pitch, and now and again a little above it. All that he said was supposed to be the inspiration of the god, and he spoke in the first person as if he were the god.

All this was done generally without any apparent emotion, but sometimes his countenance became fierce and his whole frame agitated with inward feeling: he was seized with a universal trembling, the perspiration would break out on his forehead, and his lips, turning black, become convulsed. At length tears would start in floods from his eyes, his breast would heave with the most profound emotion, and his utterance become choked. Then these symptoms would gradually subside. It should be mentioned, however, on the authority of Mariner and other writers, that before the paroxysm came on, he would eat as much as four hungry men could possibly devour. The fit having gone off, he would remain for a time calm, and then take up a club that was placed by him for the purpose, and regard it attentively; he would look to the left, and then to the right, then suddenly raising the club, he would, after a moment's pause, strike the ground: immediately the god was supposed to leave him, and he would rise up and retire to the people at the back of the king.

There was no assumed agitation for the purposes of popular deception on the part of these Tongan priests. It was the result of a strong effort of the will, and the mind thus given to a certain defined course of action controlled the whole body. The records of every religion bear a common testimony to the truth of these religious phenomena, and they range from the visions of St. Paul, or the ecstasies of St. Bonaventure, down to the 'waltzing around' of American shakers.

Tongan hospitality is as thorough as their other national characteristics. Some 70 or 80 years ago, when they first made the acquaintance of white men, they were intensely puzzled by what they considered the selfishness of the white man's way of living in procuring everything for himself and family by purchase, and only allowing his friends to partake of his good things by invitation. They used to remark that the Tongan custom was far better; that they had nothing to do when they felt hungry or thirsty, but to go into any house where eating and drinking was going forward, sit down with the company without invitation, and partake of what they had. The selfish isolation of the *papalagis* has passed into a Tongan proverb, and when any stranger comes into their houses to eat with them, they will sometimes say jocosely:

'No! we shall treat you after the white man's manner: go home and eat what *you* have got, and we shall eat what *we* have got.'

England at one time was almost Tongan in this matter of open-hearted hospitality, even if it was confined to the monasteries. When we became 'reformed,' however, we did away with the monasteries and built workhouses—to the great satisfaction of the hungry poor, and complete abolition, as we all know, of uncalled-for voluntary charity.

Mariner tells us that when Captain Cook visited the Tongans cannibalism was scarcely thought of among them, but that their interference in Fijian affairs soon taught it to them. A famine which happened some time after the Fiji invasion rendered the innovation in the matter of diet almost necessary, and about seventy years ago there can be no doubt they did occasionally eat their prisoners. But the new-fangled Fijian ideas were never permanently established as Tongan habits. In this regard they seem to have been a race standing midway between the peaceful Samoans and the bloodthirsty Fiji cannibals of the 'older days,' before the much-abused missionary reached the latter group.

The Tongans have a variety of traditions, many of which are very interesting. I will give two of them, the first of which will serve perhaps to form the basis of a Christmas moral story for young folk, with some such title as 'The Greedy Giant, or Gluttony's Reward.'

Once upon a time, there was a Tongan adventurer named Cau Moola, who desired to 'rectify some frontiers' belonging to the Fijians. If he had succeeded in his benevolent purpose, for which he would have 'accepted' canoes and other things in payment, he would then have returned to his native group and shown practically what advance he had made in the art of fighting by his residence in distant Fiji. Contrary winds, however, prevented his accomplishment of the 'shortest passage on record,' and he and his fellow-politicians (shall I say financiers ?) had to remain for a space on an island called Lotooma. Received right hospitably by the natives ('where ignorance is bliss, 'tis folly to be wise'—especially if fighting men are scarce), the Tongans were shown some very big bones, and this is how they say those bones came there.

Many years ago, before men of common stature lived at Tonga, two enormous giants resided there, who happening on some occasion to offend their god, he punished them by causing a scarcity on all the Tonga islands, which obliged the giants to go and seek food elsewhere. As they were vastly above the ordinary size of the sons of men nowadays, they were able with the greatest imaginable ease to stride from one island to another, provided the distance was not more than about a couple of miles; at all events, their stature enabled them to wade through the sea without danger, the water in general not coming higher than their knees, and in the deepest place not higher than their hips. Thus situated, no alternative was left them but to splash through the water in search of a more fruitful soil. At length they came in sight of the island of Lotooma, and viewing it at a distance with hungry eyes, one of them thought that this small island could not supply more food than would be sufficient for himself at one meal, and resolved therefore wisely, out of pure consideration for his own stomach, to make an end of his companion: this he accomplished—by what process tradition does not say.

When he arrived at Lotooma he was no doubt very hungry, but at the same time very sleepy; so resolving to have just forty winks, he made a pillow of Lotooma, and not caring to lie all night in the water (for it was eventide when he decided on his nap), he stretched his legs over to the island of Fortuna, making a sort of bridge from one place to the other. By-and-by he snored to such a degree that both islands, particularly Lotooma, were shaken as if by an earthquake, much to the alarm of the inhabitants.

The people of the latter island being roused from their slumbers by this unreasonable and extraordinary noise, repaired to the place where the head of the giant lay, and discovering that he was fast asleep, determined on killing him, lest on awaking he might eat them all up. 'Defence, not defiance,' was their maxim. Every man armed himself with an axe, and at a given signal they struck the giant's head at the same moment. Up he started with a tremendous roar, and recovering his feet, stood aloft on the island of Lotooma; but falling again with his head and body in the sea, and being unable to recover himself, he was drowned, his feet remaining on dry land. As evidence of these facts, the Lotooma people showed our Tongan friend (since dead) two enormous bones, which, by the way, were supposed by more scientific observers to be the relics of some marine monster.

The second story is also one of Cau Moola's, and relates to the enormous lizard he heard of when diplomatically engaged (with troops) in Fiji. The natives of Bau in that group told him that on one occasion when sleeping on the beach, they saw by the light of the moon a gigantic lizard leap out of the water. They were aroused from their slumbers by the screams of one of their companions, whom they afterwards missed. Next morning a young lad bathing in the sea was snatched up, and a few days later a woman was similarly destroyed. The Fijians were now in arms, and threw stones into the bay. The animal being disturbed rushed out, when he was pursued by a number of men who threw spears at him; but these were of no avail, as his hard scales proved impenetrable to their weapons. This confirmed them in their original idea that the animal was a god, sent as a punishment for some offence they had committed. After he had destroyed about nine or ten people in the island, an old warrior, who was sceptical as to this animal's divinity, noticed that he came ashore every morning at one particular place, near which he concealed himself.

Between the beach and the sea was a large tree, and the old man's plan was to procure a long rope, and passing it over a strong branch of this tree, to let one end, at which there was a running noose, hang near the ground, whilst the other end was to be in the possession of about fourteen or fifteen strong men concealed at a little distance in the high grass. When next the lizard-shaped 'god' made his appearance, he rushed towards the veteran, who retired to his station behind the noose. The animal put his jaws through it, the signal was given, and the cord drawn tight. The active Fijians soon commenced to beat him about the head and pierce him wherever they could, until, as they described it to the Tongan filibuster, 'after much hard work he was quite dead.' Their toil over, they resolved at once to see if he was good for a meal; and selecting the parts they thought the tenderest, they baked them, and doubtless had a fine dinner off a wandering crocodile. According to a New Orleans journal, a fowl stuffed with dynamite is placed near an alligator's resort, and then the editor says sadly, 'When that alligator indulges in that poultry, he knows his place no more.' According to the Tongan tradition, the Fijian's simple noose was too much for the 'big lizard' from the East Indies.

CHAPTER XXXIII.

TONGAN TRADITIONS.

As in Fiji, rank is very strictly observed in Tonga. In the old days there existed two chiefs in that group who claimed a sort of divine power; these were the Tuitonga and Veachi, the first of course meaning chief of Tonga, which island has always been considered the most important and noble of all the Tongan Group. In Tonga all the greatest chiefs resided, and were buried near the tombs of their ancestors, and this is how it is that the appellation *tabu* was given it—the latter word meaning sacred or holy.

Tuitonga and Veachi were both supposed to be descended from chief gods, who had formerly visited Tonga. The respect formerly shown to Tuitonga, and his high rank in society, were entirely of a religious nature, and in secular matters the king was supreme. Once a year (about October), the first-fruits were offered to Tuitonga. There were peculiarities in the ceremonies of his marriage and burial. Moreover, Tuitonga was not circumcised as the other men were; nor did he ever tattoo. Again, he was spoken of differently, and words were exclusively reserved for him, and only with respect to him.

After the nobles came the *mataboöles,* who seem to have been the business agents of the aristocracy. Certain professions were hereditary, and to some extent this, I believe, continues to the present day. These are canoe builders, cutters of whale's teeth ornaments, and superintendents of funeral rites. Next in rank to these came the *mataboöles,* or the class immediately below that very important body of men.

Old persons of both sexes have from time immemorial been reverenced in Tonga, and the first moral and religious duty impressed on a Tongan was to reverence the gods, chiefs, and aged persons. Women have always been treated in Tonga with the greatest respect, and rank descends through them.

The old religion of the Tongans was really a complicated piece of heathenism. It was based on the idea of gods who had existed from all eternity; but there were other degrees of gods of inferior rank, these being mainly recruited from deceased chiefs and *mataboöles.* The nobles and *mataboöles* were allowed to possess souls, but not the *tooas,* or common people, for whom there was no future after death. They maintained that the human soul during life is not a distinct essence from the body, but only the more ethereal part of it, which exists in Bolotoo (or paradise) in the form and likeness of the body the moment after death. Here is a curious approach to the Christian doctrine of the resurrection of the body. The Tongans believe firmly in supernatural appearances of the gods, and that they occasionally use the bodies of animals as their earthly covering; but at other times they would appear to mortals in all their glory.

Human merit or virtue consisted chiefly in paying respect to gods, nobles, and the aged, in defending one's hereditary rights, in honour, justice, patriotism, friendship, meekness, modesty, fidelity of married women, parental and filial love, observance of all religious ceremonies, and forbearance.

All rewards for virtue and punishment for vice are bestowed on men in this world only, Bolotoo being considered a sort of place to which rank entitled a man, more than a paradise of delights as a reward for a good life. Killing servants, or one of the lower classes who had given provocation, and theft of property not consecrated, were considered matters of indifference.

Bolotoo was supposed to be an island lying to the north-west. It was said to be much larger than all their own islands put together, was well stocked with all kinds of useful and ornamental plants, and the whole atmosphere was redolent with the scent of flowers. Birds of gorgeous plumage carolled ceaselessly in Bolotoo, and of every variety of food there was an inexhaustible supply; for as soon as a hog was killed, another one immediately took his place. The Tongans used to tell a story of one of their canoes, which was driven by stress of weather to Bolotoo. The men were ignorant of the place they had reached, and seeing the country abound in all sorts of fruits, the crew landed, and proceeded to pluck some bread-fruit; but, to their unspeakable astonishment, they could no more lay hold of it than if it were a shadow. They walked through the trunks of the trees and passed through the substance of the houses without feeling any resistance. They at length saw some of the gods, who recommended them to go away immediately, as they had no proper food for them, and promised them a fair wind and a speedy passage. They accordingly put directly to sea, and in two days' sailing with a tremendous velocity they arrived at Samoa. Here they stayed for two or three days, and soon afterwards reached Tonga, where in course of a short time they all died, not as a punishment, but as a natural consequence, the air of Bolotoo being the certain cause of a speedy death.

The Tongan gods were as follows: Tali-Toobo (literally, 'Wait there, Toobo'). This personage was a god of war. Tuifua Bolotoo, or chief of all Bolotoo, and supreme god of that place. Alo Alo (literally, 'to fan'), who took charge of wind, weather, rain and harvests. Tangaloa, god of artificers and arts; and a few others. The Tongan account of the creation is very much akin to that given by the Maori of New Zealand.

One day, many years ago, Tangaloa, intent on fishing, let down his hook and line from the sky into the wide expanse of ocean that then only existed. Suddenly he felt a great resistance, and believing that he had caught a gigantic fish, he exerted his utmost strength, and presently there appeared above the surface several points of rock, which increased in number and extent the more he drew in his line. The rocky bottom of the ocean in which it was now evident his hook had caught was thus fast advancing to the surface, and would have made one vast continent, when unfortunately the line broke, and the islands of Tonga remained to show the imperfection of Tongaloa's earth-fishing. The rock in which the hook was fixed was already above the surface, and used to be shown to the curious in one of the islands. The hook was in the possession of the Tuitonga family till about 100 years ago, when it was accidentally burnt with the house in which it was kept. Tongaloa soon made his islands something like Bolotoo, but of course very inferior, the trees, flowers, and plants being subject to decay and death. Being willing that Tonga should also be inhabited by intelligent beings, he commanded his two sons thus (I give, as near as possible, a literal translation of the actual words of the Tongan tradition, as told by Mr. Mariner seventy-four years ago):

'"Go and take with you your wives, and dwell in the world at Tonga. Divide the land into two portions, and dwell separately from each other."

'They departed accordingly. The name of the eldest was Toobo, and the name of the youngest was Vaca-acowooli, who was an exceedingly wise young man, for it was he who first formed axes, and invented beads, and cloth, and looking-glasses. The young man named Toobo acted very differently, being very indolent, sauntering about, and sleeping, and envying very much the works of his brother. Tired at length with begging for his goods, he bethought himself to kill him, but concealed his wicked intention. He accordingly met his brother walking, and beat him till he was dead. At that time their father came from Bolootoo, with exceeding great anger, and asked him:

'"Why have you killed your brother? Could you not work like him? O thou wicked one! Begone! go with my commands to the family of Vaca-acowooli, and tell them to come hither."

'Being accordingly come, Tongaloa straightway ordered them thus:

'"Put your canoes to sea, and sail to the east, to the great land which is there, and take up your abode there. Be your skins white, like your minds, for your minds are pure; you shall be wise, making axes, and all riches whatsoever, and shall have large canoes. I will go myself, and command the wind to blow from your land to Tonga, but they (the Tonga people) shall not be able to go to you with their bad canoes."

'Tongaloa then spoke thus to the others:

'"You shall be black because your minds are bad, and shall be destitute; you shall not be wise in useful things, neither shall you go to the great land of your brothers. How can you go with your bad canoes? But your brothers shall come to Tonga, and trade with you as they please."'

Mr. Mariner tells us he took particular pains to make inquiries respecting the foregoing tradition, and found that although the chiefs and *mataboolες* were acquainted with it, the bulk of the people were entirely ignorant of it. This led him at first to suspect that the chiefs had obtained the leading facts from the missionaries that had stayed a short time previously in the group; but the oldest men affirmed strongly that it was an ancient traditionary record, and founded on truth. It agrees with many of the Fijian and Samoan legends, in which, as I have pointed out, there is a strong Mosaic element, and I am inclined to think that the story is correctly described as veritable Tongan tradition of great antiquity. It certainly seems strange that they should believe an account which serves to make them a degraded race, the cursed descendants of the murderer of his brother.

The chastity of the married women was considered of the highest importance: divorce, however, was a common practice, and a woman thus divorced would marry again. As in Fiji, prostitution was simply unknown, the men being generally very true to their wives.

Children were occasionally strangled as sacrifices to the god, but with the greatest reluctance, as the Tongans have been for centuries most devoted parents. The chief widow of the Tuitonga was, however, strangled on the day of her husband's burial, that she might be interred with him. The funeral of a

Tuitonga was performed with marked ceremonial, the peculiarities of which may be here described.

The day after his death, which was the day of the burial, every individual in every island the news had reached—man, woman, and child—had the head closely shaved; this is a peculiarity, and so is the custom of depositing some of his most valuable property along with the body in the grave, such as beads, whales' teeth, Samoa mats, etc. The time of mourning for a Tuitonga was four months. The *tabu* for touching his body or anything he had on when he died, extended to at least ten months. Every man would neglect to shave his beard for at least one month, and during that time merely oiled his body and not his head.

In the afternoon of the day of burial, the body being already in the *fytoca* (or burial-place), the men, women, and children, all bearing torches, used to sit down at about 80 yards from the grave. The assemblage being complete and quiet, one of the female mourners would come out of the *fytoca*, and call out to the people, 'Arise ye, and approach;' whereupon the people would get up, and advancing about 40 yards, would again sit down.

Two men from behind the grave would now begin to blow conch-shells, and six others, with large lighted torches about 6 feet high and 6 inches thick, would descend from the raised *fytoca* and walk round one after the other several times, waving their flaming torches in the air.

After this ceremony these six leaders would ascend the mount again, and the moment they did so the people issued *en masse*, and following the six men with the big torches, ascended the mount in single file. As they passed the back of the grave the first six men would deposit their extinguished torches on the ground, an example which was followed by the others. The place was then cleared; the people separated according to their localities, and repaired to their temporary homes.

Soon after dark certain persons stationed at the grave began again to sound the conch, while others chanted, partly in an unknown language and partly in Samoan, a sort of song. The natives could give no account of what this language was, nor how they originally came to learn the words. While this was going on, about sixty men would assemble near the grave for the performance of a ceremony which I suppose has no parallel in the burial rites of the world. It being perfectly dark, the men would approach the mount and pay their devotions to the goddess Cloacina, after which they retired to their homes. At daybreak next morning all the women of the first rank, the wives and daughters of the greatest chiefs, would assemble, and with expressions of the most profound humility would make the place perfectly clean; and this extraordinary ceremony was repeated for fourteen nights, as was that of the burning torches. With these singular exceptions, the funeral of a Tuitonga was identical with that of a Tongan king.

CHAPTER XXXIV.

NEUTRAL TONGA.

THE present condition of Tonga is a very satisfactory one; the soil, it is almost needless to add, is inexhaustibly fertile, and it is also industriously cultivated, and intersected by good roads. Tonga is a succession of gardens, and want, beggary, or squalor are unknown. All the people are clothed, all read and write, all are professed Christians. They still retain a good deal of their old Tongan pride, but are courteous to strangers.

The Government is a monarchy, the reigning King being George of Tonga, who is assisted by a Council, or Parliament. On each of the great islands there resides a governor. These are men of intelligence who speak English, dress well, and live in imported houses of the European fashion. The Governor of Vavau in 1874 was named David—all the Tongans take great delight in scriptural, or English names. He was a man of huge stature and majestic presence, and looked very well in a handsome uniform he had made for him in Sydney, at a cost of about £200. A friend of mine gave me the following curious account of this personage, with whom he stayed. David's house would be regarded in the Australian colonies as a fitting residence for any high official below the rank of a Viceroy. It is constructed of imported materials, all the interior panelled and polished; the furniture of every room being elegant and costly, and imported from New South Wales. In the centre of the building is a large dining-hall with stained-glass doors at either end, which is only used on state occasions. Here the table is laid with every requisite, fine linen, plate, and cut glass. The cook is a Chinaman, the butler a negro. A better, or more elegantly served dinner one would scarcely expect in Sydney: everything is in profusion, even to champagne and soda-water. This David, like all his colleagues, apes the manners of a British officer. One remark he made was very characteristic of the man. My friend perceived on a Sunday afternoon that he did not leave the house, although his people were all at church for the second time. He inquired the reason, and the Governor replied, 'I have been this morning; too much church is not good. I have been told that English gentlemen do not go to church more than once a day. We got our religion and laws from the English. Why then should we not imitate their religious customs?'

The religion referred to is that of the Protestant missionaries, and, of course, the established religion is Protestant; but toleration of all other creeds is the rule in Tonga, and no oppression of minorities is permitted. It is a far cry from Livadia to Tongatabu, but 'Holy' Russia might take a lesson from the 'savages' of the South Sea, and possibly be able to reduce her Polish garrisons.

The Tongan laws are generally just, and are very strictly enforced. The statutes are printed, and distinctly understood by all the people. There is a strong flavour of Sabbatarianism about some of the edicts, which of course indicates their origin; but it seems to me that it is far better for the Tongans to hold curiously strict notions as to how to conduct themselves on the first day of the week—or, as they would call it, in Jewish parlance, the Sabbath—than to strangle children in sacrifice to heathen deities.

The laws of Tonga forbid the sale of land to foreigners, but it is permitted to be leased on such liberal conditions and for so long a term as to be tantamount to an actual sale. All traders, planters, or permanent foreign residents not in the service of the Government, are obliged to take out a license. Spirits and some other articles pay a heavy duty. All the people contribute to the support of the state, the tax being on an adult male about six dollars per annum.

All the great islands are traversed by broad roads laid out by a European engineer. They are formed and kept in repair by the labour of convicted criminals. There is an efficient police force, and for the defence of the country all able-bodied men are supplied with arms (*i.e.*, a musket and bayonet), and are required to attend drill twice a week. The musketry instructors are generally Europeans of experience, and the other European servants of the Government, excluding those holding very high office, are the King's private secretary, a land-surveyor, a surgeon, and many skilled mechanics.

The German Government have a treaty with King George, and I believe that a permanent treaty with Her Majesty has been ratified.

In connection with Germany, it may be mentioned that when the Franco-Prussian War broke out in 1870, the Tongan King issued a solemn proclamation of neutrality! Whether the 'inspired press' of France and Germany have continued ever since to denounce the 'perfidious selfishness' of this South Sea Group I do not know.

As in the case of Samoa, the trade of Tonga is or was practically a monopoly of the Hamburg house of Godeffroy, who here, as elsewhere, mainly confine their attentions to copra. Coffee, arrowroot, and tapioca are not forgotten, and of these there are, or were some two years ago, very successful plantations.

The *masi*, or *tappa*-tree, is extensively cultivated in Tonga. It is propagated by cuttings, 2 feet or 3 feet apart in plantations. It is allowed to grow from 10 to 15 feet high, when it is about the thickness of a gun-barrel. The fibres growing wild in the Friendly Islands are as numerous as those in Fiji. One of the most useful of the raw materials to be met with in the Pacific can be obtained from the stalks of the *puraka* plant, a gigantic species of *arum*, of which the leaves are as much as 6 feet long by 4 feet in width, and the root sometimes as large as a five-gallon keg. From this fibre some beautiful fabrics are made; a sample of it was many years ago sent home here and made into a bonnet, and presented to the Queen. An endeavour was made at the time to introduce it in the London market, but it now seems to be forgotten.

In the Friendly Islands, as well as in all the neighbouring groups, great quantities of the *ti*, or dragon-tree, are found. The root when cooked contains an extraordinary quantity of saccharine matter; indeed, it seems as if it had been boiled in syrup. Rum is distilled from it in the Friendly Islands, as well as from the sugar-cane. What applies, however, to Fiji applies also to Tonga for the most part, and a repetition of the riches of the Pacific groups is unnecessary. Some day my countrymen will understand and appreciate them. Until quite recently we have had an incurable preference for investments in the loans of South American republics, or for lending our money at high rates of interest to the 'sick man' by the Bosphorus.

CHAPTER XXXV.

THE LINE ISLANDS.

POLYNESIAN 'labour' is mainly recruited from the Gilbert and Kingsmill Groups on the Equator. The natives are called Tokalaus (or North-Eastern) in Fiji; Tapitaweans in Samoa, from the largest island of the Kingsmill Group; and Arorais in Tahiti or Marquesas, that being the island from which they were first brought to Tahiti. They live on islands little more than large sand-banks surrounded by coral-reefs, and their principal food consists of cocoa-nuts, fish, and the dried fruit of the screw-palm. With cocoa-nuts their islands are well supplied, and numbers were planted every year even in the old days. Since white traders have come among them, and they have found a sale for their copra, they plant cocoa-nut trees regularly, and in great numbers.

It is impossible to give the exact population of these groups of atolls on the Line; but I do not think I am very far out in estimating that of the Kingsmills at 3000. This shows a great decrease over what it must once have been; as their inveterate toddy-drinking, with its invariable sequel of a free-fight and consequent loss of life, has thinned the islanders for years.

The natives do not seem to know how they first learnt to make their terrible intoxicant, but I am inclined to believe that the art was taught them by whalers, perhaps fifty years ago.

The *modus operandi* of a Line Island distillery is as follows: The centre-shoot of the cocoa-nut tree is bent in an incline towards the ground, and each morning the men pare off an eighth of an inch, when the sap exudes, and drops into a bottle suspended beneath. By this process two to three pints a day are obtained. This liquid, if kept for twenty-four to thirty-six hours, becomes very intoxicating, and if fermented produces one of the strongest drinks in the world. A wine-glassful is quite sufficient to make a powerful man, accustomed to plentiful libations of whisky or other spirits, 'mad drunk.' The devotee at this particular shrine of Bacchus always gets up a fight, and will without the slightest provocation attack anybody and everybody he may meet. When whole villages have been having a 'sociable evening' with this toddy, the result may be imagined—if the reader can realise the pastime of a horde of demons.

Being perfectly well aware of the results of a drop too much being taken by a bosom friend, the Line islanders decline to live, so to speak, on the ground-floor, and perch their houses on poles. In the centre of the floor is a hole with a ladder, which they carefully take up with them when they 'go home.'

Their powers of fishing amount to an instinct, not only superior to those of any white people, but to those of such good fishers as the Samoans. In the use of both fish-traps and rod and line they excel. They never lose their love for cocoa-nuts and fish, and do not take kindly to porridge of corn-meal, unless there is a certain amount of cocoa-nut mixed with it. They are straight-haired, and of the copper-coloured Polynesian race, called by most authorities the Micronesians. They are all great navigators, and many of them build large boats not unlike those to be found in the Indian Seas. Their arms are fairly made, and they manufacture a very elaborate suit of armour from the husk of the cocoa-nut, which covers the entire body. I brought home with me a corslet, which is really a magnificent specimen of defensive armour.

I do not think that as yet Christian teachers have made much impression among the Line islanders. Little is generally known in the Pacific as to their traditions. Mr. Whitmee says that when he visited the group, the natives were strict in the observance of their rites, and the shrines of their gods were numerous. Every house contains a domestic shrine, to which offerings of food are presented. The gods are chiefly the spirits of their ancestors, the priesthood and chieftainship being commonly combined in the same persons.

They believe that for three or four days after death, the form of a deceased person hovers around his home about dusk, and that his friends may see him and hear him whistling. Their dwelling after death is across the sea—in what direction I never could find out.

The traditions of the Tarapon race are numerous, and in many cases resemble those of the other groups to the south-east of them, such as Fiji, Tonga, and Samoa. Their traditions chiefly relate to the origin of the islands and the people. They assert that some of the latter came from the West, and that these were met by some from the East. Most of the descendants of those arriving from the East were however destroyed by the others, who were more numerous.

They tattoo their backs, but never their faces, and both sexes can fight very courageously. The men are very jealous of their many wives. As used to be the case in Samoa (and is so now to a certain extent), the man who marries the eldest girl of a family has a right over all the other daughters, and if he, perhaps wisely, declines to 'marry the whole family' (I have heard of this being practically done outside the Kingsmills), the lovers of his sisters-in-law don't ask the consent of the parents, but the husband of the eldest young lady.

These people have been described as ferocious, but their ferocity is the natural result of gross ill-treatment. Like many other Polynesians, they have no idea of the sanctity of truth, and when it suits them can lie with sublime indifference.

They are decidedly the best labourers in the Pacific, as they understand the length of service on which they enter (four years), bring their women and children with them, work well, and if kindly treated are happy and contented. Their wants are small, and though they may have no word for gratitude, they are easily pleased and do not quickly forget a white man's kindness.

On the Samoan plantations their wages are $2 a month and their rations. In the Hawaiian kingdom they are paid from $5 to $6 a month; while in Tahiti the men receive $6, and the women $4 a month. On the plantations of Samoa (chiefly those of the Messrs. Godeffroy) they are paid in 'trade,' *i.e.* goods, while in Tahiti and Hawaii cash is the rule.

For reasons best known to themselves, the Line islanders have acquired a very decided reluctance to having anything to do with the Messrs. Godeffroy, whereas they willingly go to Fiji, Tahiti, and Hawaii.

In the year 1879, the German firm despatched three labour-vessels to the Line Islands, and these three vessels returned respectively with seven, six, and one, labourers. It is to be supposed that Messrs. Godeffroy will not court any more Line Island rebuffs. Prior to their recent failure, the great Hamburg house employed on their plantations 1000 Line islanders and 200 people from the New Hebrides.

The largest of the Kingsmill Group is the Island of Apemama, the population of which may be set down at about 5000. This is ruled over by a king called Tem Baiteke, who has also sway over Kuria and Aranuka, these two islands having a total population of 2500. His power is absolute; he even allows no man of his own people to look him in the face. His guards are armed with muskets, cartouche-boxes and swords. His dwelling consists of a very large house and several smaller ones, with stores for cocoa-nut oil and other produce. He has European furniture, and articles of utility and luxury of various kinds, and his quarters are surrounded by a stone wall with twelve pieces of cannon of various calibre. He boasts of a schooner of 60 tons, which is armed with four guns, and has also good whale-boats, besides war-canoes. He dresses in European fashion, usually in black trousers, linen shirt and a black alpaca coat, and he is blessed with numerous wives.

Tem Baiteke is a Polynesian king of the blood and iron order. He is no mild-spoken advocate of a Permissive Bill: if his people get very drunk, he never fines them forty shillings, but immediately puts them to death; and near his house is a very interesting collection of human heads set on spikes, *pour encourager les autres.* Tem Baiteke has also great ideas of the nobility of labour—for himself. So his people are kept hard at it all the year round, making cocoa-nut oil and fishing for *bêche-de-mer*, which he disposes of to the Sydney traders.

According to the latest information no European has been for years resident in any of the three islands ruled by Tem Baiteke, or even permitted to land in any inhabited part of it, with the single exception of the captain or trading-master of the ship with which he may be dealing. When a vessel is seen entering his harbour, she is boarded three miles from the town by the pilot, who is the king's brother, and can speak a little English, having years ago sailed in a whale-ship.

The pilot inquires all about the new-comer's business, and having seen the anchor put down, returns directly with his report to the King. If it be his pleasure the vessel is brought up to an anchorage near the village, and a small uninhabited islet is shown to the strangers as a place where they can, if they choose, land and display their goods to the natives, who will meet them there; otherwise they must do their business on board the ship. A number of women are allowed to go on board the vessel, and remain with the crew while she is in port. The captain or trader goes ashore, eats and drinks with the King, and is allowed perfect liberty. The King, as I have stated, claims all the produce of his people's labour, and receives all the pay, a portion of which, however, always consists of casks of tobacco, which he distributes justly among his subjects. In addition he serves out to them knives, axes, and other prized articles.

If the European vessel be not filled at Apemama, the King takes passage in her to his other two islands, his schooner keeping company. This latter craft is navigated by his own people, as he refuses to employ white sailors, having a rooted dislike to the *papalagi*.

On one occasion Tem Baiteke was offered a quantity of Oregon timber, and the services of an English carpenter to build him a handsome house.

'No!' he replied. 'If I never have a house to live in, I will never have a white man to live with me while he builds it.'

It was not always so in Apemama, and the rigid exclusion which Tem baiteke maintains is due to a horrible story of European avarice, lust, and murder, which would be a difficult business to intelligibly relate here.

The Line islanders all speak one language, in which consonants are more freely used than in the Sawaiori languages of the brown Polynesians of the Eastern Pacific. This is a great advantage in employing them as labourers, as it is easier to get on with them in their own tongue than in broken English.

Eighty per cent. of them are subject to a disease which often incapacitates them from work from four to twelve months. This is called in Fiji *thake*, and in Samoa *lepauni*. I have not heard that it exists in either the Marquesas or Tahiti. It appears in the form of sores, which vary from the size of a threepenny piece to 6 inches long. They are generally circular or oval; but when two or more join, the sore assumes all sorts of shapes; its edge is clearly defined, raised, and filled with yellow matter. A week or two after its first appearance the body is covered, and the patient becomes very weak, and suffers much from rheumatic pains and stiff joints.

Sometimes the sufferers waste away and die; but this may

be owing to their revolting practice of eating the scab, and so poisoning themselves internally.

In the Fiji, New Hebrides, Tongan, and Samoan Groups, nearly every native child has this strange disease between the ages of one and five, being afterwards exempt from it. White men have been known to take it occasionally. I never heard of any remedy, except a sea voyage to a place where the disease does not exist.

In the Kingsmills is to be found a certain cure for all inflammation of the mucous membrane. I have, I regret to say, forgotten the name of the plant; but several of my Samoan friends are aware of its existence, and probably know what the natives call it. A friend of mine used to prepare this drug, but he kept the manipulation a secret.

The other Polynesian labourers come from the New Hebrides, a group which extends from lat. 13° 16′ to 20° 15′ S., and from long. 166° 40′ to 170° 20′ E., and consists of eleven islands, the largest of which is Espiritu Santo. This island is 22 leagues in length, and half that in breadth.

The natives of the New Hebrides Group are dark in colour, of moderate stature, and in some places, as at Pentecost and Malicolo, are robust, muscular men with woolly hair. Generally, however, the Papuan race to which they belong are small, with thin limbs, and physically weak. In their natural condition they are invariably cannibals, and are broken up into small hostile tribes, constantly at war with each other. So great is the 'confusion of tongues' among these people, that the inhabitants of six native towns in the same island speak six different languages.

Women in the Papuan Islands are merely the slaves and tools of the men, who care for little else than fighting. In every respect the original condition of the inhabitants of the

New Hebrides is that of intense degradation. They have no traditions, and their religion resembles fetish worship. Kindness, gratitude, or even natural affection (except perhaps that of a mother for her child) are unknown. But in some of the islands Christian missions from Samoa have been very successful, especially in Antietum, where cannibalism has ceased for about twenty years, and the natives are all nominal Christians.

A few traders have settled among the group. The employment of labourers from the New Hebrides is certain to advance the civilisation of its people; but time will be required, remembering their inherent degradation, and the fact that much of the prevalent licentiousness is due to the pernicious influence of some of the whites who took up their abode among them many years since.

The climate of this group is damp, and sometimes considered unhealthy. Cotton and the usual products of Polynesia, including the sugar-cane, nutmegs, and cocoa-nuts, grow abundantly. The canoes of the people are rude in shape, and very clumsily fitted. Their arms are clubs, spears, and arrows, the latter generally supposed to be poisoned. Their gods, or 'devils,' are usually faces not unskilfully cut out of wood. Sometimes they are images of chiefs, made of clay and bamboo. Circumcision is practised universally. As in an island nearer home, the pigs share a Malicolo man's house, and the children and pigs sleep comfortably in the dust together. Infanticide is common, and the funeral ceremonies are like those practised in Fiji in the olden times.

Reference has been made to Nieuè, or Savage Island, so named by Captain Cook, on account of the extreme ferocity with which its natives attacked his landing detachment. It is about 36 miles in circumference, and about 200 feet high at the highest point. It consists of upheaved coral, and has no lagoon. There is a fair anchorage in several places, and great pools of fresh water exist in caverns on the coast. The inhabitants number about 3000, all of whom are professed Christians, and dress in European fashion. The soil is good, but not nearly so fertile as in other parts of the Pacific. Fungus is plentiful, and cocoa-nuts have been introduced into the island from Samoa. The trade is almost entirely in the hands of Messrs. Godeffroy.

Some 500 miles eastward of Nieuè is Palmerston Island, the first discovered in the South Pacific—being the San Pablo of Magalhaens. It has no harbour, but there is a good anchorage in a bight on the western side of the island. The land lies very low, in the form of a coral ring, upon which there are nine or ten islets from 1 to 3 miles long, enclosing a lagoon about 8 miles in diameter. Though many valuable plants grow wild there, little attention has been paid to the group, and a few years ago there were no permanent inhabitants. *Damana* timber is very plentiful there, and so is a wood called *Nangiia*, generally found in the Pacific on desert shores, or on the brink of lagoons where its roots are bathed by the tide. Its characteristics are great weight, intense hardness, and closeness of grain, and it would probably be very valuable as a substitute for boxwood for engravers. I think I have met with *Nangiia* under another name. Certain samples sent home to England by me from the Pacific had every appearance of making a first-class 'boxwood' but I regret to say they somehow miscarried *en route*, and I have not since heard of them. The logs of *Nangiia* found at Palmerston were about 18 inches in diameter. A few turtle-fishers and *bêche-de-mer* curers were the only inhabitants of Palmerston Island for years, and these were merely sojourners for a time.

Some detached islands, comparatively unknown, lying in the direction of the Marquesas Group, are also commercially interesting. One of the most remarkable is 500 miles due east of the Navigators, and is known as Suwarrow. This is a coral atoll of a triangular form, 50 miles in circumference, the reef having an average width of half a mile across the narrowest place, though divided by two rocks 200 yards apart into three channels 5 fathoms deep at the lowest tides, with a level bottom and no concealed dangers. Inside is a secure anchorage of varying depth, from 3 to 30 fathoms, offering accommodation for all the ships in the Pacific to ride in safety in all weathers, with room to beat out with a fair wind half-way round the compass, in or out.

Suwarrow was uninhabited when I was in the Pacific, and unclaimed by any nation. It is quite out of the track of hurricanes, which have never been known to extend so far eastward in this direction of the Pacific. There are nine or ten islets in the reef, two of them about 1½ mile in length, which are covered with tall timber. Upon the one next to the entrance into the lagoon are a great many cocoa-nut trees, and about 40 acres of rich soil not encumbered by forest. There is no fresh water on the surface, but undoubtedly this would be obtained by digging. The place would support, at any rate, about 100 Polynesians, and if properly superintended and supplied with boats, seeds of vegetables, and other requisites, would repay any arrangements of mercantile men for the introduction of native labour, even at double the average rate of wages, inasmuch as *bêche-de-mer* is found here of good quality, and in sufficient quantity to furnish a good annual cargo. The shoal water of the lagoon also abounds in pearl-shell of the largest size and finest lustre. The harbour could be utilised as a depôt for the collection of various cargoes, which could be obtained from the surrounding isles; and it would thus become a very valuable property, if worked by a business-like corporation, based perhaps on the lines of Messrs. Godeffroy's.

CHAPTER XXXVI.

'FROM ISLAND UNTO ISLAND AT THE GATEWAYS OF THE DAY.'

THE selection of 'trade' for an all-round cruise requires experience and judgment. It used to be a foolish saying in England, 'Oh, anything will do for the colonies;' but anything WON'T do for the islands. The following chapter is devoted to a *résumé* of information picked up while accompanying a friend on various lengthy cruises to the outlying archipelagoes of the Pacific, during which we found out over and over again that what would suit one group would be quite unsaleable in the next. Certain goods can always be safely taken, and a large profit can be relied on, even on Levuka prices, which for many articles of 'trade' are much higher than London figures. If a suitable vessel were chartered in London, with good passenger accommodation, and loaded with quick-selling cargo, it would be comparatively easy for any persons whom this book may interest to study things Polynesian themselves in a very comfortable fashion. In addition to an exceptionally beautiful cruise, with almost certain fair weather and calm sea, money should be made by those interested, and arrangements might be entered into which would lay the foundation for a profitable growing trade. I merely throw out the hint to gentlemen who may be glad to learn that there is still a region which, although discovered in great measure by a certain Captain

Cook, is as yet uninvaded by the satellites of the modern tourist of that name.

The islands of the 'Low Archipelago,' or the Tuamotus (sometimes called Paumotus, signifying a 'cloud of islands'), well deserve a short account. The group, or groups, extend over 16 degrees of longitude, and consist of 78 islands, all coral atolls, which with the exception of three are surrounded by lagoon reefs, varying in size from a few miles to over 100 miles in circumference. The population may be set down at 5000, of which perhaps only a fifth is in a state of primæval barbarism.

In former times these people were so famous for their bravery that Pomare the Great, of Tahiti (called so by reason of his conquests), invariably employed them as his guards.

All who know the Tuamotans say they feel safer in their company than in that of any other natives of the Pacific, and under circumstances of difficulty and danger this is especially noticeable. The Tuamotans are naturally independent, and they demand of their employers good pay and good usage. They are nearly all Catholics, and make very good converts; but they have a great predilection for rum, and are rather fond of an occasional free fight. On the Manga Reva Island there is a Catholic bishop and a body of clergy.

Of the 78 islands in the group 35 are known to contain pearl-shell in their lagoons, and there can be little doubt that the large pearl which was purchased by the Queen for £6000 came from these islands. The majority of the islands are incapable of any cultivation except for the growth of the cocoanut, as they consist almost entirely of coralline sand, with very little soil. Limes, however, flourish, and fig-trees attain great luxuriance. A few of the islands (notably Manga Reva, a basaltic island over 2000 feet high) possess fertile soil. Manga

Reva has five islands within its reef, one of which is clothed with forest and watered abundantly.

I have before mentioned the pandanus, or screw-palm ; this remarkable tree flourishes most abundantly in the Tuamotus ; though it is to be found more or less all over the islands of the Coral Sea. This is a most valuable product, and deserves to be better known. It is a very suggestive fact that the pandanus, custard-apple, and other tropical productions of this region are found in a fossil state in the Isle of Sheppey, in England. The pandanus is called 'screw-palm' for the reason that it grows with a twist, like the screw of an auger. Its height is generally from 20 to 40 feet, the stem being straight like a column, sending forth branches at regular intervals in such a form as sometimes to remind one of the golden candlestick in the tabernacle of Moses. Each of these limbs terminates in a tuft of long drooping leaves, having in the centre a large yellowish flower, of an overpowering odour, very agreeable, but sickly by reason of its intensity. Underneath this tuft hangs the fruit, which is of a dark green colour, outwardly of the size of a man's head, and a form resembling a pineapple, or more exactly that of the cone which on ancient sculptures is made to surmount the thyrsus of Bacchus. This fruit is commonly regarded by white men not only as unpalatable, but even as uneatable ; nevertheless, it constitutes almost the sole subsistence of thousands of natives in the Kingsmill and Marshall Groups, where no vegetable food exists.

When the fruit is ripe it easily comes to pieces, and is found to consist of a multitude of separate capsules, each of the form of a truncated cone, with square corners, the small ends being arranged around a central cone. Their surface is bright and smooth as ivory : in one species yellow, in the other blood-red. The outer end is as hard as a stone, the inner soft, of the consistence of sugar-cane, and containing an equal if not larger proportion of saccharine matter. The interior of the capsule is fibrous. The custom of the natives is to chew the soft end, and having thus extracted all the nutriment, to throw on one side the hard portion, which they let lie in the sun till thoroughly dry, when they crack it between two stones and extract the *kiko* or kernel, which is similar to a filbert and very wholesome. The ripe fruit when boiled down produces a large percentage of excellent molasses; also, when steamed in the Sawaiori oven and mashed up in warm water, it yields an intoxicating liquor when fermented, and a strong spirit by distillation. But the chief use to which it is devoted is the preparation of what is called on the equator *kabobo*, which serves the savage of the more barren isles in the place of bread. The soft parts of the fruit are grated, and the pulp so obtained is dried in the sun. Its appearance is then that of coarse pine sawdust, of a dark-brown colour and sweetish taste. It is packed in baskets, solidly trodden into a hard mass with the feet, and will keep for any length of time. When required for use, it is moistened, kneaded, and baked on the stones. It is a strong food, easily digested and wholesome, but not very palatable to an European.

The pandanus tree grows usually upon coral, gravel, and clean sand, where there is no particle of mould, or soil, so that it seems beyond measure surprising that its roots could there find either moisture or nourishment. Nevertheless it contains a superabundance of oily sap which exudes freely wherever it is cut with an axe. Growing as it does on the sea-shore, it would be liable to be blown down easily by a strong wind, were it not for a most marvellous protection given it by a beneficent God. From the ground upwards, round and round the stem in a spiral row following the twist of the tree (to the height of about 12 feet), are what at first appear to be excrescences, looking like warts; these continue to protrude in the form of horns growing downwards, straight, and about the thickness of a man's arm, until they touch the ground, where they take deep root and send out suckers in all directions, thus forming a series of stays round the tree on every side, so that it safely defies the power of the most furious storms.

These stays, when macerated and freed from their oily pulp, yield a fibre similar in appearance to jute, exceedingly white and exceedingly strong. The trunk of the pandanus tree, at maturity, is as hollow as a stove-pipe; the wood, never more than a few inches thick, is as hard as bone, and takes a very fine polish.

The leaves of the pandanus tree are more than 6 feet in length, and from 2 to 4 inches wide, of a bright green, with a rib down the centre, and edged on both sides with a row of sharp prickles. Roofs of houses, sails of canoes, flooring mats, and clothing of all sorts are manufactured from the leaf. Wonderful and beautiful fabrics are made from it, all plaited by hand and dyed various colours. Waist-cloths and sashes, as white as linen and as soft as silk, are also made from the leaves of this rich tree.

I do not know of anything that will approach the leaves of the pandanus tree as a paper-making material. The tree grows from one end to the other of Coral Lands. Its leaves can be had for the trouble of the cutting, and all that is wanted is to steep them in salt water, pound them and bleach them in the sun, and they will become as soft and white as a linen rag.

As in other groups, a good number of small traders cruise around the Tuamotus to pick up cargoes of copra and other produce, for the central depôts of German and other firms at Samoa, Tahiti, and Tonga. The goods exchanged with the natives for this copra, which is roughly valued at two to three cents per pound, realise never less than one hundred and oftentimes three hundred per cent. profit. Thus inferior kinds of prints which cost the trader about eightpence and ninepence per fathom are retailed at two shillings. Shirts which cost fifteen shillings a dozen, at Sydney, are sold at six shillings a piece; needles a penny each; and a small reel of sewing cotton one shilling. Combs, looking-glasses, and gilt ornaments command high prices, as also do fish-hooks, files, and tools of all sorts. Ribbons and dyed feathers are in keen demand. Tobacco generally fetches a dollar a pound (it can be had in London or Sydney for about sevenpence to one shilling per pound in bond). A regular trader—and these gentlemen must on no account be associated with the runaway rascals to whom I have had occasion so often to refer—will, when known, make an advertisement of his wares in this fashion. He will put on a pair of trousers of the kind he is most anxious to sell, and a shirt of some gaudy colour; round his waist he will wind a crape sash, or piece of handkerchief of imitation silk; on his head he will wear a felt hat, with a huge buckle and a great bunch of dyed feathers of the most gorgeous description. His ears will be pierced and loaded with gilt rings; round his neck are several yards of ribbon, strings of beads and chains, and his clothing is saturated with bergamot, verbena, or some similar perfume, as by these strong scents the Polynesians are as irresistibly attracted as rats are by that of aniseed, or dogs by a red herring. Thus attired, regardless of expense, he is looked upon as a sublime personage, and marches up the village street escorted by a dense crowd of simple islanders, bursting with admiration. Fashion is as supreme in Coral Lands as it is under the direction of Worth of Paris, and the shrewd trader will take care to make a present of what he most wants to sell to the chief. Once he is seen in public with it, all his subjects desire to be like him, and pay almost any price for the luxury. These islanders may be very simple and very 'savage,' but they would easily perceive the consummate wisdom of the 'Alexandra limp.'

Near to the tenth parallel, but north of the latitude of the Samoan Group, are a number of coral atolls which abound in natural resources which might be turned to profitable account. The nearest to Samoa is the Danger Island of Commodore Byron, or the San Bernardo of Mendana, or Pukapuka as it is called by the natives. It is, however, anything but dangerous to the voyagers who frequent this part of the Coral Sea. It is out of the track of hurricanes, and a vessel may stand off and on, making fast to the reef with a kedge anchor, for nine months out of the twelve, in a horse-shoe bight on the lee side of the land.

San Bernardo is a great triangular reef of about 35 miles in circuit, enclosing a lagoon mostly shallow, but in some places having a depth of 50 fathoms. This lagoon encloses three large cays, one of which is 5 miles in circumference. Some years ago it was thickly inhabited, but Peruvian slavers have since carried off the great bulk of the people.

The inhabitants are of a light copper hue and of very pleasing countenance; they never tattoo themselves, and crimes of violence are not known among them.

They are simple-minded people, honest and contented, but anxious to learn from white people, and speak a language which approaches more closely to that of the Maoris of the North Island of New Zealand than that of any other inhabitants of the Pacific.

They profess Christianity, and a Hervey Island teacher resides among them. The products of the place are cocoa-nuts and *bêche-de-mer*. The groves of the former are remarkably luxuriant and produce about 100 tons annually, which is mostly wasted by the natives, as they live on them; they drink no water, and choose the young nuts for the quantity of the milk they contain.

With a little labour (and the natives work well) and care in the cultivation of trees, this island would in seven years' time produce at least 500 tons of copra per annum, or, at the London price of the day, more than the value of £10,000. Very few ships call at San Bernardo, and unless things have strangely altered since I was in the Pacific, a splendid opening is offered for organised enterprise in this matter of copra alone.

Bêche-de-mer is in abundance, but good pearl-shell is rare. The *Damano* trees grow to an enormous size on the islands; they run from 6 feet to 12 feet in diameter (one has been measured more than 20 feet), and to about 200 feet in height. As explained when dwelling on Fiji, this wood is very valuable for ship-building and ornamental purposes, and is very like the best Spanish mahogany. Other trees of commercial utility flourish on the cays of San Bernardo, notably the screw-palm, and the *Nangiia* or boxwood tree.

Forty miles to the south-east of San Bernardo is the island of Nassau, or Motungongau, as the natives call it. I believe it is uninhabited; it certainly was so in 1876. The island contains about 2000 acres of rich soil; has wells of fresh water; cotton grows wild over it, and cocoa-nuts were planted there about ten years ago.

To the east of San Bernardo is the island of Manihiki, or Humphrey Island, about 30 miles in circumference; the interior lagoon of which contains a vast deposit of pearl-shell of good quality. This lagoon has never been systematically fished for more than twenty years, but a Tahiti firm obtained from it when last fished over 100 tons of shell in less than eighteen months. The women of Manihiki are especially handsome, and being much sought after by the strolling kidnappers of the Pacific, the labour supply of the Tahitian traders failed them, and they abandoned Manihiki, as in this place lagoon-fishing is exclusively the province of the weaker sex, and the introduction of other labour would have necessitated a repetition of the violent measures they were obliged first to adopt in the establishment of the fishery. I believe that now the Manihikans would welcome the advent of renewed commerce on other arguments than the 'click' of a revolver, as they are a well-disposed and highly-intelligent people, professing Christianity, able to read and write, and having a resident minister.

The Manihikans are wonderfully ingenious and skilful in all mechanical arts. They live in stone houses, and build excellent whale-boats, which they manage with great skill. They dress like Europeans, in cotton fabrics, which they have received from ships in exchange for cocoa-nut oil, or as wages at guano diggings. They have carpenter's tools, and most necessaries of all sorts.

The cocoa-nut groves of Manihiki alone would, under proper supervision, yield 300 tons of copra a year.

One of the most extraordinary isles in the Southern Sea is that of Rakahanga, about 30 miles from Manihiki. Here the traveller finds himself face to face with a civilisation of no mean order. The inhabitants of Rakahanga, numbering about 500, live for the most part in a village built of stone; the houses are large and substantial, plastered with coral lime; they have panelled doors and Venetian blinds, and the floors are covered with most skilfully made mats. The natives make good furniture from the wood of the island, and their hats, similar to those called Panama, are really excellent.

These people possess excellent whale-boats, and have a church in the middle of their village handsomely decorated within; the woodwork being inlaid with mother-of-pearl. The vessels which they use for their sacramental rites are of solid silver, and were purchased by them from traders who had procured them from a wreck.

I think Rakahanga (sometimes called the Island of the Grand Duke Alexander), although quite 20 miles in circuit, is one of the least-known atolls of this part of the Pacific, probably for the reason that its village being built out of sight, and the anchorage difficult to find, the ordinary run of mariners have passed it by as uninhabited. The density of the cocoa-nut trees on Rakahanga is very remarkable.

The inhabitants have just laws well administered by themselves, and invariably extend the kindest hospitality to any wandering or shipwrecked sailors. No Europeans reside among them, their teacher being one of their own race who was instructed in Christianity by a Polynesian missionary.

It is when encountering this sort of thing, after having supped on Fiji horrors of the past, that one becomes absolutely indignant at what I must call the insufferable assumptions of shallow writers, who, because it is fashionable, I suppose, are perpetually abusing the missionaries of every creed.

At the risk of being called 'a narrow-minded clerical,' I have come to the conclusion, after mature reflection, that from a purely commercial point of view, the inhabitants of a Pacific island devoted to, say Wesleyanism, are infinitely better people to trade with than if their 'right of private judgment' took the form of devil-worship, and their freedom from a 'soul-enslaving superstition' the sweet liberty of cannibalism.

There are brilliant exceptions to the mission-haters; and one of these has inseparably woven his honourable record into the tiny history of Rakahanga. He was true to the noble traditions which ought to associate themselves with his name, for it was that of English, and he was a merchant mariner of Honolulu. In about 1860, he instituted a cocoa-nut oil manufactory on one of the Fanning's Group, and, looking for labour, he found these people and employed them. He supplied them with useful articles, and taught them handicrafts, for which they display extraordinary aptitude. He supplied them with the seeds and cuttings of valuable plants and trees adapted to their soil, notably tobacco and figs, which last have grown to great perfection, and he was regarded as their great benefactor. What became of Captain English I do not know. I am told commercial misfortunes overtook him; at any rate, his connection with Rakahanga ceased.

What his creed was I neither know nor trouble about, but I am inclined to the opinion that, even if he possessed the ability, Captain English never wrote 'smart' articles against the extension of Christian teaching. Perhaps he was not even a 'scientist' of this infallible age of progress—but this I know, he behaved kindly to the Rakahangans, and taught them agriculture.

Since the manufacture of copra superseded that of cocoa-nut oil, these remote communities of Rakahanga and Manihiki have refused to trade with the vessels that have visited them, or, at any rate, this was the case a few years back, for the following reasons. While the American whalers frequented their neighbourhood they were in the habit of buying from these islanders great quantities of cocoa-nuts for sea-stock.

The price was always $1 per hundred (*i.e.*, its equivalent in trade); it takes fifty of them (the wild cocoa-nut of the Pacific) to make 1 gallon of oil; consequently, for a gallon they usually asked and obtained half a dollar, or its equivalent, two yards of cotton print. One hundred cocoa-nuts when dried weigh only 50 lb., for which traders usually refuse to pay, upon the spots where the nuts are grown, more than 1½ cent per pound, equal to 75 cents per hundred nuts, instead of $1 per hundred. The natives do not allow for the fact that drying the meat of the cocoa-nut involves less labour than making it into oil, nor do they understand the old business maxim of a reduction on taking a quantity, and therefore refuse to submit to what they look upon as an unfair reduction in the rate.

To the north of the Tuamotus is the Marquesas Archipelago, which is composed of two tolerably distinct groups, lying between the parallels of latitude 7° 50′ and 10° 31′ S., and longitude 138° 39′ and 140° 46′ W. They are all of volcanic origin, and may be seen in clear weather for a great distance. The French exercise a kind of protectorate over the group, but, as is the case with all French colonies, both politically and commercially, the Marquesas constitute no very favourable example of what may be made of a new country. The population I have no exact means of estimating, but from what I learnt in the Pacific and in the vicinity of the islands, I should put it down at about 6000; they are, however, like most of the Polynesian races, steadily declining in number.

The principal island, called Nukahiva, is about 17 miles from east to west. The most populous and fertile is that of Dominica, where there are Catholic clergy who shepherd, I fear, only nominal Catholics. It is true my informant was a somewhat vigorous Protestant, but I am not very sanguine about the religious results of some hard-working missions in the Southern Sea, whether they are in the bark of Peter or in frailer crafts.

The Catholic clergy have very successfully cultivated cotton, and their profits from this source may be fairly set down at from £2000 to £3000 a year. 'Every inch upon which vegetation can find a hold is covered with it,' says Sir Edward Belcher, of Dominica; and this is perfectly true. The island is 20 miles long by 7 broad. The country is hilly, with gullies running down to the sea. The highland natives are afraid of coming down to the coast, and dig deep pits to prevent the incursions of the fishermen, thus completely reversing the order of things that used to exist in Viti Levu, Fiji. Like the Tarapons of the Kingsmills, the Sawaioris of Dominica are exceedingly fond of strong cocoa-palm drink; and when they do indulge, they play a very ugly game in which murder is often a leading feature.

When killed, the victim is generally eaten, as (although denied by some writers who have not had access to reliable sources of information) there can be no question some of the Marquesans tenaciously cling to cannibalism; but it is only fair to add that it has never been with them a religion, as it was in Fiji. At any rate they have large flat stones with holes in them (like the end of a bagatelle-table), about 4 to 5 inches in diameter and 2 inches deep. Human bodies are cut up on these, and each man interested in a particular hole drinks the blood found in it.

If a chief dies, a head must be found—that is to say, the mourning natives go in search of some unhappy straggler, a lonely fisherman in a canoe, or the like, whose head is immediately taken off and buried as a resting-place for the feet of the deceased potentate.

The men tattoo their faces in black patches, the women

their lips and the lobes of their ears. The women are very pretty and light coloured.

In some islands morality can scarcely be said to exist, and the European beachcombers have not improved matters.

The French Protectorate is little better than a farce. Beautiful as some of the Marquesas Islands are, and bountifully blessed by nature in nearly every respect, their present condition is that of a huge garden gone to waste; peopled for the most part by savages, and demoralised by white influences, while a few zealous priests fight a hopeless battle, sustained in some degree by the French navy, but regarded with irreligious indifference by their official fellow-countrymen on shore.

The five islands of the Austral Group, to the south of the Society or Tahitian Group, *i.e.* Rapa, Raivavai, Tubuai, Rurutu, and Rimatara, are chiefly noticeable on account of the fact that European products are readily acclimatised in them as well as tropical vegetables. They lie between the tropic of Capricorn and 27° south. They average from 15 to 25 miles in circumference each (Rapa being the largest), and the population may be put down at about 3000 souls. The climate is delightful. For nine months in the year the wind blows from the south-east, and from the westward for the remainder. Sugar, cotton, coffee, and tobacco might be well cultivated in the group by an organised English company, and the inhabitants being inoffensive, hospitable, and intelligent, would gladly welcome some such enterprise. They have an almost extravagant affection for the English, even more so than the Tongans. In view of the probable completion of the Panama Canal at no very distant date, by the indefatigable M. de Lesseps, it is a matter of very great regret that Great Britain does not possess one single coaling station on the route which the Australian steamers would certainly adopt. This would be slightly to the south of the Austral Group. In the columns of the *Times*, Mr. Coutts Trotter, Mr. T. H. Haynes, and myself have called attention to the rapid growth of French influence all over Eastern Polynesia, but the words of warning have been as yet unheeded.

I next come to the Hervey Group, with its seven magnificent islands, of which Rarotonga is chief. Rarotonga is about 3000 feet high, and is clothed to the very top of the mountains with unsurpassed vegetation. It abounds in streams, sloping lands, and alluvial valleys. The Rarotongans are in an advanced state of civilisation. Their laws are just, and well administered. Their houses are built of stone and lime; they plant coffee and cotton, and export great quantities of oranges, besides carrying on manufactures by means of cotton gins which have been introduced. Their only weakness is a liking for a mild form of intoxicating drink, made from the juice of oranges and crushed China bananas.

In 1864 the inhabitants made a humble petition to Her Majesty's Government, praying for either the protection of, or annexation to, Great Britain, and there can be no doubt but that they entertain the same feeling still. If this were gratified, a new era of prosperity would dawn upon the Hervey Group. *Bêche-de-mer* and turtle are found in great quantities on Hervey Island itself, which had very recently only one permanent inhabitant—an aged American beachcomber. Cocoa-nut trees flourish to a great extent, and a friend told me that he noticed 400 nuts on one tree on Hervey Island.

On the direct route between New Zealand and Tahiti, lie the islands of Huon Kermadec, so-called after that unfortunate French commander, who, in company with M. D'Entrecasteaux, was despatched in search of La Perouse. There are three islands—Raoul, or Sunday, Island, Curtis, and Macaulay. The two latter are not inhabitable, nor is it possible to land on them. Curtis Island discharges great quantities of steam, which spouts out of the crevices of the rocks. Sunday Island, which has been inhabited at various times by people of European extraction, is 12 miles in circumference, and about 1600 feet in height, and has very rich soil. The ground is so warm in some places that food may be baked in it, as in an oven.

Very large turtle come up at this place, both the green kind and hawk's-bill, which is the more valuable. There is almost a mystery about this species of turtle, as it is never found westward—or, in Pacific parlance, to leeward—of the one hundred and eightieth meridian of longitude; so it is called by the natives *honu no te opunga*, the 'turtle of the going down of the sun.'

In places where the hawk's-bill turtle are plentiful it is the ustom of the natives to strip them of their valuable plates by introducing a hot knife under the laminæ, and then letting the creature return to the sea.

Wallis Island, to the west of the Samoan Group, enjoys as fertile a soil as those just described. It has a large population of devoted Catholics, under the superintendence of the Bishop of Oceania, who is assisted by numerous clergy and a sisterhood of nuns. A handsome cathedral of cut-stone has been substituted in Wallis Island for the cannibal temple, and notwithstanding the complete absence of Nihilism, Socialism, and other 'advanced' theories, the contented natives manage to do a very good business in copra.

The Fanning's Group consists of four islands in the North Pacific, discovered by Captain Edmund Fanning, an American navigator. They stretch from 1° 47′ N. to 5° 49′ N., and from longitude 157° 27′ W. to 162° 11′ W.

The most westward, and evidently the last formed of the

group, is Palmyra. Calden Reef, which is 40 miles to the northward of Palmyra, had not, in 1876, assumed the distinctive features of an island; however, according to Dr. T. H. Streets, of the United States Navy, from whose interesting paper in the 'American Naturalist' I draw most of my data on scientific matters in connection with this group, it will soon become so.

Palmyra represents the second stage in the formation of a coral island; it now consists of fifty-eight small islets, thickly clothed with vegetation, and arranged in the form of an elongated horseshoe, opened to the westward, and enclosing four lagoons, which is, generally speaking, an exceptional formation. The interest attaching, however, to the Fanning's Group concentrates itself in Washington Island. This is in fact an obliterated atoll. In place of the usual salt-water lagoon there is a lake of fresh water, 1 mile long and half a mile wide, with a depth of 4 fathoms in its deepest part. No shore platform comes out from the land at low water, but the sea at all stages of the tide breaks directly on the beach, except at the angles of the island, where reefs extend a certain distance into the sea. The beach shelves rather abruptly towards the water's edge. The highest point of the land is only 15 feet high. All traces of the former passage from the sea into the lagoon have been obliterated.

The water of the lake is perceptibly brackish, and the only life it is said to contain is a species of eel and shrimp, both of which are different from anything found in the water surrounding the island.

The Fanning's Group is noted for its handsome breed of Polynesian parrots, which are distinguished by the predominance of red in their plumage.

Captain Fanning discovered the islands which bear his name in 1798, and the following extract from his 'Voyages' bears on the *Coriphilus kuhli* here referred to: 'Amongst the birds was one species about the size of our robin, with a breast of scarlet-coloured feathers, the under portion of the body being finished off with bright red, the neck of a golden colour, back of a lively green, with a yellow beak, except the very points, which were of a bright dun colour, the wings and tail being both of a jet black, and the last tipped off with white; it was a most beautiful and lovely bird, with its brilliant and richly variegated plumage.'

These birds are still to be had on Washington Island, but, though easily caught by the intervention of a tame bird and an active islander, they cannot bear confinement, and soon die.

Dr. Streets says: 'When caged aboard the ship they exhibited as pretty a picture of love as one can imagine, well meriting their name of love-birds. They sat billing and smoothing each other's feathers for hours, and, as night came on, two would get together and sleep with their heads turned towards each other.'

The gigantic land-crab is an inhabitant of the Fanning's Group. He lives in burrows underground, and feeds on the cocoa-nuts as they fall from the trees. He first tears off the husk, and then, with his strong pincers, breaks through the shell at the extremity that holds the eyes. The strength of his claws is sufficient to crush a lath in two, and he can suspend himself on the branch of a tree for an hour or more. It may be useful to know that if, when intruding on their privacy, a human hand is grasped by them in a manner more engaging than desirable, a gentle titillation of the soft under parts with any light material will directly cause the crab to loose his hold.

The population of Fanning's Island is estimated at 150 people, who inhabit an area of about 8 miles wide, with a circumference of 30 miles. Many of us are unaware that this little place is part of the British Empire, the Union Jack having been hoisted there by Admiral Richards in 1859. The natives, chiefly from the Hervey Group, are all Christians ; can read and write, and have excellent schools. The trade is entirely in the hands of an eminent London firm, and confined to guano. About twelve ships a year used to leave the island, of about 1000 tons burden each. The value of the exports may be stated at about £60,000 per annum, while the imports are merely nominal. By the most recent advices I learn that the guano deposits on this interesting place are nearly exhausted, so my correspondent will require to seek pastures new.

North of the Kingsmills lie the Marshall Group, or what are called the Ralick and Radik chains. There are about forty-six islands, almost equally divided between the two ranges, from 60 to 100 miles apart. They are all of one description, low atolls, some of them of great extent. The largest are Mille and Aur, upon which the king of the whole group resides. These islands are fertile, for which reason they were named by Alonzo de Saavedra, who first discovered them, Los Buenos Jardines. They are covered with herbage and great trees, besides cocoa-palms and pandanus, in abundance ; they boast the usual plants, and several species of arum, which is excellent food, and yields a capital fibre, as I have already stated. Fish is plentiful, and fresh water is found in wells. The people are good-looking and strong, remarkably courageous, and of kind disposition. It is true some white men have been killed by these people, and ships burnt, but these affrays were invariably brought about by the Europeans. In regard to these islands the blame must chiefly rest with the Spanish Americans from Mexico and their cousins from Manilla, some of whom, after doing the natives the honour of settling amongst them, treated them with the greatest cruelty, and succeeded eventually in making them as bad as themselves.

On the other hand, the American missionaries, who have resided on the group for years, have always met with the greatest kindness and respect. Whether their converts are more than merely nominal Christians I cannot say. The Marshall islanders are as a rule more intelligent than those from the Kingsmill Group, and are very ingenious in the manufacture of their canoes. They are skilful navigators, and will leave their homes for a year or two and cruise from one island to another for trade in such articles as they make.

Both men and women wear fine clothing of dyed *tappa*, from across the chest to below the knee. The trade of the group is confined chiefly to copra and *bêche-de-mer*, large quantities of which are exported to Samoa for shipment by Messrs. Godeffroy.

As regards the Marshall Islands, and the other groups near them, it may be said that there is now springing up a race which will, beyond doubt, exercise in time a most powerful influence on the destinies of the Pacific. They are remarkable for superior intelligence, patience, skill in navigation, and a faculty for acquiring all the mechanical arts. They are the progeny of European and American mariners by Japanese mothers, and in them are to be found combined the grandest elements of success in life—that is to say, all the courage and spirit of adventure which distinguished their wild and roving fathers, mingled with the acuteness, ingenuity, and concentration of purpose which is so characteristic of the Mongolian, and especially of the Japanese. Some of these men would, in any organised effort to develop the trade of Polynesia by British capitalists, prove invaluable as local agents, interpreters, and as authorities on the intricate navigation of their respective groups.

The principal islands of the Ellice Group, viz., Funafuti (Ellice Island), Vaitupu (Tracy Island), Nukufetau (De Peyster Island), and Nanomea (St. Augustine Island), are all lagoon atolls; concerning which I may repeat with equal truth the remarks I made upon such atolls as the Marshall and Tuamotu Groups. Perhaps the system adopted by the natives in the cultivation of the taro, bananas, etc., in these islands is worthy of being recorded, as showing their patient industry in supplementing their ordinary fare of cocoa-nuts, pandanus fruit, and fish.

They dig large trenches, like wide moats, along the centre of the islands. Some of these are from 100 to 200 yards across them, and from 6 to 8 feet deep.

The natives, in order to make the most of the scanty soil Providence has given them, on the moist low level of these moats or trenches throw decayed wood and leaves, and plant everything that requires cultivation in the soil thus formed. Nothing edible, except the cocoa-nut and pandanus, grows on the upper sand.

A sort of *meke-meke* obtains among them, but being intoned on two notes only, it is rather a distressing performance; while the same kind of salutation which is common in Samoa is also included in Ellice Island etiquette, *i.e.*, touching the back of the visitor's hand with the nose. The Polynesian custom of cutting off the third finger of the right hand on the loss of a child or very dear relative, was common before the introduction of Christianity; but Mr. Whitmee tells me the custom was more practised by the women than the men.

As a race these people are very quiet and peaceable. Quarrels are scarce, and ordinary disputes are settled by the authority of the king and leading chiefs, and on some of the islands war is simply unknown.

The people of the island of Nanomea are a race of giants; they average quite 6 feet in height, and are proportionately muscular. When Mr. Whitmee visited the group, ten years ago, he was asked condescendingly, 'Why the whites were all such little men?' his interrogator adding that 'they looked as if they wanted a good meal.'

CHAPTER XXXVII.

POLYNESIAN TRADITIONS.

ALL the traditions of the origin of the world that I heard of in the Pacific agree in one particular; viz., that 'in the beginning' the earth 'was void and empty, and darkness was on the face of the deep.' The Samoans say that that being the case, a certain Jupiter of their mythology sent from heaven his daughter in the form of a snipe to find dry land. After many unsuccessful visits one bare rock furnished a resting-place for this weary wanderer. Repeated descents of the bird-disguised goddess still found the same rock barren, till her father at length deigned to send a little earth and a small creeping-plant to furnish the tiny continent. Watched carefully by the supernatural snipe, the plant was found to have got withered and was replaced by worms. Anyone who has noticed the important part which the earth-worm plays in the breaking up of the pent subsoil of a garden, or has read a recent work on the formation of vegetable mould by the late Dr. Darwin, will find no difficulty in seeing how the Samoans made their connection between the weed and the worm. In fact this tradition is simply a rude account of what we know does take place when naked rocks first exposed to the air become covered with vegetation more or less rapidly, according to the temperature and other physical conditions.

The New Zealand Maoris and the Tahitians all connect the creation of the world with a rock. In the Windward Islands of the Society Group they used to say that the existence of the world was due to the procreative power of their chief god who was called Taaora, who embraced a rock which immediately brought forth the earth and sea. After this stupendous birth, the heralds of day, the dark and light blue sky, appeared before Taaora and asked for a soul for his offspring—the then lifeless universe. The reply of the god was, 'It is done;' and directed his son, the sky-producer, to carry out the mandate. The son looked up to the heavens, and they brought forth new skies and clouds, sun, moon, and stars, thunder and lightning, rain and wind. He then looked downward on the earth, and the soul of the God being breathed into the mass, it soon became changed, and earth, mould, mountains, rocks, trees, herbs, and flowers, beasts, birds, and insects, fountains, rivers and fish, took their rightful places in creation. The blueness of the sea and the submarine rocks and corals, and all the inhabitants of the ocean, were afterwards created by the same Raitubu, or sky producer.

The idea of development is apparent in both the Samoan and Tahitian traditions, and in fact, as far as I know, is universally shared by all races of mankind.

I do not think that the Samoans ever heard of Dr. Darwin or of Professor Mivart; but it occurred to me, as a friend leisurely retailed these native legends with that slight American drawl which is rather common in the Pacific, that the theory of evolution is at least as old as the native races of the great South Sea; and in corroboration of this it may especially be noted that the Samoans have a tradition that all higher forms of animal life, even up to the human race, are developed from the original worm. Whether man is a distinct creation, as the Tongans have it, or is a very much improved ape, they do not say. On this matter I am, to slightly alter a well-known remark of the late Lord Beaconsfield, 'On the side of the—Tongans.'

These people used to have, by the way, a curious tradition that the earth rests on the shoulders of their god; and when an earthquake occurs, he is supposed to be shifting his burden from one to the other. This Pacific Atlas must have enormous 'staying powers,' as earthquakes are few and far between in the Friendly Islands.

One of the best of my friend's Samoan legends was his quaint version of their discovery of fire. It seems that centuries ago—how long back he could not say, but he 'guessed it was before the Declaration of Independence'—there was a great fuss about gastronomy in Samoa, and the people were very much agitated on this important subject. It was agreed on all hands that the *menus* were anything but satisfactory, and that insular habits of feeding resulted in chronic dyspepsia and postprandial inconvenience of all sorts. Many were the remedies suggested, when a brave young chief addressed the conference we may suppose, and said the wretched condition of their stomachs and the unsatisfactory nature of their meals might wholly be attributed to their barbarous habit of eating their food uncooked. What they wanted was fire to cook it with, and that was the reform he urgently demanded in the name of his outraged liver. Asked by some indignant Conservative admirer of the old days, before these new-fangled ideas were talked of, where he was to get it from, he replied that the same force that caused earthquakes, upheavals of the earth, and boiling seas could furnish fire for them; and though warned by his friends, he stated his intention of at once repairing to the cave where the god of the earthquakes and boiling springs lived, and ask for fire to enable them to make progress in the 'art of dining well.'

He was as good as his word—and calling on the rocks to divide, passed into the fearful presence of the fire-god. The young aristocrat seems to have 'jockeyed' the deity into giving a few cinders; but after a time, the latter repenting his weakness in yielding to the audacity of his petitioner, sallied forth, and by one fierce gust drove cooks, ovens, fire, and food all over the place. The prince, nothing daunted, again sought his deity, and is said to have entered into a personal combat with him.

Knowing full well that the digestions of thousands of his countrymen depended on his prowess, he fought the battle of 'cooking reform' with unsurpassed devotion, and in the end succeeded in severing one of the arms of the fiery god, whereupon the latter asked for terms, as he said he wanted the other one to maintain the balance of Samoa. An offer of a hundred wives was indignantly refused by the young man. What he had come for, what he had fought for, was fire; and the possession of that, and at once, was the only condition he would make. He carried his point, and great was the jubilation in the Samoan South Kensington School when he returned, and the banquets of roast and boiled with which he was regaled are matters about which the natives talk to this day. By the self-devotion of Prince Ti-it-iti, Samoa passed in one day from the fearful regimen of cold (raw) leg of mutton to the possible enjoyment of a triumph of Delmonico's *chef.*

When the shock of an earthquake occurs in Samoa, the natives will sometimes say: 'Ah! if brave Prince Ti-it-iti had not cut off one of the arms of Mafuie, what a terrible shaking he could have given us.'

The Samoans still joke about Mafuie as seated down below, and with a long stick amusing himself by 'stirring up' the islanders whose ancestors got fire from him. Like the Tahitians, the Samoans have a tradition that one of their goddesses conceived by looking at the sun; and bringing forth a son, he received the name 'Child of the Sun.' As he grew in years he became acquainted with his origin; and when about to marry, he was directed by his mother to appeal to the sun, his father, for a fitting dower for his bride.

Availing himself of a very high tree, he ascended to the sun, and on making his request, he was asked whether he would have blessings or calamities. He naturally chose the former, and received them—Pandora-like—in a basket.

Here the story rather abruptly ended, but I learned subsequently that the 'Child of the Sun' had, after obtaining the blessings in his basket, continued to have some influence with his father, inasmuch as on one occasion, his mother finding the day too short for her mat-drying, she requested him to get his father to improve matters, and this is how the filial youth went to work: just as the first rays of his father's effulgence appeared above the horizon of the broad sea, his earth-born boy threw a noose over him, with the result of nearly strangling his parent, who of course was still rising, and who naturally indignantly inquired the reason for his son's eccentric behaviour. The dutiful boy at once suggested the difficulty his mother had in getting her mats dried, and good-natured Sol gave a ready assent, and the hours of sunlight have been longer in Samoa ever since.

Whenever anything in nature seems unusual, the idea of physical force at once enters the heads of all the Pacific islanders; one simple instance will suffice to illustrate this very popular characteristic:

Of all that wonderfully fruitful, food-producing order, the bananas, the only one which stands upright is the mountain plantain. The Samoans say a war arose among the bananas, and the plantain conquering, the rest hung their heads in token of their vassalage.

The animal kingdom is treated in much the same fashion. The rat and bat are both well known in Samoa, and the natives having always maintained that they are relatives, the wing difficulty is thus disposed of:

Once upon a time the original rat had wings, while the bat was not so favoured; whereupon the latter, being 'uncommonly smart,' borrowed 'for a few minutes' his companion's organs of air locomotion; but the minute he found that he liked air-travel better than trudging it on foot, he quietly went away, leaving his legs for his friend to utilise as best he could.

Some of the sayings of these people are interesting, and I will give two or three which I have had related to me. If I remember correctly, the following were attributed not to Samoa, but either to Tonga or Fiji; although I never met with them in either place. One on greediness may roughly be translated:

> 'Your evil eye esteems your share too small,
> And prompts you quick to aim at all.'

Another on a brutal husband, which may apply with especial force to some very gallant specimens of our Christian, civilised, and evangelising people, may be rendered as follows:

> 'Oh, what a valiant man you are!
> Who beat your wife, but dare not go to war!'

A Tongan who had visited San Francisco was once asked by his compatriots whether it was true that the country of the *papalagis* was much better than their own. He had not proceeded far in his reply when he was told he was a 'prating fellow and a liar.' 'It was natural for a foreigner to talk thus, but unpardonable in a Tongan.'

It will be noted that travellers' tales are regarded with the same scanty respect in Tonga that they sometimes receive elsewhere.

CHAPTER XXXVIII.

WHO BUILT THOSE FORTS?

WESTWARD of the Marshall Group extends the great archipelago of the Carolines, covering the sea from the Ralick chain to the Palaos, a distance of over 2000 miles, and containing more than 500 islands, most of which are very little known. Some of them, especially towards the westward, are uninhabited, the population having been transferred by the Spaniards for the colonisation of the Ladrones. Others are very populous, but, with the exception of that particular group known as the Seniavinès, at the eastern end of the archipelago, and Yap at the opposite extremity, have been brought into contact very little with civilised man.

The most important of the eastern Carolines is called Kusaie, or Strong Island. It is lofty and basaltic, about 80 miles in circumference, and possessed of two secure harbours for the largest class of vessels. The inhabitants, who number about 2000, have a king of their own, and are naturally industrious and well disposed, though they have been a little demoralised by *bêche-de-mer* fishers and the crews of whaling vessels, who sometimes frequent the place. The antagonism of ruffianly white traders, both rich and poor, to the missionaries all over the Pacific, has done more to obstruct the material progress or conversion of the natives, than any inborn savagery or heathen ignorance. The time has surely arrived when British commerce, legitimately carried on, and restrained within its own vocation, should reap the just reward of well-organised enterprise among these fabulously rich archipelagoes, leaving the missionaries, Catholic and Protestant, to continue their spiritual labours unmolested by word or deed, provided they, on their part, confine themselves strictly to their proper province. Some readers may consider this a dream, but I have seen an approach to the reality in Fiji and elsewhere.

The Kusaie islanders are evidently capable of a higher civilisation than most of the Polynesians. There can be no doubt that, at one time, they were in a much more enlightened and advanced state than they are to-day. Large tracts of their land are covered with ruins of the most massive description, built upon a general plan which could only have been designed by men of great intelligence, and acquainted with mechanical appliances for raising enormous weights, and transporting huge blocks of stone considerable distances, both by land and water. Like the Samoans and Tongans, they have ancient traditions and forms of government. Traditional laws exist as to the intercourse of different castes. The nobles converse by signs and speech not understood by the majority of the people, and words are tabooed in the Carolines as they are in Tonga.

The inhabitants of Kusaie are of large size and strongly built, with a nut-brown complexion. Their hair grows long in curling tresses, which they confine in one knot at the back of the head. Tattooing is generally practised, and, as is the case with other Polynesian races, fragrant flowers are worn, as a wreath round the head, or through the pierced cartilage of the nostrils, while tortoise-shell ornaments for the ears are in great request. I met a beachcomber named Wilson, who had resided for a long time in Kusaie; but owing to a 'family' dispute, he had left the Carolines, and settled in the Marquesas at the other end of the Pacific. He told me he had received nothing but kindness from the Caroline islanders, and such is the general testimony of men who know how to conduct themselves among Polynesian races with tolerable decency.

When a chief dies, they make a mummy of the body, and swathe it in coloured bandages. It is watched for a whole year, a fire being kept beside it, which is never allowed to go out. Records are kept by wooden beads and knotted cords, which they carefully preserve and refer to when they want to tell what happened in a bygone time.

The timber of their houses is invariably squared. They possessed, from remote times, the arts of pottery and weaving with a loom; and the traditions they repeat of their ancestors, point to the conclusion that at some very distant date they were a rich, numerous, and powerful people.

The ruins in Kusaie were supposed, by early writers on the Pacific, to be the work of Spanish buccaneers; but this is an almost ludicrous supposition, inasmuch as D'Urville says 'that the stones measure 8 and 10 feet in length, are squared upon six sides, and have evidently been brought hither from some other country, there being no other stone in the island similar to them;' whereas Mr. Sterndale, who eight years ago stayed on the island, says: 'The stones are in many cases much larger than here described, in fact as large again. They are basaltic prisms quarried on the land itself, as I have seen. It would have taken all the labour of the Spanish pirates, from the days of Balboa till now, to build all the monstrous works that exist in Strong Island.'

Kusaie, or Strong Island, is exceedingly productive, especially in a very valuable timber which successfully resists all attacks of the salt-water worm. The piles of a dry dock and wharves at Shanghai, and other China ports, have been built with wood brought from Kusaie.

The Island of Ascension, or Ponape, is very similar to Kusaie, excepting that it is larger and contains considerable tracts of nearly level country, irrespective of the low valleys and flats along the sea coast. It is the garden of the Carolines. Grand streams run in all directions, and cascades which could turn mills abound, while the streams in the valleys have sufficient volume to float rafts, and render possible the navigation of large-sized boats.

The interior is altogether uninhabited, although covered with the ruins of ancient civilisation. The natives have a superstitious dread of going into the interior. A few years ago the population was estimated at about 7000.

Ascension has three good harbours: Metalanien, Rouankiti, and Jokoits, and each of these are within a coral reef. The island is divided into five districts, presided over by chiefs. A few white men have settled here, and have handsome half-bred children. The natives are well armed with muskets, which they use principally for shooting pigeons, which abound in the woods.

The ruins on Ascension resemble those of Strong, though they are much more extensive.

Mr. C. F. Wood, in his 'Yachting Cruise in the South Seas,' says in reference to these ruins of Ponape: 'On the bank of a creek is seen a massive wall, built of basaltic prisms, about 300 feet long and 35 feet high. A gateway opening on to the creek has a sill about 4 feet high made of enormous basaltic columns laid flat, on passing which the traveller finds himself in a large court enclosed by walls 30 feet high. Round the whole of this court, built up against the inside of the outer walls, is a terrace 8 feet high and 12 feet in width, also built of basaltic prisms. The whole of this court is not visible at once, owing to the dense vegetation; but on clambering about among trunks and creepers, it is found to be nearly square, and to be divided into three parts by low walls running north and south. In the centre of each of these courts stands a closed chamber 14 feet square, also built of basaltic columns, and roofed over with the same, not very closely laid. The walls at the base, including the terrace, are 20 feet thick, and above it 8 feet; and some of the stones, especially those in the front wall near the gateway, are 25 feet long and 8 feet in circumference.'

Pearl-shell of great size and fine quality is found here, which, with copra, cocoa-nut oil, fungus, and *bêche-de-mer*, form the chief exports; but the riches of Ascension cannot be fully stated without incurring the suspicion attaching to a traveller's tale. When Great Britain takes her proper position as a competitor for the trade of 'Coral Lands,' they will be fully realised.

Westward of Ascension is the great atoll of Hogoleu. This consists of a vast lagoon somewhere about 300 miles in circuit, which has three main channels of entrance, safe at all times for the largest ships. Within the lagoon are four great islands, each from 20 to 35 miles in circumference, and more than twenty smaller uninhabited *cays*, covered with cocoa-nut and other trees. There is still water and good anchorage everywhere within the outer reef.

The inhabitants of Hogoleu have been accused of treachery and ferocity; certain it is that they have attacked becalmed vessels, and massacred their crews without any apparent reason. I think I can give a clue to the mystery. In 1793 the English ship *Antelope* was wrecked on the Palaos Islands. The islanders treated the shipwrecked mariners with hospitality for four months; and yet these Palaos islanders are now described as infamous pirates. This deterioration in their character has doubtless been brought about by the schooling which they have since undergone at the hands of a set of white traders, who, as all Pacific travellers know, are even now occasionally to be found about these seas, making themselves at home among the simple-minded people, and instructing them in every vice and villainy.

The lagoon of Hogoleu contains an immense deposit of pearl-oyster of the largest and most valuable kind, and there is practically an inexhaustible supply of *bêche-de-mer.* Sandal-wood is supposed to be plentiful, as the natives make their canoes and paddles of it.

On the prospects of trade in the Caroline Group, but especially in regard to the great atoll of Hogoleu, and perhaps other islands I have named, I will quote the words of Mr. Sterndale, merely prefacing them by the remark that in my opinion British trade should be pushed in the Pacific not by 'commercial adventurers,' as the words are usually understood, but by a powerful company, which would include in its scope all Polynesia, and whose name should be a synonym for fair dealing and honest purpose, from America to China, from Honolulu to Auckland.

If such an idea were reduced to practice, Englishmen or Americans possessing great local knowledge, skilled in the language and habits of the various groups, and trusted by the natives for their integrity, should be appointed agents in the different localities; and I know where these can be found.

'That the first Europeans who can succeed in establishing a permanent agency upon Hogoleu will make their fortunes in a very short time, is an unquestionable fact. The island presents to the commercial adventurer such an opportunity as is scarcely to be found elsewhere in the world, not alone from the valuable products of the land itself, but from the possession of so magnificent a harbour for shipping, from which the ramifications of a trade on a large scale could be developed throughout the great Caroline Archipelago. That there is any risk in the attempt, I do not for a moment believe. All that is necessary is to find men of character and determination, who are acquainted with the Caroline tongue. These, after winning the protection of a chief by the bestowal of suitable presents, and by marrying into his family—which would inevitably be expected of them—might develop a trade to any extent they pleased on behalf of their employers.'

Of the other islands in the Carolines known to Pacific traders, it may be said, as of Pacific voyages, if you describe one, you describe all in great measure. Mortlock and Monteverde Islands are very rich in pearl and tortoise shell. How the Messrs. Godeffroy got to Yap, their most western station in the South Sea, is another romance of the Pacific.

Some twelve years ago a sailor of Hamburg was wrecked in this neighbourhood. He found his way to Yap, and was well treated by the people. They took him to Palaos, to which they trade by sea; from thence he reached the Moluccas, and managed from there eventually to return to Europe. He related his experience to Mr. Cæsar Godeffroy, who gave him charge of a vessel, and supplied him with means to purchase a tract of land from the chiefs of Yap to form a settlement there. This he did accordingly, and for two years traded between the Carolines and China, chiefly in *bêche-de-mer*. At the end of that time, an accident happened to him by the unintentional discharge of a needle-gun. He went to Europe for medical advice, and has returned to the islands no more. He certainly came destitute into the service of Messrs. Godeffroy, from whom, with the exception of his percentage, he received small pay, and yet from the time of his return to Europe he has been living at Baden-Baden, and other fashionable German spas.

The following account of Easter Island will, I am sure, be read with interest, bearing as it does on the ruins of Kusaie and Ponape just described: This lonely outpost of Polynesia, in 27° 8′ S. latitude and 109° 24′ W. longitude, and only 2400 miles from the coast of South America, is about 11 miles long and 4 wide, and in shape something like a cocked-hat, being higher at both ends than towards the centre. It is entirely volcanic, with many large extinct craters, one towards the centre of the island being over 1000 feet high. There is no running water, but several springs near the shore, and deep pools in some of the craters. There are no trees, the tallest vegetation being bushes of *Hybiscus*, *Edwardsia*, and *Broussonettia*, 10 or 12 feet high. Decayed trunks of trees are, however, found, and the paddles and other wooden articles in possession of the natives show that formerly there must have been wood in abundance. The natives are fair Polynesians, resembling those of Tahiti and the Marquesas; but they are said to be cannibals occasionally. Both sexes are tattooed, but the women more elaborately. Their weapons are clubs, spears, lances, and double-headed paddles, which seem to be peculiar to them. Their houses are long and low, like a canoe bottom upwards, with a small opening at the side of about 20 inches, serving for door and window.

This island is celebrated for its wonderful remains of some prehistoric people, consisting of stone houses, sculptured stones, and colossal stone images. At the extreme south-west end of the island are a great number (eighty or a hundred) stone houses built in regular lines, with doors facing the sea. The walls are 5 feet thick by 5½ feet high, built of layers of irregular flat stones, but lined inside with upright flat slabs. The inner dimensions are 40 feet by 13 feet, and they are covered in by their slabs overlapping like tiles, till the centre opening is about 5 feet wide, which is then covered in by long thin slabs of stone. The upright slabs inside are painted in red, black, and white, with figures of birds, faces, mythic animals, and geometric figures. Great quantities of a univalve shell were found in many of the houses, and in one of them a statue 8 feet high and weighing four tons, now in the British Museum.

Near these houses the rocks on the brink of the sea cliffs are carved into strange shapes, resembling tortoises, or into odd faces. There are hundreds of these sculptures often overgrown with bushes and grass. Much more extraordinary are the platforms and images now to be described. On nearly every headland round the coast of the island are enormous platforms of stone, now more or less in ruins. Towards the sea they present a wall 20 or 30 feet high, and from 200 to 300 feet long, and built of large stones often 6 feet long, and accurately fitted together without cement. Being built on sloping ground, the back wall is lower, usually about a yard high, leaving a platform at the top 30 feet wide, with square ends. Landwards a wide terrace, more than 100 feet broad, has been levelled, terminated by another step formed of stone. On these platforms are large slabs serving as pedestals to the images which once stood upon them, but which have now been thrown down in all directions, and more or less mutilated.

One of the most perfect of the platforms had fifteen images on it. These are trunks terminating at the hips, the arms close to the side, the hands sculptured in very low relief on the haunches. They are flatter than the natural body. The usual size of these statues was 15 or 18 feet high, but some were as much as 37 feet, while others are only 4 or 5. The head is flat, the top being cut off level to allow a crown to be put on. These crowns were made of red vesicular tufa, found only at a crater called *Terano Hau*, about 3 miles from the stone houses. At this place there still remain thirty of these crowns waiting for removal to the several platforms, some of them being 10½ feet in diameter. The images, on the other hand, are made of grey, compact, trachytic lava, found only at the crater of Otouli, quite the east end of the island, and about 8 miles from the 'crown' quarry. Near the crater is a large platform, on which a number of gigantic images are still standing, the only ones erect on the island. The face and neck of one of these measures 20 feet to the collar-bone, and is in good preservation. The faces of these images are square, massive, and disdainful in expression, the face turned always upwards. The lips are remarkably thin—the upper lip being short, and the lower lip thrust up. The eye-sockets are deep, and it is believed that eyeballs of obsidian were formerly inserted in them. The nose is broad, the nostrils expanded, the profile somewhat varied in the different images, and the ears with long pendent lobes. The existing natives know nothing about these images. They possess, however, small figures carved in solid dark wood, with strongly aquiline profile, differing from that of the images, the mouth grinning, and a small tuft on the chin.

Wooden tablets, covered with strange hieroglyphics, have also been found; but it is evident that these wooden carvings, as well as those of stone, are the relics of a former age. The people have a tradition that many generations ago they emigrated from Oporo or Rapa Iti, one of the Sorò Archipelago, and 2300 miles to the westward. Hence they call their present abode Rapa Nui, or Great Rapa, to distinguish it from

Rapa Iti, or Little Rapa. An implement of stone, a mere long pebble with a chisel-edge, is believed to have been the chief tool used in producing these wonderful statues; but it is almost incredible that with such imperfect appliances, works so gigantic could have been executed, literally by hundreds, in an island of such insignificant dimensions, and so completely isolated from the rest of the world. This difficulty is so great that some writers have suggested an ancient civilisation over the Pacific as the only means of overcoming it. The forces of distant groups of islands might then have been combined for the execution of these remarkable works in a remote island, which may perhaps have been the sanctuary of their religion, and the supposed dwelling-place of their gods.

At present Easter Island is the great mystery of the Pacific, and the more we know of its strange antiquities, the less we are able to understand them.

CHAPTER XXXIX.

THE SOLOMON ISLANDS.

VERY little is known of the Solomon Group of islands, discovered by Mendana in 1668 (40° 36′ S. lat., and 151° 55′ E., and 162° 30′ E. long.), and that little is not, as a rule, of a pleasant character. They are inhabited by dark-skinned, woolly-headed Papuans, and though the Fiji Government-conducted labour-vessels are breaking the ice and demonstrating that every white man is not necessarily a man-stealer, it has been for years past a *terra incognita* to those profoundly versed in other islands of the Southern Seas.

The group consists of a double row of islands extending nearly 700 miles in a north-west and south-east direction. The four northern islands vary from 120 to 150 miles in length and from 20 to 30 miles in width. The northern point of Bougainville Island (10,171 feet high), the largest, is 130 miles east of the southern point of New Ireland, and adjacent are Choiseul, Ysabel, and Malayta Islands, the straits between them varying from 15 to 50 miles in width. Parallel with these and some 30 miles distant are the islands of New Georgia, Guadalcanar (8006 feet high), and St. Christoval (4100 feet high), the first opposite Choiseul Island, the last extending nearly 100 miles farther to the south-east than Malayta Island.

The whole group is volcanic, and there is an active volcano in Guadalcanar Island.

Labourers are to be got in fair numbers from the Solomons, and a good number of them are now working well for white settlers in Fiji. I had for some time a Solomon Island servant, and found him willing and obedient. One thing grievously offended him, and that was to tell him that if he was sent home 'his friends would cook and eat him.' The Solomon Islanders at present are still cannibals, but this 'boy's' indignation at the idea of his being eaten, shows that even the Solomons are rapidly going ahead.

A few white traders dwell in the group, and manage to dwell in peace with the natives; but the progress of the Solomons is inseparably bound up with the labour-trade of the Fiji Islands. Men returning from a three-year term of service, well treated, and well fed, and fairly paid by white men, will in the end act as first-class missionaries of civilisation among these people, and prepare the way for better things.

The Solomon Islanders are skilful in carving and canoe-building, and most of their implements are inlaid with mother-of-pearl. Although strictly of the Papuan race, they are crossed with brown Polynesian blood, and most of their rites and ceremonies are like those I have described in dealing with Fiji and Tonga. In one of their islands, however, the dead are all buried at sea. At St. Christoval the corpse is kept till the flesh drops from the bones, the skull and finger-bones are then retained as heirlooms, and the remainder of the body exposed on a high platform. Infanticide is common, women are killed on the death of a chief, and the wife or sister of a deceased man first stupefies herself, and then commits suicide by hanging. A kind of suttee, evidently derived from the East, prevails, or has prevailed, in most parts of Polynesia.

The formation of St. Christoval is uniform throughout; it is a long chain of lofty mountains, with gentle slopes towards the sea; the shores are low, and are often furnished with a belt of mangroves, the edge of which is washed by the tide. An active and vigorous vegetation, of the usual tropical description, covers every inch of the soil, which in fact is hardly to be seen. Large rivers descend from the hills, and the climate is good. My brother is one of the few Europeans that I know who have resided in the Solomon Islands, and he fairly astonished me with his account of the fertility of the soil of other islands in the group which I did not visit, and their capacity for producing agricultural wealth of all sorts.

The ivory or Corrossos-nut is to be found in abundance, while betel-nuts are also plentiful. The Solomons seem to be a favourite resort for those extraordinary-looking birds, the hornbills, which grow to a size exceeding that of the domestic fowl, while their enormous bill resembles that of the grossbeak of South America.

There are orchids peculiar to the group, and a large tree

grows there (I have forgotten the name) whose leaves are edible and much resemble those of the domestic cabbage, which in most of the coral islands will not grow. A great future lies before the Solomons. I believe that a few years more will find this dreaded group well on the high road of civilisation; but it wants the helping hands of British justice and British gold. The success of the Crown Colony of Fiji is in a small way demonstrating what may be done by means of the former; the latter would in time assuredly acquire rich interest.

CHAPTER XL.

THE SOCIETY ISLANDS.

FRANCE and England are the only two European powers that possess Polynesian Colonies, Fiji being under the Union Jack, while the islands of Tahiti and New Caledonia and the Tuamotus, are recognised possessions of the French Republic; and a sort of protectorate is claimed by it over the Marquesas and the Austral Islands.

The Society Islands are eleven in number, and form a chain running from north-west to south-east, and are divided by a wide channel into the Leeward and Windward Groups. The names of the principal islands in the Leeward division are: Huahine, Raiatea, Tahaa, and Borabora, which it should be noted have maintained their independence, the two splendid islands first named having had it secured to them by virtue of a treaty, of which the terms were guaranteed by England in or about the year 1847. In view of the very recent formal annexation of Tahiti to France, this fact of the guaranteed independence of the Leeward Group should not be lost sight of.

The Windward Group includes Eimeo or Moorea, Maitea, and Tahiti, which is centrally situated. The area of the group may be set down at 650 square miles, and the population at some 15,000 souls.

The island of Tahiti itself has about 600 square miles, and 9745 inhabitants. It is very mountainous, and a series of coast-ranges form a kind of amphitheatre around the central peaks. The climate is delightfully healthy, vegetation of the richest order flourishes in true tropical profusion. The romantic valleys leading to the interior, with the noble outlines of Mount Orohena 7340 feet high, are gems of Pacific scenery, and are described in rapturous terms by those who have seen a little of other groups outside the Society Islands.

Civilisation of the 'spiritual' order has done its fatal work in Tahiti as in other parts of 'Coral Lands;' and the natives are not only steadily diminishing in numbers, but are by no means such physical perfections as they are described by Cook and early visitors to the group. As it is, they are fine specimens of the brown-coloured or Sawaiori race of Polynesians, with slightly protruding lips, beautiful teeth, black hair (generally curly), and a little beard.

As the policy of the French Government has never been to encourage the natives in habits of agricultural industry, by showing them how to turn the resources of their land to account, they do little else than grow sufficient for their daily wants, so at present any organised attempt of capitalists to colonise the rich lands of Tahiti would have to rely on Polynesian or coolie labour, as was found necessary by the Messrs. Stewart when they established their estate at Atimano, and which is on the south side of the island. I have heard that this magnificent estate is now again being worked, by a French syndicate, and I hope such is the case. There is plenty of room for enterprise in the Society Islands, and in Tahiti alone a Land Mortgage Company would prove a great blessing, especially if—as I understand the French Government intend, now that the island is an absolute possession—its systematic cultivation were encouraged.

The Tahitians are inveterately fond of orange-toddy, which they make by fermenting the juice of the fruit in much the same manner as the Line islanders deal with the sap of the cocoa-nut palm; and the consequence is, that intoxication of a somewhat mild type is very prevalent among them. This is certainly a very undesirable result of the growth of knowledge; but to lay this drunkenness at the door of the missionaries, whether Catholic or Protestant, as the result of their forbidding the unspeakable obscenities of some of the national dances, is to my mind beside the question altogether.

The representatives of the Government will have other instructions, I should hope, than to countenance the preservation of 'national songs,' however wittily improper, and 'national dances,' however suggestively indecent. I am no Puritan, but I should certainly hesitate on commercial grounds before I exchanged my admiration for the works of the Marist Fathers of Oceania for the voluptuous delights of a *can-can* in Tahiti. In thinking as I do that the Tahitians would, under a system of taxation like that of Fiji, rapidly advance in the ways of industry and prosperity, I am perhaps something of an optimist, as most of my friends were of decided opinion that the laziness of the Tahiti natives was incurable, and that the introduction of civilisation and Christianity had by no means helped them to appreciate the nobility of labour. In fact Mr. Sterndale says:

'Many lamentations have been poured forth by persons interested in South Sea missions concerning the evil influences of French domination over the Society islanders; but their premises are groundless and their arguments unsound. The Tahitian race could never be rendered systematically industrious or truly enlightened; they were always and still are indolent, luxurious, superstitious, and incurably vicious.'

I quote this authority, but I venture to doubt that the progressive advance of the Society islanders would be as hopeless as he makes out, if their group was under British rule, with Mr. Thurston as Colonial Secretary or Governor. I do not myself believe that they will ever become good labour hands, but they might be made large producers, and that would be a grand step in the right direction. In this matter of the material improvement of native races, there are three courses open for the governing class: either the natives must be reduced to abject slavery, or allowed by drink and disease to perish off the face of the earth, or else they must by degrees be educated up to a higher standard by means of labour like that of agriculture which they can understand. The Spaniards adopted the first course; in Fiji we are developing the idea contained in the last.

In Tahiti, as in other islands, the policy of letting the natives 'drift' is bearing its bitter fruit in their depopulation. If a choice must be made, I would prefer the simple slavery of the Spaniard to the carelessly indifferent 'Am I my brother's keeper?' which has been the rule in Tahiti and elsewhere.

Some account of the *Areoi* society as it existed in the Society Islands, and also to a certain extent in the Caroline Islands, is worth giving here.

As stated in the account of the Tahitian tradition of the deluge, Taaroa was the Creator-god, and he created two inferior divinities named Orotetefa and Urutetefa, and these remained in a state of celibacy. Oro, the son of Taaroa, desired a wife from the daughters of Taata, the first man; and having reached earth by means of a rainbow, he married the fair damsel of his choice. Oro used to visit his earthly home every day, and his frequent absence from the celestial regions caused Orotetefa and Urutetefa to go in search of him. Having discovered their high-born companion—for the two last-named divinities were very inferior in rank to the son of Taaroa—and after offering some presents (a pig and some red feathers), Orotetefa and Urutetefa were by Oro constituted as *Areois;* and as the two brothers were celibates themselves and had no descendants (though they did not enjoin celibacy on their devotees) they insisted on the murder of all the offspring of those who would consent to join the society.

The *Areois* were a sort of strolling players and privileged libertines, who spent their days in rambling from island to island, exhibiting their pantomimes, and spreading a moral contagion throughout society. They had various sorts of public entertainments, which included dances which cannot be described. There were seven regular classes of *Areois*, and in addition there were a number of persons of both sexes who attached themselves to these South Sea Island followers of the motto of the 'monks' of Medmenham Abbey, and who performed a variety of servile offices for the duly initiated members. These people, who were called *Fanaunau*, were not obliged to destroy their offspring, but took more or less part in the public rites of this horrible confraternity.

The *Areoi* society was open to all classes, but admission was attended with a great number of ceremonies; a protracted noviciate followed, and it was only by progressive advancement that any were admitted to the superior distinctions. If the candidate had any children, he had at once to destroy them.

The 'manners and customs' of the *Areois* in their diabolical orgies, I shall not further refer to. The worst pollutions of which it is possible for man to be guilty, were the organised amusements of a society of human beings in an earthly paradise, for such the Society Islands are.

A number of singular ceremonies were always performed at the death of an *Areoi*. The *oto hua*, a general lamentation, was continued for two or three days. During this time the body remained at the place of its decease, surrounded by the relatives and friends of the departed. It was then taken by the *Areois* to the grand temple, where the bones of the kings were deposited. Soon after the body had been brought within the precincts of the place, the priests of Oro came, and standing over the corpse, offered a long prayer to his god. This prayer and the ceremonies connected therewith were designed to divest the body of all the sacred and mysterious influences the individual was supposed to have received from the god, when in the presence of the idol the perfumed oil had been sprinkled upon him, and he had been raised to the order or rank in which he died. By this act it was thought they were returned to Oro, by whom they had been originally imparted. The body was then buried, as the body of a common man, within the precincts of the temple in which the bodies of the chiefs were interred.

The *Areoi* idea of paradise, or *Robutu Noanoa*, approached the Mahometan in character: an eternity of bestiality in a lovely climate free from all earthly defects, was to be the future of the *Areoi* in the life beyond the grave. The devil of the *Areoi* tradition has, in great measure, been exorcised by the teachings of Christianity, and in a certain degree the inhabitants of the Society Islands may be said to be 'seeking rest and finding none'—nearly all their old religion and amusements being things of the past, while as yet they but imperfectly understand or appreciate the new faith and the new civilisation which have followed in their stead. Time works wonders, however, and it is quite possible that if they were educated a little commercially, by the benevolent action of the French authorities, they would in a generation or so become a changed people.

The capital of the Society Group, Papcete (or Papeite)—the population of which district is 2861, of which about 800 are Europeans—is situated at the end of a semicircular bay, and extending from the dwellings of the white men on the beach are roads running up to the hill-sides, well-shaded by the orange, bread-fruit, palm, and cocoa-nut trees. These streets are all named after Parisian models—such as 'Rue de Rivoli'—and in them are numerous well-stored shops and two good hotels, besides grog-shops and cafés. There is a Palais de Justice and a Catholic cathedral, while in the Rue de Pologne there are a row of Chinese stores and tea shops, the number of Chinamen in the island being 600. At Point Venus, at the northernmost end of the island, is a lighthouse, and it was from this place that Captain Cook in 1769 observed the transit of Venus—hence its name.

The island of Moorea, to the north-west of Tahiti, has a population of 1427, of which 34 are Europeans; while that of Maitea (somctimes spelt Mehetia) is inhabited by a few natives of the district of Tautira in Tahiti.

Like the Fiji and Samoa Groups, the agricultural wealth of Tahiti can hardly be exaggerated. The value of the exports of Tahiti for the year 1878 was 2,800,000 francs, and consisted of cocoa-nut oil, cotton, oranges, mother-of-pearl shell, and guano. Sugar, vanilla, yams, and arrowroot, are all cultivated in Tahiti, and three mills for the former have been established in the island; while I learn from a French official source that it is estimated there are 3,000,000 of cocoa-nut trees, and 125,000 orange trees.

Tahiti thus at present enjoys a considerable trade, which of course might be almost indefinitely increased.

In addition to numerous San Francisco schooners and traders from Fiji, Sydney, and Auckland, the firm of Messrs. Tandonnet of Bordeaux send six ships a year to the island, and each month a schooner leaves with the mails for San Francisco.

CHAPTER XLI.

IS NOTHING TO BE DONE?

THESE are my notes on Coral Lands. I plead guilty to the charge that throughout the whole of the preceding pages there has been a marked commercial tone. To put it very plainly, I ask the race which speaks the English language to consider the South Sea Island question. I regret I cannot appeal to them on the grounds of a common religion, our 'unhappy divisions' would put me out of court; but I can do so both in the name of humanity and commerce.

Commerce, rightly understood, has a very noble side. It is a truism to say so, but generally speaking the South Pacific is ignorant of the fact. The majority of the islanders of Polynesia have learned little good and much evil from 'commercial men,' whose operations have been more akin to those of highway robbers than anything else.

I do not think I exaggerate when I say that the future of Polynesia is a British responsibility. Our sons and daughters have made Australia a great dominion, and their children will assuredly fulfil the destiny of the Anglo-Saxon race in ultimately ruling most of the islands between the City of the Golden Gate and New Zealand.

With the exception of the Archipelago of Fiji, which we reluctantly annexed (and of which even now the great majority of our people know little or nothing), we are as ignorant of the fund of wealth that lies before us in the Pacific Ocean as we are of the moral duty that is bound up with its utilization. On the basis of high-minded commerce we can all unite in shaping the future of the islands which inevitably will fall into the custody of our race.

Throughout the whole length and breadth of the Great South Sea the ordinary Englishman or American is regarded by the natives with goodwill. The Spaniard or Spanish American is, I am sorry to say, hated with an intensity which it is impossible to describe in words; while, as regards Germans, the success of Messrs. Godeffroy's Line Island labour-ships, in the year 1879, is a sufficient commentary. Taking the whole world into consideration, we alone seem able to deal successfully with the great native question. It is true that at times individuals may be cruelly overbearing in maintaining that superiority of race to which we have a very ample title, but with all our shortcomings—and I am the very last Englishman to believe in British infallibility—I know that under the flag of England the native races confided to our care are honestly and fairly dealt by.

If I did not think so I would not advocate British protection for, and more extended British commercial relations with, Polynesia.

I am fully aware that this is Imperialism, and that of a very gross order, inasmuch as it means an increased trade. However, if an honest recognition of the moral, political, and commercial responsibilities and profits arising from the position which the Anglo-Saxon race holds in the world be Imperialism, then I am Imperialist heart and soul.

To understand these things I hold to be statecraft: to undervalue or despise them is to demonstrate incapacity for its acquirement.

There is an old adage, 'Trade follows the flag.' Of Coral Lands it may safely be said that if British capital were systematically and cautiously introduced into its islands, the flag would, sooner than a great many people think, have to follow the trade. Great Britain spent twenty-seven millions in freeing the slaves: why should she not do a little, even if it be also a very profitable business, for the people of the Southern Sea?

These people are looking to us for help, and that help can be handsomely repaid.

They may not have been the victims of 'Bulgarian atrocities,' but what treatment they do occasionally receive the preceding pages should demonstrate to every thoughtful mind.

What is being done in Fiji can be repeated outside that group. The field is now open, and the harvest is bound to follow. It may seem tall talk, but it is simple folly to shut one's eyes to the manifest destiny of the grand Imperial race to which we belong. Overcrowded Britain needs fresh outlets for the splendid energy of her people. The noblest republic the world has ever seen, that of the United States of America, was created by men with English blood in their veins, and their grandsons have seen the rebellious colonies become a mighty State, with fifty millions of English-speaking people, and a territory extending from Atlantic to Pacific.

Our penal settlement in Botany Bay has developed into an Australian Dominion, which, in company with New Zealand, will be the future home of millions of our working-classes. We are just now appreciating the wealth of the great North-west of Canada, and it will be our people that assuredly will reap the rich wheat-fields of Manitoba. Our position in South and Central Africa has not been fully realised by placid stay-at-homes, but unless I am very much mistaken, there is a tendency northward from the Cape of Good Hope; and unless we become emasculated, I suppose that tendency will develop and increase in its intensity.

These outlets are mainly for what are called the working-classes, and in the countries I have named there is room for all and to spare. There is no fear for the future of our surplus farmers and labourers, if they will but seek the soil waiting for their advent.

Coral Lands require a different class of colonists. The rich archipelagoes of the Southern Sea demand for their advancement, not only adequate capital, but intelligence of no mean order. What I have said about the men that are wanted in Fiji applies to the whole Pacific; but I am of decided opinion that in the present state of the outlying islands a hearty co-operation of brains and money on a large scale would be not only the best means of securing a just reward for judicious enterprise, a future for educated men willing to work, and a new field for our manufacturers, but would be the means of preserving and civilising peoples worthy of our care, and of ultimately building up a Polynesian Dominion under the British Crown, of which even the race which colonised America and governs India might be reasonably proud.

If anybody thinks this a dreamer's vision, let him take a Mercator's chart of the world, and observing the exact position of Australia and New Zealand in regard to the islands of the great South Sea, he will see at once the commercial importance of Coral Lands, and understand the reason why I ask the question, Is nothing to be done?

APPENDIX.

COLONY OF FIJI.

RÉSUMÉ OF TOTAL EXPORTS FOR YEARS 1879 AND 1880.

Article.	1879. Quantity.	1879. Value. £	s.	d.	1880. Quantity.	1880. Value. £	s.	d.
Arrowroot	560 lbs.	28	0	0	6272 lbs. ..	243	0	0
Bark	..	..			6 tons 19 cwt. ..	139	0	0
Beans..	360 bushels ..	260	0	0	256 bushels ..	256	0	0
Bêche-de-mer ..	47 tons 9 cwt. ..	2,532	0	0	19 tons 11 cwt.	1,044	0	0
Candlenuts	181 tons.. ..	1,809	10	0	177 tons 10 cwt.	1,801	10	0
Canes	4 bundles ..	4	0	0	..	..		
Cocoa-nuts	202,500 nuts (834 bags 1 case)	613	15	0	360,784 nuts (2925 bags 1 case)	800	7	4
Coffee	9600 lbs... ..	400	0	0	180,744 lbs. ..	7,595	0	0
Copra	4089 tons 15 cwt.	61,353	10	0	7265 tons 12 cwt.	106,985	10	0
Cotton	373 tons 8 cwt.	44,020	0	0	386 tons 4 cwt.	45,530	0	0
Cotton Seed ..	533 tons 10 cwt.	553	10	0	221 tons.. ..	221	0	0
Curiosities	228 packages ..	1,586	0	0	271 packages ..	2,312	0	0
Fibre	85 tons 17 cwt.	2,739	12	0	182 tons 9 cwt...	4,920	0	0
Fibre Dust	4 tons	20	0	0	3 tons 6 cwt. ..	16	10	0
Fruit (Dried) ..	4 packages ..	4	0	0	26 cases	26	0	0
Fruit (Green) ..	43069 bananas (1984 cases 2 packages) ..	3,146	9	0	79,409 bananas (2419 cases) ..	5,189	19	0
Fungus	7½ cwt.	26	8	0	11 tons 14 cwt.	772	4	0
Ginger	..	..			8 cwt.	40	0	0
Guano	..	..			131½ tons ..	2,630	0	0
Gum	..	..			4 cwt.	5	0	0
Hair (Angora) ..	32 lbs.	4	0	0	462 lbs.	59	10	0
Hides	572 hides ..	228	16	0	436 hides ..	174	8	0
Ivory	150 lbs.	15	0	0	150 lbs.	15	0	0
Ivory Nuts	..	..			8 tons	65	0	0
Lime Juice	584 gallons ..	162	0	0	2016 gallons ..	504	0	0
Live Stock	83 cattle ..	830	0	0	..	..		
Maize	71,008 bushels ..	10,651	4	0	64,072 bushels ..	9,610	16	0
Molasses	26,534 gallons ..	2,050	0	0	19,924 bushels ..	1,691	0	0
	Carried forward	£133,037	14	0	Carried forward	£194,646	14	4

Article.	1879. Quantity.	1879. Value.	1880. Quantity.	1880. Value.
	Brought forwd.	£133,037 14 0	Brought forwd.	£194,646 14 4
Mats	20 mats	2 0 0	899 mats ..	89 18 0
Oil (Cocoa-nut) ..	2 tuns 76 gallons	90 0 0	2 tuns 88 gallons	120 0 0
Peanuts	124 tons 3 cwt.	3,477 0 0	125 tons 10 cwt.	3,514 10 0
Pearl	..	..	1 package ..	5 0 0
Pearl-shell	343 cwt... ..	1,032 0 0	274 cwt... ..	822 0 0
Pepper	112 lbs.	4 10 0	..	..
Plants	36 cases	180 0 0	8 cases 205 bundles ..	342 10 0
Sandalwood	1 cwt.	3 0 0	..	..
Shark-fins	6 cwt.	24 0 0	5 cwt.	16 0 0
Shell (Tortoise) ..	720 lbs.	360 0 0	900 lbs.	450 0 0
Sennit	30 lbs.	1 10 0	..	..
Skins	1375 skins ..	75 15 0	1350 skins ..	67 10 0
Spirits, Colonial Refined	10,866 gallons ..	1,593 10 0	9724 gallons ..	1,318 10 0
Sugar	785 tons.. ..	26,687 9 0	593 tons 5 cwt...	20,920 14 0
Sugar-cane	7 tons	20 0 0	3 tons	2 14 0
Tallow	12 cwt.	20 0 0	..	..
Tappa	1 bale	10 0 0	2 bales	20 0 0
Timber	2 logs	2 10 0	72 pieces 3 logs	33 0 0
Tobacco	10 tons 1 cwt. 3 qrs.	1,122 0 0	9 cwt.	50 0 0
Turtles	3 turtles ..	10 0 0	5 turtles ..	25 0 0
Wax (Bees')	..	..	6 cwt.	45 0 0
Wool	5 tons 5 cwt. ..	509 0 0	6 tons 5 cwt. ..	655 0 0
Yams	145 tons.. ..	724 10 0	237 tons 10 cwt.	1,188 10 0
Yagona (*Angona*) ..	4 cwt. 3 qrs. ..	54 0 0	9 tons 16 cwt. ..	2,196 0 0
		£169,040 8 0		£226,528 10 4

TOTAL VALUE OF IMPORTS, WITH THE DUTY COLLECTED THEREFROM FOR THE YEARS 1879, 1880.

Ports.	Value of Articles Imported into the Colony. 1879.	Value of Articles Imported into the Colony. 1880.	Total Amount of Duty Collected. 1879.	Total Amount of Duty Collected. 1880.
Levuka	125,075 12 5	160,955 4 0	18,072 14 10	21,579 5 1
Suva	17,127 13 6	24,581 19 10	2,235 6 10	2,227 16 8
Loma Loma* ..	9 5 6	203 10 0	0 10 7	20 10 0
	£142,142 11 5	£185,740 0 0	£20,308 12 3	£23,827 11 9

* Loma Loma has now ceased to be a port of entry.

ABSTRACT OF METEOROLOGICAL OBSERVATIONS AT BAU FOR 1879.

TAKEN AT BAU, FIJI.
Latitude 16° 38 S. Longitude 178° 37 E.
Height above sea-level 77 feet, distance from sea 1 mile.

1879.	Barometer, mean atmospheric pressure.	Self-Registering Thermometers.				Rainfall.				
		Mean temp. in shade.	Max. temp.	Min. temp.	Mean daily range.	Total amount, inches.	Greatest daily fall.	No. of days it fell.	Hours' rain.	Average previous 8 years.
January ..	29,825	79·9°	92·4°	70·1°	13·0°	25·89	4·66	20	103	24·11
February ..	29,825	79·0	91·8	69·8	12·0	19·62	3·10	20	100	15·77
March	29,871	81·6	96·8	71·7	14·9	7·83	1·36	16	18	21·00
April	29,910	80·0	92·7	69·6	13·7	8·01	1·10	22	44	9·33
May	29,928	79·1	90·6	66·3	15·6	3·98	1·10	8	24	4·70
June	29,978	78·9	90·4	64·4	15·3	5·28	2·65	11	24	2·17
July	29,990	78·2	90·2	63·1	16·9	2·83	1·02	8	13	2·00
August	30,007	77·2	90·8	63·2	17·2	0·96	0·38	6	9	4·40
September ..	29,987	77·6	89·4	63·3	15·9	4·22	0·90	13	22	3·41
October	29,947	79·1	93·7	64·6	16·8	7·63	2·04	12	26	5·79
November ..	29,885	79·5	91·0	68·0	15·4	8·36	2·17	14	27	5·68
December ..	29,780	79·8	91·4	68·0	15·0	10·60	2·57	16	54	7·83
Year 1879 ..	29·911	79·1°	96·8°	63·1°	15·1°	105·16	4·66	166	404	106·19
1878 ..	..	80·4	98·6	56·7	15·8	56·87	2·45	125	249	..
1877 ..	..	78·9	97·6	56·3	16·1	80·53	14·08	106	312	..
1876 ..	..	79·3	97·0	60·0	16·3	91·36	5·73	135	388	..
1875 ..	..	79·1	95·8	58·5	15·8	126·64	7·65	146	553	..
1874 ..	..	79·3	94·1	61·3	15·6	103·48	4·85	165	405	..
1873 ..	..	78·9	94·5	60 3	15·8	104·10	2·82	181	470	..
1872 ..	..	78·9	97·5	59·3	15·7	127·03	5·05	180	502	..
1871 ..	..	79·4	97·7	63·2	15·0	159·51	14·95	180	..	..
8 years ..	.. ..	79·3	98·6	56·3	15·8	106·19	14·95	152	411	..

N.B. The results contained in the above table have been reduced from observations taken daily throughout the year at 9 a.m., except the barometers. Thermometers by Cassella. Rain-gauge by Negretti and Zambra, 5-inch circular, fully exposed; orifice 2 feet 7 inches above ground.

NOTES ON 1878.

Extreme range of temperature in shade 33·7°, or from 96·8° on March 7th to 63·1° on July 9th.

Highest mean temperature for any twenty-four hours, 85·5° on 7th March.

Lowest mean temperature for any twenty-four hours, 70·0° on 2nd September.

Greatest daily range, 25·3° on July 9th.

Least daily range, 3·8° on February 11th.

MERCURIAL BAROMETER.

By Negretti and Zambra, compared with the standard in the Sydney Observatory, and through it with the British standard at Kew; index error 0·007. Readings were taken throughout the year at 9 a.m., 3 p.m., and 9 p.m. The monthly and yearly means have been deduced from the morning and afternoon readings, omitting the night, and are corrected for index error, reduced to 32° Fah., and sea-level. The greatest and least pressure of the atmosphere during the year was 30·141 on 12th July, and 29·404 on 11th December, all corrections applied. The 3 p.m. readings averaged 0·069 lower than those taken at 9 a.m. The 9 p.m. readings exceeded the 9 a.m. by an average of 0·007 in December, January, and February; while during the remaining nine months of the year the 9 a.m. averaged ·015 higher than the 9 p.m. observations.

RAINFALL.

The total fall for the year 1879—105·16 inches—was short of the previous eight years' average by 1·03 inches. During the dry season—June to September—13·24 inches were collected, against 11·98 inches average for same four months in previous eight years. No floods occurred from excessive rainfall at any one period. Rainfall for week ending Saturday the 15th was 9·73 inches in 64 hours. The following are the only noteworthy entries, showing amount of precipitation in stated times:

4·66	inches in	14	hours on	Jan. 20.
4·58	„	19	„	Jan. 28.
1·72	„	1	„	Jan. 26.
1·58	„	45	minutes	Nov. 25.

WIND.

On January 11th and 12th, heavy squalls of wind and rain occurred from N. to N.W. February 11th was stormy and very wet; from the 9th of that month till the morning of the 14th no sun was visible, being the longest overcast period on record here. On 11th December there occurred a strong gale with only light rainfall. It began from S.E. with thunderstorm, passing round to N.E., whence it blew hardest at nightfall. Barometer minimum at 3 p.m., viz., 29,404—all corrections applied. During the night the wind passed to westward, and fell to a moderate breeze with clear sky on the morning of the 12th. On this coast the damage done was very slight, yet it was the hardest blow felt here since the hurricane of 1871.

WATER.

Analysis of sample of water taken from hot springs, Savu Savu Bay, Vanua Levu, Fiji, supplied by H. Stonehewer Cooper:

Total solids at 212° F.	·8796 per cent.
Do., ignited	·7726

The residue consists of:

Free sulphuric acid (SO_3)	·0049
Calcium sulphate	·0260
Calcium chloride	·4355
Magnesium chloride	·0021
Potassium chloride	·0415
Water	·1070
Sodium chloride	·2641
	·8811 per cent.

(*Signed*) H. ROCHOLL.

INDEX.

ACREAGE of Fiji, 11.
Admiralty Islanders, xxiii.
Adenosma triflora (Bot.), 134.
Afoo (Tongan chief), 292.
Albino parrot, found in Fiji, 138.
Alexander's, Prof. W. P., 'Synopsis of Hawaiian Grammar,' xix.
Allender, Mr. H. Phipps, Preface.
Allspice, 155.
Alo-Alo (Tongan mythology), 304.
Ambati (Fijian priest), 65.
Amboyna, Candle-nut found in, 190; dialect, xxiii.
America, Western States of, more suitable market than Europe for Fijian produce, 156.
America, Elevation of south coast, 16.
Andrews', Judge, 'Hawaiian Grammar and Dictionary,' xix.
Anemones (British), 265, *footnote.*
Angau (Fiji), 17.
Anglo-Saxons destined to develop the resources of the Pacific, Preface; 'Anglo-Saxons of Pacific,' Tongans so-called, 286.
Angona, 10, 29, 32, 98. (*See also* Kava.)
Angora goat, 161, 162, 205.
Aniwa, xxii.
'Annatom or Aneityum,' philological work on dialect, xxii.
Anselm, Mr., 231.
Antelope, The wreck of the, 354, 355.
Antietum (New Hebrides), 320.
Antiquities, Fijian, 112, 113; Tuamotu, Kentucky, Ohio, and Tennessee, 62; Pitcairn's and Fanning's Islands, 63. (*See also* Ruins.)
Anudha dialect, xxiii.
Apemama (Kingsmill Group), 316, 317, 318.
Api dialect, xxiii.
Apia (Samoa), 212, 216, 217, 218, 226, 227, 228, 232.
Apolima Island (Samoa), 212.
Aranuka (Kingsmills), 316.
Areoi Society, The, 366-368.
Argo reef, The, 17.
Armies, Kamehameha's Hawaiian, 2.
Arorais, 312.
Arrowroot, 98, 155, 198, 199, 224, 311, 370.
Arum, Gigantic species of, 311, 341.
Ascension Island, or Ponape (Caroline Group), xvii., xxii., 353-354.
Atimano (Tahiti), 364.
Atolls (coral), their formation, 14; difficulties in accounting for their foundation, 15; their subsidence, 16; overwhelmed by tidal waves, 16, 17.
Auckland, distance from Fiji Group, 11; steam communication with Levuka, 56.
Aunu'u Island (Samoa), 212.
Austral (Orient s.s.), 165.
Austral Islands, peopled by Sawaiori race, xiv.; various, 223, 336, 363.
Australia, physical characteristics of aborigines, ix.; suitable colony

for working classes, 163; pearl fisheries on north coast, 246; first named by Spaniards, 267.

Ba (Fijian province), 50, 207, 210.
Ba River (Fiji), Battle on banks of, 69.
Bamboo, used in Fijian house-building, 92, 93.
Bananas, 54, 98, 141, 156, 205, 337, 343.
Banking Companies, 'The Fijian' and 'New Zealand,' 57, 58; Levukan, 58.
Banks Islands, xxiii.
Banyan tree, 275.
Barley, 224.
Barrack, Captain, 177; quoted in reference to measles epidemic, 27, 28.
Barracouta, H.M.S., 222.
Barrier reefs, their formation, 14, 15; examples, 17.
Bath, Mr., 179, 180, 182.
Batimona (Fijian mythology), 65.
Battle of the Beach, The, 190, 191.
Bau (Fiji), its dialect, xxiii.; work on dialect, xxii.; average velocity of the wind, 12, 378; King Cacobau (q.v.), 18; an episode in the history of Bau, 19; distress of the inhabitants from measles epidemic, 26; its political importance, situation, etc., 31, 209; Tongan tradition concerning, 300, 301; meteorological observations at, 377, 378.
Bauro dialect, xxiii.
Beachcombers, 218, 256, 257, 260-263, 336, 337.
Bêche-de-mer, found in all the lagoon islands of Pacific, 263; various names by which it goes, 263; its appearance, form, habits, etc., 264; different varieties, 264-266; its value per ton in China, 266; virulent nature of the poison it discharges; its growth and gregarious habits, 266, 267; the demand in China, 267; Chinese fisheries, 267, 268; variations in the quality of the supply, 268; curious characters engaged in the trade, 268-270; method of collecting and curing the fish adopted by the regular traders, 270-272, 275-278; labour contracts with natives, 272, 273; life at a fishery, 273-275; precautions necessary in shipping, 278; artifice resorted to by fishers, 279; various, 125, 140, 160, 161, 245, 317, 321, 322, 330, 337, 342, 354, 355, 356.
Belcher, Sir Edward, 335.
Belladonna (plant), 225, 226.
Benga Island (Fiji) conquered by Maafu, 21; Fijian tradition concerning, 64.
Bete (chief of Vanua Levu), 21.
Bethell, Messrs. Chas. and Co., 165, 166.
Bhering, The, 212.
Bible, The, translated into Hawaiian, xix.; Pacific ideas concerning its teaching, etc., 269, 270.
Biblical history, parallel in Fijian tradition, 61, 62; in Tongan, 305, 306.
Billyard, Mr., 201.
Bird (Beachcomber), 256, 257.
Birds of Fiji, 137, 138.
'Bismarck of Pacific' (term applied to Maafu), 20.
Bismarck, Prince, 237, 239.
Black, Mr., 183, 187, 190, 191, 193.
Bligh, Captain, 18.
'Blows.' (*See* Hurricanes.)
Boat Building. (*See* Canoe Building.)
Bolivian coin, 236.
Bolotoo (Tongan paradise), 292, 303, 304.
Borabora (Society Group), 363.
Bose ni Tikina (Fijian council), 94, 126.
Bose vaka Turanga (Fijian council), 94.
Bose vaka Yasana (Fijian council), 94, 126.
Botanical Gardens, their introduction into Fiji suggested, 154.
Bougainville Island (Solomon Group), 361.
Bowring, Sir John, 158.

Brander, Mr., 231.
Brazil, 122.
Bread-fruit, 205.
Bretheret, Father, 48, 49.
Bridges, Fijian, 181, 182.
Brinsmead, Messrs. John and Sons, 141.
Bua (Fijian province), 50, 69.
Bua (Fijian chief), 21.
Building, or house construction, Fijian, 92, 93.
Bukalo (human flesh). (*See* Cannibalism.)
Bukutia (Fijian town), 41.
Buli (Fijian rank of chieftainship), 33, 50, 91, 94, 101.
'Bully Hayes' (notorious pirate), 195, 196, 239-245.
Bure (Fijian temple), 40, 42, 68.
Burial ceremonies and customs, Fijian, 76, 89; Hawaiian, 62; Marquesan, 335; Tongan, 307, 308.
Burnand, F. C., quoted, 186.
Buschmann's work on Marquesas and Tahiti languages, xx.
Buzacott's 'Grammar of Hervey Islands dialects, xx.
Byron, Commodore, 329.

Cacobau, King, King of Viti, 18; the pronunciation of his name, 82; threatened by Maafu, 21; difficulties with United States Government, 22; grant of land to Melbourne speculators, 22, 23; ditto to the Fiji Commercial Co., 57, 58; formation of the Woods Administration, 23, 24; introduction of measles epidemic by Cacobau's sons, 24; address to the people upon the occasion of Sir Arthur Gordon's reception, 29; adopts Christianity, 30, 87; the education of his sons, 30; the treatment he has received at the hands of the British Government, 30; his actions at the native ceremony inaugurated in honour of Sir Arthur Gordon, 30-34; his postal system and issue of notes, 57; his presence at the funeral of Tui Cakau, 82; doggerel rhymes concerning, 191-192.
Cadell, Capt., 246.
Calden Reef (Fanning's Group), 339.
Calliope, H.M.S., 75, 76.
Calvert, Rev. J., xxiii.
Camphor, 155.
Camphor-wood boxes, 166, 167.
Canada, suitable colony for working classes, 163.
Canal (Fijian), of native construction, 207, 208.
Candle-nuts, 141-160; 189, 190.
Cannibal forks, why used, 72.
Cannibalism, Fiji, 34-43, 59, 67-73; in Tonga, 297; in Marquesas Group, 335; on Wallis Island, 338; on Easter Island, 357; in Solomon Group, 361.
Canoe-building, Fiji, 89; Samoa, 221; Marshall Group, 342; Rakahanga, 332; Solomon Islands, 361, 362; turtle-shell used in, 279.
Caoutchouc, 158.
Carew, Mr., 33-35, 39, 41, 95.
Carnarvon House (Levukan hotel), 52.
Caroline Islands, peopled by Tarapon race, xiv.; languages of Ponape and Yap, xxii.; pearl fisheries, 247; position and extent of the group, 350; Kusaie or Strong's Island (q.v.), 350-353; Ascension or Ponape, 353, 354; Hogoleu atoll, 354-356; Mortlock, Monteverde, and Yap, 356; the establishment of Messrs. Goddefroy at Yap, 356, 357.
Cau Moola, Tongan traditions originated by, 298-301.
Centipede, found in Fiji, 137.
Ceylon pearl-shell, 246.
Chalmers, Mr., 198, 199.
Chichia (Fiji), 12, 202.
China, payment of taxes, 121; *bêche-de-mer* trade, 266-268.
Chinchona, 154, 225.
Chinese, The, their lot in Sandwich Group and California compared, 6; excluded from the employ of the

Colonial Sugar Refining Co., 152; scheme for using them in Samoa, 237; Tripang fisheries (*see Bêche-de-mer*).
Chippindall, Mr. Edward, 182, 183, 187, 188, 196.
Chlorodyne, 218.
Choiseul (Solomon Group), 361.
Christianity, its introduction into Sandwich Islands, 2, 3; in Fiji, 93; in Tonga, 309; in San Bernardo, 329; in Manihiki, 331; in Rakahanga, 332; in Wallis Island, 338; in Marshall Group, 342; in Tahiti, 365.
Cigarettes, Fijian use of, 119. (*See also* Silonies.)
Cingalese pearl-divers, 257.
Cinnamon, 141, 155, 224.
Circumcision, Fijian rite of, 66.
Citron, found in Fiji, 54.
City of New York (mail steamer), 7.
Clarkson, Mr. Howard, 58.
Climate, of Sandwich Group, 7; of New Hebrides, 320.
Cloacina, The goddess, 308.
Cloves, 155.
'Club dance,' Fijian, 117.
Cockroaches, in Fiji, 166.
Cocoa, 154, 237.
Cocoa-nut tree, 14; used by Fijians in house-building and fitting, 92, 93; manufacture of sinnet, 76; Fijian custom of anointing the body with the oil, 107, 108; indigenous to Fiji, 141; the nut converted into copra, 142-144; the growth of the tree and value of its yield, 144-148; various, 201, 202, 205, 287, 312, 313, 317, 320-322, 324, 229-334, 337, 341, 343, 354, 369, 370. (*See also* Copra.)
Cocoa-palm drink, 313, 335.
Coé-o-le-Sasa o le Tuanasaga (a Samoan belle), 227, 229.
Coffee, 6, 153, 154, 170, 201, 202, 205, 224, 225, 311, 336, 337.
Coir. (*See* Fibre, Cocoa-nut.)
Colonial Sugar Refining Co., 152, 153.
Commerce of the Southern Seas, 370. (*See also* Products and Exports.)
Cook Islands, peopled by Sawaiori race, xiv.
Cook, Captain, Preface, 4, 7, 18, 63, 286, 288, 320, 324, 364, 369.
Coolie labour, used in Fiji, 130, 131.
Cooper, Mr. H. Stonehewer, visits Honolulu, 4, 5; arrives off Galoa (Fiji), 8; reaches Levuka, 11; present at Fijian *meke-mekes*, 114, 196; proceeds to Savu-Savu Bay, 176; to Vuni-wai-Levu, 177; to Wai Wai, 181; to Valaga, 192; to Koro, 198; his experiences in Samoa, 227-230; an amusing transaction with a native Fijian servant, 105; his analysis of water taken from hot springs at Savu-Savu Bay (Fiji), 378.
Cooper, Mr. Walter Stonehewer, 177-178, 192.
Copra, Fijian trade in, 141; process of manufacture, 142-144; price obtained respectively by the government and Fijian natives, 129; manufactured in Tonga, 311; various, 201, 205, 313, 327, 328, 330, 331, 333, 342, 354.
Coral reefs, their formation, 12, 13; their utility, 13; their relative position to the shore, their resistance to the waves, and their channels or outlets, 14; their varieties, 14, 15, 17; theories in regard to their formation, 15; formation of Fanning's Group, 339; of Samoan Group, 213-215.
Corossos nut, 362.
Costume, of Hawaiians, 5; of Fijians, 9, 109, 110; of Samoans, 219, 220; of Europeans at Levuka, 55, 56.
Cotton, 141, 142, 199, 202, 224, 225, 320, 335-337, 369. (*See also* Sea Island Cotton.)
Coutts, Trotter, Mr., 337.
Crab, The gigantic land, 284, 340.
Croton plant, 141.
Crown Grants. (*See* Land-transfer.)

Crusoes, Nineteenth century, 269.
Cumming, Miss Gordon, 178.
Curtis Island (Huon Kermadec Group), 337, 338.
Customs. (*See* Habits and Customs.)
Cuvu (Fiji), 38.

Daku, Distance from Levuka, 176.
Dalo. (*See* Taro.)
Damana timber, 158, 321, 330.
Damon, The Rev. Dr., 240.
Dampier, the explorer, Preface.
Dancing, Fijian, 114-118.
Danger Island, 329, 330.
Danidani, a Fijian shrub, 133.
Darwin, The late Dr., quoted in regard to coral formations, 14-16.
David (Governor of Vavau), 309.
Davilai, Fijian tradition concerning, 138, 139.
Demerara sugar estates, 131.
De Peyster Island (Ellice Group), 343.
Devil temple, Fijian, 40, 42.
'Devils' (Fijian devil-worshippers), 36, 39, 41, 59.
Dido, H.M.S., 24.
Dilo nut, its oil, 134-136, 157, 158.
Discovery, aided by Chinese tripang-fishers, 267, 268.
Doane's, Rev. E. T., Sketch of Ebon language, xxii.
Dods, Mr., 183, 192, 193, 195, 197, 198.
Dogfish, Chief, 272, 273, 275.
Doko (Fijian instrument used in agriculture), 98.
Dolphin, U.S.S., 252.
Dominica (Marquesas Group), 334, 335.
Dragon tree, 312.
Draiba (Levukan cemetery), 46.
Drek river (Fiji), 178, 179.
Dress. (*See* Costume.)
Drury, Mr. Charles, 168.
Duauru dialect, xxiii.
Dunn, Mr. Archibald J., Preface.
D'Urville, Dumont, the Polynesian traveller, Preface.
Dutch East India Company, 240.
Dye barks, 141, 195.
Dysentery, 27, 167, 218.

Easter Island, 357-360.
Ebon, peculiarities in language, xvi., xvii.; works bearing on the language, xxii.
Ebony, 158.
Eddystone Island dialect, xxiii.
Efate (New Hebrides), xxii.
Eggs, Turtle, 283, 284.
Eimeo or Moorea (Society Islands), 364, 369.
Elephantiasis, its prevalence in Samoa, 217, 218.
Elisa, Wreck of the brig, off Fiji, 19.
Ellice Island (Ellice Group), 343.
Ellice Islands, probable origin of dialect, xix.; its resemblance to that of Samoa, xxi.; particulars concerning the group, 343, 344.
Ellis, Mr., 62.
Elloz, Monseigneur, 227.
Elphinston, Mr., Preface, 193, 195.
Emma, Queen of Sandwich Group, 5.
English, Captain, 333.
English, The, how regarded by the South Sea Islanders, 371.
Eno's Fruit Salt, 167.
Entrecasteaux, M. d', 337.
Eoa (Tonga), 286, 287.
Erromanga, philological work on dialect, xxii.
Espiritu Santo Island (New Hebrides), 319.
Eugenie, The Empress, her pearl necklace, 258.
Exports, Amount of, from Fiji in 1879, 141; from Tahiti in 1878, 369, 370; from Fanning's Island per annum, 341.

Fanning, Captain Edmund, 338, 339.
Fanning's Group, 258, 259, 333, 338-341.
Fanning's Island antiquities, 63.
Fate dialect, xxiii.
Fee simple, the only principle of land-tenure recognised in Fiji, 172, 173.
Fibre, Cocoa-nut, converted into

sinnet, 76 ; its commercial value, 144 ; its growth and utility, 146 ; white plantain, pine-apple, aloe, and arum, 159 ; machinery for preparation of, 159.
Field, The, newspaper, quoted, vi., met with in Fiji, 183.
Fig-trees, 324.
Fiji, physical characteristics of inhabitants, ix. ; peopled by the Papuan race, xiii. ; influence of Sawaiori race on language and inhabitants, xxi. ; direct passenger service to islands temporarily suspended, 1 ; Kandavu Island, description of natives, etc., 9 ; Ovalau ; Levuka ; position and extent of group, its acreage, soil, and climate ; the Rewa river, 11 ; the climate, rainfall, and wind velocity characterising the group ; population, 12, 377, 378 ; the surrounding coral reefs, 13; history of the islands previous to their cession to Great Britain, 18-24 ; probable unity of islands at an early period under one rule, 18, 19 ; unconditional transfer of the sovereignty to Great Britain, 24 ; ravages of measles epidemic, 24-28 ; reception of Sir Arthur Gordon, 28, 29 ; native homage-ceremony, 30-34 ; native practices previous to going into battle, 42 ; cannibal outbreak of 1876, 34-43 ; defence of early Fijian colonists (their character), 47, 48 ; Levuka, 43-50 ; life at Levuka, 50-56 ; ocean communication with Levuka, 56, 164, 166 ; postal arrangements, coinage, etc., 57 ; financial companies, 58 ; religion, ancient traditions, and ceremonies, 59-67 ; cannibalism, 67-73 ; superstitions, 74, 88 ; Fijian treatment of the sick and infirm, 74, 75 ; ceremonies observed at the death of a chief, 75, 85 ; courtship and marriage, 85, 86 ; classes of society, rank and polygamy, 87 ; treatment of children, 87, 88 ; native mariners, 88, 89 ; construction and capacity of native canoes, 89, 90 ; a long swim, 90 ; the present system of administration, 49, 50, 91-96 ; social organisation, 91-93, 95, 98 ; divisional and municipal authorities and their duties, 50, 93, 94 ; Fijian irony, 97 ; native estimation of English law, 95, 96 ; physical characteristics of the natives, 97 ; cultivation of the land, 97-99, 123 ; native manufactures, 99 ; social and domestic economy, 99, 100 ; moral characteristics of natives, 100, 101, 103, 104, 123 ; Kava-drinking, 102, 103 ; the relative positions of native and white man, 105-107 ; Fijian love of extreme unction, 107, 108 ; Fijian games and pastimes, 108 ; hair-dressing, 108, 109 ; personal adornment, 109, 110 ; tattooing, 110, 111 ; remarks on the language, 111, 112 ; native manufactures, clubs, bows, arrows, curios, etc., 112, 113 ; conch-shell trumpets and their use, 113 ; practical jokes, 114 ; *Meke-mekes* (or native dances), 114-118 ; native pottery manufactures, 118, 119 ; the use of tobacco, 119 ; the percentage of native population, 120 ; the difficulties which confronted the present government, 119, 120 ; taxes (whether to be collected in specie or produce), 120-125, 129, 131 ; the arrangements under which the latter system is carried out, 126, 127 ; its result, 128 ; the opinion of the natives, 128, 129 ; the labour supply, 105, 130, 131 ; the amount levied in taxes in 1879, 131 ; the mosquito, 132 ; comparative insensibility of natives to pain, 132 ; diplomatic poisoning, 132 ; medicinal plants and herbs, 132-137 ; beasts, birds, reptiles, and fishes found in the islands, 137-140 ; extract from a lecture given by Sir Arthur Gordon on the prospects of Fiji, 140, 141 ; Fijian products, 141-162, 170 ;

grants of land under the old *régime*, 22, 23, 57, 58; distance from natural markets for produce, *i.e.*, Sydney and Auckland, 156; live stock, 160-162; internecine war, 161; the class of colonists required, 163, 164; climate beneficial in cases of consumption, 166; what to take out, 166, 167; precautions against disease, 167; bathing, 167; price of land, 169; advice to a new-comer, 168, 169, 170; quotation from letter bearing on prospects of Fiji, 170; transfer of land, 171-175; Levuka to Savu-Savu Bay, 176, 177; Vu-ni-wai Levu, 177, 178, 181; Wai-Wai, 179, 181-183, 189, 192; beach-combers, 179-182; prevalent native disease, 319; atmospheric disturbances, 184, 186; the scenery of Savu-Savu Bay, 186, 187; a storm at Wai-Wai, 187, 188; a *meke-meke* (native dance), 196; the candle nut, 189, 190; the 'Battle of the Beach,' 190, 191; the cultivation of the yam, 193; of taro, 193, 194; dye barks, 195; everyday life of a settler, 182, 183, 184, 186, 187, 188, 189, 192, 195-197; hot springs, 198; Koro Island, 198, 199; cultivation of arrowroot, 199; Taviuni, 198, 199-202; Mango Island, 202-205; Suva, 206, 207; the Rewa river, 207-210; description of an estate in Viti Levu, 210, 211; general remarks on the future of Fiji, 211; the native Fijians compared with the native Samoans, 219.
Fiji Argus, The, 49.
Fiji Times, The, 47, 49, 57.
Fil (Efate, New Hebrides), xxii.
Finoo (Tongan chief), 289, 290-295.
Fishes of Fijian waters, 138, 139.
Flinders, Captain, 267.
Floyd, Rev. W., 49.
'Flying Fox dance' (Fijian), 116, 117.
Forbes, Mr. Litton, 61.
Fortuna Island, Tongan tradition concerning, 298-300.
Fotoo (Tongan chief), 292.
Fotuna, xxi.
Franco-Prussian war, Tongan declaration of neutrality, 311.
French, The, their system of colonisation as exemplified in Tahiti, 366.
Friendly Islands. (*See* Tonga.)
Fringing-reefs, their formation, 14.
Fruits; tropical compared with those of temperate latitudes, 194; Fijian, 54, 155, 156.
Fulanga, quantity of *bêche-de-mer* found at, 160.
Funeral rites, 75-85. (*See also* Burial Ceremonies, Fijian.)
Fungus, 321, 354.

Galoa (Fijian harbour), 8.
Gambier Islands, xxi.
Gannet Cay Island, fishing contract, 272, 273.
Gaussin's Tahitian Grammar, xx.
Gaussin's Polynesian Grammar, xviii.
George, King, of Tonga, 20, 309, 311.
Gera dialect. (*See* Guadelcanor.)
German emigrants, Messrs. Godeffroy's scheme for the supply of, 237.
German government, treaty with Tonga, 311.
Germans, The, in Samoa, 224; how regarded by the South Sea Islanders, 371.
Gilbert Group. (*See* Kingsmill Group.)
Gill, Rev. W. W., xx.
Gin, Schiedam, its use in Polynesia, 52, 53.
Ginger, 141, 155, 224.
Giovanni Appiani, The schooner, 240.
Goat Island (Samoa), 215.
Godeffroy, Messrs., their *Journal du Museum*, xxii.; the firm represented in Fiji, 138; in Samoa, 227; their history, 231-233, 237-239; islands which contained their representatives in 1873, 234; their system of business and instructions to employés, 235, 236; their estate at Apia, 232; valuable shipment of pearls from Tuamotus,

256; trade with Tonga, 113; difficulties with Line islanders, 315, 316, 371; trade with Savage Island, 321; with Marshall Group, 342; with Caroline Group, 356, 357.
Goodenough, Commodore, 51, 60.
Gordon, Mr. Arthur, C.M.G., 10, 38-40.
Gordon, Sir Arthur, nominated to Governorship of Fiji, 24; his arrival at Levuka, 28; reception of the Vuni Valu and planters, 29; account of assembly of native chiefs convened in his honour, 30, 34; meeting with the cannibal Kai Kolos, 35; expedition to Nasaucoko, 37, 38; campaign against the cannibals, 39-43; the wisdom of his Fijian policy, 95; the opposition to his taxation scheme, 120; quoted in reference to native taxation, 126; in reference to the prospects of Fiji, 140, 141.
Gorrie, Sir J., 50.
Gourds in Fiji, 54.
Government, Hawaiian form of, 3.
Grand Duke Alexander Island. (*See* Rakahanga.)
Grapes in Fiji, 194.
'Great Council' of Fiji, 94.
Green, Rev. J. L., xx.
Grenadilla (Fijian fruit), 54.
Grey's, Sir George, works on Maori language, xviii., xix.
Guadelcanor dialect, xxiii.
Guadalcanor Island (Solomon Group), 361.
Guano, 341, 370.
Gulick's 'Grammar of Ponape Language,' xxii.
Gutta percha, 158.

Haano (Tonga), 286.
Habits and customs, Caroline Group, 352; Easter Island, 357; Ellice Islands, 343; Fiji, 30-34; 42, 65-67, 74, 75-86, 87, 88, 99, 100, 102, 103, 107-111, 113, 132, 190. Hawaii, 3; Line Islands, 313, 314, 315, Marquesas, 335, 336; New Hebrides, 320; Samoa, 213, 219-222, 228-230, 315; Solomon Group, 362; Areoi Society, The, 366-368; store houses of the gods, 252. (*See also Bêche-de-mer* and Turtle, The.)
Hair-dressing, Fijian, 108, 109; Samoan, 221.
Hale, Mr., xvii, xviii., xxii., xxiii.
Hapai (Tonga), 287.
Harding, Mr., 28, 69-72, 195.
Hawaii, or Owyhee (Sandwich Group), 4.
Hawaiian Archipelago. (*See* Sandwich Group.)
Hawk's-bill turtle, 264, 265.
Hayes, Bully (notorious pirate), his career, 195, 196, 239-245.
Hayes, Mrs., 239.
Haynes, Mr. T. H., 337.
Hazelwood's, Rev. D., 'Fijian Dictionary and Grammar,' xxiii.
Hennings, Messrs., 142, 202, 203.
Herbert, George, quotation from poem by, 148.
Hertha, The, German ironclad, 238.
Hervey Islands, works on dialects of, xx.; peaceable disposition of the natives, 223; description of the group, 337.
Heyward and Cooper, Messrs., 178.
Hill, Captain, and Co., 162.
History, Fijian, 18-24; Hawaiian, 2, 3; Samoan, 221, 222; Tongan, 288-294; 308, 309.
Hogoleu (Caroline Group), 247, 354-356.
Holmhurst (Fiji), 201.
Holothurides mollusc, 263.
Home, Mr., 211.
Home, Sir Everard, 75, 76.
Honolulu (Sandwich Group), 2, 4, 5, 7.
Hornbills, 362.
Hort, Brothers, Messrs., 231.
Hospitality, Fijian, 101; Tongan, 297.
Hotels, Levukan, 44, 50-52; Honolulu, 7.
Huahine (Society Islands), 363.
Humboldt's, William von, work on Marquesas and Tahiti languages, xx.

Humphrey, or Manikiki Island, 330, 331.
Hunter, Mr., 200.
Hurricanes, 184, 185, 187, 188.
Huon Kermadec Islands, 337, 338.

Imports, amount of, into Fiji in 1879, 141.
India, collection of taxes, 121; candle-nut found in, 190.
Indian Archipelago, the probable home of the ancestors of the Sawaiori, Tarapon, Malay, and Malagasy races, xii.; visited by Chinese fishermen, 267.
Indian corn, 155.
India-rubber, 141.
Indigo, 224.
Infanticide, its prevalence in Fiji, 88; its practice by the Areoi Society, 367.
Intoxicants, sale to Fijian natives forbidden by Government, 103; Pandanus juice, 326. (*See also* Cocoa-palm drink and Kava.)
Ipecacuanha, 136, 137.
Ivory nut, 362.

Japanese character, 342.
Jokoits (Ascension Island), 353.
Joseph, Prince, son of King Cacobau, 24-30, 83.
Journal of American Oriental Society, xxii.
Journal of Anthropological Institute, xxiii.
Juggernaut, Fijian parallel, 61.
Jute, 237.

Kabobo, 326.
Kahulai (Sandwich Group), 4.
Kai-Colos, their meeting with Sir Arthur Gordon, 35; their defeat by Captain Knollys, 41.
Kalou Rerere (Fijian mythology), 69.
Kaluakua (King David), of Sandwich Islands, 3.
Kamehameha III. accepts Christianity, 3.
Kamehameha the Great, founder of Hawaiian dynasty, 2, 3.
Kana-bogi (Fijian funeral rite), 80.
Kanakas (native inhabitants of Hawaii), 5.
Kandavu (Fiji), 8, 50.
Kanusimana (Fijian mythology), 65.
Kao (Tonga), 286, 287.
Kasavu (Fiji), 209.
Kauai (Sandwich Islands), 4.
Kava, used by Fijians as a present to their priests, 65; the bowls in which it is made, 82, 92; its manufacture from the angona root, 98; its ceremonial use, Fiji, 32, 102, 103; Samoa, 228, 229; Tonga, 293, 295; its effects, 103, 217; its flavour, 10.
Kava bowls, their construction, etc., 82, 92.
Kelsall, Mr. T. S., Preface.
Kendal's Grammar (Maori), xviii.
Kentucky, cave skeletons and other antiquities found in, 62.
Kermadec, peopled by Sawaiori race, xiii.
Kingsmill Islands, peopled by Tarapon race, xiv.; names by which the natives are known in other islands, 312; life and occupation of the natives, 312-314; population, 313; religious observances, superstitions, and traditions, 314, 315; tatooing, marriage customs, and characteristics of natives, 315; the wages they earn in other islands as labourers, 315; their refusal to serve in the employ of Messrs. Godeffroy, 316; King Tem Baiteke, 316-318; language, 318; prevalent disease, 318, 319; value of pandanus tree, 325.
Klinesmith, Mr., 138.
Knollys, Captain, 38, 41.
Kokola (Fijian mythology), 65.
Kolikoli (Fijian chief), 37.
Koro Islands (Fiji), 12, 17, 198, 199.
Koro Sea, 198.
Kotoo Group (Tonga), 287.
Kuahilo (Hawaiian god), 3.
Kusaie. (*See* Strong's Island.)
Kura (Fijian medicinal tree), 132.
Kuria (Kingsmills), 316.

Labour supply, 130, 223, 312, 315, 319, 360, 361.
Laca (Fijian medicinal herb), 133.
Ladrone Islands, peopled by Tarapon race, xiv.
Lakemba (Fiji), 12, 288.
Lali party, A Fijian, 196.
Lanai (Sandwich Group), 4.
Land-transfer, in Fiji, 171-175; in Tonga, 310.
Language, of Fiji, 18; Line Islands, 318; San Bernardo, 329; Samoa, 219.
Late (Tonga), 286, 287, 288.
Latham's (Dr. R. G.) 'Elements of Comparative Philology,' xxiii.
Lau (Fijian province), 50.
Laughing jackass, 145.
Lava-lava (Samoan waist-cloth), 220.
Lawa-ni-mate (Fijian funeral rite), 81.
Lawes, The Rev. W. G., xxi.
Layard, Mr. E. L., 24; quoted in reference to measles epidemic, 24, 25.
Leases, their legal standing in Fiji, 174.
Leefe, The Hon. R. B., 161, 162.
Leeward Islands. (*See* Society Islands.)
Lefuga (Tonga), 286.
Le Hunt, Mr., 38.
Lemons, 141.
Lemons, sweet, found in Fiji, 54.
Leonora, The brig, 241, 242.
Leopard *bêche-de-mer*, 265, 266.
Lepauni (disease), 318, 319.
Lesseps, M. de, 336.
Leveney, Mr., 207.
Levuka (Fiji), its former port of communication with San Francisco, 8; distance (navigation) from Galoa Bay, 10; situation, 11, 43; arrangement, 43, 44; hotels, shops, conveyances, promenade, etc., 44; sports and pastimes, government institutions, and commercial facilities, 45; bizarre character of population, 45, 46; banks and commercial companies, 58; sanitary arrangements, statistical returns (population), cemetery and cricket-ground, 46; devotional institutions, 48, 49; hospital, medical staff, and periodicals, 49; resident government officials, 49, 50; hotels and boarding-houses, 50-52; dietary, 50-54; bathing-place, 51; mosquitoes, 55, 218; dress, 55, 56; ocean communication, 56, 57, 164-166; good stores, 166; advice to a new comer, 168.
Liardet, Mr., H. M. Consul at Samoa, 11.
Lifu, xxiii.
Lifuka Group (Tonga), 287.
Likus (Fijian article of dress), 116.
Lime-juice, 162.
Limes, 54, 141, 324.
Line Islands, the Kingsmill Group, 312, 313, 316, 318, 319; intoxicant distilled by natives, its effect, and the precautions it has rendered necessary, 313, 314; skill exhibited by the natives in fishing, 314; their food, canoes, arms, etc., 314; religious observances and superstitions, 314; traditions, 314, 315; tattooing, marriage customs, and characteristics of natives, 315; the wages they obtain in other islands as labourers, 315; their employment in Samoa, 223; by Messrs. Godeffroy, 232; their subsequent refusal to enter the service of the firm, 316; King Tem Baiteke, 316-318; language, 318; prevalent disease, 318, 319.
Lizards found in Fiji, 137.
Loloku (Fijian rite), 75, 77-79.
Loma-Loma (capital of Vanua Balavu, Fiji), 12; visited by Maafu, 20; trading station at, 202.
Lomai Viti (Fijian province), 50.
London, a Fijian's idea of, 70, 71.
Longbeard, Captain, 272, 273, 275.
Loo Choo Islands, 16.
Lotooma Island, Tongan tradition concerning, 298-300.
Lotus, The schooner, 243.
Low Archipelago. (*See* Tuamotus Group.)

Lowest types of humanity, ix.
Loyalty Islands, peopled by Papuan race, xiii.; language of Uvea, xxi.; works on dialects, xxiii.
Lugunor (Caroline Group), 247.
Lychee tree, 155, 156.

Maafu (Tongan and Fijian chief), his early history, first appearance in Fiji, and ambitious projects, 20; successful raids in Vanua Levu, annexation of Benga, difficulties with the British Consul, and death, 21; his presence at the ceremonial recognition of Sir Arthur Gordon, 33.
Maafui (Samoan mythology), 347, 348.
Macauley Island (Huon Kermadec Group), 337.
Macauta (district), 21, 50.
Macdonald, Dr., 138, 208.
MacGregor, Dr., 167.
Mackay's (Angus) 'Semi-tropical Agriculturist,' 169.
Magalhaens, The explorer, Preface, 321.
Mahaga dialect, xxiii.
Mahogany, 158.
Mainatavasari (Fijian mythology), 65.
Maitea (Society Group), 364.
Maize, 160, 205, 211, 224.
Malagasy, The, their probable origin, xii.
Malatta Bay (Kandava, Fiji), 8.
Malayta (Solomon Group), 361.
Malietoa family (Tongan), 286.
Malicolo (New Hebrides), 319, 320; philological work on dialect, xxiii.
Malo (Fijian cloth), 99.
Malua (Fijian procrastination), 104.
Mamosi (Fiji), 208.
Manaar, Straits of, value of pearl bank in, 247.
Manga Rewa Island (Tuamotus) 324, 325.
Mango Island (Fiji), frontispiece engraving, Preface, 12, 155, 156, 202-205.
Mango Island Co. (*See* Ryder, Messrs.)
Manihiki, or Humphrey Island, 330, 331, 333.
Manilla hemp, 158, 159.
Manilla pearl-shell, 246, 247.
Manono Island (Samoa), 212, 214, 216.
Manu'a Island (Samoa), 212.
Maori language, Philological works bearing on, xviii., xix.
Maoris, 219, 274, 345.
Mara dialect, xxiii.
'Marama Levu' Appellation given by Fijians to the Queen, 70.
Marco Polo, 267.
Mari, xxiii.
Mariana Islands. (*See* Ladrone Islands.)
Mariner, quoted, 286, 291, 292, 294, 296, 297, 305.
Marist Fathers, 60, 61.
Mark Twain, quoted, 176, 188.
Marriages (Fiji) in early times, 85-87; Samoa, 213, 315; Kingsmills, 315.
Marshall Islands, xiv., xxii., 325, 341, 342.
Marquesas Islands, works on language, xviii., xx., xxi.; peopled by Sawaiori race, xiv.; their position, government, and probable population, 334, 363; the principal islands, 334, 335; unsuccessful efforts of missionaries, 334, 335; cultivation of cotton, 335; habits and customs of the natives, 335, 336; laxness of the French Protectorate, 334, 336.
Masi or Tappa, 98, 311.
Ma-siki dialect, xxiii.
Masonic, The (Fijian hotel), 200.
Mataboolès (Tongan), 302.
Matafae Mountain (Samoa), 214.
Mataqalis (Fijian), 91, 92, 98, 99.
Matantu (Samoa), 226, 227.
Matawalu (Fijian mythology), 65.
Mats, Fijian manufacture of, 92; 99, 146; custom of storing, 100; Samoan, 220, 221.
Maui (Sandwich Islands), 4.
Maunsell's, R., 'Maori Grammar,' xviii.
Mauritius compared with Fiji, 163.

Mayo, Dr., 218.
McConnell, Mr., 201.
McKissack, Messrs., 201.
Meade, Captain, 242.
Measles, introduction of the epidemic into Fiji, 24; atrocious rumour concerning its origin, 25; its terrible ravages amongst native population, 25-28; attributed to the adoption of Christianity in Fiji, 35.
Mehetia. (*See* Maitea.)
Meke-meke (Fijian dance), 114-118, 196; native dance of Ellice Islanders, 343.
Mel, xxii.
Melanesian. (*See* Papuan.)
Melbourne, speculators, 22, 23; communication with Fiji, 56.
Mendana, Alvaro de, Preface, 329, 360.
Menika. (*See Bêche-de-mer.*)
Messina, Coral banks of, 245.
Metalanien (Ascension Island), 353.
Meteorological observations at Bau, 377.
Micronesian. (*See* Tarapon.)
Milk, Cocoa-nut, 147.
Mille, xxii.
Mirage, 7.
Missionaries, at Rotuma Island, xxi.; E. T. Doane, xxii.; American in Sandwich Islands, 3; old witticism relating to Fijian, 56; general remarks on, 59-61; the French in Fiji, 61; Samoa, 227; ill-feeling existing between missionaries and traders, 236; missionaries in Tonga, 294, 310; in New Hebrides, 320; San Bernardo, 329; Marquesas Group, 334, 336; Marshall Group, 342.
Moka (Fijian), meaning of term, 36.
Moli apple (Fijian fruit), 54.
Molokai (Sandwich Group), 4.
Monteverde Island (Caroline Group), 356.
Moore, Mr., 201.
Moorea or Eimeo (Society Islands), 364, 369.
Mortgage (in Fiji), 171, 173-175.
Mortlock Island (Caroline Group), 356.
Moseley, Mr. H. N., F.R.S., xxiii.
Mosquitoes, 131, 166, 167, 206, 218.
Mota Island, Grammar of language xxiii.
Mother of Pearl. (*See under* Pearl.)
Motungongau Island. (*See* Nassau.)
Moulton, Rev. J. E., work on Polynesian Dictionary, xx.
Moumoua (Tongan chief), 292.
Mudu (chief of the Quali Mari), 38.
Mulinunu (Samoa), 226, 227.
Müller (Dr. Friedrich's) 'Sketch of Sawaiori Languages,' xviii.

Na Cagi Levu (Fijian chief), 33.
Nadi (Fiji), 38.
Na Drau (Fiji), 71.
Nadroga, Fijian province, 50; Fijian harbour, 38.
Naicobocobo (Fijian mythology), 64.
Naitisiri (Fijian province), 50, 207, 209.
Naitono (Fijian mythology), 65.
Na Lotu, massacre of inhabitants by cannibals, 72.
Namena massacre (Fiji), 81.
Namosi (Fiji), 156, 210.
Nangiia timber, 321, 330.
Nanomea Island, 344.
Naples, Bay of, surpassed in beauty by the harbour of Apia, 226.
'Napoleon of the Pacific,' Kamehameha so called, 3.
Narragansett, U.S.S., 242.
Nasaucoko (Fijian town), 37, 38.
Na-Seivau (Fiji), 210.
Nasova (suburb of Levuka), 28; episode at, 190, 191.
Nassau Island, 330.
Na Ulivou, chief of Bau, 19.
Navigators' Islands. (*See* Samoan Group.)
Navuso (Fiji), 208, 209.
Ndanthina (Fijian mythology), 65.
Ndengi (Fijian mythology), 64, 110.
Negrito Polynesian. (*See* Papuan).
New Britain, peopled by Papuan race, xiii.; philological work on, xxiii.
New Caledonia, xiii., xxiii., 363.
Newfoundland, 245.
New Georgia (Solomon Group), 361.
New Guinea, ix., xiii., xxiii., 267.

New Hanover, xxiii.
New Hebrides, xiii., xxii., xxiii., 223, 316, 319, 320.
New Holland, 267.
New Ireland, xiii., xxiii., 361.
Newspapers, Fijian, 49; Hawaiian, xix.
New Zealand. (*See also* Maori.) Physical characteristics of inhabitants, ix.; probable early settlers, xii.; peopled by Sawaiori race, xiii.; fallacy of some ideas concerning, 164.
Nichau (Sandwich Group), 4.
Nieué. (*See* Savage Island.)
Niusana trees, 209.
Nombre de Dios, a painting at, Preface.
North's (Lord) Island, xxii.
Nukahiva (Marquesas Group), 334.
Nukufetau (Ellis Group), 234.
Nukunivano fishing contract, 272, 273.
Numuka (Tonga), 286, 287.
Nutele Island (Samoa), 212, 214.
Nutmegs, 141, 155, 224, 320.

Oahu (Sandwich Group), 2-4.
Of'u Island (Samoa), 212.
Ohio antiquities, 62.
Oil-producing trees, 225.
Olive, Captain, 38.
Olosenga Island (Samoa), 212, 214.
Ono Buleanga Valley (Fiji), 210.
Oporo (Soro Archipelago), 359.
Oratory (Samoan), 223, 224.
Oranges, 54, 141, 156, 337, 369, 370.
Orchids, 362.
Orestes, The ship, 239.
Orient S.S. Line, 165.
Oro, Tahitian mythology, 367, 368.
Orohena, Mount, 364.
Orotetefa, Tahitian mythology, 367.
Otouli (Easter Island), 359.
Ovalau (Fiji), its area and position, 11; its anchorage, 43; suited for growth of coffee, 153.
Oven, a Polynesian, 276.
Owyhee. (*See* Hawaii.)

Paahua oyster, 258-260.
Pacific Mail Co., 1, 2, 4, 164.
Palaos Islands, 354, 355.
Pali (Hawaii), 5.
Palmerston Island, 321.
Palmyra (Fanning's Group), 339.
Pama dialect, xxiii.
Panama Canal, Preface, 336.
Panama pearl-fisheries, 249.
Pandanus, or screw palm, 37, 117, 155, 325-327, 341, 343.
Pango-Pango harbour, 214-216.
Papalagis or white men, Fijian tradition concerning their origin, 65.
Papeete or Papeite (Tahiti), 369.
Papuans, works on their languages, xxii., xxiii.; their physical characteristics, ix., x., 319; their origin, and treatment of women, x.; list of islands they inhabit, xiv.; approximate date of their migration, xiii.; construction of their languages, xiv., xv.
Parrots, Polynesian, 339, 340.
Patteson, Bishop, xxiii., 60.
Patioli, Samoan chief, 227, 228.
Paumotus. (*See* Tuamotus.)
Peach, The, 155.
Pea-nuts, 207.
Pearl, H.M.S., 28.
Pearl-fishing, in Fiji, 125; depreciation in value during 1867 of pearl, 233; fisheries at Nukufetau, 234; in North Australia, 246; advantages enjoyed by South Pacific fisheries, prices obtained and quality of yield, 246; different systems under which were conducted the fisheries at Tahiti and Manilla, 246, 247; value of fisheries generally, 247; fisheries in the Low Archipelago, and description of appearance they present, 247, 248; comparative safety of Pacific pearl-fishing, 249; the propagation of pearl-oysters and their partiality for certain places, 249, 250; use made by the natives of pearls and shell, 249, 250, 252; varieties of the pearl-oyster, the formation of pearls, 251, 254; method of opening the pearl-oyster, 251, 252, 255, 256; pearl-robbers, 252; state of the Tua-

motus fisheries, 253 ; the oyster's powers of locomotion, 253, 254 ; the spawn probably deposited *outside* the lagoons, in which the oysters are afterwards found, 254, 255 ; history of the Tuamotus fisheries, 256 ; large profits made by beachcombers, 256, 257 ; native pearl-divers, 257, 258 ; average cost of raising shell per ton, 258 ; the Empress Eugenie's pearl necklace, 258 ; shell used for special purposes, 258-259 ; bargaining for pearls, 259 ; pearls of the Paahua oyster, 258-260 ; found at various islands, 322, 330, 331, 354, 355, 356, 362, 369.
Pease, Captain, 241.
Peckham, Mr., 202.
Peninsular and Oriental S.S. Co., 164, 165.
Penrhyn Island, 257.
Pentecost (New Hebrides), 319.
Pepper, 155.
Perouse, La, Preface, 337.
Peru, 122.
Petherick's, Mr. E. A., catalogue of works bearing on Australia and the Pacific, xxiv.
Philippine Islands, 16.
Phœnix Islands, peopled by Sawaiori race, xiv.
Pillans, Mr., 192.
Pinard, M., xxi.
Pine-apples, 54, 141, 156.
Pinkham, Captain, 243.
Pitcairn's Island antiquities, 62, 63.
Plantains, 141, 158.
Poisoning, professional, in Fiji, 132.
Polygamy, its practice formerly in Fiji, 87.
Polynesia, the people of, ix., its commercial importance, Preface.
Polynesian Land Co., 23.
Polyparia, 12, 13.
Pomare, the Great, of Tahiti, 324.
Pomegranates, 54.
Pomelo tree, 155.
Ponape. (*See* Ascension Island.)
Population : Fanning's Island, 340 ; Fiji, 12 ; Kingsmills, 313, 316 ; Levuka, 46 ; Marquesas, 334 ; Papeite, 369 ; Samoa, 212 ; Sandwich Islands, 4, 7 ; Savage Island, 321 ; Society Islands, 364 ; Whites engaged in commerce in Fiji, 121 ; Tonga, 287.
Porpoise, U.S.S., 252, 262.
Potatoes, 194.
Pottery manufacture in Fiji, 99, 118, 119.
Pratt's, Rev. G., Samoan Dictionary, xix.
Prescott, Mr., 63.
Priests, Fijian, 41.
Prince William's Island, Fiji Group so called by Tasman, 18.
Pritchard, Mr., 21.
Products—(*see also* under separate headings, *e.g. Bêche de mer*, Pearl, Cotton, Sugar, etc.) : Ascension Island, 354 ; Austral Group, 336 ; Ellice Islands, 343 ; Fanning's Island, 341 ; Fiji, 133, 141-162 ; Hervey Island, 337 ; Hogoleu (Caroline Group), 355, 356 ; Manihiki Island, 331 ; Marshall Group, 341 ; Monteverde and Mortlock Islands (Caroline Group), 356 ; Nassau Island, 330 ; Rakahanga, 333 ; Rarotonga, 337 ; Samoa, 215, 224-226 ; San Bernardo, 330 ; Sandwich Group, 4, 6 ; Solomon Group, 362, 363 ; Tahiti or Society Group, 369, 370 ; Tonga, 133, 311, 312 ; Tuamotus or Low Archipelago, 324-327.
Proverbial sayings, 349.
Pukapuka or San Bernardo Island, 329, 330.
Puraka plant, 311.
Pyjamas, 166.

Quali Mari (Fijian tribe), 38, 40.
Qualis (Fijian), 91.
Queen, The, 33, 70, 311, 324.
Quinine, a remedy for elephantiasis, 217.
Quiros, Fernando, Preface.
Quixote, Don, quotation from, 248.

Rabi (Fiji), 153.
Ra (Fijian province), 50.

Ra Bithi (Fijian chief), massacre in honour of, 81.
Rabone's, Rev. S., Tongan Vocabulary, xix.
Race, the Polynesian divided into three classes, ix.; the Sawaiori, x.-xiii.; the Tarapon, xii.; the Papuan, ix., x., xii., xiii., 319; lists of islands peopled by the three distinctive races of Pacific, xiii., xiv.; race peopling Marshall Group, 342; Solomon Group, 360; Society Group, 364.
Radack Chain (Marshall Archipelago), xxii.; Strings', or Kusaie Island, 351.
Radik and Ralick Chains. (*See* Marshall Group.)
Raiatea (Society Islands), 363.
Railway, American Trans-continental, 1.
Rakahanga Island, industry and civilisation of the natives, 331, 332; their laws, characteristics, religion, etc., 332, 333: their refusal to trade with passing vessels and their reason, 333, 334.
Ra Kambasanga (Fijian mythology), 65.
Raki-Raki (district in Fiji), 207.
Ralick and Radik Chains (*See* Marshall Group.)
Rambi Plantation Co., 162.
Raoul (Huon Kermadec Group), 337, 338.
Rapa (Austral Group), 257, 336.
Rapa Iti. (*See* Oporo.)
Rapanui Islands, xxi.
Rarotonga (Hervey Group), xx., 337.
Ratans, 158.
Ratu Joe (son of King Cacobau), circumstances of his marriage, 86.
Ratu Savanatha, 25.
Ra Undreundre (Fijian gourmand), 68.
Ravu-Ravu (Fijian mythology), 65.
Reefs. (*See* Coral reefs.)
Religion. (*See also* Christianity.) Its observance by Sawaiori races, xii.; its introduction into Fiji, 59, 61; Tonga, 302, 303; Line Islands, 314.
Rewa (Fijian province), 56.
Rewa river (Fiji), 11, 39, 50, 202, 207-210.
Rewa tree. (*See* Vasa.)
Rheumatism, Fijian remedy for, 135.
Rice, 155, 224.
Richards, Admiral, 341.
Roberts, Mr., 207.
Robinson, Sir Hercules, 24.
Rocholl, Mr. H., 378.
Rodi. (*See Bêche-de-mer.*)
Roggewein, The discoverer, Preface.
Roko Bati-dua (Fijian mythology), 65.
Rokola (Fijian mythology), 64.
Rokora (Fijian mythology), 64.
Rokos (Fijian), 33, 50, 91, 94.
Rosewood, 158.
Rotuma Island, xxi.
Rouankiti (Ascension Island), 353.
Rowena (a Fijian servant), story concerning, 105.
Royal Gazette, The Fijian, 49.
Rugg, Captain, 252.
Ruins, Ascension Island, 353, 354; Easter Island, 357-360; Strong's Island, 352.
Rum, distilled in Fiji, 52, 160; in Tonga, 312.
Rurutu (Austral Group), 336.
Ryder (Messrs.), 141, 162, 203, 204, 205, 206.

Saavedra, Alonzo de, Preface, 341.
Sabbatarianism in Tonga, 310.
St. Augustine Island (Ellice Group), 343.
St. Christoval Island (Solomon Group), 361, 362.
St. Thomas, 185.
St. Mary, U.S.S., 22.
Sal, 158.
Samoan Group, peculiarities of the language and method of address, xi., 219; probable early settlers, xii.; peopled by the Sawaiori race, xiv.; the construction of the langnage, xv., 219; works

bearing on the language, xix., xxii., xxiii. ; the vicinity of submarine volcanoes, 16; communication by sailing-vessel with Levuka (Fiji), 56, 57, 211 ; distance from Levuka, 211 ; geographical position, extent, and population of the group, 212 ; enumeration and area of islands comprised in the group, 212; Savaii, 212, 213; Upolu, 213, 214; Olosenga, Manono, and Tutuila, 214; Pango-Pango harbour, 214-216; climate and atmospheric changes, 215-218; European and American resident population, 217; health statistics, 217, 218; physical and moral characteristics of the natives, 219, 221-223, 227 ; tattooing, 219, 220; dress, 220; mats, 220, 221; hair-dressing, 221 ; house and canoe building, 221 ; eloquence, 223, 224; fertility of the land, 224; its products, 215, 224-226; the harbour of Apia, 226, 227, 228; kava-drinking, 228, 229; a Samoan dinner, 229; probability of annexation, 230; pearl-fisheries, 259; prevalent native disease, 319; wages given to Line Island labourers, 315; curious marriage custom, 315; traditions, various, 348, 349; concerning the origin of the world, 344, 345; the development of animal life, 345, 346; the origin of fire, 346, 347.

Sandal wood, 355.

Sandwich Group, probable early settlers, xii. ; peopled by Sawaiori race, xiii. ; authorities on language, xix. ; length of voyage from London, 1 ; San Francisco route to, and general description of islands, 2; their history, 2, 3; introduction of Christianity, 2, 3; ancient rites and traditions, 3; present state of civilisation, 3-6; the army, islands comprised in group (*see also* under separate headings), and population, 4; trade, 4, 6; the inhabitants, their costume, etc., description of Pali and road to, 5; the products, labour schemes, and treaties, 6; the climate, decline of native population, and particulars concerning Honolulu, 7; burial customs, 62; sarsaparilla found by Dr. Seeman in the group, 133; yield of sugar per acre per annum, 151 ; use of candle-nut in, 190; wages obtained by Line Island labourers, 315.

San Francisco, 2, 56.

Sang, Mons. Frédéric, Preface.

San Pablo. (*See* Palmerston Island.)

Santa Cruz Island, Preface.

Sarsaparilla, 133.

Savage, Charley, 19.

Savage or Nieué Island, xxi.; 223, 232, 320, 321.

Savaii (Samoa), 8, 212, 213.

Savu-Savu Bay (Fiji), 27, 176-198.

Sawaiori races and languages, x., xv., xvii., xviii., xix., xxi., xxii.

Schiedam gin, 106.

Scotch fishermen, 125.

Screw palm. (*See* Pandanus.)

Sea Island Cotton, 141, 203-205, 224.

Sea Island Cotton seed, 205.

Seeman, Dr., 18, 64, 133, 158.

Selia Levu (Fiji), 200.

Senna, 136, 137.

Shaddocks, 54, 141.

Sheppey, Isle of, 325.

Sigatoka, town in Fiji, 39, 40; Fijian river, 36.

Silonies, 229.

Sinnet, 76.

Skull-cap, The, 278, 279.

Slave-trade, 48, 54, 55.

Smith, The Hon. J. C., 198.

Smith, Mr. Donald, 187.

Smith and Aitchison, Messrs., 201.

Smythe, Colonel, 18.

Snakes, of Fiji, 137.

Society, Fijian, six classes of, 87.

Society Islands, peopled by Sawaiori race, xiv.; political standing, geographical position, ex-

tent and population of the group, 363, 364; Tahiti (q.v.), 364-366; the Areois Society, 366-368; moral status of the natives, 368, 369; Papeete (or Papeite), Moorea and Maitea, 369; nature and value of exports from Tahiti in 1878, 369, 370; products, 369, 370; communication, 370.
Sofatabua house, 71, 114.
Sole, The, Fijian tradition concerning, 138, 139.
Solomon Group, peopled by Papuan race, xiii.; a guide to the dialects, xxiii.; position, extent, etc., 360, 361; cannibalism, and the labour trade, 361; occupations, habits, and customs of natives, 361, 362; St. Christoval, 361, 362; products, 362, 363.
Somo-Somo (Fiji), 134, 200.
Soro (Fijian peace offering), various kinds of, 66, 67, 88.
Soro Archipelago, 359.
Sotomi (Samoan chief), 222.
Spain, no longer a colonising power, Preface.
Spaniards, their system of colonisation, 366; how regarded by South Sea Islanders, 371.
Sponge fishing and cleansing, 285.
Sports and pastimes, Fijian, 108.
Squid, The great, 248, 249.
South Africa, suitable colony for working classes, 163.
Star of the South, mail packet, 9.
Sterndale, Mr., Preface, 232, 234, 259, 355, 365.
Stewart, Messrs., 258, 364.
Strauch, Captain H., xxiii.
Strawberry, The, 156.
Streeter, Mr. Edwin, 258.
Streets, Dr. T. H., 339, 340.
Strong's Island (Caroline Group), extent and population, 350; character, habits, and customs of natives, 351, 352, ancient ruins, 352.
Sturt, Mr., 206.
Sugar-cane, The, 6, 98, 141, 142, 148-153, 183, 200, 202, 211, 224, 225, 320, 336, 370.
Sulu (Fijian costume), 9.
Sunday Island (Huon Kermadec Group), 337, 338.
Superstitions, 74, 88, 209, 314.
Suva (Fiji), 49, 93, 206, 207, 218.
Suwarrow Island, 322.
Swanston, Robert S., 58.
Sweet potatoes, 211.
Sydney (Australia), 6, 11, 56, 165.

Taaora, Tahitian tradition concerning, 345.
Taaroa (Tahitian mythology), 366, 367.
Taata (Tahitian tradition), 367.
Taboo or Tabu, Custom of, xvii., 80, 88, 301, 307.
Tahaa (Society Group), 363.
Tahiti, Grammar and Dictionary of Language, xx.; use of candlenut in, 190; pearl-fishing, 246; wages obtained by Line Island labourers, 315; tradition concerning the origin of the world, 345; extent, population, and configuration of the island, 364; moral and physical characteristics of natives, 364, 365, 366.
'Tahitian shell,' 246.
Taifua Belotoo (Tongan mythology), 304.
Tai Levu (Fijian province), 50.
Tali Toobo (Tongan mythology), 304.
Talie Tabu (Tongan mythology), 292.
Tama (Fijian salutation), 31.
Tamarinds, 224.
Tana dialect, Philological work bearing on, xxii.
Tandonnet, Messrs., 370.
Tanoa (Fijian chief), 19, 75.
Tantira (Tahiti) natives, 369.
Tapioca, 141, 155, 311.
Tapitaweans, 312.
Tappa (Fijian cloth), 9, 34, 118, 342.
Tarapon race, xii., xiv., xvi., xvii.
Tarawau (Fijian mythology), 64.
Taro root, 98, 141, 193, 194, 343.
Tasman, the Dutch navigator, 18.
Tattooing, in Dominica, 335, 336; in Easter Island, 357; in Samoa and New Zealand, 219, 220.

Taumata. (*See* Skull-cap.)
Ta'u Olosenga Island (Samoa), 212.
Taviuni (Fiji), 12, 16, 153, 155, 198, 199-202.
Taxes, how levied in Fiji, 120-129; the amount collected in 1879, 131.
Tea, 154, 155, 225.
Teak, 158.
Tem Baiteke, King, 234, 316-318.
Tennessee, Cave skeletons found in, 62.
Terano Hau (Easter Island crater), 359.
Thake (disease), 318, 319.
Thurston, Mount, 177.
Thurston, Mr. J. B., Preface, 23, 24, 49, 58, 120, 122, 155, 180, 181, 191.
Tidal waves, so-called, 16.
Ti-it-iti, Samoan tradition concerning, 346, 347.
Tikina, Fijian territorial division, 91.
Timber, Fiji, 156-160; Palmerston Island, 321.
Times, The, newspaper, 337.
Timothy, Roko, 24, 30.
Toad, The, 266.
Tobacco, 98, 155, 207, 211, 224, 225, 336.
Tobi. (*See* Lord North's Island.)
Tofoa (Tonga), 287, 288.
Tofua (Tonga), 286, 287.
Togo Ahu (Tongan chief), 289, 290.
Tokelau dialect, xix.
Tokelau or Union Islands, xxi., 8, 223, 312.
Tomatoes, 54.
Tommy, One-legged, 180, 181.
Tonga Group, peopled by Sawaiori race, xiv.; vocabulary of language, xix.; Fijian tradition concerning Tongan origin, 65; existence of Sarsaparilla plant, 133; Capt. Cook, 286; position and extent of the group, 286; the principal islands, 286-288; population, 287; moral characteristics of natives, 286, 288; Tongan history, 288-294; treatment of missionaries, 294, 295; ancient invocation of gods and supposed inspiration of priests, 295, 296; Tongan hospitality, and cannibalism, 297; old traditions, 298-301, 303-306, 346; rank and chiefship, 301, 302; treatment of the old and of women, 302; Marriage, divorce, and human sacrifice, 306; funeral ceremonies, 306-308; the present condition of Tonga, 308, 309; The government and religion, 309, 310; roads, police force, and enforced military service, 310, 311; treaties, 311; trade, 311, 312; friendly feeling of natives towards the English, 336.
Tonga Island (Tongan Group), 301.
Tonga, a medicinal preparation, 137.
Tongaloa (Tongan mythology), 304, 305.
Tongatabu (Tonga), 286, 287.
Toobo (Tongan tradition), 305.
Torres, the discoverer, Preface.
Torquemada, biographer of Fernando Quiros, Preface.
Tortoise-shell, 125, 356.
Totoga Valley (Fiji), 51.
Tovi-Tovi (Fijian chief), 182.
Tracy Island (Ellice Group), 343.
Trader, Description of a Polynesian, 328, 329.
Traditions, Fiji, 61, 62, 64, 65, 138, 139; Line Islands, 314, 315; Samoa, 344 - 350; Sandwich Group, 3; Tahiti, 366, 367; Tonga, 298-301, 303-306; Tuamotus, 62.
Treadway, The late Mr., 239, 240.
Treaty or agreement for *bêche-de-mer* fishing, 272, 273.
Treaty between Sandwich Group and United States, 6.
Trenches dug by Ellice islanders, 343.
Tripang. (*See Bêche-de-mer.*)
Tuamotus Group, or Low Archipelago, peopled by Sawaiori race, xiv.; position of group, extent, population, description of the natives, their religion,

etc., 324; the products, 324-327; trade, 327-329; government, 363; tradition, 64; pearl-fisheries, etc., 247, 248, 249, 253, 256, 257, 258.
Tubuai (Austral Group, 336.
Tubu Neuha (Tongan chief), 289-291.
Tubu Toa (Tongan chief), 291.
Tui Bua (Fijian chief), 33.
Tui Cakau (Fijian king), his funeral, 76-80; contrasted with that of one of his successors, 83-85.
Tui-hala-Fatai (Tongan chief), 288, 289, 290.
Tui Ra, quoted in reference to *bêche-de-mer* fishing, 125.
Tui Thakau (Fijian chief), 33.
Tuitonga (Tongan rank), 301, 302, 306, 307, 308.
Tui Viti, Cacobau so-called, 18.
Turmeric, 141.
Turner, Dr., ix., 218.
Turtle, The Hawk's-bill, 264, 265; native customs concerning the proprietorship of turtle when caught, 279, 280; uses to which it is put, 279, 280; its weight and the value of its oil, 280; its flesh highly esteemed by the natives, 280; method of killing the turtle and withdrawing its shell, 280, 284, 338; cooking arrangements and preservation of oil and meat, 280, 281; how caught, 281-284; the instinct shown by the female in the secretion of her eggs, 282, 283; the eggs described, 284; fishers of Palmerston Island, 321; found in Hervey Group, 337; Huon Kermadec Group, 338; Fiji, 139, 140.
Tutuila Island (Samoa), 212, 214, 217.
Twain, Mark, 176, 188, 202.

Uea or Uvea dialect, xxi., xxii., xxiii.
Umi, King, of Hawaii, 3.
Union Group. (*See* Tokelau Islands.)
United States Government claim upon King Cacobau of Fiji, 22.
Upolu Island (Samoa), 212, 213, 214; Apia, 212, 216, 217, 218, 226, 227, 228.
Urutetefa (Tahitian mythology), 367.
Uvea. (*See* Uea.)

Vaca Acawooli, 305.
Vagadace, suburb of Levuka, 46.
Vakadredre (Fijian funeral rite), 80.
Vakandua (Fiji), 210.
Vakavidiulo (Fijian funeral rite), 80.
Valaga (Fiji), 192, 195, 198.
Valenza, Cardinal, Preface.
Vancouver's Island, 2.
Vanikoro (Santa Cruz Group), Preface.
Vanilla, 155, 224, 370.
Vanua Balavu (Fiji), 12, 20.
Vanua Levu (Fiji), 11, 17, 21, 105, 153, 160, 176, 210.
Vasa or Rewa, Fijian medicinal tree, 133.
Vasco Nunez de Balboa, particulars concerning, vii.
Vavau (Tonga), 286, 287, 288.
Veachi (Tongan chief), 301.
Verata (Fijian chief), 19.
Violette's, Father, Samoan Grammar and Polyglot Dictionary, xix.
Viti Levu, ii., 15, 17, 28, 34-43, 145, 153, 154, 160, 210.
Vœux, Geo. W. des, 49.
Vogel, Sir Julius, Preface.
Volcanic disturbances, 15, 16, 17.
Voyages, Long, in open boats, 63.
Vuna (Fiji), 200, 201.
Vuni Valu (Fijian hereditary title), 19.
Vu-ni-wai-Levu (Fiji), 177, 178, 181.
Vunmarama dialect, xxiii.

Wai Manu river (Fiji), 208, 209.
Wai Ndia river (Fiji), 210.
Wai-ni-kumi (Water of the beard), 209.
Wairiki (Fiji), 201.
Waitova Falls (Fiji), 51, 52, 187.
Wai Wai (Fiji), 179, 181-183, 189, 192, 202.
Wakeman, Captain, 214.

Wallis Island, 338.
Washington Island (Fanning's Group), 339, 340.
'Water of the Beard,' 209.
'Waves of the Sea' dance, 118.
Wawabalavu (Fijian chief), 70.
Webb, Mr. W. H., 214.
Webb, Rev. A. J., quoted in reference to measles epidemic, 215-217.
Weber, Mr. Theo., 232-235.
Wee (Fijian fruit), 54.
Wesleyan Mission at Levuka, 19, 49.
West Indies compared with Fiji, 163.
Whales' teeth, used by Fijians as a present to their priests, 65.
Whitmee, The Rev. S. J., his use of the term Sawaiori, x.; description of the languages of the three races of the Pacific, *i.e.* Papuan, xiv., xv., Sawaiori, xv., xvi., and Tarapon, xvi., xvii.; Comparative Dictionary of Polynesian language, xx., xxi.; on the Line islanders, 314; questioned by a Nanomea islander, 344.
Whitsunday Island, Vunmarama dialect, xxiii.
Wilkes, Commodore, 19, 67, 85, 96, 212, 213, 262, 263.
Williams, Beachcomber, 257.
Williams's, Bishop, Maori Dictionary, xviii.
Williams, Mr., 63, 66, 76, 86.
Wilson, Captain, 18.
Windward Group. (*See* Society Islands.)
Woods, Mr., 23, 24, 58, 191.
Woondel. (*See* Dilo-nut.)
Works bearing on languages of South Sea Islands, xvii.-xxiv.

Yaka plant, 61, *footnote*.
Yam, The, 98, 141, 193, 211, 370.
Yap (Caroline Group), 356.
Yasanas (Fijian territorial divisions), 50, 91.
Yehen or Yengen dialect, xxiii.
Ysabel (Solomon Group), 361.

Zoology of Fiji, 140.

THE END.

BILLING AND SONS, PRINTERS, GUILDFORD AND LONDON.

www.ingramcontent.com/pod-product-compliance
Lightning Source LLC
Chambersburg PA
CBHW032305280326
41932CB00009B/707